Tennessee's Historic Landscapes

TENNESSEE'S HISTORIC

LANDSCAPES

A Traveler's Guide

Carroll Van West

THE UNIVERSITY OF TENNESSEE PRESS / KNOXVILLE

The paper in this book meets the minimum requirements of the
American National Standard for Permanence of Paper for Printed
Library Materials. ∞ The binding materials have been chosen
for strength and durability.

 Printed on
recycled paper.

Library of Congress Cataloging-in-Publication Data

West, Carroll Van, 1955-
        Tennessee's historic landscapes: a traveler's guide / Carroll Van West.—1st ed.
            p.   cm.
        Includes bibliographical references and index.
        Contents: The interstate landscape—The urban landscape—Appalachian
Tennessee—The great valley of Tennessee—The Cumberland Plateau—Middle
Tennessee—The west Tennessee plateau—The Mississippi River country.
        ISBN 0–87049–880–0 (cloth: alk. paper)
        ISBN 0–87049–881–9 (pbk.: alk. paper)
        1. Tennessee—Guidebooks.   2. Historic sites—Tennessee—Guidebooks.
3. Landscape—Tennessee—Guidebooks.   I. Title.
F434.3.W47   1995
917.6804'53—dc20   94-18717
                                                                                    CIP

TO

OWEN WILLIAM WEST

The best traveling companion a father could have

Contents

Illustrations

Figures

Maps

How to Use This Book

All travelers can enjoy Tennessee's rich legacy of history and architecture through the pages of *Tennessee's Historic Landscapes: A Traveler's Guide*.

The introduction sets the stage as it allows travelers a glimpse of the diversity of history, places, and themes found among the historic landscapes of Tennessee. Chapter 1, "The Interstate Landscape," is for interstate travelers: it is a concise guide to significant places visible or immediately accessible from our modern highway system. In most cases, the interstate traveler needs to drive no more than six miles from the interstate to encounter the properties discussed. The chapter is arranged in numerical order of highway—I-24, I-40, I-65, I-75, and I-81.

Chapter 2, "The Urban Landscape," is for big-city visitors and residents. Memphis, Nashville, Knoxville, and Chattanooga are explored in depth, so that the visitor is encouraged to stop at, walk in, and experience directly some fascinating urban neighborhoods, downtown business districts, and local government buildings.

Chapters 3–8 are for travelers on a more leisurely pace, those who wish to explore the older U.S. highways and local byways of Tennessee. These chapters emphasize places and buildings not always visible from the roadside; to fully experience local history and architecture, tourists are encouraged to walk along the streets of our towns and rural communities in order to encounter history on their own terms. At certain areas, travelers may see patterns of exploitation that have shaped the landscape in ways not easily reversed; at others, they will find that demands of modern times have encouraged the uneasy coexistence of man, machine, and nature. The book's narrative, together with what can be experienced through direct contact, conversation, and observation, may provide travelers with a new perspective on how our physical surroundings document the history of Tennessee.

Each chapter is divided into selected geographic or thematic landscapes that best reflect the region's history. These selected landscapes are further subdivided into traveling routes based on important historical or architectural themes. For example, the Sequatchie Valley is discussed in chapter 5. To explore the area's agricultural history, take U.S. Highway 127 from Dunlap to Cumberland Homesteads, while to see historic industrial and mining sites, take Tennessee Highways 27 and 28 from Richard City to Dunlap. Here, sublime rural vistas are within miles of devastated industrial areas, a trait shared by many other landscapes in the state.

The book emphasizes sightseeing by themes and landscapes, but its index of towns, cities, and place names allows travelers to find information about any historic site in Tennessee quickly. Selected boxed sidebars also highlight historical trends and landscape patterns that several communities have in common. Properties that have been listed in the National Register of Historic Places—a documentary record of places significant in state and local history administered by the Tennessee Historical Commission and the National Park Service—are in boldface type. A handful of National Register properties are further identified as National Historic Landmarks. This federal program designates properties that are of national significance in history and architecture.

In chapters 3–8, twenty-four historical landscapes are explored. Chapter 3 covers Appalachian Tennessee, the towns and countryside north of Knoxville. Chapter 4, "The Great Valley of Tennessee," focuses on the cities, rural communities, and industrial corridors between Knoxville and Chattanooga. Chapter 5 visits the sparsely populated but beautiful Cumberland Plateau, an area stretching from Byrdstown in the north, down the Sequatchie Valley to Jasper in the south, and including the hilly land of the Eastern Highland Rim. Chapter 6, "Middle Tennessee," is the book's largest chapter, including the rich history of the Central Basin and the often different past found along the Western Highland Rim. The last two chapters discuss the history of West Tennessee. Chapter 7, "The West Tennessee Plateau," examines the railroad network that crisscrosses the region, creating such classic railroad towns as Paris, Milan, Humboldt, Trenton, McKenzie, and Jackson. The final chapter explores the Mississippi River Country, the land watered by the mighty Mississippi and its tributaries, such as the Forked Deer, Wolf, and Hatchie Rivers.

Many of the places mentioned in this book are museums, historic sites, or public institutions that welcome visitors. In most cases, travelers are free to walk along the sidewalks or streets to enjoy the exterior architecture of local neighborhoods and downtown districts. Other places are commercial businesses open to the public. Some places, however, are private and generally not open to the public. These sites are marked in the book as either (private, no access) or (private, limited access).

Always remember as well that Tennessee's historic places are often fragile and always irreplaceable. Whether public or private property, it is illegal to dig for artifacts or to remove objects from a site without proper permission. Please treat our historical landscapes with the utmost care and consideration so that their legacy may be passed on to future generations.

Acknowledgments

Many librarians, curators, historic site managers, architectural historians, and county historians from throughout Tennessee have given me invaluable help and encouragement during my research of the Tennessee landscape. A special debt is owed to the following people: Dorothy Curtis and Anne Dale of the Tennessee Department of Agriculture; Claudette Stager and Elizabeth Straw of the Tennessee Historical Commission; Martha Carver of the Tennessee Department of Transportation, as well as former agency historians Jeff Durbin and Leo Goodsell; and Ann Toplovich and Susan Gordon of the Tennessee Historical Society. I especially thank Susan, who is the managing editor of the *Tennessee Historical Quarterly,* for helping me locate several excellent historic photographs for the book. I also must acknowledge the research and friendship of my students from Middle Tennessee State University, especially Jennifer Martin, J. Michael Floyd, Lauren Batte, Steve Sadowsky, Richard Betterly, Leslie Sharp, Amy Dase, Mary Mason Shell, Susan Goodsell, Richard Quin, Mike Gavin, Ken Rush, Pat Craddock, Lisa Oakley, Jeff Mansell, Jane Laub, Missy McLeod, Lea Lewis, Tirri Parker, Jennifer Butt, Rachel Franklin, David Judkins, Kent Whitworth, Holly Rine, Bonnie Gamble, Anne Leslie Owens, Tim Zinn, David Brum, Susan Cabot, Sandi Glidden, Gail Reed, Amanda Bradley, Trina Binkley, and Ruth Nichols for their research into different aspects of Tennessee history.

My closest companions and assistants during my fieldwork research were my wife, Mary Sara Hoffschwelle, of the history department of Middle Tennessee State University, and my young son Owen, who spent many weekends traveling the back roads of the state. Without their love, support, patience, and keen eyes, this book would have never been completed.

Introduction

I have discovered that there are certain essentials for success-
ful wayfarers. Not everyone possesses a measure of wander-
lust. (Perhaps this is just as well; otherwise the world might
resemble one immense beehive with drones and workers and
an occasional queen swarming constantly to and fro.) If you
do not yearn to seek out new paths and highways, listen to
strange tongues, become familiar with different ways of
thought and living, and if you are not prepared to pay a price
in time and energy and resources for this exploration, then
home is for you and you can bear witness to Shakespeare's
sentiment, "When I was at home, I was in a better place."
Wilma Dykeman, *Explorations* (1984)

Every year, millions of tourists speed along the interstate highways of
Tennessee heading south to Florida and New Orleans, east to Virginia
and Washington, D.C., north to Chicago and Detroit, and west to Dallas and Houston. Hundreds of thousands stop in the state's major cities
to visit such worldwide tourist destinations as Beale Street and
Graceland in Memphis, Music Row and Opryland in Nashville, the Tennessee Aquarium in Chattanooga, and the Great Smoky Mountains National Park outside of Knoxville.

This book will tell interstate travelers about the landscapes and
places they see as they cruise along the interstates or stop and visit in

the metropolitan areas of Tennessee. It also hopes to entice visitors and Tennesseans alike to slow down a bit and travel the older U.S. highways and secondary roads of the Volunteer State. Tennessee's history is more than country music, Elvis Presley, crowded national parks, and river museums. It is also a story of frontier villages, railroad towns, outstanding folk architecture, Civil War battlefields, coal mines, iron forges, schools, churches, and modern engineering landmarks. Tennessee is a place worth exploring and offers experiences found nowhere else in the country. This narrative and its illustrations may open your eyes to the landscape of history—especially its patterns of settlement, exploitation, adaptation, and conservation—so you may learn better to interpret Tennessee's urban and rural places in your own way.

Tennessee has been a state for two hundred years, but people have carved a life from its land for thousands of years. Over its rivers, through its deep forests and forbidding mountains, on its flat basins and rolling hills, and along its beautiful valleys, generations of Tennesseans have molded the landscape in ways that have left an indelible record of their hopes, achievements, and disappointments.

For those prehistoric Tennesseans who left no written records, we can interpret their history only through the objects, mounds, and village sites they left behind. The fork of the Duck and Little Duck Rivers at Manchester is a striking natural landscape of falls, forests, and

Duck River Falls, Old Stone Fort State Park. This landscape had an entirely different meaning to the Native Americans than it had to later white owners.

open land where people of the Middle Woodland period built a wall-enclosed, forty-acre place roughly between the years 30 and 430 A.D. Once described as a prehistoric stone fort, and still known as the **Old Stone Fort,** archaeologists now believe that this great walled space was set aside for religious ceremonies; it was a landscape full of mystery and meaning for Tennessee's first inhabitants for well over four hundred years.

The nineteenth-century settlers of Manchester, however, looked at these same resources in a different way. The spectacular falls were perfect for powering gristmills, sawmills, and gunpowder mills. In 1879 the Hickerson and Wooten Paper Company built a factory and small industrial village where Native Americans once had practiced sacred rites.

How different people have used the same natural and physical resources for different purposes is a constant theme in the history of Tennessee's landscapes. The most striking example is a modern landscape, the reservoir and valley created by the Tellico Dam on the Little Tennessee River in Monroe County. At one beautiful spot along the river once stood the town of **Chota,** which served Overhill Cherokees as a mid-eighteenth-century political center. Trade contact, disease, warfare, and land cessions steadily contributed to the decline of Chota; by 1799, missionaries found only five remaining houses there.

In the century to follow, Chota and other old village sites became part of prosperous farms, some large and profitable enough to use slave labor before the Civil War. After the war, the population grew but farms became smaller throughout Monroe County. The opportunities at the turn of the century were not the same as they had been two generations before. In 1907 the Babcock Lumber Company of Pittsburgh came to the valley and began to systematically strip the land of its valuable timber. Nearby canning and aluminum factories, new roads, and cheap electric power continued the twentieth-century process of modernization and exploitation. Then, in 1979, the Tennessee Valley Authority finally closed the gates of the infamous Tellico Dam, and the proud and beautiful valley was flooded; its man-made landscape broken here and there by monuments that mark where the great Cherokee villages once existed. The recreation area again forces our attention upon the water, the forests, and the wildlife—the same features that helped to attract the Cherokees, then the fur traders, hundreds of years ago.

This process of change over time is what makes our landscapes historic documents. The historian John Stilgoe defines the word land-

scape as "the not-quite-understood complex of dwellings, fields, factories, and other artifacts of human work placed among natural landforms and vegetation or in totally modified space" ("Two Archetypes," 9). As the folklorist Henry Glassie has pointed out, "plowing, strip mining, laying brick upon brick in mortar, weeding, bulldozing: these are as much historical acts as scratching a pen over paper." The landscape is a truly significant record of our history; in Glassie's words, it is "a palimpsest, the people's own manuscript, their handmade history book" ("Meaningful Things," 82).

Most landscapes of history fall into one of three broad categories. A vernacular landscape is one that reflects an evolving tradition of land use, where men and women shaped their patterns of living to the patterns of the natural landscape, locating towns where salt licks stood near a river or establishing farms where rivers had left rich bottomland ready for the plow. The political landscape is comprised of the politically established boundaries that surround us. The borders of Tennessee are, of course, the largest political landscape, and within those borders there are county, city, and town boundaries, which sometimes reflect nature's course, but more often than not they follow an arbitrary

TENNESSEE'S HISTORIC LANDSCAPES

dividing line chosen by a committee of legislators or local government officials. Within those boundaries, however, officials use zoning ordinances to further manipulate land-use decisions so that in many towns, the location of neighborhoods, shopping centers, and factories follow politically chosen lines on a map rather than reflecting individual choices and preferences. The engineered landscape is a creature of the industrial revolution, a landscape where men and women prepared professional plans and specifications before they took new inventions and technology and reshaped nature's contours to meet their needs and aspirations. Railroad corridors of roadbeds, bridges, steel rails, and sidings were among the first engineered landscapes in Tennessee. Later came the enormous projects of the Tennessee Valley Authority, and today we travel from city to city on modern engineered landscapes known as interstate highways.

Deciphering the not-quite-understood complex of the landscape requires the visitor to be both a keen observer and a thoughtful detective because sometimes the history of a place, at first glance, is not what it appears to be. The small Appalachian town of **Cumberland Gap,** for example, is justly celebrated for its long association with the migration of peoples through the Appalachian Mountains into the Great Valley of Tennessee. Between 1775 and 1840, over three hundred thousand people traveled the Wilderness Road and passed through Cumberland Gap. On the Tennessee side of the gap, a post office named Cumberland Gap sat beside trading posts, inns, taverns, blacksmith shops, and small stores. Despite the thousands of potential settlers who walked by in any given year, Cumberland Gap never grew larger than a village, and it became even more desolate during the Civil War when the movement of troops back and forth across the gap destroyed almost everything that remained of the original town.

The street grid, houses, stores, and churches travelers see today in Cumberland Gap, Tennessee, have little to do with the adventures of Daniel Boone and others two hundred years ago, but they have everything to do with a small group of Canadian and British capitalists who had wanted to build the "Birmingham" of the Appalachians. From 1886 to 1891, the American Association, Limited, designed a wholly new town, built an imposing two-story brick headquarters, and introduced Claiborne County to the industrial revolution. The company's grand plans for stores, hotels, and other businesses were never completed, but its town plan and street names still define the town today. Visitors to Cumberland Gap find not an early frontier town but the remnants of

Cumberland Gap, Claiborne County. The history of a place is not always what it seems.

1D 8
CUMBERLAND GAP

First explored, 1750; Long Hunters used it until 1760, and Daniel Boone in 1769, cutting the Wilderness Trail through it in 1775. Hosts of pioneers followed even before the road was built in 1796. Postal service was established in 1795 and a post office in 1803. The Gap changed hands 4 times during War Between the States.

Hampton's General Store, Skullbone. General stores are a rapidly disappearing sight in rural Tennessee.

what was once a small industrial company town, a place where most of the buildings roughly date between 1890 and 1930.

In other words, deciphering historical landscapes requires visitors to look at their surroundings with inquisitive minds and open eyes. Each landscape has a unique combination of patterns, a result of the relationships between the man-made and the natural. By looking closely at these patterns—ranging from places that have evolved from the days of first settlement to the imposed patterns of modern technology—the careful observer quickly discovers not only that a manmade landscape can be a thing of beauty, but also that powerful ties exist between the land and the human condition. "Landscape acquires meaning from human interpretation," observes geographer Ary J. Lamme III, "and people acquire identity through association with place" (63).

Nowhere is that relationship more clear than in the rural communities of Tennessee. The Hampton Grocery at Skullbone, along Tennessee Highway 105 in Gibson County, documents the reciprocal relationship between people and the commonplace that shapes our identity. The store is a plain two-story building, with gas pumps out front, the general store and post office on the first floor, and a self-proclaimed city hall on the second. If the building served only these necessary commercial and civic functions, it would be a community landmark. (Indeed, throughout Tennessee there are other crossroads stores that served their communities in similar ways.) But its lavishly decorated exterior, complete with a regional map highlighting Skullbone as the center of rural West Tennessee, speaks to the human need to feel part of a larger whole. The Hampton Grocery might appear to be in the middle of nowhere, so

Highway directions sign, Skullbone.
A road to nowhere may also be a
road to everywhere.

to speak, but its map "proves" that it has connections to everywhere. To emphasize the point, a wooden directional sign across the road gives the mileage from Skullbone to some thirty-odd places, from the three miles to Bradford to the 11,876 miles to Sydney, Australia.

The themes represented by these four very different places in the Tennessee landscape—Old Stone Fort, Chota, Cumberland Gap, and Skullbone—will be repeated in many places throughout the state. Places that held mystery and wonder for ancient Tennesseans exist in every region; modern settlers have used some for agricultural or industrial purposes while others remain much as they were hundreds of years ago. The bloody struggle of the Civil War destroyed towns and settlements, but its aftermath gave African Americans new opportunities to create their own landscapes while new towns and farms rose from the ashes of destruction along the paths of the rapidly expanding railroads. The industrial revolution and the Tennessee Valley Authority changed the course of history for rural and urban places throughout Tennessee. Country stores, on the other hand, still contribute to local identity and help to maintain a sense of past ways in our increasingly standardized, prefabricated world.

The many different dwellings, stores, churches, place names, dams, highways, schools, farms, factories, and public buildings of the Tennessee landscape have a diverse but always interesting history. This book will introduce the reader to those I found the most compelling, but as travelers ride the highways and backroads of Tennessee, they too will find others that convey their own special meaning to themselves and their families. The landscape is what we make of it: the names we give it, the way we look at it, and the memories we take from it. I can only hope that this encounter with our historic landscapes will help guide the traveler's own understanding and appreciation of the people, history, and architecture of Tennessee.

CHAPTER ONE

The Interstate Landscape

Interstate travel, by its very name, is designed to get the driver from one state to another as quickly as possible. Many older U.S. highways were designed as scenic drives that would meander from town to town through the state. But the interstates emphasize speed, uniformity, and separation with their "limited access" design. Travelers pass through major cities then cut through open countryside with few towns or communities directly visible from the road. They can stop only at rest stops or at parking areas. They exit the highway only where it allows them to do so. They are physically separated from the countryside by an endless line of fence paralleling either side of the highway. Over the years, trees, bushes, and too many advertising signs have grown up along the fences, further obscuring the view of the countryside and compounding the traveler's sense of isolation. No wonder all interstates seem alike. This lack of personal freedom and choice is the price travelers pay for the opportunity to cover long distances in the shortest amount of time possible.

Interstates are among the best examples we have of the modern "engineered" landscape of the late twentieth century. Serious interest in divided lane, grade separated, and limited access long-distance highways began in the 1930s. By the time the influential Pennsylvania Turnpike opened in 1940, officials in Washington and in many state governments had already discussed the possibilities of a national network of modern superhighways.

Cost was a major impediment to these grandiose construction

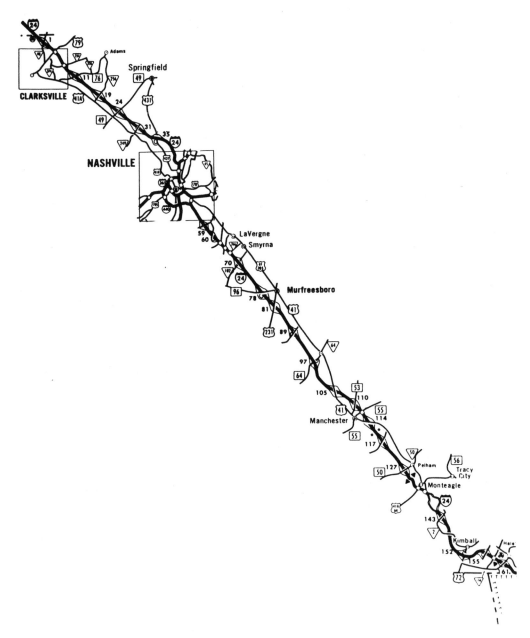

dreams. Eastern states, especially the booming urban areas, favored toll roads. Western states, lacking the population and traffic flow to support toll roads, wanted "freeways." In 1939 the federal Bureau of Public Roads reported that new direct interregional freeways were needed for the growing number of interstate commercial carriers and for the interest of national defense in mobilizing quickly the scattered resources of the armed forces. But, with the beginning of World War II, the federal government had no money for a new highway system. States filled the need with toll superhighways that by the 1950s stretched from Connecticut to Baltimore and from Philadelphia to Chicago.

Tennessee, like most other southern states, built no toll superhighway during these years and relied instead on the earlier federal highway system. Among the most important roads were U.S. 70 from Memphis to Knoxville; U.S. 41 from Springfield to Chattanooga; U.S. 31 from Nashville to Pulaski; U.S. 11 from Bristol to Chattanooga; U.S. 79 from Clarksville to Memphis; U.S. 64 from Memphis to Ducktown; and U.S. 51 from Union City to Memphis.

A booming postwar recovery, the suburban explosion, Americans' love affair with the automobile, and cold war defense needs finally convinced the federal government to fund the construction of a national system of interregional highways, defined by new routes, control of access, grade separation, and a minimum of four lanes divided by a median strip. Every interstate in Tennessee has those basic characteristics. In 1954 President Dwight Eisenhower appointed a committee to study the feasibility of an entirely new highway system. Two years later, Congress approved the Interstate Highway Act that called for the construction of forty-one thousand miles—eventually expanded to almost forty-three thousand miles—of interstate highways with the federal government bearing 90 percent of the total cost. This system of roads, cloverleafs, and rest stops now defines life on the road for most Americans.

Interstate Highway 24

Interstate Highway 24 begins in southern Illinois and ends in Chattanooga, Tennessee, serving the modern traffic needs once served largely by the Nashville, Chattanooga, and St. Louis Railroad, a company initially founded in 1845 as the Nashville and Chattanooga Railroad. Edmund W. Cole became company president in 1868, and he reorganized and expanded the railroad over the next decade. In December 1879, Cole announced plans to tie the largely Tennessee line to the ma-

jor midwestern commercial hub of St. Louis. Fearful that the Nashville, Chattanooga, and St. Louis would threaten its domination of regional commercial traffic, the powerful Louisville and Nashville Railroad bought controlling interest in the NC&St.L in 1880. Despite its domination by outside interests, the railroad remained a key transportation route between Nashville and Chattanooga through the 1950s.

The western end of I-24 in Tennessee is at Clarksville, the state's fifth-largest city and the location of Fort Campbell Military Base, home to the famous 101st Airborne Division-Air Assault of the U.S. Army. Turn west at exit 1 for access to the military base. At Gate 4, a visitor center and museum provides a history of Fort Campbell and the 101st Airborne.

Clarksville has two other interstate exits. Exit 4 (U.S. 79 and Tennessee 13) goes near the Dunbar Cave State Natural Area before continuing to Austin Peay State University and the downtown business and residential neighborhoods. A striking Colonial Revival theme dominates the architecture of the Austin Peay campus, originally founded in 1926. Much of the downtown commercial area has been listed in the National Register of Historic Places for its industrial, transportation, and architectural importance. Exit 11 is probably the best way to encounter Clarksville since U.S. 41A served for many decades as the town's major highway and many businesses and homes were located along its route. After passing through the typical shopping centers and strip development of the 1950s and 1960s, the highway becomes Madison Street, home to fashionable Victorian and early-twentieth-century dwellings and churches.

After exit 11, the next twenty miles of I-24 parallels U.S. 41A to the west. Cattle, hay, and tobacco are important agricultural products of this region; gable-roof rectangular tobacco barns are common. The highway passes through two properties that well represent the fate of family farms along the interstate system. Near mile marker 18, on the west side of I-24 in Cheatham County, are the 1827 house and associated work buildings of the Robert Elliott and Sons Farm, founded by Benjamin and Susan Elliott in 1807 and continuously operated by their descendents ever since (private, no access). Interstate construction took about ninety acres of the original farm and divided the property into seven tracts. The family had already sold land for the right-of-way of U.S. 41A a generation earlier. The two highways, however, brought little additional development to the area. The Elliott family continues to raise Angus cattle, corn, soybeans, and tobacco.

At mile marker 24, the exit for Tennessee 49, the impact of the interstate proved to be much different. About a half mile east of the exit stands the Maryama Farm, originally established by Mary Ann Naylor and her husband, Jonathan L. York, in 1864 (private, no access). Maryama Farm was noted for its tobacco and cattle, but recent development pressures have greatly reduced its size and production. In what used to be its fields, there is a new suburban neighborhood, which was built here less than a decade ago, that is populated by commuters who use I-24 to reach their jobs in Nashville. Only the house and two barns remain of the original farm.

At mile marker 44 in north Nashville, I-24 junctions with I-65 to pass through the state capital. As this junction skirts the historic neighborhoods of east Nashville and Edgefield, a very interesting view of the downtown skyline soon appears. Four skyscrapers are especially noteworthy. The Third National Financial Center (1983–86) features distinctive postmodern Egyptian Revival architecture, designed by Kohn Pederson Fox of Philadelphia. One Nashville Place (1983–85) is an octagonal dark glass skyscraper, designed by Morris and Aubry of Houston. The city's first major foray into modern architecture was the L&C Tower (1956), designed by Edwin A. Keeble of Nashville. The newest skyscraper, the postmodern South Central Bell Building (1993–94) by Earl Swensson Associates of Nashville, looms over the city's historic waterfront. This section of I-24 and I-65 also shows the city's earlier reliance on transportation and industry along the Cumberland River.

As the two interstates cross the Cumberland River, I-65 continues southwestward while I-24 merges with I-40. As these busy interstates

Interstate highway construction, Nashville. Interstates destroyed as well as created new neighborhoods in urban areas. (Courtesy of Nashville-Davidson County Archives)

run together for the next two miles, traffic becomes hectic. To relieve congestion, traffic engineers designed I-265 north of Nashville and I-440 to the south and west. Here the impact of the interstate on the urban landscape of Nashville cannot be ignored. As geographer Edward Relph has observed of urban interstates in general, wherever possible the highways are "driven along the lines of least resistance—parks, river valleys, blighted areas with low property values, or raised on columns above the rooftops of old buildings." They create a different experience of landscape, one "comprised chiefly of sequences of concrete channels and glimpses of landmarks, with sometimes dramatic views of skyscraper skylines unfolding as one drives toward them or around them" (Relph, 162). Their benefits are ambiguous. "Looked at in detail," Relph comments, "they are almost always ugly and dirty, like the railways before them, they divide up cities, separating industrial districts from residential areas, or poor ghettos from rich communities" (162). But their redeeming value—every place is accessible within a few minutes—outweighs their negative qualities in today's commuter society. For example, I-24 at exit 54 (Briley Parkway) provides good access to the Opryland entertainment complex. Exit 56 (Donelson Road) takes travelers to the modern Nashville International Airport. These standard urban interstate patterns—the division of cities, the separation of industrial areas, the heavier impact on poorer neighborhoods—can be seen throughout Nashville, or in any major urban area for that matter.

Another shared characteristic of many urban areas is the rise of "edge cities," or suburban downtowns, where huge shopping malls are surrounded by apartment complexes, shopping centers, huge grocery stores, medical and professional offices, and major discount retailers. I-24's best example of this emerging phenomenon is the commercial and residential development around Hickory Hollow Mall (1978), designed by Cooper Carey & Associates of Atlanta, at exits 59 and 60 (Bell Road and Hickory Hollow Parkway). Edge cities are our new "downtowns" where people congregate daily to shop, eat, and be entertained.

As I-24 leaves Nashville and continues for the next 118 miles to Chattanooga, it closely parallels U.S. 41 to the east. This highway was part of the legendary Dixie Highway that connected Chicago and Miami. Three miles east of exit 70, at the junction of U.S. 41 and Tennessee 102, stands the huge Nissan automobile plant. This factory—owned and operated by Japanese—began a new chapter in Tennessee's economic history when it opened in 1982. An important junction of the old Dixie Highway was the city of Murfreesboro, home to Middle Tennessee State University, a Classical Revival–style campus founded in 1911. The city has downtown commercial and residential historic districts that include **Oaklands Mansion** historic museum. North of town,

Hazen's Monument, Stones River National Battlefield. Modern industrial development threatens the future of the oldest Civil War monument in the country.

the National Park Service preserves portions of the battleground where the bloody **Battle of Stones River** was fought in 1862–63. At Murfreesboro, the Dixie Highway turned southwest toward the town of Shelbyville. Exit 81 (South Church Street) follows the Dixie route north directly to the late 1850s **Rutherford County Courthouse** at the Murfreesboro square.

The interstate passes out of the heart of Central Basin at about exit 97 where it crosses Hoover's Gap, site of a Civil War skirmish in the Chattanooga campaign of 1863. Just north of exit 110 (Tennessee 53), the road crosses the Duck River, an important water and power source for many southern Middle Tennessee towns. Manchester, which is a mile west of exit 111 (Tennessee 55), was once home to several nineteenth-century mills operating on the Duck River.

Sixteen miles farther, I-24 begins its tortuous climb up Monteagle Mountain. Engineers worked on completing this section of the highway years after the rest of the road was open to traffic. Even with modern technology, the grades are steep and the curves dangerous in inclement weather. Monteagle (exits 134–35) is a mountain resort hideaway and the location of the **Monteagle Assembly,** the oldest Chautauqua community in the South (private, limited access). Six miles to the west is the inspiring Gothic architecture of the University of the South at Sewanee. Established in 1857, the university has outstanding examples of Victorian Gothic and the later Collegiate Gothic architecture. The poet Richard Tillinghast described the place well in his *Sewanee in Ruins* (1984):

> In the 1850s the founders had envisioned
> broad avenues, fountains, Jeffersonian symmetries,
>> In the 1890s
>> the Gothic battlements their survivors built
>> served their experience,
> which told them there was something to fight against,
> and something to fight for.

To avoid the mountainous terrain surrounding Chattanooga, engineers of the Nashville and Chattanooga Railroad dipped their railroad south into Alabama before returning to Tennessee. The modern engineers of I-24 followed a similar idea, dropping into northern Georgia before approaching Chattanooga from the south side of the Tennessee River. Exit 174 is for the Lee Highway, the combined route for U.S.

All Saints' Chapel, University of the South, Sewanee. Inspiring Gothic architecture combines with the beauty of Monteagle Mountain to create a unique collegiate campus.

11, 41, 64, and 72 around Lookout Mountain and the Moccasin Bend of the Tennessee River into Chattanooga.

Between exits 174 and 178 is a splendid way to see several places that have shaped the history of Chattanooga. The city was initially founded as a river town, and the Tennessee River flows immediately to the north of the highway. Running between the river and the interstate are the former tracks of the Southern Railway and the NC&St.L Railroad, along with a railroad tunnel through Lookout Mountain on the south side of the highway. Chattanooga's growth one hundred years ago was linked to its role as a major southern railroad hub. Lookout Mountain was where the "Battle above the Clouds" took place on November 24, 1864, a decisive victory for the Union army that loosened the Confederate siege at Chattanooga. In the 1920s, local entrepreneurs developed **Ruby Falls** and Rock City on Lookout Mountain as attractions for tourists funneled into the combined routes of U.S. 11, 41, 64, and 72. Interstate travelers also have an excellent view of the U.S. Pipe and Foundry Company's works. For decades, the iron industry has contributed much to the economy of Chattanooga.

Downtown Chattanooga is accessible at exit 178 (I-124 Bypass). Important downtown buildings include the Chattanooga Choo-Choo complex, which was originally the **Southern Railway Terminal** (1909),

U.S. Pipe and Foundry, Chattanooga. The iron industry, although diminished greatly since 1900, remains part of the Chattanooga landscape.

designed by Beaux-Arts–trained architect Donn Barber, and the **James** and **McClellan** skyscrapers on Broad Street, designed by notable Chattanooga architect Reuben H. Hunt. Nearby on 730 E. Martin Luther King Boulevard is the Chattanooga African-American Museum and Research Center, which has a special display about blues singer Bessie Smith. Clearly visible to the east as the bypass crosses the Tennessee River is the Tennessee Aquarium (1992), a major new attraction along the city's riverfront, designed by the Nashville firm of Tuck and Hinton. I-24 climbs Missionary Ridge between exits 181 and 183, providing a glittering nighttime view for westbound travelers. The highway officially ends at its junction with I-75 at mile marker 185, two miles from the Georgia border.

Interstate Highway 40

Interstate 40 is Tennessee's major east-west highway, and its 451 miles are more than double the length of any other interstate in the state. The east entrance is high in the Appalachian Mountains at the northern border of the Great Smoky Mountains National Park. The west entrance is at the Mississippi River bridge in Memphis.

Eight miles after the North Carolina border at exit 443, I-40 intersects the Foothills Parkway, a short remnant of a once grandiose federal scheme to build a scenic parkway around the Great Smoky Mountains National Park. A seventeen-mile-long section of the highway also is in Blount County between U.S. highways 129 and 321.

At mile marker 425, shortly before exit 424 for Dandridge, the

Interstate Highway 40, East Tennessee. (Courtesy of Tennessee Department of Transportation, as adapted by the author)

highway crosses Douglas Lake, a 31,600-acre, man-made lake created by the Tennessee Valley Authority in 1943 when it dammed the French Broad River at a point southwest of Dandridge. Built to meet wartime demands for electrical power, the dam and lake have always been controversial because they claimed at least fifteen thousand acres of excellent East Tennessee bottomland. According to historian Wilma Dykeman, the "French Broad is a river and a watershed and a way of life where day-before-yesterday and day-after-tomorrow exist in odd and fascinating harmony" (*French Broad,* 25). Douglas Lake covers the region's largest intact Indian mound village, leading Dykeman to observe that "our most ancient relic of man and our most recent trophy of his scientific skill rest practically side by side" (*French Broad,* 25). When they looked at this landscape, Native Americans saw a perfect place for trade and cultivation. Latter-day engineers perceived the water as valuable if they could "harness" its power through modern technology. Douglas Dam can be reached from exit 412 and, as at most TVA facilities, public information and tours are available. (For more on TVA in Ten-

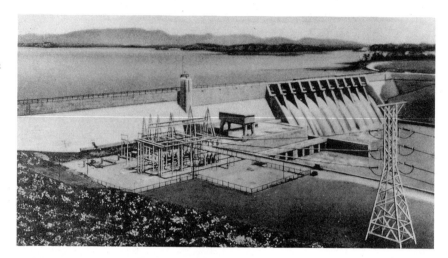

Douglas Dam, Jefferson County. An engineering achievement that forever altered the history of the French Broad country. (Photograph by June Dorman)

nessee history, see the sidebar entitled "The New Deal Built Environment" in Landscape 9 of chapter 4.)

Dandridge (1793), one of the oldest towns in Tennessee, can be reached by either exit 424 or exit 417. Douglas Lake almost covered this significant place of history and architecture, but an executive order from President Franklin D. Roosevelt forced TVA to build a dike protecting the town. Dandridge features a downtown historic district, including the Greek Revival–styled **Jefferson County Courthouse** (1845) and several excellent examples of antebellum domestic architecture.

Between exits 394 and 378, I-40 presents a complete overview of Knoxville as it passes north of the historic downtown. Knoxville was initially established in 1791 as a river port where the Holston and French Broad Rivers meet to form the Tennessee River. It served as the territorial capital, then the state capital, until 1817. Several early landmarks still stand, including **Blount Mansion,** which is a National Historic Landmark, and the Greek Revival architecture of the 1848 Knoxville **City Hall**, which was formerly an asylum for the deaf and dumb.

From 1850 to 1920, railroad construction reshaped the city, creating a new urban corridor of factories and warehouses along the route of the Southern Railway. Indeed, near the junction of I-75 and I-40 north of downtown, the yards of the Norfolk and Southern Railway are still operating. Just west of the interstate junction is exit 386, which leads to U.S. 129, locally known as the Alcoa Highway. This is a popular entrance to the University of Tennessee. The older campus buildings are excellent examples of Collegiate Gothic style, most of which were

Blount Mansion, Knoxville. The first Tennessee State Constitution was drafted on these grounds in 1796.

designed by the Knoxville firm of Barber and McMurry. U.S. 129 gives a particularly good view of the agricultural school and its various experimental farms. After exit 383, the interstate closely parallels the combined highways of U.S. 11/70. Traffic is heavy through this major commercial and suburban corridor that continues to expand west of Knoxville along the older federal highways.

As I-40 crosses the Clinch River between exits 352 and 350, the mammoth smokestacks of the Kingston Steam Plant dominate the landscape. At its opening in 1955, this Tennessee Valley Authority installation was the largest coal-fired power plant in the world. It also represented a massive change in the relationship between TVA and the landscape. When TVA began in the 1930s, it dammed rivers like the Clinch to harness hydroelectric power. But reservoirs and generators could not produce enough power to meet postwar needs, especially for places like the nuclear operations at Oak Ridge. Coal-fired plants initially met those demands and saved river valleys from flooding, but they also brought new environmental damage to Appalachian coalfields and communities as thousands of acres were strip-mined to fill the enormous appetite for coal. It is possible, for example, to see several train tracks—often full of coal cars—heading into the complex. Coal plants also meant air pollu-

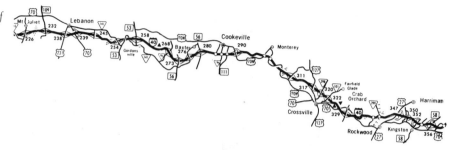

Interstate Highway 40, Plateau and Middle Tennessee (Courtesy of Tennessee Department of Transportation, as adapted by the author)

tion, and in 1976 TVA added the towering landmarks of the twin one-thousand-foot-high smokestacks in order to reduce pollution. In the name of energy production, TVA had found itself destroying the same natural resources and landscapes it had been created to protect.

The coal that powers the Kingston Steam Plant arrives on the tracks of the Norfolk Southern, a major supplier of coal from the southern Appalachian fields. Highway I-40 crosses the Norfolk Southern tracks at exit 347 (U.S. 27). Three miles to the north is Harriman, while six miles to the south lies Rockwood. Both are classic industrial towns of the late nineteenth century, with Harriman possessing large commercial and residential historic districts. Its historic **Princess Theater** is a dazzling landmark of Art Deco architecture.

After the Harriman/Rockwood exit, the interstate rides high along the Cumberland Plateau, providing spectacular scenic views in the fall, until it reaches Crab Orchard at exit 329. Crab Orchard sandstone is a bright light-brown and rose-colored stone used in many regional dwellings and public buildings. Crossville, at exit 317 (U.S. 127), has several excellent examples of sandstone use in its downtown county **courthouse,** jail, the **Palace Theatre,** and the cottages of **Cumberland Homesteads,** another National Historic Landmark in Tennessee.

From Crossville, I-40 takes a more northwest route and parallels U.S. Highway 70N. Cookeville (exit 287) is home to Tennessee Tech University (1915), which features a splendid quadrangle of Colonial Revival–style buildings. Beginning at Cookeville, the next twenty-nine miles of the interstate follows a route once dominated by the Tennessee Central Railroad. The **Tennessee Central Railroad Depot** is a railroad museum in downtown Cookeville. Organized by Jere Baxter during the depression of 1893, the railroad was based in Nashville and served towns such as Baxter and Cookeville that were previously ignored by other rail companies. From 1905 to 1908, the Tennessee Central leased

its eastern branch to the Southern Railway, but by 1912 the company was in receivership. Ten years later, the Tennessee Central was reorganized and remained a freight carrier until it ceased business in 1968.

The Cumberland River is the major river system of Middle Tennessee, and the town of Carthage, located five miles north of exit 258, is a largely intact historic river town. A few miles east of town is the family farm of Vice President Albert Gore Jr. (private, no access). Lebanon (exit 238), the next county seat twenty miles to the west, is the base of operations for the Nashville and Eastern Railroad, a short-line railroad established in 1985–86. It is also home to **Cumberland University,** one of the region's oldest private schools, dating from 1842.

A major tributary of the Cumberland is Stones River. In 1970 the U.S. Army Corps of Engineers finished Percy Priest Dam and Reservoir, creating a large recreational lake where the river once flowed. Between exits 221 and 219 to the south, the interstate gives travelers an excellent view of the dam and powerhouse. Producing twenty-eight thousand kilowatts of power, the dam is part of a massive fifty-year corps program of nine separate dams and reservoirs to improve navigation, control flooding, and produce hydroelectric power along the Cumberland River system.

The best way to see Nashville by interstate starts at exit 216 (Donelson Road/Nashville International Airport) and ends ten miles

later at exit 206 (the junction with bypass I-440). In 1779 Nashville began as a small settlement along the Cumberland River at a place called Fort Nashborough. A 1930 reproduction of the fort stands by the river in downtown Nashville. Nashville became the permanent state capital in 1843. A most impressive view of the Nashville skyline comes between exits 211 and 208. The high-pitched, gable roof of the red-brick **Ryman Auditorium,** an early home of the Grand Old Opry, the striking Greek Revival **State Capitol Building,** designed by William Strickland, and the tower of **Union Station** (1900), a railroad terminal of Richardsonian Romanesque architecture, can be seen. The last two buildings are prestigious National Historic Landmarks. Exit 209 gives access to Vanderbilt University, while exit 208 presents a view of the historic campus of **Fisk University,** one of the nation's leading African-American colleges. Its first campus was near a Civil War contraband camp where the massive neoclassical Nashville Electric Service building now stands.

As the interstate heads west of Nashville, it creates an almost entirely new route of travel, except for a stretch between exits 196 and

188 where I-40 follows the historic and scenic Harpeth River. Although no towns are visible for the next hundred miles, the interstate crosses several historic family farms. To the north of the interstate at mile marker 154 is the Mule Farmer Ranch (1869); the interstate passes directly behind the barn and cuts off the house and barnyard area from the remainder of the farm (private, no access). Founder Solomon Tidwell diversified his crops, producing peanuts, sorghum molasses, cotton, and wheat, along with raising sheep and cattle. He hired out the area's first steam wheat thresher in 1885 and even invested in the community's first metal-hub wagon, which he loaned to neighbors for long trips to Tennessee and Kentucky markets. Tidwell began with 160 acres and in modern times his descendents have farmed more than double that amount, mostly to raise cattle.

On either side of I-40 between exits 152 and 148 are fields and buildings of the Pruett Farm (1810), the oldest historic family farm in Hickman County (private, no access). The interstate right-of-way claimed thirty acres and an early log smokehouse from the original farm. William Totty controlled thousands of acres here during the antebellum period before dividing the property between his children in 1838. One hundred and fifty years later, the farm contained over six hundred acres, which yielded corn, hay, and cattle.

After exit 137, I-40 crosses the Tennessee River and enters West Tennessee. The Civil War, agriculture, and railroads have contributed much to regional history. Parker's Crossroads, at exit 108, was where Confederate cavalry and troops under the command of Nathan Bedford Forrest fought off a day-long assault from two Federal brigades on December 31, 1862. To the east, Federal commanders had just started the march to Chattanooga and were then fighting the Army of Tennessee at the Battle of Stones River. They desperately wanted to keep Forrest from returning to Middle Tennessee and supporting his comrades. The Union attack failed, however, and Forrest soon crossed the Tennessee River at the Clifton ferry.

Three years after the battle, William Pearson established Walnut Flat Farm (1865), which lies near mile marker 91 on the north side of the interstate (private, no access). Before the war, Pearson was a prosperous cotton planter in nearby Henderson County. The family history records that during the Civil War, Federal troops "with the help of the slaves freely looted and took whatever they pleased" from the plantation (West, 301). But these acts of revenge hardly left Pearson destitute. He moved to Madison County, where he purchased 1,062 acres and re-

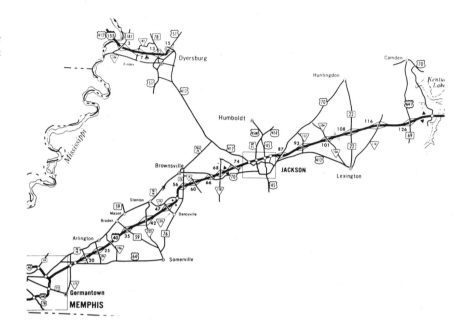

Interstate Highway 40, West Tennessee. (Courtesy of Tennessee Department of Transportation, as adapted by the author)

sumed the life of a planter. Pearson even added another 295 acres before he died in 1871. For years the family operated a cotton farm, but in recent years it shifted to raising registered polled Hereford cattle.

I-40 encounters the city of Jackson, a major transportation center and the second-largest city in West Tennessee, between exits 82 and 79. South of the interstate, via exit 82 (U.S. 45), is the historic downtown, which possesses some of the state's best Art Deco architecture, including its Madison County Courthouse, **Greyhound Bus Station,** and old Dr. Pepper bottling plant. Other important National Register landmarks include the former **Carnegie Library** (1901) and the **East Main** and **Northwood Avenue historic districts.** Jackson developed as a major regional terminal for the Illinois Central Railroad. One company engineer was the legendary Casey Jones, and his downtown Jackson home once stood at 211 W. Chester Street. After the construction of the interstate, however, city officials decided to move the house to exit 80 to improve its visibility and to serve as a tourist attraction. The house and railroad museum are now part of Casey Jones Village, typical of tourist attractions found along interstates throughout the country.

Cotton fields begin to dominate the landscape to the west of Jackson. Brownsville (exit 56) is an important trade center for the local cotton industry and the location of historic districts with several striking

Polk House, Jackson. The evolving domestic architecture of the East Main historic district documents Jackson's development as an urban center.

Greek Revival and Gothic townhouses that once belonged to the planter elite. Between exit 56 (Tennessee 76) and Brownsville is Alta Vista Farm, a historic cotton plantation that began with about a thousand acres in 1850 (private, no access). After Brownsville, I-40 parallels the old tracks of the Louisville and Nashville Railroad and generally follows the railroad until it reaches Memphis. It passes south of several small rural towns initially created by the railroad. Arlington, north of exit 25 in Shelby County, has an old general store and architecturally significant Victorian houses.

As the interstate passed through rural Shelby County and neared Memphis, new suburban developments associated with interstate travel soon destroyed some farms as the highway created new opportunities for others. The **Davies Plantation,** which features the oldest extant house (1807) in West Tennessee, once stood on both sides of I-40 between exits 16 and 14 (private, limited access). The family still retains hundreds of acres of land but sold other holdings to make way for the Davieshire subdivision and other developments in recent years. To the north of the bridge between exits 16 and 14 is the best view of the plantation.

The interstate does not enter Memphis directly; rather, the highway takes either a southern or northern loop to reach downtown and the bridge over the Mississippi River. Engineers initially planned for the interstate to also pass straight through the city, which would have destroyed acres of homes and much of **Overton Park,** the location of the city's major museums and zoo. Determined local opposition stopped these plans for destruction, but not until officials had condemned and demolished hundreds of homes along the proposed path of the interstate. Only during the early 1990s have a few new homes been built in the wide path once cleared for the interstate in the neighborhood west of Overton Park.

Most of Memphis's growth over the last two decades has taken place along the southern loop of I-240. The emergence of a new edge city is evident at exit 15 (U.S. 72), the access for Germantown. The development of multiple urban cores in our major metropolitan areas, according to urban critic Joel Garreau, is "the biggest change in a hundred years in how we build cities" ("Beyond the Urban Core," 18). In their shopping malls and easily accessible parking lots, dispersed office towers surrounded by trees and landscaping, multiple fast food restaurants, and low-rise apartment complexes, edge cities reflect our preference for suburbia and love for the automobile and mass consumerism as well as our fear of the inner city. Indeed, the evolution of edge cities may well be the "crucible of America's urban future" ("Beyond the Urban Core," 58).

The two ends of the I-240 loop meet in downtown Memphis. Important downtown landmarks include the Classical Revival–style **Shelby County Courthouse** (1909), designed by Rogers and Hale, the **Cotton Row** historic district along Front Street, and **Beale Street,** a

The Pyramid, Memphis. The new gateway to Memphis overwhelms the surrounding historic built environment.

TENNESSEE'S HISTORIC LANDSCAPES

National Historic Landmark as the birthplace of the blues. Before I-40 reaches the Mississippi River, two modern landmarks are visible. The Danny Thomas Boulevard exit is the entrance for the postmodern St. Jude's Children Hospital, to the north of the interstate. Also to the north of I-40, along the banks of the Mississippi River, is the Pyramid (1991), a thirty-two-story stainless steel addition to the city skyline. Memphis takes its name from an ancient Egyptian city along the Nile River. In the late 1980s, city officials and developers decided that a modern indoor arena, patterned after an Egyptian pyramid, would boost downtown economic development. Designed by Rosser FABRAP International of Atlanta and Venable and Associates of Memphis, the striking Pyramid dominates the interstate entrance and exit to Memphis. At the same time that Memphis officials and developers poured over fifty million dollars into their new gateway, however, historic sites, neighborhoods, and commercial areas continued to decline. A grand monument to a past that Memphis, Tennessee, shares in name only has come at the expense of the actual historic Memphis that embodied its true identity and culture.

The Mississippi River can also be crossed on the Interstate 55 bridge. I-55 enters Tennessee from Arkansas at Memphis and quickly exits through the southern half of the city into Mississippi. It presents an excellent downtown view of the waterfront and downtown districts.

At exit 5 (U.S. 51, Elvis Presley Boulevard) it provides immediate access to **Graceland,** a Colonial Revival mansion (1939) that later became home for Elvis Presley. This historic house museum about the king of rock 'n' roll is a National Historic Landmark that documents Presley's lifestyle and tastes in the late 1960s and early 1970s.

The many souvenir shops, restaurants, and other attractions that are adjacent to Graceland say little about Presley himself but say much about the present-day Presley cult and the powerful and still controversial role his career has played in modern American culture.

Interstate Highway 65

Interstate 65 is a major north-south route in Tennessee, connecting the midstate with Louisville, Indianapolis, and Chicago to the north and Birmingham and Mobile to the south. Entering from Kentucky, the highway closely parallels the route of U.S. 31W until it reaches Nashville, where it then follows U.S. 31 to the eastern outskirts of Franklin. From that point I-65 carves a new route to the Alabama state line, crossing sixty-five miles of open countryside.

Exit 117 (Tennessee 52) for Portland traverses land famous for its huge annual yield of strawberries. The town of Portland still holds an annual Strawberry Festival in mid-May. Cross Plains, about three miles west at exit 112, is a typical country crossroads town in Robertson County. Its main street (Tennessee 25) mixes the historic **Thomas Drugs** building (1915) and a 1907 bank building with nineteenth-century historic dwellings. The earliest is the **William Randolph Home and Tavern,** which dates to about 1820 (private, no access).

Fourteen miles later, at exit 98 near the junction of U.S. highways 31W and 41, I-65 meets the northern suburbs of Nashville. Goodlettsville was once a place of agricultural innovation. In 1887 local farmers organized the Goodlettsville Lamb Club, one of the first cooperative farm markets in the region. The suburban sprawl that greets travelers today makes it difficult to envision the agrarian landscape of one hundred years ago. About one and a half miles east of exit 97 is the reconstructed Manskers Station, a living history museum about the way of life along the Cumberland River when Kasper Mansker first settled there in 1779. Adjacent to the fort is the **Bowen-Campbell House** (circa 1788), an important early example of brick hall-and-parlor construction in Middle Tennessee.

Interstate Highway 65. (Courtesy of Tennessee Department of Transportation, as adapted by the author)

I-65 at exit 90 (Briley Parkway) gives quick access to the Cumberland River and the Opryland theme park and associated country music attractions. The development of Opryland dates from the early 1970s when company officials purchased open farmland along the Cumberland River in order to build a country music theme park to accompany the construction of a new theater for the Grand Ole Opry. They also built the massive Colonial Revival–style Opryland Hotel, designed by Earl Swensson Associates of Nashville, to serve park visitors. This complex welcomes country music fans year-round, as well as many regional and national conventions.

Two miles later, the highway junctions with I-24 and enters the heart of metropolitan Nashville. Northbound travelers have the best view of the Nashville skyline and its many high-rise buildings that were built in the 1980s. At exit 82, the Cumberland Science Museum for children is visible. On the hill behind the museum once stood **Fort Negley,** a federal army post built by African-American labor and garrisoned by African-American soldiers during the Civil War. The next exit, Wedgeworth Avenue, is near the famous Music Row of Nashville. During the middle decades of the twentieth century, many recording studios and publishing houses concentrated along or nearby Sixteenth Avenue South, making Nashville an internationally important music center, especially for country and gospel music. At the corner of Sixteenth Avenue South and Division, with an address of 4 Music Square East, is the well-respected Country Music Hall of Fame and Museum, which possesses an outstanding collection of artifacts about country music in the twentieth century. This museum will soon relocate its collections to Nashville's downtown.

After exit 81, I-65 heads south, closely paralleling the tracks of the former Louisville and Nashville Railroad. To the immediate east of exit 78 are the Radnor Yards, a major switching operation for CSX Railroad, which acquired the Louisville and Nashville line in 1980.

Northern Williamson County, between exits 74 (Brentwood) and 65 (Franklin), once featured many fine farms and plantations. Today suburban growth has transformed this once rural area into another emerging edge city; recent development have centered around the Galleria shopping mall at exit 69. Franklin, the seat of Williamson County, is three miles west of exit 65. Historic preservation planning and zoning have protected the town's nineteenth- and twentieth-century historic neighborhoods from uncontrolled development. A bloody Civil War battle took place here in 1864, but several antebellum homes and

Carter House, Franklin. Modern development continues to threaten the few remaining places of the Franklin Battlefield.

buildings survived the destruction, including two National Historic Landmarks. The **Carter House** (1830) witnessed some of the heaviest fighting. **Carnton Mansion** was also part of the fighting, and the adjacent **cemetery** was where many of the Confederate dead were buried. The **Hiram Masonic Hall** (1823) was the first Gothic Revival and three-story-tall building in Tennessee (private, no access).

The Saturn Parkway (exit 53) is the entrance to the modern Saturn automobile factory built by General Motors during the late 1980s (private, limited access). General Motors considered thirty-eight states before choosing land that was once part of the Haynes Haven plantation. It kept the Greek Revival plantation house as a reception area and landscaped the terrain to hide most of the factory from public view.

The last fifty miles of I-65 passes through rich and productive farmland in southern Middle Tennessee. Fewer than six miles east of exit 32 is Lewisburg, the county seat of Marshall County, which was a flourishing center for the dairy industry in the early twentieth century. Overlooking the historic town square and courthouse is the striking Queen Anne–style **Adams House** (1900), home to a former mayor and town banker (private, no access). On U.S. 31A, between Lewisburg and the interstate, the University of Tennessee operates an experimental dairy farm. In 1830 the state assembly chartered Cornersville, four miles east at exit 27, and the town has served as a trading center for local farmers ever since. Its **United Methodist Church,** built jointly by the congregation and local masons in 1852, is an excellent example of Greek Revival ecclesiastical architecture.

At exit 22, the interstate passes two historic family farms. In 1845 Henry K. Burgess established the Burgess Farm (private, no access). The highway divides the farm in half, yet the family maintains a livestock farm of cattle and swine. The Wits End Farm was originally a 413-acre antebellum cotton plantation, founded by Maj. John Gordon in 1846 (private, no access). By 1913 changes in ownership had reduced the farm to 246 acres, and it lost another thirty acres during the construction of I-65. Family members recently have produced livestock, corn, and sorghum on 185 acres.

Before I-65 meets the Alabama state line, between mile markers 7 and 6 are two more historic farms directly impacted by the construction of the interstate in 1963–64 (both private, no access). The White Cloud Plantation flanks the interstate. Dating from 1866, the farm contains the log-cabin birthplace of John C. Brown, who was governor of Tennessee from 1870 to 1874. Bert Gwaltney acquired the property after 1906 and transformed it into a model progressive farm, yielding sheep, mules, and dairy products. Once I-65 took twenty-eight acres and divided the farm in half in 1963, the family turned the eastern land into a pine, black walnut, and poplar tree farm and kept the western half for cattle, dairy, and lumber production. Also adjacent to the interstate is the King Farm (1859). The first owner, James King, produced favorite nineteenth-century crops such as cotton, corn, and wheat on his 455 acres, but by the mid-1980s the farm had grown to over 750 acres, yielding such popular modern crops as soybeans, milo, and lespedeza.

Interstate Highway 75

Interstate 75 is one of the great north-south highways in America, beginning at Sault Ste. Marie, Michigan, at the Canadian border and ending outside the Everglades in Naples, Florida. The 160-mile Tennessee section passes through mountainous terrain and narrow gorges before entering the Great Valley of Tennessee south of Knoxville and later exiting the state at Chattanooga.

For its first twenty-six miles, the interstate passes through a rugged landscape shaped by railroads and coal mining during the late nineteenth and early twentieth centuries. Jellico, immediately east of exit

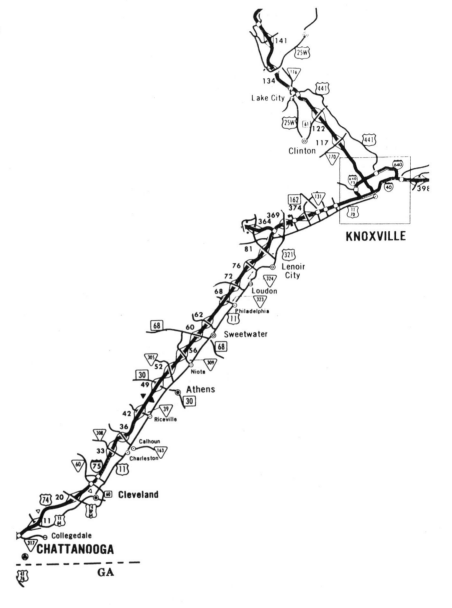

Interstate Highway 75.
(Courtesy of Tennessee Department
of Transportation, as adapted by
the author)

160, was a center of coal mining activity as early as 1881 when the East Tennessee, Virginia, and Georgia Railroad extended a spur line northward from Caryville. Mining activity intensified during the 1890s when major railroad powers, the Southern and the Louisville and Nashville, acquired local branch lines. Few early buildings exist today, however, largely because in 1907 an accidental explosion of a boxcar of dynamite leveled most of the trackside commercial buildings. The explosion killed eight people while injuring more than two hundred. During the early twentieth century in Jellico, the federal government operated a **Mine Rescue Station** that conducted classes in first aid and mine safety.

The next twenty-six miles of interstate share a gorge through the mountains with the tracks of the Southern Railway. On Stinking Creek Road east of exit 144 stands the Black Bill Baird place (private, no access). William Baird, a veteran of the Civil War and western Indian wars, saved his army pay to buy a farmstead of about 250 acres in 1873. His family kept the land in production for the next hundred years, and in 1976 the Tennessee Department of Agriculture designated it as the only Century Farm in Campbell County. Caryville, at exit 134, was another railroad shipping point for coal. Its public school, built by the Public Works Administration in 1938, faces southbound traffic on the interstate. Three miles east of Caryville is Jacksboro, the seat of government for Campbell County, initially established in 1806. The Campbell County Courthouse (1926) is a Classical Revival building designed by R. F. Graf and Sons. On the courthouse grounds is a

TVA Camp #14, Company 1229, CCC, at Norris Dam. Norris Dam and Village are excellent examples of the New Deal built environment created by such federal agencies as the Civilian Conservation Corps. (Courtesy of Tennessee State Library and Archives)

rare war memorial monument built by the National Youth Administration in 1938.

Technology and industry of the late Victorian era marked the land and communities of Campbell County. But beginning in 1933, the landscape south of Caryville between exits 128 and 122 was forever altered by the great experiment in planning and technology known as the Tennessee Valley Authority. Norris Dam (1933–36), which tamed the waters of the Clinch River, was TVA's first major construction project, and, in many ways, it remains the most interesting to visit. Exit 128 is where the interstate junctions with the remnant of the scenic Norris Parkway (U.S. 441). This approximately thirty-mile-long road connected the dam and TVA's offices at Norris to the authority's headquarters in Knoxville. The WPA guidebook to Tennessee described the freeway as "scientifically constructed to eliminate sharp turns, crossroads, and other traffic hazards" (344). As the traveler approaches the dam and powerhouse on U.S. 441, there is an excellent overlook of the complex, with interpretive markers explaining the massive land transformation.

Immediately east of exit 122 is the town of **Norris.** When TVA came to build Norris Dam, none of the surrounding towns had enough housing for its thousands of employees. The authority, therefore, developed Norris as a model residential community and owned the town until 1948 when it sold it to private individuals and developers. The still-intact town plan and the combination of Colonial Revival, Tudor Revival, and Rustic architecture makes Norris a fascinating statement of New Deal town planning. Norris is also home to two important folklife museums. Located in the Norris Dam State Resort Park, the Lenoir Pioneer Museum features a historic gristmill (1935), a threshing barn, and modern exhibits about the people and history of the Clinch River country. The Museum of Appalachia has comprehensive exhibits on regional crafts and folklife as well as a group of historic farm buildings, dwellings, and other structures moved to the museum for preservation and interpretation. Properties, including the **Arwine Cabin** and a cantilever barn from near Seymour, become the setting for living history and craft demonstrations throughout the year.

About fourteen miles south of Norris, the interstate encounters the I-640 bypass around north Knoxville. Travelers may take I-275 and go directly into the heart of north Knoxville. They will go by the large Norfolk and Southern railroad yards. To bypass the city, take I-640 west to its junction with Interstate 40. The two highways then run together for the next twenty miles until exit 84 when I-75 curves southward toward Chattanooga.

In 1978 TVA changed the course of history along another historic river, the Little Tennessee River, when it shut the floodgates on the Tellico Dam, located three miles southeast of exit 81. The Tellico project has proven to be one of the agency's most controversial, with questions raised on both economic and environmental grounds. Nearby on the Tennessee River, just above its confluence with the Little Tennessee, is Fort Loudoun Dam and Powerhouse, a TVA project of the 1940s. Both dams have shaped the growth of Lenoir City—a late-nineteenth-century planned industrial town—into one of the region's larger industrial centers.

Loudon is a historic river town about four miles east of exit 72. Established as Blair's Ferry in 1799, the settlement later took the name of Loudon and became the county seat. The **Blair's Ferry Storehouse** (circa 1835) is one of the oldest buildings left from the river days in this county seat (private, no access).

Between exits 84 and 72, I-75 passes through some of the best farmland in East Tennessee, watered from the north by the Clinch River and to the south by the Tennessee River. The interstate takes travelers near five historic family farms that document agricultural change and continuity in the Tennessee Valley (all private, no access). From 1938 to 1948, the Alexander Farm served as a TVA model farm, demonstrating new crops, fertilizers, and farming techniques. The Shipley Farm was established in 1853 and became a prosperous dairy farm in the early twentieth century. But in the 1960s, it lost ninety-one acres to the construction of I-75, reducing it to a small farm of sixty acres that produced only hay and garden vegetables by the mid-1980s.

Nearer the Tennessee River stand the Eldridge, Hotchkiss, and McQueen family farms. Established in 1798, the Eldridge property is one of the region's oldest. During the Civil War, the farm lost most of its crops and livestock to marauding Federal troops. The Hotchkiss Farm avoided the same fate only because the family had nursed a Union trooper to health, and he kept his fellow soldiers from pillaging the property. The McQueen Farm, established by Thomas and Eliza Mason in 1852, still uses five of its original buildings in its cattle operations.

Nineteenth-century railroad development largely determined the location of towns along I-75 from its Tennessee River bridge to its junction with I-24 in Chattanooga. During the 1850s, the East Tennessee and Georgia Railroad built the original line, which connected Knoxville to Dalton, Georgia. In 1869 the line became part of the East Tennessee, Virginia, and Georgia Railroad. This company controlled all of the rail traffic of the Tennessee Valley until it became part of the Southern Railway system in 1894.

The historic buildings and homes in the railroad towns adjacent to I-75 typically reflect the decades when the Southern Railway dominated regional commerce and industry. Three miles to the east at either exit 62 or 60 is Sweetwater, a name derived from the English translation of the Cherokee words "Culla Saga" for a creek that runs through town. In 1897, three years after the Southern took control of the railroad, officials incorporated the town. Its town depot, mill factories and warehouses, along with several late Victorian storefronts and homes, document the railroad's impact on local history. Notice how these buildings are oriented to the railroad tracks that pass through the heart of town; there is a similar linear pattern in almost every town south of Sweetwater.

Niota, three miles east at exit 56, has a historic **East Tennessee and Georgia Depot** (1855) that is considered to be the state's oldest existing depot. Athens, two miles east of exit 49, has a history closely tied to railroads. The region's first railroad construction took place in 1837 when the Hiwassee Railroad Company broke ground near

East Tennessee and Georgia Railroad Depot, Niota. The railroads introduced the industrial revolution to rural Tennessee as they created new towns, with specialized buildings, at regular intervals on their lines.

Athens. The old company office still stands downtown on North Jackson Street, near a neighborhood of historic public, ecclesiastical, and collegiate buildings, many of which are associated with Tennessee Wesleyan College.

After exit 36, the interstate crosses the Hiwassee River. To the east of the bridge is the huge Bowater Paper Mill (1954) at the town of Calhoun. Mist from the river sometimes produces a dense fog, and interstate signs warn drivers of this dangerous possibility. After crossing the Hiwassee, the highway enters Bradley County, the location of several historic places associated with the infamous "Trail of Tears." In 1835 federal officials produced the Treaty of New Echota, a document of dubious legitimacy that compelled the Cherokees to exchange their historic south Appalachian homeland for a new reservation in what was then called "Indian Territory" in Oklahoma. When the Cherokees protested and refused to go voluntarily, the U.S. Army removed them by force. Four miles east of exit 33 is Charleston, where the Cherokee Indian Agency operated from 1821 to 1838. East of the agency was Fort Cass (1836–38), which served as army headquarters for the forced removal of the Cherokee. In 1838 Gen. Winfield Scott brought approximately thirteen thousand Cherokee here for the westward march. The last meeting of the old Cherokee tribal council took place at nearby **Rattlesnake Springs** (private, no access).

The county seat of Bradley County is Cleveland, three miles southeast of interstate exit 25. White settlers established the town as soon as the last Cherokees were forced out of the county in 1838. A large industrial town one hundred years ago, Cleveland had its own streetcar system as early as 1886. Today the town features excellent examples of Victorian period architecture, including the Second Empire architecture of **Craigmiles Hall** (1878) and **St. Luke's Episcopal Church,** a Gothic design by Peter J. Williamson in 1887. Ooltewah, less than a mile east of exit 11, was once a county seat as well. The state legislature created James County in 1871, but in 1919 the county went bankrupt and the state legislature dissolved it, leaving only the historic **James County Courthouse** as evidence of its brief existence (private, no access).

After exit 11, I-75 enters into the eastern half of Chattanooga. At exit 4, Tennessee 153 to the north gives quick access to TVA's Chickamauga Dam (1935–40). This mammoth structure is 129 feet high and 5,800 feet long. The lake contains 35,400 acres and is almost 60 miles long. One of the recreation areas bordering the lake is Booker T. Washington State Park, built and developed by an all African-American

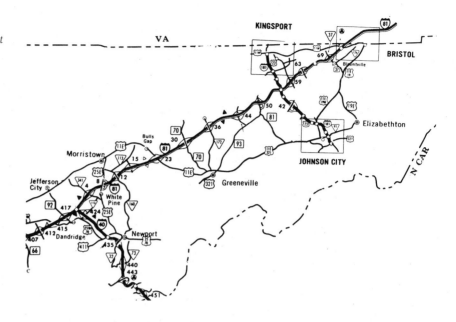

Interstate Highways 81 and 181.
(Courtesy of Tennessee Department
of Transportation, as adapted by
the author)

camp of the Civilian Conservation Corps in 1939. Until the Civil Rights laws of 1960s ended racial segregation of public places, Washington Park was one of the few state parks where blacks were welcome. Tennessee Highway 153 is also the exit for the **Tennessee Valley Railroad and Museum**, where tourists can take train rides through a slave-built antebellum **railroad tunnel** under Missionary Ridge.

Interstate 75 leaves Tennessee by combining with I-24 at exit 2 and turning southward toward Atlanta.

Interstate Highway 81

Interstate 81 cuts through the heart of northeastern Tennessee, creating a new transportation route connecting travelers from Knoxville to Bristol and on to the Shenandoah Valley of Virginia. Before its construction, travelers going east from Knoxville to Bristol took either U.S. Highway 11E, which went by Greeneville and Johnson City, or U.S. Highway 11W, which passed through Morristown, Rogersville, and Kingsport. Highway I-81 made the jaunt from Knoxville to Bristol much safer and faster.

Exit 74 leads to Bristol, a rarity among American cities because its main commercial street, State Street, is the boundary between Vir-

State Street Gateway, Bristol, Tennessee and Virginia. This electric sign proclaims Bristol's devotion to industrial development during the early twentieth century.

ginia and Tennessee, so decided by the Tennessee legislature in 1902. Standing proudly across State Street is an **electric sign** that has welcomed visitors for over seventy years. Both sides of State Street have impressive historic buildings, including the **Bristol Union Railway Station** on the Virginia border and the **First National Bank** building and **Paramount Theater** on the Tennessee side. A block south is the **Shelby Street Post Office** (1899–1900), designed in the Renaissance Revival style by James Knox Taylor. Bristol was an important Southern Railway and Norfolk and Western Railroad junction, and many of its historic buildings date from the early twentieth century when railroads and coal mining dominated the regional economy. An interesting exception is the Medieval Gothic architecture of the **Stone Castle** stadium on Edgemont Avenue. Built by the Works Progress Administration during the 1930s, local football games are played there today.

Highway I-81 also represents a cultural link between northeastern Tennessee and the Shenandoah Valley of Virginia. Many settlers from Pennsylvania and Virginia came through the Shenandoah Valley to Tennessee. Early towns, such as Blountville just east of exit 69, share characteristics in town planning, architecture, and folklife with their Virginia neighbors. Historic Main Street in Blountville, for example, documents the linear town plan often found in the Shenandoah Valley. Dwell-

Deery Inn, Blountville. This doorway shows an exuberance rarely associated with the Federal style in Tennessee.

Daniel Boone highway marker, Church Circle, Kingsport. The development of the Colonial Revival architecture of Church Circle coincided with the building of Daniel Boone Highway during the 1920s.

ings and businesses are close to the street, with little or no front yards. The **Deery Inn** was built in about 1800 and is one of Tennessee's early architectural landmarks (private, no access). It is a block of three connected row houses, with a shared cornice and prominent doorway. Another landmark is the **Dulaney House** (1802), a late Georgian brick dwelling with a Palladian portico (private, no access). Exit 69 is also the access for the Bristol International Speedway, a major stop on the NASCAR stock-car racing circuit.

The twentieth-century industrial city of Kingsport is three miles west of exit 59. Sections of the town adjacent to the **Long Island of the Holston River,** a National Historic Landmark, belong to the early settlement history of Tennessee. The **Netherland Inn and Boatyard Complex,** at 2144 Netherland Inn Road, date from the early 1800s. But the Kingsport of today is a reflection of the planned industrial city movement of the early twentieth century. The firm of John Nolen, a pioneer in American urban planning, is credited with refining and further developing the town plan of Kingsport from 1915 to 1921. The downtown **Church Circle** shows how Colonial Revival architecture and modern city planning ideas combined to produce an ideal urban landscape of the 1920s.

After exit 59, the interstate moves into the countryside. It bypasses major cities, such as Johnson City, Rogersville, and Greeneville, although in recent years, the state department of transportation has improved the interstate access roads for each city. Between exits 50 and 23, I-81 travels through northern Greene County, where almost forty historic family farms have been identified. These twenty-seven miles of pavement cross a beautiful agricultural landscape. Tobacco is a very important crop in Greene County, and most families also raise cattle. As indications of these agricultural traditions, the landscape is dotted with tobacco barns and fields of hay.

The interstate intersects U.S. 11E at exit 23, and, three miles to the west, at Bulls Gap, the settlement landscape again shifts to reveal the region's industrial and transportation history. **Bulls Gap** began as an important railroad junction on the East Tennessee and Virginia Railroad. By the 1920s, the Southern Railway turned the town into a mini division point for its eastern Tennessee lines, complete with depot, water towers, sand house, dormitory, and other support buildings.

Morristown, six miles north of exit 8, shares a similar history. The seat of Hamblen County, Morristown was organized in 1855 as the East Tennessee and Virginia Railroad was building its first section of track. It too benefited from traffic on the later Southern Railway, and by the 1930s the town had more than thirty small factories and six tobacco warehouses. The town center features the Second Empire architecture of the **Hamblen County Courthouse** (1874), designed by A. C. Bruce, at 511 W. Second Street North; the adjacent red-brick

Richardsonian Romanesque city school, now the **Rose Cultural Center** (1892); and the Renaissance-style **U.S. Post Office** (1915) at 134 North Henry. The town was also home to the **Morristown College**, a seminary and college for African Americans established in 1881 by the United Methodist Church. Later in the twentieth century, TVA projects such as the nearby Cherokee Dam spurred further growth, and Morristown became a regional commercial and industrial center. The Crockett Tavern and Museum, at 2002 E. Morningside Drive, is a memorial to the area's early history when John Crockett operated a tavern near this place in the 1790s. The present building was reconstructed in the 1950s when a Disney television series rekindled interest in John's son, the legendary Davy Crockett.

North of exit 4 is Jefferson City, the largest commercial center in Jefferson County. It too grew as an East Tennessee and Virginia railroad town in the late nineteenth century. In 1889 Carson-Newman College was located at the center of town, and the campus still retains an outstanding collection of Classical Revival buildings. North of town, visible from U.S. Highway 11E, is the **Glenmore Mansion** historic house (1869), designed by W. H. Clyce. Architectural historian James Patrick calls the dwelling "perhaps the grandest Second Empire country house remaining in Tennessee" (187).

The Tennessee branch of I-81 ends four miles from the Jefferson City exit when the highway meets I-40.

CHAPTER TWO

The Urban Landscape

Four large urban cities—Chattanooga, Knoxville, Nashville, and Memphis—anchor the Tennessee landscape. Each has its own sense of place, history, tradition, and destiny. But these real and imagined differences do not overshadow what the four cities share in common. They stand at or near former Native-American communities and trade centers of the earliest frontier years. River transportation was important to their initial growth. Chattanooga, for instance, stands along the banks of the Tennessee River; Knoxville is where the Holston and French Broad Rivers form the Tennessee River; Nashville developed along the Cumberland River; and Memphis remains an important river city on the mighty Mississippi.

Then, in later decades of the nineteenth century, railroads shaped these cities' destinies and built environments. These four cities served as important transportation crossroads for the Southern Railway, the Louisville and Nashville, the Nashville, Chattanooga, and St. Louis, and the Illinois Central. In these cities was focused the state's industrial revolution that reshaped the "New South" out of the ashes of the Civil War. Determined civic capitalists—business and political leaders who worked together to achieve mutual goals in economic development—created new alternatives for a future different from the antebellum, agrarian past. They added the necessary infrastructure of urban culture: city parks, libraries, museums, water and sewage systems, fire and police stations, and social services. The new urban culture embodied assumptions about the "good life" that contrasted with those of the countryside. Little wonder that the cities both repelled and irresistibly attracted farm boys and girls throughout Tennessee.

The late-nineteenth-century city also became a source of strength for newly established African-American communities. In the era of Jim Crow segregation, urban middle-class blacks, although few in numbers, effectively organized betterment leagues, fairs, and home-improvement clubs. They agitated for public funding for better schools and libraries. In Memphis this activism led to a series of public parks; in Nashville it gained parks, libraries, and YMCA facilities. The cities became home to the state's best educational institutions for African Americans, including Fisk University and Tennessee State University in Nashville, Knoxville College in Knoxville, and LeMoyne-Owen College in Memphis. The cities, however, could also be places of terror. In 1892, white mobs lynched three Memphis blacks and then destroyed the newspaper offices of Ida B. Wells when the outspoken editor dared to speak out against lynching. Terrible riots rocked Knoxville in 1919 when white mobs destroyed the jail, stole weapons, and proceeded to shoot up black neighborhoods.

In the twentieth century, the cities proved fertile ground for the rising civil rights movement. The sit-in protest movement struck five downtown Nashville lunch counters in February 1960; by that summer all four cities had witnessed this effective and forceful show of black solidarity and the urban lunch counter became integrated. Nashville colleges produced important leaders of the national movement, including Diane Nash and John Lewis. The cities remain centers for African-American education, business, culture, and political power.

The rise of the suburbs in the late nineteenth century, and the suburban explosion of the twentieth century, also left an indelible mark on the urban landscape. "Suburbia symbolizes the fullest, most unadulterated embodiment of contemporary culture," notes historian Kenneth T. Jackson. "It is a manifestation of such fundamental characteristics of American society as conspicuous consumption, a reliance upon the private automobile, upward mobility, the separation of the family into nuclear units, the widening division between work and leisure, and a tendency toward racial and economic exclusiveness" (4). Today neighborhoods such as Richland-West End in Nashville, Overton Park in Memphis, and Fort Sanders in Knoxville are significant historical and architectural remnants of the early suburban experience.

In the broad patterns of land use, cities often look alike. Zoning is a major reason why. Beginning in the 1920s and becoming increasingly significant every decade since, the legal tools of zoning and land-use planning have created segregated islands of industrial parks, residential neighborhoods, retail plazas, and high-rise apartment complexes within the larger cityscape. Zoning, like suburbia, has contributed much to the visual order and uniformity that characterize our cities.

Finally, as noted in chapter 1, the web of interstate highways, commercial strips, airports, entertainment complexes, and shopping malls have become important landmarks of the urban experience for most travelers. "Going to the city" is hardly what it used to be. Travelers use bypasses and overpasses of the interstate to drive by the downtown without stopping. Or they might stop, shop, eat, and visit at the exurbias and historic sites on the outskirts of the urban core. Airports long ago replaced train depots as urban transportation hubs, and, due to the vast amounts of acreage needed for modern air traffic, these new urban gateways are located miles away from the heart of downtown. Even most residents of metropolitan areas rarely go downtown, except to spend the hours of nine to five at their office desks. At night, downtowns become virtual ghost towns set in a dark concrete-and-steel canyon. After looking at the changes brought by urban renewal and interstate construction to her old neighborhood in Knoxville, poet Nikki Giovanni wondered, "I thought there may be a reason we lack a collective historical memory" (Paschall and Swanson, 261).

This chapter encourages travelers to do more than drive through or around the state's four largest cities. To experience fully the urban landscape, they should walk the downtown streets, step inside the remaining shops, department stores, and restaurants, and visit the historic sites and architectural landmarks that embodied the hopes and dreams of past generations. Their encounter with the past, as it exists in the present, may bring to mind questions about the nature of urban life before the air conditioner, the elevator, and the automobile. All three machines have indelibly changed urban experience. Downtown stores might still be the heart of commercial life if not for air conditioning, which made enclosed shopping malls possible and popular, and the automobiles that gave consumers individual access to suburban shopping areas.

As geographer Edward Relph reminds us, "Buildings, whether architect designed, hand-made, or mass-produced, are the most obvious human artifacts in urban landscapes" (7). They provide a gateway to the urban past, but one that should be used carefully. They are not isolated components of history but part of the web of city life, and they only have meaning when we consider the people who built them, used them, and altered them as the patterns of urban life have changed over the last 150 years.

Landscape 1: Chattanooga

Some say that Chattanooga is the
Old name for Lookout Mountain
To others it is an uncouth name
Used only by the uncivilised
Our a-historical period sees it
As merely a town in Tennessee
To old timers of the Volunteer State
Chattanooga is "The Pittsburgh of
The South"
According to the Cherokee
Chattanooga is a rock that
Comes to a point

Ishmael Reed, "Chattanooga" (1973)

Nestled in the "Grand Canyon" of the Tennessee River Valley, Chattanooga has served as an important transportation hub for hundreds of years. The Tennessee River winds its way through the southern Appalachians at this point, creating its famous Moccasin Bend, surrounded by rugged, craggy mountainsides. Travel by river had always been troublesome. The Native Americans developed trails that crossed the river at Chattanooga, but river transportation was difficult due to many whirlpools and rough water at this point. Settlers following those early Indian paths also found the Chattanooga area to be extremely hazardous for navigation.

Chattanooga never was much of a place until the railroad arrived in the 1850s. Indeed, the treacherous mountain approaches to the small town meant that the railroad from Tennessee had to build into Alabama and then return north to Tennessee to enter the town and connect with the Georgia railroad system that owned a large chunk of downtown real estate. During the Civil War, Chattanooga became a vital railroad junction and experienced a long occupation and a bloody battle as well. During the twentieth century, the early federal highway system followed the

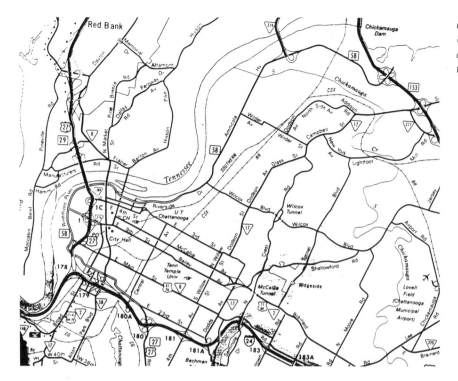

Chattanooga.
(Courtesy of Tennessee Department of Transportation, as adapted by the author)

general paths of the great steam engines. Chattanooga became the junction for U.S. Highways 11, 27, 41, 64, and 72 and emerged as a tourist town, with several attractions, such as Rock City and **Ruby Falls**, being established on Lookout Mountain.

Today Chattanooga and Hamilton County form a vital transportation center, intersected by three major interstates. The evolution of the city's transportation network is an important story, as are the stories of its early history as a Cherokee settlement and of its post–Civil War rise as an industrial center. There are four different central locations travelers might consider visiting: Lookout Mountain, Ross's Landing, the Chattanooga Choo-Choo/Market Street District, and Missionary Ridge.

Lookout Mountain

Lookout Mountain can be reached on Interstate 24 at exits 174 and 175. Here is an excellent vantage point for seeing the broader landscape patterns of Chattanooga's past. In 1905 the U.S. Army Corps of Engineers established **Point Park** near the top of the mountain and

*Point Park Gate, Lookout
Mountain, Chattanooga.*

adorned the park with a beautiful stone gateway patterned after the
castle-like insignia of the corps. The monuments at Point Park commemorate the "Battle above the Clouds" of November 24, 1863, when a
determined Federal assault dislodged entrenched Confederates overlooking the besieged town of Chattanooga. The ninety-five-foot-high
New York Peace Memorial dominates the center of the park, and other
interpretive markers explain the fighting on that foggy day in 1863. The
Robert Cravens House, on the mountain's eastern slope, first served
as the headquarters of Confederate general E. C. Walthall and then the
temporary headquarters for Union general Joseph Hooker once his
army of ten thousand soldiers had swept the Confederates off the mountain. Destroyed immediately after the battle, the house was rebuilt by
the Cravens family in 1866.

Point Park also has a stunning view of the Tennessee River at its
Moccasin Bend. Here, too, is a place to consider the natural resources,
topography, and locations of early Native-American villages that shaped
the history of the "Grand Canyon of the Tennessee" before white settlement took place.

Upriver from Lookout Mountain is the site of Dallas Island, now
submerged by the Chickamauga Dam reservoir. Native Americans of the
Mississippian culture built and occupied a large temple-mound trading
center hundreds of years ago along both sides of the river and at the
head of the island. Those who lived at Dallas Island made elaborate shell
gorgets and pottery but lived in quite simple houses. Thatch or bark
roofs were supported by wooden timbers covered with cane-and-clay

plaster. Beds were built off the ground along the sides of the building. The village plan, however, reflected the more complex nature of Dallas culture. The outdoor council ground served as a public square, which was surrounded, in turn, by three-sided buildings with their open ends facing the council ground. The west side of the square was for the chief and members of his clan; the chief's lieutenants and assistants occupied the south side. On the north side were respected warriors, while the east building was home for boys and any visitors. The Point Park vantage point also provides an excellent view of **Williams Island,** another place significant for its ancient Indian village sites (private, no access).

From Point Park, the general area where Spanish explorer and trader Hernando de Soto led the first Europeans to Tennessee can be seen. Although scholars still debate De Soto's actual route, they believe that in 1540 his party camped for about a month at the Creek Indian town of Chiaha, believed to be on an island near present-day Chattanooga. But few Spanish—or for that matter English or French—traders followed De Soto's footprints for the next 150 years.

As trade between Indians and different colonial outposts to the north, south, and east became more frequent in the late 1600s and early 1700s, the Chattanooga area served as a crossroads for several important Native-American trading routes. Moving down the Great Valley of the Tennessee, the Great Indian Warpath crossed over Chickamauga Creek at Brainerd before passing on to Citico Creek and then around Lookout Mountain. Here was one of the best places to cross the Tennessee River. A Scotsman named John McDonald established a trading post where the path crossed the Chickamauga Creek in 1770. The Chickamauga Path connected the peoples of north Georgia to Kentucky, while the Great Lakes Trail connected the Upper Midwest fur trade to the tribes of the Mid-South. Another important trail was called the Cisco and St. Augustine Trail (or the Nickajack Trace). It ran from Florida to the Cumberland River near Nashville and connected the Mid-South tribes to the Spanish trade in Florida.

From Lookout Mountain, a stretch of the river that early settlers once feared and avoided at all costs can also be seen. In 1777 Dragging Canoe led a large group of Cherokees from their East Tennessee homeland to Chickamauga Creek. The Cherokees came out of anger and frustration. Dragging Canoe had never accepted the tribe's 1775 agreement with speculator Richard Henderson to exchange millions of acres for trade goods allegedly worth some ten thousand English pounds. In 1776

Dragging Canoe and his followers waged war against the upper East Tennessee settlements. Refusing to take part in any peace negotiations, Dragging Canoe moved his followers to the Chattanooga area in the spring of 1777. Here, this splinter group of Cherokees became known as the Chickamaugans, and they controlled local trade and transportation for the next decade and a half. In the towns of Running Water, Nickajack, Long Island, Crowtown, and Lookout Mountain Town, the Chickamaugans were joined by members of the Shawnees and Creeks, who also opposed the further expansion of white settlement in Tennessee. For fifteen years these Indians mounted an aggressive defense of their homeland, supported by Spanish supplies from Florida trader and Spanish agent John McDonald.

In 1794 Middle Tennessee settlers struck back with a vengeance as Maj. James Ore and six hundred followers destroyed the towns of Running Water and Nickajack. The Chickamaugans ended their resistance and agreed to abide by the earlier Treaty of Holston (1791), which had normalized relations between the Cherokees and the new United States government. As the upper East Tennessee settlements continued to expand, most Cherokees moved southwest of the Appalachian Mountains, making Chattanooga and Hamilton County a center of Cherokee settlement. In 1802 the first federal agent established his residence in the Chattanooga area, at the mouth of Lookout Creek on the Tennessee River. Three years later, the Cherokees allowed the federal government to build the Nickajack Road, which connected Georgia and Middle Tennessee.

Peace between the settlers and Cherokees, however, led to little increase in river traffic, because no one could solve the difficulty of navigating the Tennessee River. Railroads eventually provided a transportation alternative. Directly below Lookout Mountain are the former lines of the Nashville and Chattanooga Railroad, which first reached the city in 1854 where they junctioned with tracks of the Western and Atlantic, a Georgia-owned railroad that had arrived in Chattanooga four years earlier. From Lookout Mountain, it is possible to see that most of Chattanooga is along the south bank of the Tennessee River. The town developed where it did because there was enough flat bottomland for future expansion and because the Georgia railroad tracks stopped here to intersect with commercial traffic on the Tennessee River at this point.

Huge engineering projects in the early twentieth century finally solved the centuries-old problem of navigation. The Hales Bar Lock and Dam, completed in 1913, was the first major improvement. Then, during the late 1930s, the Tennessee Valley Authority built the Chickamauga Dam and Reservoir. Dedicated by Franklin D. Roosevelt in 1940, the dam allowed TVA engineers to better control water flow and level, lessening the danger of whirlpools and eddies in the "Grand Canyon of the Tennessee." However, the new course of the river submerged many historical places, including Dallas Island and the Chickamauga villages. Today only the course of the river remains to document the area's earliest history.

Ross's Landing, Downtown Chattanooga

To reach Ross's Landing, take the Interstate 127 Loop, exit 1-C, or Interstate 24, exit 179. In about 1815 John and Lewis Ross, the Cherokee grandsons of John McDonald, established a ferry and landing on the south bank of the Tennessee River. Here is where the city of Chattanooga began, and today a river park recognizes the contributions of the Cherokees to the early development of Chattanooga. One traveler called **Ross's Landing** nothing more than a "shanty for goods and a log hut for the ferryman," but it soon became a transfer point for Cherokee-settler trade (Livingood, 13). Because of modern developments, few Cherokee sites remain untouched within the city. But the landing, along with a historic cemetery and a regional history museum, provide valuable information on these early years.

In 1816, about seven miles east of Ross's Landing along South Chickamauga Creek, Congregationalist minister Cyrus Kingsbury of the American Board of Commissioners for Foreign Missions established **Brainerd Mission** for the Cherokees. Today only the mission cemetery (off U.S. 11/64 in the Brainerd neighborhood) is intact, but the surrounding property once contained a large complex of buildings that remained open until the forced removal of the Cherokees in 1837–38. It is also possible to drive Old Mission Road, immediately north of U.S. 11/64, in the Brainerd neighborhood.

The expanding trade of the Cherokee settlements led John and Lewis Ross to build their ferry landing in 1815, but visitors to the riverfront today find a modern park, plenty of parking lots, and the massive postmodern-style Tennessee Aquarium (1992), which dominates the landscape. The aquarium exhibits were designed by Peter Chermayeff and Cambridge Seven Associates, Inc. They feature freshwater fish from the Mid-South, and they give an overview of the resources of the Tennessee Valley. The city's major commercial arteries,

Ross's Landing, Chattanooga. The sculpture Cherokee (1992), by Jud Hartmann, is a modern reminder of the Cherokee contribution to Chattanooga history.

Tennessee Aquarium. The postmodern architecture of the Tennessee Aquarium has given an entirely new look to the Chattanooga riverfront.

Broad and Market Streets, abruptly end at the landing, but the heart of the business and civic district lies about four blocks to the east. Before going there, the traveler may stop at the Chattanooga Regional History Museum, at Fourth Street and Chestnut, to view permanent exhibits about the region's prehistoric past and its significant role in Cherokee history. The museum also has excellent exhibits on later chapters in the city's urban development. Another choice lies in the opposite direction. The tourist may cross the Tennessee River by way of the **Walnut Street pedestrian bridge,** a one-hundred-year-old structure designed by Edwin Thatcher. The bridge and walkway provide an interesting view of local historic and cultural attractions, such as the Hunter Museum of Art, which is partially housed in a Classical Revival mansion overlooking the Tennessee River. In addition, the bridge provides the best overview of Ross's Landing and the one hundred and fifty years of urban development that surrounds it.

Chattanooga Choo-Choo (Southern Railway Terminal) and Market Street, Downtown Chattanooga

To visit the Southern Railway Terminal, take the Interstate 127 Business Loop, exit 1, or Interstate 24, exit 179, and follow the signs to the Choo-Choo complex.

The Chattanooga Choo-Choo was originally known as the **Southern Railway Terminal** (1909), designed by the Beaux-Arts-trained architect Donn Barber of New York City. This magnificent architectural gateway to the Deep South opened in time for the Christmas season in 1909 and served travelers until the Louisville and Nashville's "Georgian" completed its last run on May 1, 1971. Two years later, the terminal reopened as the Chattanooga Choo-Choo, a complex of hotel rooms, shops, and restaurants that was designed to attract the millions of travelers passing through the city on the newly completed interstate highway system. A stroll from the terminal down Market Street to the downtown business district shows how Chattanooga used new construction, urban renewal, and historic preservation to transform its transportation past into a modern urban landscape, a task Chattanooga has accomplished not once but twice in this century.

Urban renewal is often considered a fairly recent phenomenon, something that happened in the 1950s and 1960s. But the civic capitalists of turn-of-the-century Chattanooga also dreamed of a new future, and of a new environment, for their city. In a massive redevelopment

Southern Railway Terminal, Chattanooga. Now known as the Chattanooga Choo-Choo, this successful historic preservation project still welcomes visitors to Chattanooga.

project beginning with the Southern Railway Terminal in 1907, they carved much of the historic Chattanooga we see today.

Chattanooga in the early twentieth century was a dirty, polluted place. The city was heavily industrialized and had emerged as one of the South's major iron and steel producers. In 1910 some three hundred industries employed over twenty-two thousand workers. To escape the grime and grit of the city, middle-class and wealthy residents moved into exclusive suburbs, with the latest in architectural fashion, along Lookout Mountain, Signal Mountain, and Missionary Ridge.

The downtown environment was somewhat chaotic. An orderly street grid, focused on Market and Broad Streets, could be found from the riverfront to Ninth Street (now Martin Luther King Boulevard), where it met the boundary of the large amount of land owned by the state of Georgia for its Western and Atlantic Depot and shops. West of Ninth Street, it seemed that railroad tracks ran everywhere. A central passenger station dominated activity at Thirteenth Street and Market Street where the neoclassical **Southern Railway Office** (1922) is now at 1301 Market Street. The passenger station, however, was hopelessly overcrowded, and its major tenant, the powerful Southern Railway Company, decided to build a new depot to better route passenger traffic as well as to symbolize its importance in the regional railroad system.

On a twenty-three-acre site around the 1400 block of Market Street, the railway began construction in 1907. The company demolished the Stanton House, a circa 1870 luxury hotel, and numerous dwellings and warehouses to make way for the new gateway. From Chattanooga Choo-Choo, walking east on Market Street toward the downtown business district reveals the progression of changes that accompanied the opening of the depot in 1909. Signs of that transformation in this National Register–listed district include two-story brick buildings from the early 1900s, old warehouses, railroad freight stations, and modern high-rise office buildings.

The **Terminal Hotel,** directly across the street, also opened in 1909, while the **Grand Hotel** at 1401 Market was built within months. The north side of East Main Street soon evolved into a furniture retail center, while streetcars rushed rail passengers to downtown businesses. From about 1910 to 1920, eleven new commercial buildings were constructed along the 1200 block of Market Street. At 1206 Market Street, the railway built a new **freight depot,** which was renovated into office and commercial space in the mid-1980s as a historic preservation tax credit project. Just north of the freight depot, in the 1100 block of Market Street, stands **Warehouse Row,** a renovation of the late

1980s, which turned once busy three-story warehouses into a downtown outlet shopping mall.

From Warehouse Row, it is possible to see how a second period of massive urban renewal, directed at the old Western and Atlantic Railroad yards, changed the face of downtown Chattanooga during the 1970s. Across the street, between Market and Broad Streets, is the modern office complex and energy center of the Tennessee Valley Authority. The two-hundred-million-dollar project, involving the construction of TVA Center, a hotel, parking garage, and other business facilities, combined with the Chattanooga Runaround project of the late 1960s and early 1970s to erase most physical traces of the old railroad yards. Modern office buildings rapidly multiplied, including the Krystal Building (1978), the TVA Federal Credit Union (1978), and the First Federal Savings and Loan (1979). Similar dramatic changes had already occurred to the immediate west, where the Golden Gateway Redevelopment Project, completed in 1976, transformed over four hundred acres. The gateway project forced the relocation of fourteen hundred families and razed over eleven hundred buildings. In their place stood new highways and buildings, such as the First Baptist Church (1967), the St. Barnabas Nursing Home and Apartments (1966), and the Jaycee Towers I and II (1970–75). Only the **Read House Hotel** (1926), designed by the Chicago firm of Holabird and Root in the Colonial Revival style, serves as a reminder of the old railroad legacy of this area.

Despite the massive changes of the 1970s, downtown Chattanooga has preserved a remarkable collection of early-twentieth-century architecture along the three blocks of Broad and Market Streets between Martin Luther King Boulevard and Sixth Street. Much of this work came from the architectural firm of Reuben H. Hunt, who practiced in Chattanooga from 1885 to the 1930s. His architecture spans the gamut of styles from those years, from late Victorian Romanesque to the stripped-down classicism of Art Deco. In time, Hunt emerged as one of the region's most important architects, and his firm designed projects in almost every southern state, as well as in South America. In Chattanooga his best work came during the Classical Revival of the early twentieth century when his new buildings coincided with the building boom associated with the construction of the Southern Railway Terminal. Representative examples of his designs in this style include the **Hamilton County Courthouse** (1911–12) at Sixth and Georgia, the **City Hall** (1908) at East Eleventh, and the **James Building** (1907)— the city's first skyscraper—at 735 Broad. Another significant classical design is the adjacent **Maclellan Building** (1923–24) at 721 Broad. Hunt's flair for Renaissance Revival architecture is exhibited in the seven-story **Soldiers and Sailors Memorial Auditorium** (1922–24) on McCallie Avenue. He also proved adept at the new modern styles of the 1930s. First came the Art Deco **Medical Arts Building** (1928) on McCallie Avenue. His **U.S. Post Office** (1933) on Georgia Avenue at Martin Luther King Boulevard was praised for its Art Deco design, and, in 1938, the American Institute of Architects selected it as one of the best "modern" buildings in the country.

Many other significant public and commercial buildings designed by R. H. Hunt and Company stand in Chattanooga. Most have been listed in the National Register of Historic Places in recognition of Hunt's contribution to Tennessee architecture. As the *Chattanooga Free Press* of May 29, 1937, noted at his death, the work of "no man's life has been more thoroughly woven into the progress of Chattanooga during the past half century than that of R. H. Hunt."

Missionary Ridge

There are two ways to reach Missionary Ridge. From Interstate 24, take exit 181 and then U.S. 41S to South Crest Road. From U.S. 11E (Bailey Avenue), turn on Shallowford Road and then take North Crest Road.

A drive along Missionary Ridge along either North Crest Road or South Crest Road puts travelers back in touch with two persistent features of the Chattanooga landscape: monuments to the great Civil War struggles that happened here in 1863 and the great diversity of domestic architecture represented by the city's many neighborhoods.

The Confederate siege of Chattanooga followed its significant victory at the Battle of Chickamauga, which took place about seven miles south in Georgia in September 1863. Control of this railroad junction was vital to the planned Federal invasion of the Deep South; the South desperately wanted to retake Chattanooga. The Confederate Army of Tennessee, under the command of Braxton Bragg, entrenched itself on Lookout Mountain to the west and all along Missionary Ridge to the east. Initially, the siege appeared successful. But then President Abraham Lincoln used the regional rail system to reinforce his army with the commands of Gens. Joseph Hooker and William T. Sherman. Union hero Gen. Ulysses S. Grant also arrived to assume overall command. In late November, the Federal army began its counterattack.

On November 24, Gen. George Thomas, who had been appointed commander of the Union Army of the Cumberland, took Orchard Knob and stood just west of the base of Missionary Ridge, threatening the center of Bragg's army. The National Park Service maintains interpretive markers and monuments at **Orchard Knob,** between Ivy and Fifth Streets. The next day, General Hooker routed the Confederates from Lookout Mountain. The day after, November 25, 1863, Grant launched Hooker against the Rebel left and Sherman against the fortified right high on Missionary Ridge. But the unified assault quickly bogged down as Hooker was slow to attack and a spirited defense by Patrick Cleburne's undermanned and undergunned Confederates stopped Sherman.

With his attack stymied, Grant ordered General Thomas to take the Confederate rifle pits at the base of Missionary Ridge. Embarrassed by the defeat at Chickamauga and eager for vengeance, Thomas's army charged hard. The Union command thought that a direct frontal assault on the Confederate position would be futile and would lead only to a bloodbath. But as the Federal troops took the rifle pits, they realized that Confederate fire from the top of the ridge would turn their exposed position into "a hideous slaughter pen." Many chose not to stop and madly began to climb the ridge, to the amazed horror of the senior Federal commanders. Gen. Gordon Granger remarked to Grant: "When these men get going, all hell can't stop them!" (McDonough, *Chattanooga,* 165, 168).

And so it couldn't. Despite "a terrible shower of shot and shell," Thomas's men took Missionary Ridge in one of the most breathtaking charges of the war (McDonough, *Chattanooga,* 171). The road to Atlanta was open once again. Today along the North Crest Road overlooking the city, there are many regimental markers that explain the development of that confusing day of bloodshed. Several markers and monuments are now on private property, but the National Park Service maintains six small interpretive areas—called reservations—where pivotal moments in the battle are marked and explained. From these positions, especially the **Bragg Reservation** and the **DeLong Reservation,** it is possible to look over Missionary Ridge and imagine the terrifying sight of thousands of Union soldiers wildly climbing up this rugged ridge on a late fall afternoon in 1863.

Interspersed with the monuments are many dazzling homes, mostly built in different revival styles between 1900 and 1940. North Crest Avenue is home to the **Shavin House** (1950), Tennessee's only dwelling designed by the famous American architect Frank Lloyd Wright (private, no access). This house of Tennessee limestone is a good example of the "Usonian-style" design from the latter period of Wright's career.

The ridges and mountains surrounding Chattanooga became popular suburbs as the downtown environment became more foul and polluted during the turn-of-the-century industrial explosion. Lookout Mountain was incorporated as early as 1890 and soon became a haven for the wealthy and a playground for tourists. In 1895, investors established the famous **Lookout Mountain Incline Railway** to boost tourism and development further. Civic capitalist Charles E. James developed the community of Signal Point City—later Signal Mountain—during the 1910s.

Other interesting historic neighborhoods are located closer to the downtown area. **Ferger Place,** along Evening Side and Morning Side Drives off U.S. 41, was the city's first planned restricted private park. Developed by the Ferger Brothers Real Estate firm in the early 1910s, the neighborhood of mostly two-story Colonial, Dutch, and Spanish Revival dwellings was built to meet the housing needs of the city's expanding business class.

Older neighborhoods are adjacent to the University of Tennessee at Chattanooga campus along McCallie Avenue. Established in 1886 and first named U.S. Grant University, the institution's original quadrangle features excellent examples of the Collegiate Gothic style, especially the chapel designed by H. B. Downing. Just northeast of the university, along Fort Wood Place, Vine, and Oak Streets, is the **Fort Wood historic district.** Most of the dwellings date between 1880 and 1920, with Queen Anne, Romanesque, and Classical Revival styles predominating. Particularly notable are the Byzantine Revival–style Warner House (1891) at 800 Vine, the home (1888) of future Secretary of Treasury William McAdoo at 829 Vine, the grand Colonial Revival–style Jo Conn Guild Home (1899) at 950 Vine, and the Queen Anne home of Benjamin F. Thomas, one of the founders of Coca-Cola, at 938 McCallie Avenue. Thomas, along with Guild and Warner, were among the important civic capitalists leading Chattanooga into a new century of economic change (all private, no access).

The workers who built these buildings, however, lived in much simpler neighborhoods, often near their place of employment where it was impossible to escape the ill effects of industrial pollution. In 1916, George Haynes worked with the local Negro Business League to establish the Central Community Betterment League to improve the public health and living conditions in the African-American neighborhoods near the steel mills in South Chattanooga and in St. Elmo, Churchville, and Tannery Flats. Later, in 1925, these neighborhoods became the only ones in Tennessee to support a chapter of the Universal Negro Improvement Association, a national black pride and unity organization started by Marcus Garvey. Urban renewal has eliminated many of the city's working-class neighborhoods, but Lupton City, on the north side of the Tennessee River, still remains, and it represents what was considered a model mill village in the early twentieth century.

The people who lived in Lupton City worked at the Dixie Spinning Mills, a textile factory established by the prominent Chattanooga attorney and capitalist J. T. Lupton in 1922–23. The company first only built sixty houses for employees, but, as the mill increased production to thirty thousand spindles, the number of houses grew to two hundred by 1929. The well-planned company town had concrete sidewalks, a gymnasium, movie house, post office, church, brick school, and commercial establishments. Of course, within this totally designed industrial environment, the workers had little freedom but to accept the wages and conditions set by the company. The company town atmosphere stayed largely intact until the 1950s when Dixie Yarns began to sell the mill housing. By the mid-1980s, the company owned only the homes of the superintendent and assistant superintendent.

Landscape 2: Knoxville

Lying in the heart of the Great Valley of Tennessee, Knoxville stands where the Holston and French Broad Rivers form the Tennessee River. James White first moved here in 1786, and five years later William Blount, governor of the Southwest Territory, negotiated the Treaty of Holston with the Cherokees. The land that became Knoxville was formally opened to settlement.

Knoxville dominated the early political history of Tennessee. The city was the territorial capital; after 1796 it became the state capital. The town served as the capital three different times, for a total of seventeen years. In 1817 state officials moved the capital to Murfreesboro; it would not return to Knoxville. Due to its location in the river system of East Tennessee, Knoxville also emerged as a regional commercial center. By 1835 steamboats were regularly carrying goods between north-

Knoxville. (Courtesy of Tennessee Department of Transportation, as adapted by the author)

ern Alabama and Knoxville. Within a generation, however, the new technology of railroads eclipsed the importance of river traffic.

Shortly before the Civil War, Knoxville became the rail center of southern Appalachia. The city was the midpoint for the East Tennessee and Georgia Railroad, which arrived in 1855, and the East Tennessee and Virginia, which began operations the next year. By 1858 track connected Knoxville to Dalton, Georgia, and Bristol, Tennessee. The railroads brought about dramatic growth in the urban population, and many new immigrants were Irish. They established the city's first Catholic congregation in 1854 and thirty-two years later built the beautiful Church of the Immaculate Conception.

Knoxville entered the Civil War years with a population of more than fifty-three hundred residents. Its rail network, together with its traditional role in supplying meat—especially pork—to all of the southern states, made it a very strategic place. In September 1863, a Federal army under the command of Gen. Ambrose Burnside occupied the city, and, despite the determined efforts of Confederate general James Longstreet to recapture Knoxville two months later, the city remained under Federal control for the remainder of the war.

After the war, Knoxville quickly rebuilt its railroads, emerging as a regional warehouse and manufacturing center. In 1867 Hiram S. Chamberlain, who had been Burnside's quartermaster during the war, established the Knoxville Iron Company on the northern edge of the city. Around this large factory grew the industrial neighborhood of **Mechanicsville.** Between 1880 and 1887, ninety-seven new factories were built in and around Knoxville. The city, as of 1885, was already the fourth-largest wholesale market in the South. It was also home to a much larger African-American population than ever before, comprising 32.5 percent of the population in 1880. **Knoxville College,** established by the United Presbyterian Church in 1875, evolved from earlier Freedman's Bureau efforts in public education. The campus at 901 College Street, NW, has served as a focal point for American-American education and culture ever since. A more recent African-American history institution is the Beck Cultural Exchange Center at 1927 Dandridge Avenue.

The depression of 1893 and the great Gay Street fire of 1897 only slowed the city's remarkable expansion. From 1895 to 1904, for instance, five thousand new homes were built in the Knoxville area. During these years of industrial expansion, the city's business district became concentrated in an area bordered by Gay Street between its Tennessee River bridge to the Southern Railway Terminal and by Broad Street between the Henley Street Bridge and Louisville and Nashville Depot.

A change in the city's ethnic mix coincided with the new urban industrial growth. By 1910 African Americans made up only 21 percent of the population. Middle-class whites also left the city to establish new suburban communities at places like Sequoyah Hills and **Talahi** off Kingston Pike (present U.S. Highway 70). Late Victorian factories, with outdated equipment and less demand for their products, found it difficult to respond to changing market realities. Knoxville Woolen Mills, once the region's largest millworks, had closed by World War I.

Deterioration of the city's industrial core continued for another generation. By the 1940s, descriptions of Knoxville were none too flattering. John Gunther, in his *Inside U.S.A.* (1946), described the Knoxville urban landscape as "an intense, concentrated, degrading ugliness." Knoxville was "the ugliest city I ever saw in America, with the possible exception of some mill towns in New England. Its main street is called Gay Street; this seemed to me to be a misnomer" (McDonald and Wheeler, *Knoxville,* 67).

Yet, these years of decline also witnessed the rise of the Tennessee

Downtown Knoxville skyline along Gay Street. The dreams of nineteenth- and twentieth-century boosters stand together on Gay Street.

Valley Authority and the University of Tennessee, two institutions that did much to reshape Knoxville's future. The Tennessee Valley Authority located some initial offices in Knoxville and gave new hope and encouragement to the city's business class. By 1940 fifteen hundred Knox County residents worked for the agency. During World War II, TVA dam-construction projects, together with the federal atomic energy program at Oak Ridge, attracted millions of dollars in federal funding to the Knoxville area. A generation later, during the early 1970s, new agency leadership built the twin TVA Towers at Market Square and joined with the city in ambitious urban renewal projects. The agency is still one of the city's most important employers.

The University of Tennessee, according to a census count, had just fifty-one hundred students in 1950. During the 1950s and 1960s, however, the university boomed, and soon the once confined campus of Collegiate Gothic–style buildings on "The Hill" sprawled all over the city's west end. By the mid-1970s, well over twenty thousand students were in attendance. The university supplied significant numbers of skilled workers, high-tech innovators, and daring entrepreneurial go-getters to the city's major employers. The massive neo-Colonial Revival business building of Whittle Communications on Gay Street in downtown Knoxville was a recent example of local economic boosterism from University of Tennessee graduates.

In the early 1980s, the civic and business leaders of Knoxville had gained enough confidence to host a World's Fair. The event was envisioned by local boosters—led by banker Jake Butcher—as an ideal way to clean up the run-down Second Creek area and to reconnect the downtown business district to the bustling university campus. The fair opened in 1982 as an energy exposition. It never proved to be the success its promoters had promised. After closing, the fair buildings were mostly abandoned; dreams of a high-tech business and research center connecting the university and downtown came to naught. The largest building, the once grand United States pavilion, was demolished. Today the fair's Sunsphere stands as a lonely monument to unfulfilled dreams of Knoxville's modern-day boosters.

These changing patterns of the Knoxville urban landscape over the past two hundred years are still visible today from four central locations: Blount Mansion, the Southern Railway Terminal, the historic Knoxville City Hall, and the University of Tennessee.

Blount Mansion

Blount Mansion can be reached by taking Interstate 40 to exit 388. Then take the downtown business loop (Tennessee 158) and follow signs to the house.

The cradle of Tennessee government, **Blount Mansion** is a National Historic Landmark located along the Tennessee River at 200 W. Hill Avenue. A new visitor center and museum are currently under development to greet strollers on adjacent Gay Street. The earliest section of the house—a hall-and-parlor floor plan—is believed to date to the 1790s, but probably not until 1830 did the house evolve into the three-part Georgian-like mansion that can be seen today. Behind the house is Gov. William Blount's original office, which basically served as the territorial capitol from 1792 to 1796 and was where Blount and others drafted the first state constitution. Related outbuildings have been reconstructed, and a formal colonial garden was added during the property's initial restoration. Recent archaeological research has focused on determining the size and location of the dwellings of Blount's slaves.

William Blount came to Tennessee from North Carolina, where he had been a prominent politician, serving as a state delegate to the federal Constitutional Convention in Philadelphia in 1787. He was also an avid land speculator, and he eagerly accepted his appointment as governor of the Southwest Territory in 1790. Blount first lived at **Rocky Mount** in Sullivan County, where he established the first seat of territorial government. After negotiating the Treaty of Holston in 1791, he moved the territorial seat to the junction of the Holston and French Broad Rivers.

Blount held the Cherokee negotiations at the fort settlement of James White, who had arrived in 1786. White's two-story log dwelling, which has been moved at least twice since 1791, is part of the reconstructed James White's Fort, located just a few hundred yards east of the Blount Mansion, at 205 E. Hill Avenue. After completing the negotiations, Blount bought from White land for sixty-four lots, roughly bordered today by Church, Central, and Walnut Streets and the Tennessee River. Charles McClung surveyed the property, and an auction of lots on October 3, 1791, began the city of Knoxville.

The city slowly expanded as a frontier trade center. A visitor in 1794 noted the town's seven taverns, not counting tippling houses, ten stores, a courthouse, and several frame homes with brick chimneys. Urban growth has obliterated most of the physical remnants of early Knoxville that once surrounded Blount Mansion. One notable architectural exception is the adjacent Federal-style **Craighead-Jackson House** (1818). Three blocks north on State Street is the First Presbyterian Church cemetery where such town founders as Blount and White are buried. To the southwest, at 422 W. Cumberland, is the **Sevier-Park House** (private, no access). John Sevier first owned the property and built its foundation in 1797; Joseph Park later finished the house around 1812.

A better way to experience the domestic architecture and lifestyle of the early settlers is to take a side trip to three historic homes on the outskirts of Knoxville. In northeast Knox County, on Emory Road, is the **Nicholas Gibbs Homestead** (private, limited access). This two-story log cabin, with modern additions, dates from 1793 and is an excellent vernacular example of beaded interior paneling and square notching of the logs. Built for a second-generation German American, Gibbs's house is a significant example of German log construction techniques and was once part of larger German settlement that later established the first Lutheran congregation in East Tennessee.

Next, take U.S. 441 to the John Sevier Highway (Tennessee 168) and follow this road southwest to Neubert Springs Road. Here is the **Marble Springs** state historic site, approximately six miles south of Knoxville. By 1792 John Sevier, the famous frontier hero and early Tennessee politician, had established his Marble Springs farm. He and his family periodically lived in the single-pen log cabin, with attached kitchen, until 1815. This dwelling is another important example of log architecture on the Tennessee frontier.

Then, continue on Tennessee 168 northeast to Thorngrove Pike. Turn east at the historical marker to arrive at the **Ramsay House,** a two-story stone late Georgian dwelling built for Francis A. Ramsay between 1795 and 1797. Ramsay was a colleague of Sevier, Blount, White, and other important early settlers. A wealthy planter with over two thousand acres, Ramsay hired as his architect Thomas Hope, an English-trained builder who had moved to the territory from Charleston, South Carolina, in 1795. Hope gave his patron a magnificent achievement in masonry design and construction. He took the basic three-bay Georgian style and added stone quoins, a string course of beautiful blue limestone, and classically inspired consoles at the roof eaves. In another twist, Hope located the kitchen wing not as a separate rear building or even an L-addition to the house, but as flanking block to the dwelling. His striking interior designs embraced molded chair rails and a cornice.

Knoxville City Hall

From Interstate 40, take exit 388. Then take the downtown loop (Tennessee 158) to the Summit Hill Drive exit.

At the corner of Summit Hill Drive and Broadway is the old **Knoxville City Hall** (1848, 1905), the city's best remaining example of Greek Revival architecture. Built by Jacob Newman, it originally served as the Tennessee Asylum for the Deaf and Dumb. Both Confederate and Federal armies used the school as a hospital during the Civil War. After a new school was constructed in 1924, the city maintained its offices here until 1980. The building stands on the south slope of Summit Hill, which was used as a Confederate artillery position during the summer fighting of 1863. But today, the Summit Hill area gives a commanding view of three key urban institutions: the Louisville and Nashville Railroad passenger station, the 1982 World's Fair grounds, and the city's historic Market Square.

At the opposite street corner, is the **Louisville and Nashville Depot** (1904). Company architect Richard Monfort designed the station in the Renaissance Revival style. The new depot was a direct response to the competition represented by the new Southern Railway Terminal on Gay Street. Abandoned by the railroad during the early 1980s, investors adapted it into a modern restaurant to serve visitors to the adjacent World's Fair.

Market Square, Knoxville. Well-intentioned urban renewal almost killed Market Square before the area stabilized in the 1980s.

The site of the 1982 World's Fair is behind the depot, with the Sunsphere—the fair's symbolic heart—standing tall, proud, and empty over the skyline. Before the fair, this area served as L&N railroad yards. Today several of the fair buildings remain closed, but other places, like the Court of Flags and the Tennessee Amphitheater, are reminders of the excitement that gripped the city in the summer of 1982. Arts and cultural institutions have moved to the area. The Knoxville Museum of Art (1990), for example, has opened a new exhibit building.

To the immediate east of old City Hall along Summit Hill Avenue are the twin TVA Towers. Nearby is **Market Square,** another area of the city transformed by urban renewal projects in the 1960s. In 1853 William G. Swan and Joseph A. Mabry donated this land to the city for a public market. For the next one hundred years, the Market House was where local farmers sold produce and meat. In the 1950s, however, urban planners and developers began to envision a new future for Market Square and the old Market House. In an attempt to ease the parking shortage in the downtown business area, one expert even suggested building a parking garage on top of the old Market House. However, the original deed of Swan and Mabry forbade any such multiple uses.

Then, in 1960, fire destroyed the Market House; planning a new future for this prime downtown location began in earnest. The Downtown Knoxville Association first considered widespread demolition before opting for a rehabilitation plan called the Market Square Mall. Canopies, landscaping, and an open-air market were combined to create an alleged urban oasis for downtown shoppers. But the reality was something quite different from the architects' vision. The modern canopies dramatically clashed with the architectural traditions conveyed by the facades of the older historic buildings. Business did not improve as the planners had hoped.

After the construction of the TVA Towers (1974–75), Market Square experienced another facelift. The large office complex provided a necessary "anchor" for new businesses, mostly restaurants and other service-related stores. The canopies came down and the historic facades were refurbished, some were even restored. In 1984 the city rebuilt an open-air pavilion where farmers could once again sell their produce to city residents. The new pavilion, designed by Bullock, Smith, and Partners, uses historic architectural details to suggest continuity with the old Market House tradition.

Another important change occurred in 1983 when Charles Krutch, a former TVA photographer, donated money to build Krutch Park, an imaginatively landscaped park in the heart of downtown. At the south end of Krutch Park is the old **U.S. Post Office and Customs House** (1871–73). Federal architect Alfred B. Mullett, whose other important designs include the splendid Executive Office Building next to the White House in Washington, D.C., designed this Second Empire building in Tennessee marble. It is now home to the East Tennessee Historical Society, which has recently opened a regional history museum. The building also has an important regional research center that includes the Calvin M. McClung Historical Collection and the Knox County Archives.

Southern Railway Terminal and Gay Street District

From Interstate 40, take exit 388. Turn onto the business loop exit (Tennessee 158) and exit at Gay Street signs. Travel north on Gay Street to the railroad overpass; the terminal is located to the east.

In the aftermath of the depression of 1893, international banker J. P. Morgan financed and organized the consolidation of various small, regional railroad lines into a new giant company known as the Southern Railway. As the corporation improved its facilities during the following fifteen years, many Southern towns found their old urban landscape transformed. In Knoxville, for example, the construction of a

Southern Railway Terminal, Knoxville. Although its clock tower is gone, the restored Southern Terminal remains a Knoxville landmark.

modern **Southern Railway Terminal** in 1904 stimulated the development of nearby food-processing factories and increased the city's already sizeable warehouse business. The terminal, designed by railroad architect Frank P. Milburn, is off Gay Street at 306 Depot Avenue (private, limited access). From this point, take either Gay Street south or Jackson Street east or west and glimpse the many light industrial and commercial storage buildings that surrounded the railroad complex. The solid-brick construction and the largely unadorned facades of these tall buildings reflect their function and provide an opportunity to imagine past days when the adjacent streets and sidewalks hummed with activity.

Next door at 106 Depot Avenue is the **White Lilly Foods Company** (1890–95), which still produces cornmeal and flour. To the west, over the tracks, is the **Gay Street Viaduct** (1918–19), designed by the railway to separate the increasing amount of automobile traffic from the busy railroad lines. The date of construction of these structures pinpoints the time when automobile traffic took precedence over railroad traffic. The Renaissance Revival architecture of the **Emporium Building** (circa 1903–4) at 102 S. Gay and the ten-story **Sterchi Furniture Building** (1921) document the changes in Gay Street that coincided with the opening of the terminal. Buildings along this block served more direct commercial functions than the warehouses nearer the tracks; therefore, their facades are often decorated with eye-catching cornices and other architectural details. The four-story **Commercial Building** (circa 1891), decorated with Italianate detailing, is from the earlier period of this vital commercial artery.

Portions of East Jackson Street have recently undergone historic renovations and adaptive reuse. **Sullivan Saloon** (circa 1889) at 100 E. Jackson blends elements of Queen Anne and Romanesque architecture. The other seven commercial buildings in the 100 block of East Jackson either date from or were built after the Southern Railway Terminal and are much less stylized in appearance. West Jackson Avenue features more of a blend of late Victorian commercial architecture and the more modern facades of early twentieth-century warehouses. The **Carhart Building** (circa 1900) at 121–23 W. Jackson has a particularly interesting Romanesque influence in its three-and-a-half-story facade.

Gay Street has always been the principal commercial address in Knoxville. It has witnessed most of the city's important parades and political rallies. In the spring of 1960, for example, at lunch counters of the town's major department stores, students from Knoxville College staged successful sit-in demonstrations during the early days of the civil rights movement in Tennessee. Today many of those same department stores are no longer in business. Indeed, despite spirited efforts by preservationists and investors, Gay Street has become more of a business and office center, dotted here and there with restaurants and other service-oriented enterprises, than the commercial emporium of Knoxville.

A few of the grand storefronts of sixty to a hundred years ago remain in commercial use. **Woodruff's,** at 424 S. Gay, has been a family business for 130 years. Its current home dates from 1904, the year the Southern Railway Terminal opened, which is about the same time the adjacent five-story **Kimball's Jewelers Building**, at 428 S. Gay, opened for business. On the sidewalk next to the building stands Knoxville's last Gay Street clock (circa 1915); once, several stood along the street to remind busy shoppers of the correct time. The **Cowan, McClung, and Company Building** (known now as Fidelity Bankers Trust), at 500–504 S. Gay, is one of the street's oldest buildings. Constructed as Knoxville began to rebuild from the Civil War in 1871, the building was updated in 1929 to reflect the best of Second Renaissance Revival architecture. Just off Gay Street, at 311–13 State, is the three-story **Cal Johnson Building** (1898), built by a middle-class African-American businessman to serve a large black community.

Gay Street also features the city's best modern commercial architecture. The S&W Cafeteria chain picked dazzling Art Deco facades for most of its restaurants. The Knoxville **S&W Cafeteria,** at 516–20 S. Gay, is no exception. Nearer the riverfront, across from the historic county courthouse, are the gleaming glass skyscrapers that once symbolized the banking empire of Jake Butcher and his brother C. H. Jake Butcher's United American Bank and C. H. Butcher's City and County Bank system both failed in the early 1980s. Convicted of fraud and banking violations, the brothers spent time in prison. The modernism of the skyscrapers stands in sharp contrast to the neo-Colonial Revival, campus-like complex of Whittle Communications, completed across the street in the early 1990s.

The **Knox County Courthouse** (1886, 1921, 1989) is one of the state's most important examples of the designs of Palliser and Palliser, a New York firm that produced many different pattern books of high Victorian architecture. The courthouse is described as "eclectic" in architectural terms: it is a mixture of different styles, including Colonial Revival, Romanesque, and Queen Anne.

Ayres Hall, "The Hill," University of Tennessee Campus

From Interstate 40, take exit 386. Either the Seventeenth Street ramp or the U.S. 129 ramp will lead to West Cumberland Avenue.

The state's major land-grant institution, the University of Tennessee, dates from 1794, when Blount College was established in the tiny territorial capital. This school operated for the next thirteen years until 1807 when the name was changed to East Tennessee College, but it soon closed and did not reopen until 1820 after a merger with Hampden-Sidney Academy. In 1826 the two schools went their separate ways; the college located to a new campus on top of "Barbara Hill," now simply known as "the Hill," on present-day West Cumberland Avenue. By 1840 the school was known as East Tennessee University.

During the Civil War Confederate and later Union soldiers occupied the campus because of the commanding views available of the surrounding landscape. After the war, college activities temporarily moved to the School for the Deaf (old City Hall) until the campus could be cleared of fortifications and the buildings prepared for classroom use once again.

In 1879 the college officially became the University of Tennessee. The buildings of today's modern campus were mostly constructed in the twentieth century, many in the last thirty years. But high on the Hill are several early-twentieth-century buildings that reflect different

Common Styles in Tennessee Architecture

Late Georgian: 1780–1820 generally, but remained influential in Tennessee domestic architecture until 1860. The style is characterized by symmetrical three- or five-bay facades, a steep gable roofline, delicate, understated ornamentation and use of classical detailing, and a central-hall interior plan. Often described as "Tennessee Federal" to reflect its period of greatest popularity. Cragfont in Sumner County is an excellent example (see the photo of Cragfont in the Landscape 16 section of chapter 6).

Greek Revival: 1820–1860. A temple-form building (since the entrance is on the gable end), characterized by a two-story classical portico comprised of columns with either Corinthian, Ionic, or Doric capitals that support an entablature and pediment. The more common form in Tennessee is a Greek Revival portico added to a late Georgian building. The state capitol, a nationally significant example of the Greek Revival–temple style, is the most famous Greek Revival building in Tennessee (see photo of the capitol in the Landscape 3 section of this chapter).

Gothic Revival: 1840–1900. A popular style for church buildings in Tennessee, especially after the Civil War. Verticality is a key element, which is expressed best by spires, towers, and sharply pitched roofs. In Gothic-style churches, the Tudor arch and buttresses are common elements. St. John's Church in Maury County is a representative example (see the photo of St. John's Church in the Landscape 18 section of chapter 6). In domestic architecture, the style is characterized by a cross gable, with its incline decorated by gingerbread designs, at the center of the facade, by corbeled, decorative chimneys, by hood window moldings; and by a sharp roof slope. Carpenter Gothic refers to a frame Gothic-style church or house covered with board and batten. Most of the historic houses and the Episcopal Church at Rugby represent Carpenter Gothic style (see photos of the Rugby Free Library and Christ Church Episcopal at the end of chapter 5).

Italianate: 1850–1880. A very popular style in domestic and commercial architecture during the decade before and after the Civil War. The style is characterized by a two- to three-story tower, wide eaves with brackets, pronounced window moldings, a low-pitch roof, and brick construction. A good Tennessee example is the McNeal Place in Bolivar (see photo of the McNeal Place in Landscape 21, chapter 7).

Second Empire: 1860–1880. Derived from a French architectural movement of the 1850s, Second Empire style in Tennessee is historically associated with the New South Era of 1865 to 1880. It is characterized by a mansard-style and multicolored tinplate roof, by projecting two- to three-story central block, by arched hood window moldings, by cast-iron cresting, and by elaborate dormer windows. Craigmiles Hall in Cleveland is a rare example of a Second Empire commercial building (see photo of Craigmiles Hall in Landscape 11, chapter 4).

Queen Anne: 1875–1900. This style is primarily used in domestic architecture, although elements of Queen Anne style can be seen in commercial buildings of the late nineteenth century. The composition of the building is asymmetrical, with turrets and towers becoming primary decorative elements. Other characteristic elements include fish-scale shingles, bay windows, tall, thin chimneys, and a multiplaned roof. The Clark-Roche farmhouse outside of Wartrace is an exquisite example of Queen Anne style in Tennessee (see photo of the Clark-Roche farmhouse in Landscape 17, chapter 6).

Classical Revival: 1895–1940. A widely popular movement in public, commercial, and domestic architecture. Differs from the earlier Greek Revival movement in that its classicism is heavy and pronounced, with monumental paired columns and enriched cornices and pediments. The George Peabody College for Teachers in Nashville has several excellent examples of the many different expressions of Classical Revival (see photo of the Social and Religious Administration Building of Peabody College in Landscape 3 of this chapter).

For more on architectural styles, see the Blumenson and the McAlester and McAlester entries in the suggested readings.

periods of the university's growth and expansion. The oldest is South College (1872), the only remaining structure from the days of East Tennessee University. The most impressive is Ayres Hall (1921), named for Brown Ayres, a former university president. Its 125-foot-high Collegiate Gothic tower, designed by the Chicago firm of Miller, Fullenwider, and Dowling, instantly became a city landmark and has ever since served as a symbol for the university. Collegiate Gothic architecture was a modern adaptation of the late medieval Gothic buildings at the famous English colleges of Oxford and Cambridge. Many universities, such as Princeton and Duke, had already constructed new buildings in the style. During the 1920s and 1930s, the University of Tennessee followed this nationally accepted standard for university architecture in most of its new buildings.

In 1927 Gov. Austin Peay approved a bill that gave the university five hundred thousand dollars a year for the next five years for the construction of new campus buildings. Out of this funding bonanza came Hoskins Library, directly across West Cumberland Avenue from Ayres Hall. Surrounding Ayres Hall itself were Ferris (Engineering) Hall, Hesler (Biology) Hall, Dabney (Chemistry) Hall, a new Physics and Geology Building, and Alumni Memorial Auditorium and Gymnasium, with seating for forty-five hundred people. The Knoxville firm of Barber and McMurry designed these Collegiate Gothic buildings between 1928 and 1935. With its own Gothic tower, Hoskins Library is perhaps the most impressive of the lot.

During the 1960s and 1970s, a new construction boom shifted the center of campus activity away from the Hill westward toward new university streets south of West Cumberland Avenue. Using urban renewal funds in 1963, the Knoxville Housing Authority first demolished 341 buildings and moved 400 families. Then a new modern campus expanded along Volunteer Boulevard, Andy Holt Avenue, and Circle Park.

The firm of Barber and McMurry designed several of the new buildings, such as Clement Hall and the Music Building (1966). But in the late 1960s and 1970s, architect Bruce McCarty, together with several different partners, gave the campus a more modern, innovative look. The skyscraper-like McClung Plaza and Tower (1967) and the stair-step look of the Hodges Library (1987) are merely the most stunning examples. Other important buildings are the Communications and University Extension Building (1969) at Circle Park, the Clarence Brown Theater (1970), Andy Holt Tower (1973), and the Art and Ar-

chitecture Building (1981). Another creative building is the seven-story tower of the Stokely Center for Management Studies, designed by Robert Church, a former dean of the university's school of architecture. The Frank H. McClung Museum on Circle Drive has rotating exhibits on art, history, anthropology, and technology.

The largest building on campus is Thompson-Boling Assembly Center and Arena, which can seat 24,535 for college basketball games. The most famous is Neyland Stadium, where almost a hundred thousand devoted fans can be found cheering on the University of Tennessee football team during autumn afternoons.

West of the university campus, where West Cumberland Avenue (U.S. 11) intersects with U.S. 129, the agricultural campus can be visited by turning south. Here are over twenty buildings, with the oldest structures, especially Morgan Hall (1921), sharing the Collegiate Gothic theme of the main campus.

At this same intersection of U.S. Highways 11 and 129, Cumberland Avenue becomes Kingston Pike, which once was the city's primary western link to Nashville. Nearby are two historic house museums. The Armstrong-Lockett House (1934) at 2728 Kingston Pike displays decorative arts and landscape gardening. The circa 1858 **Bleak House** (or the Confederate Memorial Hall) at 3148 Kingston Pike is a fifteen-room Italianate mansion, used by Gen. James Longstreet as his headquarters during the Battle of Knoxville in 1863.

After the turn of the century, when a streetcar railway was built along the road, Kingston Pike became popular as a suburban hideaway from the harsh realities of life in the city. Some of Knoxville's best designed and preserved examples of domestic architecture now face this street. John Russell Pope, an American architect famous for his neoclassical designs, including the Jefferson Memorial in Washington, D.C., designed the neoclassical **Dulin House** (1915–17) at 3100 Kingston Pike. **Westwood** (1890), at 3425 Kingston Pike, features Queen Anne and Richardsonian elements and was designed by the important Knoxville firm of Baumann and Baumann.

Next there is the stone gate entrance to Sequoyah Hills, the city's first planned subdivision, as well as the entrance to **Talahi,** an elaborate 1920s expansion of the earlier development. Cherokee Boulevard and Southgate Road are only two of the streets in the combined development that highlight important examples of the different revival designs of Barber and McMurry. These two suburbs provided safe havens for upper-class businessmen and middle-class professionals who wished to escape the pollution of downtown Knoxville. The streetcar, and later the automobile, made commuting to the downtown business district and university relatively easy. Both subdivisions used deed restrictions to control landscaping, house styles, and setbacks. In Talahi, elaborate parks, foundations, and gardens were scattered throughout, and many of these landscape features remain today.

The firm of Barber and McMurry, as the buildings at the university and Sequoyah Hills document, played a significant role in the architectural history of Knoxville. The firm's founder, George F. Barber, also holds an important place in the history of American domestic architecture. In 1889 he became the first American designer to make available by mail entire prefabricated dwellings. Barber did so perhaps out of desperation rather than inspiration. Lacking clients, he discovered a steady market for complete homes shipped by rail. In addition Barber sold building plans and published architectural pattern books, including *The Cottage Souvenir* (1891), *New Model Dwellings* (1894), *Artistic Homes* (1895), *Art in Architecture* (1902–3), and *Modern Dwellings* (1901–7). Barber established a monthly magazine to promote his designs further.

The **Park City** neighborhood, in the east Knoxville area of E. Fifth, Jefferson, Woodbine, and Washington Avenues, contains probably the largest concentration of George Barber–designed houses in the country. This area began in 1892 as a typical streetcar neighborhood, with streets running parallel to the streetcar right-of-way on Magnolia Avenue. Building continued here until World War II, with the more recent construction clustered around the Standard Knitting Mills at the west end of the community.

Barber resided in a Queen Anne–style home at 1635 Washington; he later lived at 1724 Washington, and in the 1700 and 1800 blocks of this street are seven other Barber-designed homes, typical of his designs in that they combined intricate Victorian detailing into creative individual architectural expressions. Barber would even mix the fish-scale shingles, turrets, and bays of Queen Anne style with such classical elements as Ionic capitals and Palladian windows.

Planned neighborhoods like Talahi and Park City were hardly the norm in Knoxville. Mountain View was a historic black neighborhood where the Hyatt-Regency Hotel now stands. Before urban renewal in the 1960s, it was considered the city's worst slum. According to the 1960 census, it rated almost at the bottom nationwide in terms of the quality of its housing. **Mechanicsville,** in north Knoxville, was home to skilled artisans who worked in the nearby railroad yards or factories. On Deaderick Street, the cast-iron fences that were produced at the Knoxville Iron Company are notable.

Landscape 3: Nashville

Along the Cumberland River, in the heart of Tennessee, is the city of Nashville, the state capital since 1827. At this point on the river, a great

Nashville. (Courtesy of Tennessee Department of Transportation, as adapted by the author)

salt lick existed that had attracted animals and, in turn, Indian hunters for centuries. In about 1710, the French established a trading post nearby, and the place became known as French Lick.

It was a tiny outpost on the fringes of the North American fur trade until 1763, when the Treaty of Paris transferred the land to England. Sometime during the 1760s, Timothy Demonbreun, a French-Canadian trader, moved there and can be considered the area's first settler. In the winter of 1779–80, James Robertson and John Donelson brought English settlers. A 1930 re-creation of Fort Nashborough, their first residence, faces the river on First Avenue North. In its initial decades Nashville grew as a river port for an increasing number of surrounding rich farms and plantations in Davidson, Sumner, and Robertson Counties. The first steamboat arrived in 1818, and by 1829 the local wharf totaled 112 steamboat arrivals.

Nashville became the temporary state capital in 1827, and sixteen years later it was named the permanent capital. The 1840 census found almost 7,000 residents in Nashville. During the next decade, the city continued to grow, largely in response to the construction of new turnpikes—410 miles of completed roads by 1840—that connected Nashville to the rural hinterlands.

Just as they were in Tennessee's other major cities, the 1850s were years of prosperity and expansion in Nashville. The grand Greek Revival **State Capitol** and the twin towers of the Egyptian Revival **First Presbyterian Church,** both by the important American architect William Strickland, dominated the downtown landscape. Adolphus Heiman, a German-trained engineer and designer, added other architectural landmarks, including his Gothic Revival **University of Nashville** at Second Avenue South. Around the **Church of the Assumption,** designed by Jacob Geiger, a large and prosperous German community had been established in north Nashville at a place now known as Germantown. By 1857 taxable property in Nashville was worth eleven million dollars, and there was more wealth in the surrounding countryside. Several grand mansions were constructed during the decade, including the elaborately landscaped **Belmont** (1850s), the remodeled **Belle Meade** (1853), **Two Rivers Mansion** (1859), and **Clover Bottom** (1858).

Nashville's transportation evolution from steamboats to turnpikes to railroads had much to do with the new prosperity. Completed in 1854, the Nashville and Chattanooga Railroad, supported by $872,000 in city subscriptions, connected Nashville to the Chattanooga rail junction. In 1856 railroad president Vernon K. Stevenson and others launched the Nashville and Northwestern to link the capital to the Mississippi River at Hickman, Kentucky. (During the Civil War, however, Union generals commandeered the eastern end of the line and used contraband African-American laborers to finish it to New Johnsonville on the Tennessee River.)

Outsiders controlled the second important Nashville railroad. The Louisville and Nashville Railroad was completed in 1859 and connected Nashville to the Ohio River and to the midwestern railroad system. Smaller lines also fueled the city's railroad boom. The Edgefield and Kentucky ran from the city's first suburb to Guthrie, Kentucky. The Nashville and Decatur Railroad linked Nashville to the rich plantations of Maury County before connecting with the Memphis and Charleston line at Decatur, Alabama.

Nashville was an occupied city for most of the Civil War. As a base for Federal operations, the city was surrounded by a ring of defensive forts. The most important was **Fort Negley,** built mostly by recently freed African Americans in 1862. It represented the first heavy use of newly freed blacks in the Federal war effort, and it influenced the later creation of "contraband" labor camps in Nashville, Chattanooga, Clarksville, Murfreesboro, Tullahoma, and other Mid-South towns (see sidebar entitled "Contrabands in the Civil War," Landscape 20, chapter 7). The fort stood on St. Cloud Hill, behind the present-day Cumberland Science Museum, but it escaped heavy fighting until December 15–17, 1864, when the Confederate Army of Tennessee, under the command of Gen. John B. Hood, launched a futile attack on the well-fortified army of Gen. George H. Thomas.

After the war, new patterns of growth and development, similar to those of other major "New South" cities, marked Nashville's history. By 1884 the Louisville and Nashville securely controlled the city's many different railroad lines and set limits on local economic development. The city's wholesale grocery business dominated Mid-South markets. The flour industry was large enough that Nashville claimed to be the "Minneapolis of the South." Textile mills were another key to the local economy. The Tennessee Manufacturing Company, established in 1869, opened a huge four-story mill in 1871. By 1890 the mill had one thousand looms and thirty-five thousand spindles, worked by eight hundred employees. The factories of the Nashville Cotton Mills employed some six hundred and fifty workers. Nashville also became a regional education center. Northern philanthropists helped to establish Fisk University, Roger Williams University, and Vanderbilt University in an effort to uplift the defeated South; in the early twentieth century, initiatives for rural reform created the George Peabody College for Teachers.

Nashville was slow to recover from the depression of 1893, and, while growth continued, its rate was greatly diminished from the heady days of the 1880s. Urban competitors such as Memphis, Birmingham, and Atlanta surpassed Nashville in population and economic power. Nashville joined the middle tier of southern cities.

In 1920 Nashville's population of 118,342 was dispersed over a wide area of Davidson County as suburban life took hold. **Edgefield** (1868), east of the river, was the first suburb. At the turn of the century came several more enclaves for middle-class professionals and businessmen. Subdivided in 1890, the **Belmont-Hillsboro** neighborhood boomed in 1901 once a streetcar line was completed. Seven years later, another streetcar suburb, the **Hillsboro-West End** neighborhood, was developed to the west. The **Woodland-in-Waverly** and **Richland-West End** neighborhoods emerged at roughly the same time. Today the Richland area contains the city's best collection of American Four-Square and bungalow residences. Working-class neighborhoods abounded as well. During World War I, Du Pont Corporation built the town of **Old Hickory** for employees at its huge ammunition plant. "The plant was so big and had so many people on its payroll," remembered Nashville businessman and historian Stanley Horn, "that Nashville was just turned around" (Burns, 70).

The city once again boomed in the next decade. Education facilities continued to expand. The Classical Revival campus of **George Peabody College for Teachers** and the beautiful Collegiate Gothic campus of **Scarritt College** (1928), designed by Nashville architect Henry C. Hibbs, added significantly to the city's architectural traditions. By 1930 Nashville residents totaled 153,866 people, a 30 percent increase in ten years.

The Great Depression witnessed further changes in the urban landscape. The failure of the financial house of Caldwell and Company in late 1930 shocked the business community and shook the state's banking institutions to their core. New Deal agencies replaced slum housing with the Cheatham Place housing project (white) and the Andrew Jackson Courts project (black), both designed by Nashville Allied Architects. The Works Progress Administration restored the Fort Negley historic site, designed a controversial steeplechase course at the **Percy and Edwin Warner Parks,** and built Berry Field, a new Nashville airport. New government buildings, shining in their PWA Modern classicism, surrounded the state capital in downtown Nashville. Dominating the old public square was the city's most dazzling piece of modern architecture, the **Davidson County Courthouse** (1937).

In the post–World War II era, however, the city's expansion slowed as new suburban communities grew in size. A population of 167,000 in 1940 had increased to only 170,000 twenty years later, despite the growth of the country music business, the addition of important new industries such as Vultee Aircraft (now Textron Aerostructures), and the successful Capitol Hill Redevelopment Project. The latter venture used federal funds to replace slums with new offices and larger parking lots and built the James Robertson Parkway (1957) to improve access to Capitol Hill.

The 1960s were a decade of great change in Nashville. The most dramatic came at downtown lunch counters in early 1960 when a group of dedicated African-American activists from Fisk, Tennessee State, and the American Baptist Theological Seminary staged successful nonviolent sit-ins to protest segregation. The civil rights movement soon gathered momentum, and by 1964 segregation had almost disappeared in public accommodations. The face of local government changed as well. In April 1963, Nashville and Davidson County had

Downtown Nashville skyline, 1990. A skyscraper boom during the 1980s gave a modern look to the Nashville skyline.

become the first local governments in Tennessee to merge into a metropolitan government.

Throughout the decade and continuing into the 1970s, the Downtown Urban Renewal Project almost totally rebuilt downtown Nashville. The Andrew Jackson Hotel and other historic buildings fell victim to the wrecking ball. A new skyline of skyscrapers and office buildings took their places. In 1974 the Grand Ole Opry left the historic **Ryman Auditorium,** just off Lower Broadway, for the new Opryland entertainment park out in the suburbs. Downtown businesses had lost another important anchor.

In reaction to the recent wholesale destruction of historic architecture, Nashville looked with a more favorable eye toward historic preservation. The former grand Colonial Revival estate of the Cheek family, **Cheekwood,** became a horticultural and fine arts center, bringing nationally important art exhibits to the midstate. The museum is located off Tennessee 100 in west Nashville. Projects in the 1970s and 1980s saved the historic warehouses along **Second Avenue North** and led to a rebirth of the **Lower Broadway** district. **Union Station,** a magnificent railroad terminal built by the Louisville and Nashville Railroad in 1900, was renovated after years of neglect and abuse. The old **Grassmere** estate became a wildlife park. Reserved tours of the grand antebellum mansion also are available at the park, which is located on Nolensville Road (U.S. 31/41A). Nashville, like other Southern cities, discovered that the past could serve as the foundation for a better future.

Perhaps Nashville's recognition of the importance of its past is one reason novelist Peter Taylor found a ray of hope for the city in his *A Summons to Memphis* (1987):

> Even with its present-day vulgar, ugly, plastic look and sound there is a little something else left for anyone who was once under Nashville's spell. As one walks or rides down any street in Nashville one can feel now again that he has just glimpsed some pedestrian on the sidewalk who was not quite real somehow, who with a glance over his shoulder or with a look in his disenchanted eye has warned one not to believe too much in the plastic present and has given warning that the past is still real and present somehow and is demanding something of all men like me who happen to pass that way. (24–25)

Nashville has four central locations to begin to explore the city's history and architecture: 1) Davidson County Courthouse, 2) state capitol, 3) Fisk University, and 4) Vanderbilt University and Peabody College. Because of the importance of plantation agriculture to the city's early decades, this section on Nashville concludes with a tour of surrounding historic farms and plantations.

Davidson County Courthouse

There are two routes from highways to the Davidson County Courthouse. From Interstate 40, take exit 211. Follow Second Avenue north to the courthouse. From Interstate 24/65, take the James Robertson Parkway exit to the courthouse.

Construction over the last sixty years makes it difficult to see and to understand the patterns of early settlement in downtown Nashville. The best way is to leave Interstate 40 at the Second and Fourth Avenue ramp (exit 211) and turn north on Second Avenue, which runs by several major landmarks of nineteenth-century Nashville. To the east, behind Howard School, is the former **Literary Department** of the University of Nashville (1853), a Gothic Revival design by Adolphus Heiman. At the bottom of the hill, at the intersection of Second Avenue and Broadway, is Riverfront Park, formed from the old steamboat wharfs on the Cumberland River.

Traveling up the hill, visitors pass by the historic riverfront ware-houses of the **Second Avenue historic district.** These buildings, with their multicolored Victorian facades and prominent cornices, show the city's development as a wholesale grocery and supply center from 1870 to 1890. At that time, this street was called Market Street because it directly linked the wharfs and warehouses to the merchants at Nashville's Public Square. Its name changed to Second Avenue in 1903; today interpretive markers along the sidewalks explain important his-torical events.

The **Davidson County Courthouse** stands at the center of what was once the Public Square. In 1784 Thomas Molloy prepared the first town plat, providing for 165 one-acre squares with four squares re-served for a public square. Here was the focus for local politics and com-merce in early Nashville. Today, however, it is difficult to envision what the square looked like since many buildings have been demolished to make way for parking lots, new roads, and new buildings in the twen-tieth century.

The most radical changes came in 1936–37 when the Public Works Administration demolished the antebellum Davidson County Courthouse (a magnificent Greek Revival design by Francis Strickland), along with the historic Market House and city hall, to make way for the sparkling new Davidson County Public Building and Court House. In an attempt to mute local criticism about the destruction of the Greek Revival landmark, the new courthouse expressed a strong classical fla-vor in its commanding facade of Doric columns. Designed by Frederick Heirons of New York and Emmons Woolwine of Nashville, the mix of classicism and Art Deco elements at the courthouse makes it an out-standing example of what is often called "PWA or WPA Modern" style, depending on which agency designed and funded the project. Like the New Deal itself, the style represents a curious blending of the old and new to create a building that is visually modern but that also evokes the past. The interior has federally sponsored murals by the artist Dean Cornwell that represent industry, agriculture, statesmanship, and com-merce (also see sidebar entitled "The New Deal Built Environment," Landscape 9, chapter 4).

In 1880 the Public Square was still the commercial heart of Nash-ville, but by the turn of the century, retail shopping had shifted more to the west, especially along Union and Church Streets. In 1906 Caster-Knott Dry Goods Company opened the city's first large department store at Seventh Avenue and Church. Three years earlier, Daniel C.

The Arcade, Nashville. Arcades were innovative solutions to the demands for more downtown retail space in turn-of-the-century urban centers.

Buntin had established the **Arcade** between Fourth and Fifth Avenues as a glass-covered urban retail center where busy shoppers, safe from inclement weather and free from dodging carriages, taxis, and animal droppings, could choose from forty stores. This early stab at the idea of an enclosed shopping mall is one of the few remaining downtown arcades in America. The Arcade demonstrated, so claimed a Nashville newspaper, "a new spirit—one of industrial enterprise, of financial activity, of prosperity" (Doyle, 74).

Another grand symbol of the "new spirit" stood several blocks to the southwest at 1001 Broadway. **Union Station,** constructed by the Louisville and Nashville Railroad in 1900, is a magnificent example of

Richardsonian Romanesque architecture and features a unique iron and steel train shed that measures 250 feet by 50 feet with a clear span of 200 feet. Company engineer Richard Montfort designed both the station and the shed, and the complex is listed as a National Historic Landmark for its architectural and engineering significance. The station, which has been renovated into a hotel and restaurant, symbolized the L&N's control over Nashville commerce and served as the western boundary for the grand public and commercial buildings of downtown Nashville.

From 1870 to 1900, Broadway evolved into an avenue of political and commercial significance. The buildings nearer the train terminal include such key public buildings as the Art Deco **U.S. Post Office** at 901 Broadway, designed by Nashville architects Marr and Holman, and the Federal Building at 801 Broadway (1949), where the Nashville Centennial of 1880 took place. Across the street is **Christ Episcopal Church** (1887–92, 1947), one of the city's best examples of High Victorian Gothic architecture. The trendsetter for that style—the **U.S. Customs House** (1876–87, 1903, 1916)—is on the next block, at 701 Broadway. Federal architect William A. Potter, who was already famous for his Victorian buildings at Princeton University, designed the building's original central block, and its cornerstone was laid on September 19, 1877, by President Rutherford B. Hayes. A later federal architect, James Knox Taylor, designed the compatible 1902–3 addition.

Sadly, only the great spire (1884–86) remains from the adjacent First Baptist Church, which once matched the customshouse for its Victorian splendor. Across the street from the church and customshouse are two important buildings from the early twentieth century. The old **Hume-Fogg High School** (1912, 1916) is on the site of the first public school in Nashville. Its Tudor Gothic facade also reflected the architectural traditions embodied by the earlier First Baptist Church and the customshouse. However, the Masonic Grand Lodge (1925) directly across from the church was a decided neoclassical departure, designed by the Nashville firm of Asmus and Clark.

As Broadway edged downhill to the waterfront, the nature of activity and architecture changed. The most important building, **Ryman Auditorium,** stood north just off Broadway at 116 Fifth Avenue. In the late 1800s, Tom Ryman, a successful steamboat captain, was converted to the message of the gospel and agreed to fund the construction of the Union Gospel Tabernacle for revival meetings. But soon the huge building—renamed the Ryman Auditorium in 1905—was used for secular

Ryman Auditorium, Nashville. A recent restoration has once again made the Ryman a popular concert stage.

Lower Broadway historic district, Nashville. For over ten years, historic preservationists, urban renewal experts, bankers, and developers have experimented with new uses for the old stores and warehouses of Lower Broadway.

purposes as an all-purpose auditorium. Popular music performances featured such diverse talents as Enrico Caruso, Will Rogers, Marian Anderson, Jascha Heifetz, Sarah Bernhardt, and Roy Rogers. Then, in 1943, WSM Radio moved its weekly Grand Ole Opry program to the Ryman to better accommodate country music fans who wanted to watch their favorite stars. The Ryman remained the Opry's home until 1974, and during those thirty years it carved a special niche in the annals of American popular music. In 1993–94, the Ryman was renovated, and it opened in the summer of 1994 as a music performance hall once again.

The shops near the Ryman on Broadway between Fifth and Fourth avenues catered to the music crowd. The turreted **Merchants Hotel** (1892) was once a cheap hotel for aspiring country music stars; today it is a classy restaurant and jazz bar. **Tootsie's Orchid Lounge** at 422 Broadway is the most famous juke joint; Ernest Tubb Record Shop, across the street at 417 Broadway, once hosted its own program after the Opry closed every Saturday night. After crossing Fourth Avenue, activity changed again. The next two blocks once served as the center of the Mid-South furniture business. Of special note is the neoclassical-style corner building at 301 Broadway, once the old **American National Bank**. Nearer the waterfront, hardware stores and feed and

seed stores became common. The **Acme Feed and Seed Store** at 101 Broadway is one of the oldest family-owned businesses in this National Register district.

Tennessee State Capitol

To reach the capitol from Interstate 24/65, exit at the James Robertson Parkway; to reach the capitol from Interstate 40, take exit 209 and turn east on Charlotte Pike.

William Strickland, born in New Jersey in 1788, was one of the best American architects of the Greek Revival style, which dominated American public architecture in the first half of the nineteenth century. He gained fame and popularity in Philadelphia with designs such as the Second Bank of the United States (1818–24) and the Philadelphia Exchange (1832–34). After recovery was slow to follow the depression of 1837, however, Strickland accepted an offer from the state of Tennessee to design and supervise the construction of its permanent state capitol building in 1845.

Strickland considered the **Tennessee State Capitol** his ultimate statement in Greek Revival. He used all three Greek orders: a Doric basement, Ionic porticoes, and a Corinthian cupola. The design inspiration for the main section of the building came from the Erectheum in Athens while the idea of the cupola came from another gem of Athens antiquity, the Choragic Monument of Lysicrates. Unfortunately, Strickland died before the building was completed and, in respect for his wishes, was buried in a tomb in the east facade. His son Francis Strickland supervised the remaining construction, and the building was finally finished in 1859. The interior of the capitol is as compelling as the exterior, especially the state library and the house chambers. Informative guidebooks to the building's architecture, and its many paintings and monuments, are available at its information booth.

To the east and west of the capitol is the heart of a complex of state government buildings while to the south lies the central business district. Immediately west of the capitol are the Supreme Court Building, a Public Works Administration project of the 1930s designed by Marr and Holman of Nashville, and the neoclassical State Library and Archives (1952–53), designed by H. Clinton Parrent Jr. To the east is the Cordell Hull Building, another PWA project named in honor of Tennessee native Cordell Hull, who was the secretary of State during Roosevelt's New Deal. The adjacent John Sevier State Office Building has a construction history much like that of the Davidson County Courthouse. It too was designed by Heirons and Woolwine, and it has federally sponsored murals depicting Tennessee history by Dean Cornwell. The three New Deal–period public buildings that surround the capitol—all exhibiting different aspects of PWA Modern style—document the enormous impact of the Roosevelt years on the urban landscape of Nashville (also see sidebar entitled "The New Deal Built Environment," Landscape 9, chapter 4).

The next major building period came from the mid-1960s to mid-1970s. The boxy Andrew Jackson Building, southeast of the capitol, dates from 1970, while the multiple-use James K. Polk Building at 505 Deaderick was constructed from 1976 to 1980. Part of the building houses state offices; another part holds the Tennessee Performing Arts Center, which features three theaters. The largest is the twenty-five-hundred-seat Andrew Jackson Hall. The Polk building also holds the Tennessee State Museum, which relies on its collections and those of the

Tennessee Historical Society to interpret the state's social, cultural, and political history from the prehistoric era to the twentieth century. The museum also has temporary gallery space for special exhibits on history and art.

Tennessee military history is interpreted in gallery space in the basement of the historic War Memorial Building (1925), which is located directly west of the Polk building. Designed by the New York firm of McKim, Mead, and White, with Nashville's Edward Daughtery as associate architect, the War Memorial Building is one of the city's best expressions of the Classical Revival movement of the early twentieth century. It was the first building, besides the capitol, constructed for state government use. Its central atrium, surrounded by Doric columns, highlights a bronze statue of "Victory" by Belle Kinney and Leopold Scholz. Its auditorium seats twenty-two hundred.

The Legislative Plaza (1974), designed by Steinbaugh, Harwood, and Rogers, enhances the splendid classical architecture of both the capitol and the War Memorial Building by creating a landscaped vista. Architect Charles Warterfield has described the plaza as a "unique sort" of architecture, "not visible as such to the passerby, a kind of inner world of its own, with its subterranean main street, side streets, and very important places along the way" (Orr, 59).

From the Legislative Plaza, the important architectural landmarks of the downtown business district are visible. Directly south at Union and Sixth Avenue is the historic **Hermitage Hotel** (1910), designed by Edwin Carpenter in the style of Beaux-Arts classicism. Next, walk to the north end of the plaza and turn east in front of the capitol on Charlotte Avenue. At the intersection with Fifth Avenue is an antebellum Greek Revival landmark, **St. Mary's Roman Catholic Cathedral** (1845–47), designed by Adolphus Heiman. It was the first permanent Catholic church in Tennessee. By continuing south along Fifth Avenue, visitors will encounter a historic district that preserves late-nineteenth- and early-twentieth-century commercial buildings. At the Deaderick intersection, however, it may be a good idea to turn east for one block to Fourth Avenue. There stands the restrained neoclassical **Morris Memorial Building** (1924), designed by Nashville's McKissack and McKissack, which was the first American architectural firm to be organized and staffed by African Americans. Moses McKissack III, the grandson of a freed slave who was a mason and contractor, and Calvin McKissack established the firm in 1922.

At the corner of Fifth and Church, two significant architectural landmarks face each other. The brick building is the twin-towered **Downtown Presbyterian Church** (1849–51), a National Historic Landmark designed by William Strickland in Egyptian Revival style. The Egyptian Revival in American architecture was popular for only a brief time in the antebellum era and produced relatively few buildings. The style can be identified by the reeded columns, cavetto cornice, and winged sun disk. The interior also features Egyptian motifs, believed to be the work of local artist William Davies during an 1881–82 renovation.

Across the street is the Third National Financial Center (1983–86), designed by the New York firm of Kohn Pederson Fox. The skyscraper is one of the country's most important monuments of postmodern architecture. This recent architectural movement combines historical details with the modern shine of the glass and steel skyscraper. In this case, the building reflects the architectural traditions of Strickland's earlier Egyptian Revival church.

Fisk University

From Interstate 40, take exit 207; Fisk University is located on Jefferson Street at Seventeenth Avenue North.

Fisk University, one of the most famous African-American private colleges in the nation, is at the heart of Nashville's black community. The creation of the university dates to the Reconstruction period immediately after the Civil War when various reform and religious groups came to the South to help blacks adjust to their new freedom in a still segregated and racist society. The American Missionary Association of New York City and the Western Freedmen's Aid Commission of Cincinnati, assisted by Gen. Clinton B. Fisk, head of the state's Freedmen's Bureau, established Fisk School in 1866; the following year, the school was chartered as a university. Unfortunately, the Reconstruction reformers soon lost interest, and federal funding from the Freedmen's Bureau abruptly ended in 1870.

Fisk administrators turned to their students for help. In 1871 college treasurer George L. White organized a group of Fisk students into a choir that would travel in the North and raise money for the college. The tour began slowly; to attract larger audiences, the students began to perform slave songs and spirituals and took the name "Fisk Jubilee Singers." Their performances met with wide critical and commercial success; they even sang before President U. S. Grant at the White House

and brought back twenty thousand dollars to their financially strapped university. A tour of Europe in 1873 raised fifty thousand dollars more. With this money, the college built the magnificent Victorian Gothic **Jubilee Hall** (1873–75), a National Historic Landmark at the center of the Fisk campus. Stephen D. Hatch of New York was the architect.

The campus has other historic buildings that document different periods of the university's history. The recently restored **Memorial Chapel** (1892), by William B. Bigelow of New York, was built with twenty-five thousand dollars from the estate of General Fisk. Andrew Carnegie provided the funding for the **Academic Building** (1908), which was originally a Carnegie Library, designed by Moses McKissack. The **Administration Building** (1930), by Henry C. Hibbs of Nashville, served first as the university library. It has murals by Aaron Douglass, an African-American artist of the Harlem Renaissance period who founded the school's art department. The **Carl Van Vechten Art Gallery** is in the old 1888 gym, remodeled in 1949 to serve as the university art gallery. Van Vechten was a major critic and patron of the Harlem Renaissance and an important photographer in his own right. He inspired the famous artist Georgia O'Keefe to donate her husband Alfred Steiglitz's art collection to the university. Consequently, Fisk has the best collection of early modern art in Nashville, including paintings by Aaron Douglass, O'Keefe, Picasso, and Cézanne.

The small antebellum black community of north Nashville soon centered around Fisk University, and by the 1920s Jefferson Street became the commercial heart of the neighborhood. Many businesses closed forty years later, due to the integration of downtown businesses and the heavy impact of interstate highway construction, which claimed the historic Ritz Theater and adversely affected 626 homes and 128 businesses. North of Jefferson Street, along Heiman, Scovel, and Jackson Streets, remains a largely intact historic black neighborhood of small cottages, bungalows, and "shotguns"—an urban folk housing form of three interconnected rooms with no interior hallway that originated in Haiti. At the corner of Seventeenth Avenue North and Jo Johnston is the historic Pearl High School, designed by McKissack and McKissack and built with PWA funds in 1939.

To the immediate west of the Fisk campus, at 1005 D. B. Todd Boulevard, is Meharry Medical College, which began as the medical department of Central Tennessee College in 1876. The school was originally located on First Avenue, but in 1930–31 a new twenty-six-acre campus of four red-brick Collegiate Gothic buildings, designed by Gordon and Keebler, was established adjacent to Fisk University. The college was the first medical school for African Americans in the United States, and it remains the largest private school for the training of black medical professionals. As of the early 1990s, almost 40 percent of all black doctors and dentists in American practices were Meharry graduates.

Continue west on Jefferson Street to its intersection with Twenty-eighth Avenue North; from here, John Merritt Boulevard gives access to the campus of Tennessee State University, opened in 1912 as the state's teacher-training college for blacks. Its original name, Tennessee Agricultural and Industrial State Normal School, reflected the belief of white reformers that African Americans should be educated primarily for work in the fields or in the factories. Yet, college administrators worked hard to insure that their students received a broad education. Under the leadership of William J. Hale, Tennessee State became an official college in 1922 and greatly expanded its facilities during the 1920s and 1930s. Harned Hall and a new library were constructed in 1927; four years later came the James E. Elliot Building. Together, the new and old buildings created a dignified campus of Classical Revival architecture, largely designed by the firm of McKissack and McKissack.

Vanderbilt University and George Peabody College for Teachers

To reach Vanderbilt and Peabody, take Interstate 440 to exit 3. Twenty-first Avenue S (U.S. 431) leads to both campuses. An alternate route to Vanderbilt is to take Interstate 40 to exit 209. West End Avenue (U.S. 70S) leads to the campus.

For many years Nashville has been recognized for its educational institutions. Vanderbilt University, like the earlier Fisk University, helped to shape the city's self-proclaimed reputation as the "Athens of the South." In 1872 the Methodist Episcopal Church South chartered the college as Central University, but after Bishop Holland N. McTyeire prodded New York railroad magnate Cornelius "Commodore" Vanderbilt to donate $500,000—an amount soon increased to over a million dollars—the name changed to Vanderbilt University in honor of his generosity. The Commodore's son, William H. Vanderbilt, gave additional funds a few years later and together the two Vanderbilts donated $1.2 million.

The university opened its doors in 1875 as a Methodist-sponsored institution, not as a denominational college. (Ties between the church and the university were completely severed in 1914.) The original campus was noted for its carefully landscaped grounds and picturesque Victorian Gothic buildings; the 1878 university *Register* listed 306 different trees and shrubs. The **Old Gymnasium** (1880), at West End and Twenty-third Avenue North, was designed by Peter J. Williamson of Nashville. Sharing a similar Victorian Gothic look is the former Science Hall (now Benson Hall). The historic **Mechanical Engineering Hall** is a more Romanesque-influenced design that has been incorporated into the new Owen Graduate School of Management Building. Kirkland Hall, the main administration building, also dates to the college's early years, but in 1905 a disastrous fire left only the shell of the twin-tower original administration building. In its reconstruction, only a single tower, the campus's most recognized landmark, was repaired and left standing.

Today the university reflects the 1905 campus plan of George Kessler, who changed the prevailing architectural style from Victorian Gothic to the faddish Collegiate Gothic. In 1907 Furman Hall, at that time the most modern chemistry and pharmacy building in the country, opened as the first building in the new style. No more new campus buildings were constructed until the mid-1920s when new donations and a new campus plan by Charles S. Klauder of Philadelphia brought

about a two-million-dollar medical school complex, the Alumni Memorial Hall, Neely Memorial Auditorium, along with Buttrick, Garland, and Calhoun Halls. All of these buildings were designed in a restrained Collegiate Gothic style.

By the Jazz Age, Vanderbilt's counterpart to the south, the **George Peabody College for Teachers,** had completed its new campus, which had been influenced by the plan and architecture of Thomas Jefferson's much earlier University of Virginia. Peabody, like Vanderbilt, owed its financial base to northern philanthropists. But its mission—to prepare teachers to uplift the rural South from its ignorance and backwardness—was quite different from Vanderbilt's reputation for graduate studies and professional colleges of medicine and law.

Peabody's intellectual and historical roots lie with the University of Nashville, the city's primary antebellum educational institution. After the Civil War, the university began training teachers with money provided by the Peabody Fund, establishing the Peabody State Normal School of the University of Nashville in 1875. Three years later, the medical school and other departments were closed so the institution could better concentrate on training teachers. The college became known as State Normal College, then Peabody Normal College in recognition of the continued support of the Peabody Fund, even though the college also received state funds on a regular basis.

The college campus at this time stood on Rutledge Hill off Second Avenue South in downtown Nashville. Today the old campus location is marked by the Gothic Revival **Literary Department** (now home to the Metro Planning Commission) along with the **Litterer Laboratory,** which was home for the University of Nashville Medical School until Litterer gave the building to Vanderbilt for laboratory use in 1915.

In 1905 the board of the Peabody Fund used its remaining monies to establish a regional institution for educating a new generation of southern teachers at the old Peabody school in downtown Nashville. With additional funds from the powerful General Education Board, an education foundation established by the Rockefellers, college administrators planned and built a remarkable modern campus along Twenty-first Avenue South adjacent to Vanderbilt University. Part of the land had earlier belonged to Roger Williams University, a college for African Americans first established as the Nashville Institute by the Home Mission Society in 1867. After changing its name to Roger Williams University in 1883, the Second Empire–designed school remained in business until 1905. Other acreage for Peabody College came from Vanderbilt because its administrators wanted to be close to what was then perceived as the most important development in southern education.

Classes began at the new campus in 1914, and the Home Economics Building was the first hall to be opened. By 1925 the college had added eight other classroom buildings and offices, following a campus plan by the Boston architects Ludlow and Peabody. Their Social and Religious Building, with its monumental Corinthian portico and dome, served as the symbolic heart of campus. The firm also designed the Psychology, Industrial Arts, and Home Economics Buildings (all in 1914). Leading American architects contributed other neoclassical buildings. McKim, Mead, and White of New York added the Administration Building and the University School (1925), as well as the Fine Arts Building two years later. Henry C. Hibbs designed the library (1918) along with the east and west dormitories (1921–23). In 1929 Raymond Hood of New York contributed the Graduate Dormitory and Granberry Jackson was the architect for the United Daughters Memorial Hall in 1933. The end result was the city's most magnificent collegiate landscape, a perfect symbol of the high hopes reformers placed in education in the early-twentieth-century South.

In 1924 another new college moved to Nashville, about two blocks south of Peabody, along Nineteenth Avenue South. On a nine-acre campus, Henry C. Hibbs of Nashville designed the exquisite stone **Scarritt College** campus, completing the primary buildings of his Collegiate Gothic vision in 1928. The well-proportioned and beautifully detailed Gothic tower of the college chapel is especially inspiring. The chapel, together with the other buildings of the original campus, represent the state's most coherent expression of the Collegiate Gothic style, and in 1929 Hibbs's work received the prestigious gold medal from the American Institute of Architects. "The Scarritt College campus sits in its quiet elegance and beauty expressing its clients' aspirations to Christian service," observes current Nashville architect Harriet Hall Cates. "It ranks in quality and design with the best of this genre in America" (Orr, 11).

The neighborhoods directly around the colleges became popular addresses for Nashville's middle-class professionals. Many of the city's finest examples of early-twentieth-century residential architecture are located along Hillsboro Pike and West End Avenue west of Vanderbilt or Peabody, particularly past Interstate 440. East of the interstate, commercial development is claiming an increasing number of homes. West of the interstate, however, the neighborhoods have few intrusions and several are listed in the National Register of Historic Places.

The colleges of west Nashville, which include Belmont University and David Lipscomb University, are the educational roots of Nashville's reputation as the "Athens of the South." Directly north of the Vanderbilt football stadium, in Centennial Park on West End Avenue, is a document of the architectural roots of that city slogan: the **Parthenon.** It is a full-scale replica of the Parthenon of ancient Athens. A replica of the Parthenon had housed the Fine Arts Museum for the 1897 Tennessee Centennial Exposition. From 1920 to 1931, the city rebuilt the replica in concrete based on plans by Nashville architect Russell E. Hart and New York architect and archaeologist William B. Dinsmoor. George J. Zolnay reproduced the Doric frieze. Nashville artists Belle Kinney and Leopold Scholz added the reproductions of the original Ionic frieze, as well as fifty-four classic statues in the tympana of the pediments. A statue of Athena by Nashville sculptor Alan LeQuire dominates the east room of the main hall. Other sections of the building house office space and art galleries. The building is in the wrong color—marble was too expensive and the concrete produced a buff color—but there is no better symbol of Nashville's pretensions as the "Athens of the South" than the Parthenon. Architectural critic Paul Goldberger has called it "a piece of earnest, well-meaning Americana" (*New York Times,* March 5, 1989).

Belmont Mansion, Nashville. A modern college campus now occupies what was once an ornately landscaped plantation.

Antebellum Agriculture in Davidson County

Outside of a few public buildings and private dwellings, little remains of Nashville's antebellum urban landscape, but surrounding the city are many historic farms and plantations that reflect the lifestyles and architectural tastes of the wealthy class. These same places also document the contribution to Tennessee's pre–Civil War economy and culture made by African-American slaves. In many cases, skilled slave laborers built the elaborate mansions; at every plantation, the slaves provided the back-breaking labor and agricultural expertise that made the plantations richly profitable. The resulting antebellum landscape was as much theirs as it was that of the white masters who actually owned the properties. This brief section will introduce a selection of those plantations, most of which are popular historic house museums.

Southwest of the Parthenon, just off the intersection of Twenty-first Avenue South and Wedgewood, is Belmont University, the location of **Belmont Mansion** (1850s), the most significant Greek Revival house in Nashville. A pair of fluted Corinthian columns dominates the front entrance, and the intact historic interior reflects the grandeur of the 1850s. Its richly appointed salon features Corinthian columns, chandeliers, paintings, and statuary. When initially designed by Nashville architect Adolphus Heiman, the mansion was the centerpiece of elaborately landscaped grounds, in the manner of an Italian villa. The Italianate-style 105-foot-high water tower, marble fountains, and cast-iron gazebos stand west of the house, but other major elements of the original landscaping, such as the deer park, zoo, and bear house, have disappeared as the private Belmont University has evolved over the last hundred years.

Belmont was the home of Adelicia Acklen, who might have been the wealthiest woman in late antebellum America. She had large land-holdings in Louisiana and Texas as well as in Middle Tennessee. Her Belmont mirrors not only her extraordinary wealth but also her pretensions toward the highest possible standards of taste and refinement.

From Belmont traveling west on Twenty-first Avenue South to Interstate 440, take the interstate north to the next exit, for West End Avenue, and continue west until signs indicate **Belle Meade Mansion.** In 1853 Belle Meade became a Greek Revival showplace when William Giles Harding probably designed and added a commanding Greek Revival portico of six limestone columns to the family home in addition to making lavish alterations in the interior. The grounds also have the original plantation home (circa 1807): a dogtrot house of two single-pen cabins connected by a common gable roof.

One of Tennessee's leading antebellum horse breeders, Harding managed a large and prosperous farm. According to an account of 1864, the plantation could "vie with those of the old manorial estates of the English barons. His buildings were very extensive—great barns, and outlying tenements for his tenants and his slaves" (Warden, 9). The slave quarters stood on five acres in an open court plan, with small houses arranged along three sides of the quarter. The outbuildings at Belle Meade today, however, mostly date from a later period. In 1886 Harding's son-in-law, William Hicks Jackson, inherited the fifty-three-hundred-acre plantation and enhanced even further its reputation as a thoroughbred farm. In 1903 the vast estate was broken up, and around the mansion grew one of the city's most exclusive suburbs, named Belle Meade.

From Belle Meade, it is possible to return to U.S. 70S and again travel west to its junction with Tennessee Highway 100. Take this highway past Warner Park to Hicks Road where a historical marker locates **Devon Farm,** a Tennessee Century Farm that has operated for two hundred years (private, no access). John Davis founded the farm in 1795. His daughter Fanny later married David M. Harding, the brother of John Harding of Belle Meade, linking the history of these two famous antebellum plantations. The farm name dates from the late nineteenth century when owner Edward D. Hicks II specialized in breeding English

Devon cattle. Today the farm has five hundred acres, the original brick farmhouse, and three other early outbuildings.

Interstate 65 actually cuts through some of the original land of **Travellers Rest,** a plantation established by John Overton in 1796. Take exit 78, turn south on the Franklin Pike (U.S. Highway 31A), and follow the signs to the historic house. The Louisville and Nashville Railroad bisects the property, and the collective impact of the railroad, interstate, and suburbs means that now little is left to document the agricultural history of the plantation. The oldest section of the house dates from the early 1800s and was built by carpenters David Cumming and Frederick Pinkley. Later additions in 1812, 1828, and 1885 give the mansion the distinctive appearance it still retains and show the evolution of a farmhouse into a comfortable country seat. A prominent antebellum politician, Overton practiced law with Andrew Jackson and later served as his presidential campaign manager. Together with James Winchester and Andrew Jackson, he also founded the city of Memphis.

To the east of Travellers Rest, also off Interstate 65 at exit 78 on Edmondson Pike, is the Oscar Farris Agricultural Museum, where the Tennessee Department of Agriculture maintains a valuable collection of artifacts related to the state's agrarian past. The collection is housed in a historic horse barn, once part of the vast Brentwood Hall estate of Rogers Caldwell, who brightened the city's financial horizons during the Roaring Twenties with his imaginative financial speculations. But his private banking house, Caldwell and Company, failed spectacularly during the Great Depression, taking with it several other financial institutions and millions in state funds. The state government eventually received Brentwood Hall as part of a settlement with Caldwell, who continued to live there until 1957. Shortly thereafter, the state moved its agricultural department to the estate, and the property is now known as the Ellington Agricultural Center. The department's main offices are in Brentwood Hall (1927), a replica in red brick of Andrew Jackson's Hermitage.

The actual **Hermitage** stands just off Lebanon Pike (U.S. Highway 70) in the town of Hermitage. The 1829–37 administration of President Andrew Jackson was one of the most influential and controversial in American history. The state's first federal congressman and an early chief justice of the state supreme court, Jackson gained a national reputation in the War of 1812 when he repulsed a British army that attacked New Orleans in 1815. From that point on, Jackson was often mentioned as a presidential candidate, but he lost his first major campaign in 1824 when a three-way race left no winner in the electoral college and a controversial vote in the House of Representatives selected John Quincy Adams. Four years later, Jackson swept into the White House where he diligently worked for a balanced budget, no national banks, wider suffrage for white adult males, and removal of southeastern Indians to lands in the West.

Although parts of the house date from 1819–21, the Hermitage reflects Jackson's presidential years. In 1831 Jackson remodeled the house in a more classical orientation, adding dining and library wings along with a one-story classical colonnade across the front. But only three years later, a fire severely damaged the house. From 1834 to 1836, Stokely Donelson, Jackson's nephew, supervised the reconstruction, which produced a more elegant Greek Revival dwelling with its two-story, Corinthian-column facade.

Behind the mansion are several original buildings of the plantation, which totaled one thousand acres at the time of Jackson's death in 1845. English gardener William Frost in 1819 designed the garden where Jackson and his beloved wife, Rachel, are buried. Two log houses of the original Hermitage complex document a much earlier construction tradition in Tennessee architecture at this National Historic Landmark estate.

Across the highway from the Hermitage is **Tulip Grove** (1836), the impressive Greek Revival home of Andrew Jackson Donelson, the president's nephew and private secretary. On this estate also stands the Old Hermitage Church (1823), built by Jackson for Rachel. Building a plantation church for use of the family, neighbors, and the farm's laborers began as a southern colonial tradition, but few of these churches survived into modern times.

Andrew Jackson was a gambling man, and he loved to race his horses at Clover Bottom, an early area of settlement along the Cumberland River. In 1805 Jackson, John Coffee, and John Hutchings developed a tract into a boat yard and racetrack, including a tavern and general store. The commercial venture failed, but the racetrack remained popular. On another tract of land, John Hoggart established Clover Bottom Farms, and, during the boom years of the 1850s, he built **Clover Bottom Mansion,** which features a commanding portico that combines elements of both Greek Revival and Italianate architecture.

The farm continued operating into the twentieth century until the construction of U.S. Highway 70 cut through the farm and gave its owners real estate opportunities. During the 1920s Robert D. Stanford Sr. developed a portion of the farm into a new residential neighborhood. Then the state purchased the house and outbuildings as the campus for the Tennessee School for the Blind. Today the mansion is being restored and converted into state government offices.

Landscape 4: Memphis

Memphis has been part of the rich and vibrant history of the Mississippi Delta for over 150 years. The first settlers were Native Americans, who lived there hundreds of years ago; a large prehistoric Mississippian village once stood along the riverbanks. Today the **Chucalissa historic site** and museum interpret the architecture and way of life of the Mississippian peoples. The Chickasaw Indians later established farms and residences in the Memphis area. The name of Memphis, taken from a Egyptian city on the Nile, comes from outside sources, unlike the Cherokee origins of Chattanooga and the Revolutionary War origins of Nashville and Knoxville. Established in 1819, Memphis is Tennessee's largest city, with 610,337 people in 1990, and has the state's largest African-American population. Unlike the other three cities, no major Civil War battles altered the Memphis landscape. Nor are any major federal dams and reservoirs nearby. Memphis's notoriety lies with more recent events. Music superstar Elvis Presley grew up here and made his adult home at **Graceland.** In 1968 Memphis witnessed the most infamous event of violence during the civil rights movement: the assassination of Dr. Martin Luther King Jr. No other Tennessee city has been so marked.

Three famous early Tennessee heroes—Andrew Jackson, John Overton, and James Winchester—founded the city in the spring of 1819. While Winchester came up with the name, Jackson and Overton owned the initial five thousand acres along the Chickasaw Bluffs of the Mississippi River. Jackson later traded his part to John C. McLemore, who became a fourth founding father. Growth was slow at first, but then as more and more settlers moved into West Tennessee—and discovered land perfect for cotton cultivation—Memphis emerged as an important Mississippi cotton port. The Cotton Exchange and different cotton factors still in business along Front Street reflect the influence of the cotton trade on the city's history.

In 1849 Memphis and its neighbor South Memphis (Union Street was the original border between the two) merged, and the following year's census listed the expanded city's population at almost nine thou-

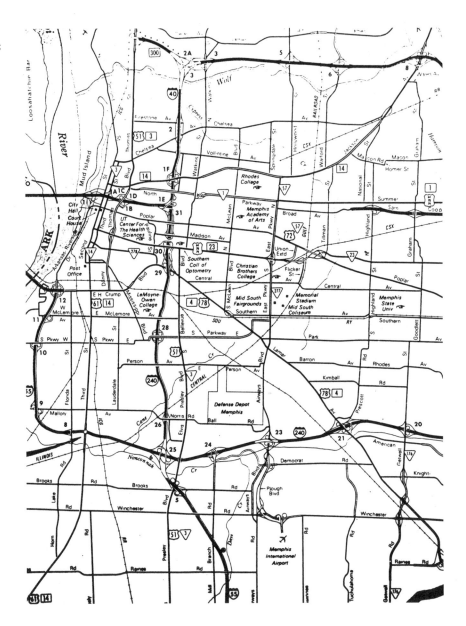

sand. Like the state's other major cities, Memphis mushroomed in the 1850s, with railroad construction leading the way. The Memphis and Charleston Railway, completed in 1857, linked the Mississippi River to the Atlantic Coast. (The route of U.S. Highway 72 in Tennessee generally follows the railroad.) Two years later, Memphis gained almost fourteen hundred new buildings in a single year, and, by the end of the decade, the city had twenty-two thousand residents, making it the largest city in Tennessee.

During the Civil War, Memphis served as a major headquarters for black Union soldiers; with the end of the war, many of the soldiers stayed while African-American field workers came to Memphis looking for new and better opportunities. The largest contraband camp in Tennessee, for example, was on nearby President's Island (see sidebar entitled "Contrabands in the Civil War," Landscape 20, chapter 7). By 1866 African Americans made up about 60 percent of the population of the city, and most of them were crowded into south Memphis. Shamed by their defeat in the war and outraged that blacks had the temerity to demand freedom and employment, hundreds of whites invaded the African-American community in May 1866. They killed forty-six, raped five black women, and destroyed four black churches and eight schools. Even though federal troops still occupied the state, the authorities did nothing in response. For decades to come, the white community would periodically use violent means to keep African Americans "in their place."

Racial violence was not the only force reshaping Memphis. In 1873 yellow fever swept through the city and claimed over two thousand lives, followed in 1878 by a much more serious yellow fever epidemic that virtually closed the city. At least 5,150 died of the disease, and so many businessmen and officials abandoned Memphis that it went bankrupt and lost its charter in January 1879. The legal entity of Memphis became the "Taxing District of Shelby County," which had lost, according to the 1880 census, 20 percent of its population from the previous decade.

A new generation of city leaders took bold steps to re-establish Memphis, and their legacy from 1880 to 1930 is documented in many historic downtown buildings. In the 1880s alone came a new sewage system, deep artesian wells for a safe water supply, electric streetcars, and electric streetlights. During the Gay Nineties, Memphis extended its railroad connections westward when the **Frisco Bridge** opened in 1892 as the only railroad bridge south of St. Louis. The city became a distribution point for southeastern freight businesses; the warehouse district along **Wagner Place** belongs to those days. In 1893 the state restored the city's municipal charter. Symbolic of its rise to new levels of prominence, the **D. T. Porter Building,** designed by E. C. Jones and others, opened on Main Street as Memphis's first skyscraper two years later.

As the city recovered, African Americans struggled for basic civil rights. Ida B. Wells sued a railroad for discrimination in 1882, but lost the case the following year. Memphis African Americans were also involved as plaintiffs in the famous decision of the *Civil Rights Cases* (1883) in which the U.S. Supreme Court gave legal sanction to public segregation. Demanding an end to public segregation, T. F. Cassels led a tiny black delegation in the Tennessee General Assembly. Few in the assembly listened; indeed, new restrictive race laws meant that by 1889 no blacks served in the state legislature, a situation that lasted until 1965. In Memphis segregation went hand-in-hand with the city's recovery, and, during this period, black businessmen and citizens, including Robert Church Sr. and Robert Church Jr., developed Beale Street into a center of local African-American commerce and culture. By the new century, white city leaders had turned the ideology of segregation into a physical reality. Beale Street and the area south was a recognized black neighborhood; by 1905 the city had established two new African-American neighborhoods to the north (Douglass Park) and to the east (Orange Mound).

The city also developed a parkway system (1902–10) that, together with the increasing popularity of the automobile, encouraged middle-class whites to move away from the central city and to relocate in new suburbs to the east. The city soon annexed these neighborhoods, and by 1930 the city's population stood at more than two hundred and fifty thousand. The **Memphis Parkways,** designed by George Kessler, reflected the latest ideas in urban planning, what is called the "City Beautiful Movement." As architectural historian Marcus Whiffen has emphasized, the movement's grand neoclassical public architecture reflected the widely shared belief that "some variation of the formal, classical facade expressed civic virtue" (281). In Memphis the connection between classicism and public works was well expressed in the new **Shelby County Courthouse** (1906–9), designed by James Gamble Rogers and Herbert D. Hale, and in the adjacent **Fire Engine House #1** (1910) and **Central Police Station** (1911) on Adams Avenue.

Compared to Nashville, the New Deal era in Memphis shaped its public housing more than its governmental buildings. The WPA did expand the city zoo at **Overton Park,** adding many display areas, including Sea Lion and Swan Pool (1936). The CCC carried out archaeological excavations at the Chucalissa Indian Village. But the biggest change came in two old, dilapidated neighborhoods where the federal government developed the Colonial Revival–style Lauderdale Courts (1935–38) along North Third Street for whites and the modernist Dixie Homes Project (1935–38) on Poplar Avenue for blacks. Due to its sensitivity to the contemporary trends in housing design, in fact, Dixie Homes has been described by architectural historians Eugene Johnson and Robert Russell Jr. as "one of the high moments in the history of Memphis architecture" (126). The flood of refugees—estimated at between fifty to sixty thousand—rushing to Memphis to escape the great Mississippi flood of 1937 stretched public housing capacity beyond its limits. The black population of Memphis increased by almost 45 percent during the Depression years.

Urban planning and renewal became the norm for postwar Memphis as more businesses and industries moved east toward the suburbs and left the downtown area increasingly empty. The city annexed vast tracts of new land—two hundred and fifty square miles from 1945 to the mid-1970s. In the late 1950s, city and state officials designed a set of interstate expressways to encircle north and south Memphis while Interstate 40 would cut eastward and divide older neighborhoods and Overton Park in half. Fortunately, spirited citizen protest later stopped part of the I-40 extension, saving Overton Park. But other urban renewal projects continued unabated. Along historic Beale Street, the city began a series of construction projects that left a few blocks intact but also destroyed the African-American neighborhood that had created and sustained the street as the cultural birthplace of the blues. Unfortunately, urban renewal continued here until Beale Street stood alone, physically segregated with open fields between its noisy nighttime strip and the surrounding African-American neighborhood.

What happened on Beale Street was repeated in other older and mostly black neighborhoods. The Memphis Housing Authority and other agencies demolished much of the city that had stood since the late Victorian era. From 1955 to 1978, for example, three thousand buildings in eleven project areas were lost to urban renewal. Destruction of old buildings for new projects is one thing; leveling buildings to leave empty lots is another. One city official complained, "You can stand on Main Street now and see to where the city limits were 50 years ago and it's all vacant land" (Biles, "Epitaph for Downtown," 280).

Downtown Memphis from Mud Island. The northern entrance of the Mississippi Delta, as viewed from the imaginary "end" of the Delta on the scaled model Riverwalk at Mud Island.

Deteriorating race relations and continuing urban renewal projects have created a city fragmented: between the north and south, between the downtown, midtown, and the suburbs, and between the commercial strips along Sumner and Poplar and the large malls positioned on or near the interstates. Memphis is no longer a river city, except when special events, like the month-long celebration of "Memphis in May," bring people to the waterfront. Recent attempts to bolster downtown have a mixed record. The "Mid-American Mall" conversion of Main Street into a pedestrian shopping mall lasted only from 1974 to 1991—over the last few years, the city has ripped out the concrete planters and walkways in favor of a streetcar line that connects the Pyramid and Convention Center to Beale Street. The Mud Island Museum and Park, opened in 1983, no longer receives the attention it once commanded. Current hopes lie with the giant and gaudy Pyramid along the Mississippi.

Four central locations—the Cotton Row Historic District along Front Street, the Shelby County Courthouse on Adams, the Peabody Hotel on Union, and Overton Park—are good focal points to see and assess the people, events, and places that have shaped the history and urban landscape of Memphis.

Cotton Row Historic District

To reach the Cotton Row Historic District from Interstate 40, take exit 1 to Riverside Drive; from Interstate 55, take exit 12 to Riverside Drive.

Cotton was king in Memphis long before Elvis Presley. The city's early growth was closely tied to cotton shipping and selling, and from Riverside Drive to Front Street the many buildings and places associated with Memphis's role in the central Mississippi cotton trade can still be seen. In general, the buildings are multistoried and date from the late Victorian era to the Art Deco craze of the twentieth century. Some are still in the cotton business. A cotton factor needed a certain type of commercial building. First, it had to be well lighted for the classing—or grading—of cotton before it could be marketed. Classing is an art based on a keen eye and experience; Memphis graders were among the best. Note the many large windows on the buildings along Cotton Row. Second, the first floors had to have wide openings so that bales of cotton could be moved easily about. Along Front Street, it is still possible to find bales of cotton blocking the sidewalks.

To explore the **Cotton Row historic district,** start at Confederate Park (1908), which lies between North Front Street and Riverside Drive. Initially, the park was a city dump, but during the City Beautiful Movement in Memphis, Robert Galloway of the Park Commission decided to turn the vacant lot into a memorial to the Confederacy, complete with a statue of Jefferson Davis. By creating new urban places like this, city leaders across the South linked respect for the "Lost Cause" to their emerging system of Jim Crow segregation in all phases of southern life. The park gives an excellent view of the cobblestones of the waterfront, where boats still dock. Also note how the railroad tracks closely parallel the riverbank here. To the east, the park is an excellent vantage point for several of the city's major twentieth-century skyscrapers: the modern Morgan Keegan Tower (1986), the **D. T. Porter Building** (1895), the **Lincoln-America Tower** (1924), and the **Exchange Building** (1910).

From Confederate Park, walk south to the **Falls Building** (1909–12) at 20–22 North Front Street. Several cotton factors established their offices here because the wide front windows allowed for plentiful natural light for the classing of cotton. In 1914 the Alaskan Roof Garden opened on top of the building, and in November of that year legendary bluesman W. C. Handy gave the debut performance of his "St. Louis

Cotton Row historic district, Memphis. Cotton is still king on this Memphis street.

Blues." After crossing Madison Street, enter South Front Street. On the first block is the neoclassical **U.S. Customs House, Courthouse, and Post Office** (1876, 1903, 1929), which has evolved over time from the designs of James Hill, James Knox Taylor, and James A. Wetmore. When Wetmore greatly enlarged the building in 1929, he gave it a decided classical look, although the front facade's colonnade of paired columns came at the insistence of U.S. Senator Kenneth D. McKellar. Here, merchants and factors could obtain the necessary federal paperwork to ship products or import other goods.

Along South Front Street is the heart of Cotton Row, beginning at the **Mid-South Cotton Growers' Association Building** (1936), designed by Walk C. Jones Jr. and Walk C. Jones Sr. in the Art Deco style. Next door, at 48 South Front, is the **Hart Building** (circa 1899), with the words "Cotton/Fulton and Sons" emblazoned between two massive stone arches on its front facade. Also on this block is the former office of **Armistead and Lundee** (circa 1890) at 66–70 South Front. The oldest cotton offices on South Front stand on the east side, closest to the river. **Howard's Row,** at 77, 81, and 85 South Front, was first constructed in about 1843; the connected buildings are the oldest commercial structures left downtown and were restored in 1974.

The grandest building on Cotton Row is, quite naturally, the **Cotton Exchange Building** (1925) at 84–86 South Front, where the business of selling cotton takes place daily. The architecture of this twelve-story building mixes Gothic and classical elements in a restrained manner. A more architecturally consistent facade is a few doors to the south at the **Joseph N. Oliver Building** (1904, 1909) at 99–103 South Front. Designed by Alsup and Woods, this rare commercial example of Beaux-Arts architecture reflects its date of construction when the ideas and styles of the City Beautiful Movement were very popular in Memphis. Unlike the other buildings detailed above, however, the Oliver Building was used as a cold-storage warehouse; it is now a popular restaurant.

Shelby County Courthouse

To reach the Shelby County Courthouse, take Interstate 40, exit at Danny Thomas Boulevard and go south to Adams Avenue. Turn west on Adams and the county courthouse is at 140 Adams.

With the **Shelby County Courthouse** (1906–9) and the Brooks Museum of Art (1916), James Gamble Rogers of New York City gave Memphis two major landmarks of Classical Revival architecture. The courthouse was built when Memphis was reinventing its urban landscape with grand civic buildings and the monumental parkway system that surrounded downtown. The massive Ionic porticoes of the courthouse proclaim, in architectural terms, the turn-of-the-century belief in good government and civic virtue. Statues by sculptor William Rhyne represent Wisdom, Justice, Liberty, Authority, Peace, and Prosperity, and they—along with the richly appointed pediments at each entrance—add to the classical symbolism of the courthouse.

When he designed the courthouse, Rogers already was regarded as a master of classical architecture. He began his formal training in the independent Paris atelier of Paul Blondel, a teacher of such noted American architects as Ernest Flagg (who designed the Singer Tower in New York City) and Donn Barber (who designed the Southern Railway Terminal in Chattanooga). Under Blondel's direction, Rogers gained a love for the classical tradition and met his most important partner, Herbert D. Hale. An earlier important Rogers and Hale design was the Italian Renaissance town villa of Edward Harkness in New York City, built in 1905. Many other Rogers designs stand in New York City and at Yale University, where he designed Gothic architecture.

To the west and north of the courthouse is the current heart of government in Memphis: a cluster of modern rectangular buildings asymmetrically placed on the Civic Center Plaza, an arrangement influenced by the urban-planning principles of Le Corbusier, the French master architect and urban theorist. This urban renewal project dates from the late 1950s and 1960s when Le Corbusier's ideas about monumental civic centers were popular. Francis Gassner was the principal designer for the Hill State Office Building (1964–65) and the Shelby County Administration Building (1969). The Clifford Davis Federal Building (1961–63), designed by A. L. Aydelott and Associates with Thomas Faires and Associates, is the oldest building on the plaza. The firm of A. L. Aydelott also designed the Memphis City Hall in 1966.

The new symbolic heart of Memphis government was planned and constructed after the death of E. H. Crump, whose political machine effectively ran the city of Memphis, and much of Tennessee politics, from 1909 to 1954. Appropriately, Crump's old insurance office building stands at the edge of the grand Civic Center Plaza, at 110 Adams Avenue.

One block north of the Shelby County Courthouse are two of the city's best examples of Victorian Gothic architecture, the **First United Methodist Church** (1887–93), by Jacob Snyder, and the First Presbyterian Church (1884), by E. C. Jones of Memphis. Antebellum statements of Gothic Revival style include **Calvary Episcopal Church** (1843, 1881), which stands to the immediate south of the courthouse. To the east are the twin Gothic towers of **St. Peter's Catholic Church** (1852), designed by church architect Patrick C. Keeley of New York.

The four churches serve as a transition between the civic buildings of Memphis and the residential neighborhood that once stood on Adams Avenue, stretching for blocks to the east. Buildings on the first two blocks form the **Adams Avenue historic district.** The **Magevney House,** at 198 Adams, is one of the oldest dwellings in Memphis. Probably built before 1837, the original house had two rooms. In December 1837 Eugene Magevney, an Irish schoolteacher who had arrived in Memphis four years earlier, acquired the property and added a parlor and upstairs by 1840 and then a one-story wing during the Memphis boom of the 1850s. Magevney left teaching in 1840 and became a real estate speculator and politician. A founder of St. Peter's Catholic Church, he served as a city alderman and is credited with beginning the public school system. Magevney died in 1873, one of the many victims of that year's yellow fever epidemic.

The historic homes along the 200 block of Adams reflect local

Mallory-Neely House, Victorian Village, Memphis. Mansions of Victorian grandeur stand as isolated historic preservation monuments, leaving the historic streetscape of Adams Avenue to the visitor's imagination.

high-style domestic architecture at the time of the great epidemic of 1873. The houses at 239, 246, and 253 Adams were built between 1869 and 1873 (all private, no access). Memphis architect M. H. Baldwin designed the **Toof House,** a finely detailed Italianate townhouse, at 246 Adams. Current architectural critics consider it to be the best on the block.

Commercial development and modern highway construction have wiped out most of the historic dwellings between the 300 and 600 blocks of Adams Avenue. Many grand examples of late-nineteenth-century architecture were lost in these urban renewal efforts. But traveling east on Adams reveals very interesting late Victorian mansions that partially document what the Adams Avenue neighborhood was once like. This area is now known as the Victorian Village, and it is home to several historic house museums. What was once part of a larger neighborhood has become an oasis of historic preservation, and the museum setting of the village is in sharp contrast to surrounding businesses, offices, and homes. This area shows how historic preservation can add to our sense that the past is a foreign country, as geographer David Lowenthal has observed. There is a public parking lot at the village.

The **Mallory-Neely House** (1852–90s) at 652 Adams is one of the most intact Victorian mansions in the country. Although the first sections date from the late antebellum period, Memphis merchant James C. Neely extensively updated and enlarged the house in the 1880s and again in the 1890s when the tower was added. As the house changed on the outside, the family constantly purchased new furniture for the lavish interior—including stained glass from the 1893 Chicago's World Fair—and installed elaborate stenciling, gilding, carved mahogany mantels, and parquet flooring until the mansion represented one of the city's ultimate statements in interior design. Neely's daughter lived there until 1969 and changed little in the house. Today this intact Victorian interior is a remarkable artifact of the decorative arts of the late nineteenth and early twentieth centuries.

The Greek Revival cottage known as the **Massey House** (1844–49) at 664 Adams is the earliest house in the village. Next door at 680 Adams is one of the state's grandest Second Empire–style mansions, the **Woodruff-Fontaine House** (1870–71), designed by Memphis architects E. C. Jones and M. H. Baldwin. Its builder was Amos Woodruff, a former president of the city council and local capitalist involved with railroads, hotels, banking, insurance, cotton, and lumber. In 1883 he sold the home to Noland Fontaine, a local cotton factor, whose family lived here for the next forty-six years. This house, as well as the adjacent **Goyer-Lee House** (1848, 1871–73) at 690 Adams, are properties administered by the Association for the Preservation of Tennessee Antiquities (APTA). Both are important examples of Second Empire architecture. With its prominent tower and mansard roof, the Woodruff-Fontaine House is an original, coherent statement of that style. The Goyer-Lee House, however, shows how architects updated older homes in new Victorian styles after the Civil War. E. C. Jones and M. H. Baldwin designed the early 1870s addition that featured a commanding and detailed entrance tower with mansard roof and overstated brackets.

Across the street are two homes in different styles (both private, no access). The **Pillow-McIntyre House** (1852) has a restrained, two-story Greek Revival portico of four Corinthian columns. After the yellow fever epidemic of 1873, the house was the residence of Gideon J. Pillow, a former Maury County planter who was a close political ally of President James K. Polk in the antebellum period. He also served in the Mexican War and as a controversial Confederate general in the Civil War. The **Mollie Fontaine Taylor House** (1886–90) at 679 Adams is directly related to the Woodruff-Fontaine house. Noland Fontaine built the Queen Anne home as a wedding present for his daughter Mollie.

Two blocks to the southeast is one last mansion of note, the Romanesque-styled **Lowenstein House** (1890–91) at 756 Jefferson Avenue. Elias Lowenstein, a local department store owner, was the first owner, and his family lived there until 1920 when the dwelling was turned into a home for rural women seeking work in Memphis. It is now a halfway house (private, no access).

Peabody Hotel

To reach the Peabody Hotel from Interstate 40, take exit 1A to Union Avenue; the hotel is at 149 Union.

Standing tall and proud with its Spanish-influenced design, the **Peabody Hotel** opened in 1925 as one of the great southern hotels, a place to be and be seen for politicians, matriarchs, businessmen, debutantes, and social climbers alike. Designed by Walter Ahlschlager of Chicago, the hotel features an expansive lobby with a wonderful fountain in the center. A great Memphis tradition began here in 1932, when the hotel manager placed some ducks in the fountain. Quickly the ducks became the hotel's symbols, and hundreds daily watch the ducks march between the fountain and their roof-garden roost.

The Peabody symbolizes the confidence of the Memphis business community before the dark days of the Great Depression. The view of the city from its old roof garden is especially valuable. From there several architectural landmarks of downtown Memphis are visible. To the west is the Art Deco ornament that tops the Memphis Business Journal Building (1927) at 88 Union. Originally called the Farnsworth Build-

Beale Street, near Second and Third Streets, circa 1970, Memphis. (Courtesy of Tennessee State Library and Archives)

ing, the skyscraper was designed by E. L. Harrison and Noland Van Powell, who later designed the excellent Art Deco **Fairview Junior High** at 750 East Parkway South. To the north is the **Sterick Building**, initially conceived as a Gothic skyscraper by Wyatt C. Hedrick of Fort Worth. When it opened in 1930, the twenty-nine-story building was the tallest in the region.

To the south, however, is the most interesting view. Two blocks away the remnants of the historic **Beale Street** neighborhood, once home to a thriving African-American community and culture, can be seen. Note how buildings between Beale and the black neighborhoods to the south have been demolished, leaving large empty spaces. Note too how parking lots for the tourists who visit Beale Street have added to the destruction of the district's historic fabric. New streets have also altered the earlier urban landscape. On the street itself, some buildings have been totally gutted, left with only their streetside facades, evidence of the disease of "facadism" that swept through portions of the historic preservation community during these years. Much of what you see today, both good and bad, resulted from decisions by the Memphis Housing Authority and federal authorities during the 1960s and early 1970s.

Beale Street, from the Peabody Hotel roof, Memphis. The vacant acres around historic Beale Street show what ill-conceived methods of preservation and urban renewal can do to a historic neighborhood.

The Beale Street Urban Renewal Program involved 113 acres of a mostly African-American neighborhood; when completed, about 65 buildings remained, ready for further preservation and adaptive reuse. But about 560 buildings were gone—eliminating much of the soul of Beale Street. Today the street is "preserved" and retains many buildings worthy of a closer look, but it is not the same street or neighborhood where southern African Americans created and popularized the blues during the early twentieth century. By demolishing so much of the neighborhood, Memphis also destroyed a large part of what made the city the northern cultural entrance to the Mississippi Delta.

A tour of Beale Street could begin near its western end at its intersection with Main. Here is the **Orpheum Theater** (1927) by the Chicago architects Rapp and Rapp, who specialized in designing grand movie palaces for American cities. To the east is Elvis Presley Plaza, which features a 1980 sculpture of the king of rock 'n' roll by Eric Parks. The music and culture of Beale Street certainly influenced Presley, and his fusion of black and white southern traditions has received much comment. But Beale Street seems an odd location for this monument: why not the suburbs where Presley's rabid fans lived and listened to his records? His Graceland home on Elvis Presley Boulevard seems a more appropriate location for this sculpture.

As a teenager, Presley liked to shop at **Lansky's,** a clothing store at 126 Beale that had flashier clothes than blue jeans and button-down shirts. This business survived urban renewal but then closed in the early 1990s. Another early retailer is **A. Schwab's** general merchandise and hardware at 163–65 Beale. This store is part of a group of historic buildings in the 100 block that conveys, at least, a little of the original Beale Street environment, although the modern landscaped sidewalks and clean streets of today certainly did not exist then. At 130 Beale is the Center for Southern Folklore, which maintains an active program of recording, documenting, and interpreting the folk music, art, and traditions of Memphis and the Delta. The museum maintains permanent and temporary exhibits about regional folklife.

The steel braces holding up the 1891 facade of the Gallina Building at 177–81 Beale reveals the reality of the preservation disaster that occurred here a generation ago. The "white face" that Beale presented to outsiders is preserved while the people who made the building come alive are gone forever. Diagonally across the street is Handy Park, between Second and Third Streets. The first urban renewal efforts began here in 1959–60, when whites and blacks joined together to establish a park and erect a statue to W. C. Handy, the acknowledged "father of the blues." The sculptor was Leone Tomassi of Italy. Across from the park are storefronts from the late nineteenth century. Ironically, later extensions of the park and new road construction to improve access to the park and Beale Street led to the demolition of P. Wee's Saloon, which stood at 317 Beale. Here is where W. C. Handy actually wrote "Memphis Blues" in 1909.

Several other important buildings, however, remain on the 300 block of Beale Street. The eclectic **Old Daisy Theater** (1914) at 329 Beale and the Art Deco architecture of the **New Daisy Theater** (1942) across the street are reminders of the popularity of movies in urban areas, black or white. The twin towers of the **Beale Street Baptist Church** (1867–81) at 379 Beale are meaningful landmarks to the local African-American community. Designed by Memphis architects E. C. Jones and M. H. Baldwin, the church was the first in Memphis built by blacks for an African-American congregation, and its lofty Gothic towers speak to the confidence and prosperity of the African-American community in the Reconstruction era. Its stone exterior was painted white in 1964.

Next door is a vast public space also of great symbolic meaning to the local community. In late-nineteenth-century America, Robert R. Church Sr. was one of the most successful black businessmen in the country. His Solvent Bank of Memphis was the financial heart of local black commerce. One of his entrepreneurial efforts was creating **Church Park** at 391 Beale Street in 1899. Memphis blacks had no large public space; Church created one that charged a nominal admission for access to the playground, bandstand, auditorium, and gardens designed by his wife. This park became the public meeting place for Memphis's African Americans. His son, Robert Jr., kept the park open after his father's death in 1912. Robert Church Jr. established the Lincoln League, a black Republican organization that represented what little political power blacks had in Memphis and West Tennessee during the first half of the twentieth century. Later, during the civil rights movement, the park was the scene of demonstrations and planning meetings. Today none of the original park buildings remain, but the public space is there, enhanced by a monument (1986) to the auditorium by landscape architect J. Ritchie Smith.

From the park, it is a short walk east to 485 Beale, at its intersection with Danny Thomas Boulevard, where the Dr. Martin Luther King Jr. Labor Center (1978) stands. Harold Thompson designed this modern office center. A block south, on Linden Avenue, are two more architectural monuments. The African-American firm of McKissack and McKissack of Nashville designed the Universal Life Insurance Company (1949) in a rare Egyptian Revival style. The great intellectual, political, and cultural achievements of ancient Egypt have long been a source of pride for many African Americans, and the design of McKissack and McKissack reflects that cultural heritage in this imposing office building. Created in 1923 by Dr. J. E. Walker, assisted by A. W. Willis Sr., Universal Life Insurance Company now serves ten states and Washington, D.C. To the east is the Mt. Olive CME Cathedral, a Classical Revival design built in 1910.

West of the intersection of Beale Street and Danny Thomas Boulevard, at 533 Beale, is a rare remnant of the upper-class residential architecture that populated Beale Street in the late antebellum era. The Hunt-Phelan House (1828–32, 1851) is an impressive Greek Revival mansion that served as headquarters for both armies during the Civil War and then as an administrative and educational center for the Freedmen's Bureau in the Reconstruction era. Now undergoing restoration and scheduled to open to the public in 1996, the mansion is an excellent place to explore how different people—masters, slaves, Confederates, Federals, and Freedmen's Bureau teachers—with different outlooks on life lived at and used the same place over a brief span of ten years.

The view from the roof of the Peabody Hotel includes buildings to the south of Beale Street that are part of an active African-American neighborhood. One of the greatest tragedies of modern American history—the assassination of Dr. Martin Luther King Jr.—took place along these streets in April 1968. South of Beale Street, Main Street leads to an older brick building that is now the home of the Memphis Center for Contemporary Art (1912, 1982) at 416–18 South Main Street. Here, from an upper window, a white murderer fired the shot that killed Dr. King. One block east at 406 Mulberry stands the balcony of the former Lorraine Motel where Dr. King stood at the moment of his murder. The Lorraine Hotel, which later became a motel, welcomed black patrons for over fifty years before its conversion into the National Civil Rights Museum (1991), with a new exterior designed by McKissack and McKissack. The museum retains portions of the original motel facade, including the room where Dr. King stayed and the spot where he fell. But most of the building gave way to modern, high-tech exhibits devoted to the history of the American civil rights movement from the nineteenth century to the brutally violent—but ultimately successful—days of the 1960s.

South of E. H. Crump Boulevard is where Dr. King gave his last great public address, known as the "Mountain Top" speech, at the **Church of God in Christ National Temple and World Headquarters** at 958 Mason Street. In this vast public auditorium, before a crowd of at least three thousand, King proclaimed:

> We've got some difficult days ahead. But it doesn't matter with me now. Because I've been to the mountain top. And I don't mind. Like anybody, I would like to live a long life. Longevity has its place. But I'm not concerned about that now. I just want to do God's will. And he's allowed me to go up to the mountain. And I've looked over and I've seen the promised land. I may not get there with you. But I want you to know tonight, that we, as a people will get to the promised land. And I'm happy tonight. I'm not worried about anything. Mine eyes have seen the glory of the coming of the Lord! (Garrow, 621)

The next day, King was murdered and the civil rights movement changed forever.

Several of the leaders of the civil rights movement had been students at nearby LeMoyne-Owen College, which is about five blocks east of the Mason Temple at 807 Walker Avenue. This small campus features a mix of Colonial Revival architecture, such as Brownlee Hall (1933–36) by George Awsumb, and more modern architecture as represented

Japanese Gardens, circa 1940, Overton Park, Memphis. During the anti-Japanese hysteria following the bombing of Pearl Harbor, local officials demolished the Japanese Gardens at Overton Park. (Courtesy of Mississippi Valley Collection, Memphis State University)

by Hollis Price Library (1963) by the Memphis firm of Gassner, Nathan, and Browne. The early **Steele Hall** (circa 1914) is named in honor of Andrew J. Steele, who was principal at LeMoyne from 1879 to 1908. Established in 1869–71 as the LeMoyne Normal and Commercial School, with funding from F. Julius LeMoyne and the American Missionary Society of the Congregational church, the college began as a northern sponsored and directed school for newly freed African Americans. In 1934 it became a four-year college, granting a bachelor's degree, and it dropped its elementary and high school programs. In 1968 school officials decided to merge with Owen Junior College, creating the present institution.

Overton Park

Overton Park is bounded by Poplar Avenue, East Parkway, and North Parkway, west of Interstate 240. Follow the signs to the Memphis Zoo to reach the park.

Overton Park (1905) anchors the historic midtown of Memphis and serves as an excellent central location for several key elements of the early-twentieth-century urban landscape. In his massive **Memphis**

Parkways plan, based in part on his earlier urban plan for Kansas City, landscape architect George Kessler designed Overton Park out of the city's 335-acre purchase of Lea's Wood in 1901. His U-shaped parkway system then made Overton accessible to all white neighborhoods in Memphis. Today the park has a public golf course, recreation areas, and several of the city's most important cultural institutions.

The Memphis Brooks Museum of Art is the most impressive building in Overton Park. James Gamble Rogers designed the original Brooks Museum in an appropriate Italian Renaissance style with more than a nod toward the influential design of the Morgan Library in New York City by McKim, Mead, and White. As its collection grew in the postwar years, the museum needed more space, and during the 1950s Everett Woods designed its first expansion. Architects Walk Jones and Francis Mah in 1970–73 added a second wing in Brutalist style. Then, in 1987, the Houston office of Skidmore, Ownings, and Merrill, with Rick Keating and Craig Taylor as designers, replaced the earlier Woods addition with another new wing, greatly expanding the building and creating a postmodern entrance.

The Memphis Academy of Arts (1956), by Mann and Harrover, is a classic statement of 1950s American architecture, which won an award from the magazine *Progressive Architecture*. The Memphis Zoo dates from the earliest days of the park, but many of its buildings and display areas were created with WPA assistance during the 1930s. The WPA also funded the construction of the Raoul Wallenberg Memorial Shell (1936), designed by Max Furbringer in the Art Deco style (see sidebar entitled "The New Deal Built Environment," Landscape 9, chapter 4).

Directly north of Overton Park, at 2000 North Parkway, is the campus of **Rhodes College,** formally Southwestern at Memphis. The City Beautiful plan of Memphis attracted the college's trustees, and in the early 1920s they decided to move the school from Clarksville to a new 124-acre campus across from Overton Park. The trustees hired the landscape architects Day and Klauder as advisory architects and then picked Henry C. Hibbs of Nashville to design the campus and its buildings. Collegiate Gothic is the unifying architectural theme, reflecting President Charles E. Diehl's belief in the superiority of the English collegiate system. Although later administrations altered the campus design, many early buildings remain intact. Palmer Hall, Kennedy Science Building, and the Neely, Robb, and White dormitories all date to the college's Memphis opening in 1925. Completion of the original campus plan and architecture, however, had to wait for the administration of President Peyton N. Rhodes, who supervised the construction of almost one new building a year during the 1950s and 1960s.

The college's second major architect was H. Clinton Parrent, the former chief draftsman in Hibbs's Nashville office. Parrent added the soaring Gothic spire of Haliburton Tower to Palmer Hall in 1961. Indeed, the continuity in sandstone building materials at Rhodes is impressive. Most of the brown sandstone comes from the same quarry in Arkansas, and even buildings constructed in the last decade share the same stone-and-slate roofing material.

Around Overton Park, the adjacent parkways, and Rhodes College would soon evolve the city's pre-eminent early-twentieth-century neighborhoods. Outstanding examples of American domestic architecture, especially Tudor Revival, Colonial Revival, and bungalow, can be found along any street in this area. The house at 705 North University, for example, is a Colonial Revival design by E. L. Harrison built by the Federal Housing Authority and local groups in 1935 as a demonstration model home (private, no access). Stonewall Street (private, no access) is wonderfully eclectic in its architecture, ranging from the Beaux-Arts duplex (1917–18) at 200 Stonewall Place to the American Four-Square and bungalow designs of the firm of Mahan and Broadwell. The firm's Samuels House (1922–23) at 449 Stonewall is recognized as the city's most impressive bungalow. Another outstanding local example of bungalows is next door at 457 Stonewall where Memphis architect Eugene Woods once lived.

East of Rhodes College along North Parkway is the Hein Park subdivision with Classical Revival, Colonial Revival, and Tudor Revival residences (all private, no access). Of particular note is the Rhodes College President's House (1926) at 671 West Drive, a Tudor design by Herbert Burnham and J. Frazer Smith.

South and east of Overton Park are additional neighborhoods of architectural distinction. A delightful series of southern Colonial Revival cottages, designed by J. Frazer Smith in 1938, can be found along Williamsburg Lane (private, no access). The **"Pink Palace" Museum and Planetarium** at 3050 Central Avenue was once the Clarence Saunders mansion. Saunders, who founded the Piggly Wiggly grocery store chain, began the mansion in 1922 as part of a large 155-acre estate. Memphis architect Hubert T. McGee designed the mansion in what he called a "Romanesque American rambling design" using pink marble from Georgia. "If I never did anything else," Saunders once boasted, "I sure gave Memphis a landmark" (Chumney, 8). His financial empire, however, failed before he even lived in the house. Acquiring the property in 1926, the city turned the huge mansion into its first natural history museum, and, during the Depression years, the Works Progress Administration added murals to the lobby. Today the Pink Palace is among the region's best natural history museums.

Farther east of the Pink Palace, at the intersection of Central Avenue and East Parkway, is the **Fairview Junior High School** (1938), an Art Deco masterpiece by E. L. Harrison. Another Art Deco landmark stands at the intersection of Central Avenue and Hollywood Street: the National Guard Armory (1941–42), a compelling vision of American nationalism and modernist styling by Walk C. Jones Sr. and Jr.

The University of Memphis (1912), on Central Avenue, was the city's original state teachers' college, initially named the West Tennessee State Normal School. It became Memphis State University in 1957 and changed its name to the University of Memphis in 1994. Although more recent construction dominates the campus environment, several original buildings remain. The Classical Revival–style Mynders Hall (1912–13), a women's dorm, was probably designed by Mahan and Broadwell. The original athletic dorm, Scates Hall (1921), was the contribution of architect Everett Woods. In 1929 Mahan and Woods collaborated on Manning Hall, which exhibits both Doric and Ionic orders in an almost overstated classical entrance. Another important building is the **John Willard Brister Library,** which houses valuable archives on Mississippi Valley history.

One last statement of the popularity of the twentieth-century Classical Revival in Memphis is the Hugo Dixon House (1940), now the Dixon Gallery and Gardens at 4339 Park Avenue, southeast of Memphis State University. John F. Staub of Houston designed a heavy two-story Ionic portico for the mansion's central block, with flanking one-story wings. Hope Crutchfield designed the lovely gardens. Like the Memphis Brooks Museum, the Dixon Gallery has recently expanded in recent years, with additions by Daniel Bingham in 1977 and 1986.

CHAPTER THREE

Appalachian Tennessee

The northeast corner of Tennessee—the country between Knoxville and the Tri-Cities of Bristol, Kingsport, and Johnson City—is an ideal place to begin a detailed, more backroad, exploration of the state's historic landscapes. Not only did the first settlers of Tennessee stop here over two hundred years ago, but also the subsequent development of farms, communities, and towns introduces common historical themes found elsewhere in the state. Ethnic groups in Appalachian Tennessee shaped the land in their own distinctive way as they would later at places like Gruteli and Belvidere. Farmers of Appalachian Tennessee practiced many different types of agriculture, from scratching out a subsistence living on the rocky hillsides of Hancock or Union Counties to cultivating cotton along the rich river bottomland of the Tennessee Valley. Railroad development in the nineteenth century proved just as important in this region as it was in the settlement of West Tennessee. In the late nineteenth and early twentieth centuries, mining and industry lay a heavy hand on the people of Appalachian Tennessee just as it did in Grundy County or at Bemis in Madison County. Indeed, the industrialization of Appalachian Tennessee created many of the region's towns—Alcoa, Jellico, Coalfield, Embreeville, Kingsport, and Bristol, just to name a few.

Yet, within the valleys, hills, mountains, and hollows are special spaces that convey the uniqueness of Appalachian culture and history. The Unaka Range of the Appalachian Mountains, according to geologist Edward T. Luther, is like a great "eastern rampart" that separates Ten-

Pemberton House and Oak Tree, Sullivan County. West of Bristol on U.S. Highway 421, the massive oak tree on the historic Pemberton Farm was one of the gathering places for the Overmountain Boys before the decisive Battle of King's Mountain. It is the only tree individually listed among the Tennessee properties in the National Register of Historic Places.

nessee from its East Coast neighbor, North Carolina (75). The difficulty of crossing this great natural barrier profoundly impacted the settlement landscape. Most early settlers came from the north, traveling the more accessible gaps along the Kentucky and Virginia borders and pouring into the large valley created by the French Broad, Holston, Clinch, and Nolichucky Rivers. The mountainous land along the Appalachian ridge later became prized for its magnificent beauty. The Great Smoky Mountains National Park is the most popular natural and scenic landscape in the country. Millions come to breathe the mountain air, to soak in the beauty of preserved wilderness, and to traverse the Appalachian Trail.

The Smokies, however, are not the only exceptional natural landscape in Appalachian Tennessee. The Cherokee National Forest runs to the north and south of the park. Carter County has Roan Mountain State Park, where the mountain becomes a rainbow of colors when its wild rhododendrons bloom every spring. To the north in Johnson County, U.S. Highway 421 actually crosses the Appalachian Trail, while a spectacular automobile tunnel runs through the mountains at Backbone Rock on Tennessee Highway 133 north of Shady Valley. Frozen Head State Natural Area in Morgan County is a place of stark beauty and rugged isolation, while in Fentress and Scott County lies the region's newest federal park, the Big South Fork National River and Recreation Area, that protects scenic landscapes and historic sites in both Kentucky and Tennessee.

Soil quality, rugged terrain, and climate led to different patterns of land use in Appalachian Tennessee than those in Middle and West Tennessee. Farming is a constant, but cotton was not. In turn, slavery was never as prevalent in Appalachia as it was in other areas of the South. When the Civil War began in 1861, many East Tennesseans remained loyal to the Union because of their own cultural traditions, their suspicions of planter culture, and their own distaste for slavery. On the courthouse square in Greeneville is the typical Civil War monument of the turn of the century: a heroic statue of a gallant soldier. But this monument is to the Union cause, making it a bold, permanent memorial to regional loyalty during that terrible conflict. Another legacy of the Civil War is the region's political loyalty to the Republican party of Abraham Lincoln. Upper East Tennessee, in particular, has been a Republican stronghold since the 1860s. Huntsville, just off U.S. Highway 27 in Scott County, is home to former U.S. Sen. Howard Baker, who represented Tennessee in the Senate for over twenty years before serving as chief of staff under President Ronald Reagan.

Vast acres of productive bottomland disappeared as human hands carved many upper East Tennessee river valleys into popular recreational places during the twentieth century. East Tennesseans love to boast of their many lakes, which are ideal for fishing, water sports, and sightseeing. But the most popular waterways—Norris, Cherokee, and Douglas—were created when the Tennessee Valley Authority shut its gates on dams along the Clinch, Holston, and French Broad Rivers, forever altering the landscape and the history of Appalachian Tennessee. Middle and West Tennesseans have also felt the hand of this great New Deal experiment in social planning, design, and engineering, but East Tennessee is the heart of the Tennessee Valley Authority. What happened north of Knoxville set the tone for many of the agency's programs and initiatives, establishing the basic patterns of the TVA landscape that remain today (see sidebar entitled "The New Deal Built Environment," Landscape 9, chapter 4).

The proximity of TVA power combined with the topography of the Appalachian foothills to create the most unique place in the region, perhaps even in Tennessee. When military planners during World War II searched the country for an ideal place to develop nuclear weapons, they needed vast quantities of electricity and a location that was near a major transportation center, but they also needed an area that was isolated, where the natural topography could serve as a barrier against disaster if an accident happened. Oak Ridge—the instant "Atomic City"—proved to be their answer. And into the stereotypical "backwoods" of Appalachia came the most modern ideas in science, engineering, and technology, ideas that planners naively hoped to use to build a new world of peace and prosperity through the "magic" of atomic reaction.

Many ways exist to explore the historic landscape of Appalachian Tennessee. In discussing the landscape of settlement, this chapter will follow routes created by the federal highway system, beginning at Knoxville with U.S. 70 to Newport, then taking U.S. 321 north to Elizabethton in the northeast corner of the state. Next, the narrative will return to Knoxville via U.S. 11W starting at Kingsport. The second half of the chapter is devoted to the industrial landscape of Appalachian Tennessee. To describe this landscape, a mix of road systems will be referred to, from the interstate between Kingsport and Erwin to the narrow state roads connecting Norris and Oak Ridge. The chapter closes by returning to the Great Smoky Mountains for a discussion of the conservation landscape represented by the national park and its surrounding national forests.

Landscape 5: The Upper Tennessee Valley

The first permanent English residents of Tennessee settled during the American Revolution, over two hundred years ago. Most came down the Shenandoah Valley of Virginia into the Great Valley of the Tennessee River, navigating rafts, canoes, and flatboats down the many tributaries and creating homes where land was fertile and hunting was rich. On the Watauga River at Piney Flats, William and Lydia Bean established one of the earliest farms, named **Rocky Mount,** in 1770–72. It is the oldest original territorial capitol in the United States and is now a historic house museum that interprets early settlement lifestyles and culture. The early settlers on the Watauga, Nolichucky, and Holston grew quite quickly in number, but in 1771 colonial officials discovered that many lived outside of treaty boundaries and were squatting on Cherokee land. British officials ordered the settlers to leave, but the pioneers refused, and in order to protect their land claims they established the Watauga Association in 1772. The association soon negotiated a lease

Mauris-Earnest Fort House, Chuckey. A rare extant example of the transition between German and English folk architecture on the Tennessee frontier.

with the Cherokees for the disputed land, and new waves of immigrants moved along the tributaries of the Tennessee.

In 1775 at Sycamore Shoals, along the Watauga River in present-day Elizabethton, land speculator Richard Henderson of North Carolina negotiated a bold and greedy land purchase for millions of acres of land in what later became Kentucky and Middle Tennessee. This immense transfer of property—called the Transylvania Purchase—encouraged further immigration. A year after the Declaration of Independence, for example, Henry Earnest (his original name was Heinrich Ernst) of North Carolina established a farm along the Nolichucky River near the present-day town of Chuckey. Ever since, family descendents have lived here and cultivated its hundreds of acres, making Elmwood Farm the oldest historic family farm in Tennessee. Two family dwellings remain: the **Mauris-Earnest Fort House** (circa 1784) reflects German log construction traditions while a brick Tennessee Federal farmhouse (1820s) demonstrates the family's assimilation of English cultural traditions.

A third tributary of the Tennessee—the Holston River—received the most attention from the early "Overmountain" settlers because at present-day Kingsport stood the Long Island of the Holston, an already established trading place for the colonists and Cherokees. Nearby passed the "Great Indian Warpath," an ancient Native-American road of warfare and commerce. The Indians considered the island to be ideally located for trade as well as full of wild game, especially buffalo, elk, and deer. Early settlers also appreciated its strategic location. In March 1775 Daniel Boone began to build the Wilderness Road here, moving northwest through Cumberland Gap to the Kentucky River, opening up the Transylvania Purchase of his patron Richard Henderson. About eighteen months later, settlers constructed Fort Patrick Henry along the South Fork of the Holston. Military raids from this post soon led to the Treaty of Long Island (also known as the Avery Treaty) in 1777, which erased all Cherokee claims to Tennessee land already occupied by the settlers. Then, two years later, Col. John Donelson left Long Island with a hardy band of pioneers headed for the French Lick at Nashville, taking the first step in the settlement of Middle Tennessee. In 1780 John Sevier twice led a rag-tag group of pioneers from a camp on a fourth major tributary, the French Broad River, to successfully attack Cherokee villages on the Little Tennessee River and end the Revolutionary War in Tennessee.

Permanent towns soon dotted the countryside, creating a vernacular landscape of isolated, tiny settlements surrounded by a few scattered farms and acres upon acres of wilderness. Jonesborough was the oldest, founded in 1779; by the end of the century, small urban settlements existed at Rogersville, Dandridge, Blountville, Knoxville, and Greeneville. Within two generations, however, a hundred thousand settlers resided where only a handful had lived before. The roads that pass through these towns consequently reflect more than the early settlement landscape; they also document how railroads connected upper Tennessee towns into larger regional and national markets and communication systems during the nineteenth century. Railroad companies, especially the mammoth Southern Railway, left a lasting mark on the landscape. They not only linked the region to larger metropolitan centers of commerce, but they also introduced the industrial revolution to Appalachian Tennessee, forever changing the look of the land and the rhythms of life.

Route A: The French Broad River

East of downtown Knoxville, U.S. Highway 70 crosses the Holston River just above its confluence with the French Broad River. But as the highway continues east and approaches the Appalachian Mountains, it follows closely the route of the French Broad River. "A river is not only a highway in itself," observed historian Wilma Dykeman, "but frequently it also provides, like the ancient buffalo trails and Indian traces, the route of least resistance and marks the way for thoroughfares to follow" (*French Broad*, 136). So it was for the French Broad as it "carved a passage for commerce" through the Appalachians to the fertile valley of the Tennessee River.

For twenty-nine miles between Knoxville and Dandridge, U.S. Highway 70 passes through open farmland, broken here and there by small, rural suburban developments, dairy farms, cattle herds, tobacco farms, and the modern commuter farm, where the owners typically live in a variation of the ranch-style house and own a small amount of adjoining land. These residents probably work in Knoxville or one of the adjacent cities, yet they are farmers, too, and own a few beef cattle while farming garden vegetables or specialty crops. In 1992 the number of farms in Tennessee actually increased from the year before, temporarily reversing decades of decline. But many of these farms are of the commuter variety, providing rural people with a foothold in their rural past while they earn most of their livelihood in the modern commercial and industrial world.

The productive countryside of today, however, is not what travelers of U.S. Highway 70 found sixty years ago. A century of agricultural cultivation, devoid of conservation practices like crop rotation, contoured plowing, and terracing, left the land in miserable condition. "Between Dandridge and Knoxville," noted a WPA writer in the late 1930s, "many acres were so badly eroded that they were not suitable for cultivation until the CCC improved them" (*WPA Guide*, 434). Throughout the 1930s, the Civilian Conservation Corps reclaimed thousands of acres of Tennessee farmland and forests, a legacy—unless a historical marker has been erected documenting the camp's activities—that is little recognized today (see sidebar entitled "The New Deal Built Environment," Landscape 9, chapter 4).

Dandridge, the seat of government for Jefferson County, was once a busy steamboat port on the French Broad River. But during the 1850s, the railroad built to the north and created the new town of Jefferson City. Dandridge lost its commercial prominence and settled into life as a small county seat. Lack of growth during the seventy years between the Civil War and the arrival of the Tennessee Valley Authority at nearby Douglas Dam enabled the town to keep its mid-1800s appearance. Today few towns can match Dandridge for its outstanding examples of public and domestic architecture from the antebellum period.

The heart of the **Dandridge historic district** lies around Main, Meeting, and Gay Streets. The **Jefferson County Courthouse** (1845) is a Greek Revival design that was very similar to the 1842 Knox County Courthouse. On either side of the courthouse on Main Street, there are interesting variations of late Georgian architecture, most with some sort of Greek Revival detailing. Geographers have described this symmetrical two-story design, with a central hallway and chimneys located at the gable end, as an I-house or a central-hall house. Many Tennessee historians will describe these homes as examples of the "Tennessee Federal" style because they were built during the early Republic years. Yet, their architectural origins actually belong to the Georgian architectural period of the late eighteenth century.

Main Street in Dandridge has several variations in the Tennessee Federal style. The **Hickman House** (circa 1840) at 15 Main Street is a five-bay design with stepped gables that is reminiscent of homes found in the Shenandoah Valley of Virginia during the same time period. Farther up the street is the more austere **Roper Tavern** (circa 1817) that has somewhat heavy pilasters added during the Greek Revival era. The **Rogers-Miller House** (1860), with its two-story Greek Revival portico decorated with Italianate brackets and a Victorian bargeboard, is one of the most striking dwellings in East Tennessee. Other important homes surrounding the downtown core include the **Fain House** (1843), another five-bay Tennessee Federal house, and the classical pilasters and Italianate bracketing of the **Swann-Hampton House** (circa 1855) on Cherokee Drive (all dwellings are private, no access).

Four miles east of Dandridge on U.S. 70 is the rural village of French Broad. At the turn of the century, along the riverbanks now flooded by Douglas Lake stood the original canning factories of the Stokely Brothers, today recognized worldwide as the Stokely-Van Camp Corporation. What is now a bucolic scene was once a place that witnessed the merging of nineteenth-century agriculture, consumer mar-

Common House Plans

In early Tennessee architecture, the single-pen cabin was the most common dwelling type and served as a building block for other types of houses. The single-pen log cabin typically was built of yellow poplar logs and usually measured about twenty-by-seventeen feet, with a single chimney at the gable end. They were one-story buildings, but the steep gable roof created a loft for storage and perhaps for sleeping. Some cabins had windows cut into the walls, but in many the only ventilation was provided by doors cut into the long sides of the house. Since these houses vary so little in exterior appearance, a basic tool for distinguishing log architecture is the notching used to the connect the four corners of the house. The dominant notch in most areas of Tennessee was the half-dovetail, apparently an American adaptation of earlier log-notching techniques. The second most popular was the V-notch.

To double the size of the house, some builders favored saddlebag construction; that is, a house with a central chimney on either side of which was a single-pen log room. No central hallway existed in this type of house; indeed, most had no connection between the two rooms so each side had its own front door. The double-pen house also shared this trait of two front doors, but there was no central chimney; rather, each pen had its own chimney at the gable end.

The dogtrot house, however, allowed families to add a log pen to the existing house and create three spaces at the same time. The dogtrot combined two single-pen cabins under a commonly shared gable roof. The open passageway between the two pens, where people, dogs, and other animals could freely pass, is where the name "dogtrot" comes from. This space could be used for storage, food preparation, and even sleeping in the hot summer months. Later owners sometimes would clapboard the entire house, filling in the open passageway to create a simple three-room, central-hall dwelling.

Another vernacular dwelling found throughout Tennessee is a two-story dwelling of either log- or braced-frame construction, with a central hallway and chimneys of either limestone or brick at the gable ends (see photo of the Houston House in the Landscape 13 section of chapter 5 and the photo of the Warner Price Smith House in the Landscape 16 section of chapter 6). The windows and doors are placed symmetrically on the front facade while the interior is arranged around a central hall with typically four rooms on each floor. Geographers coined the term "I-house" for this dwelling type. Many historians will describe these homes as examples of "Tennessee Federal" architecture because they were built during the early years of the Republic, from 1780 to 1820. Another term for this house in the literature is "Plantation Plain," a reference to the prosperous landowner, merchant, or politician who most often had the resources to build such a large home. But whatever the name, the architectural antecedents of this statewide style—especially the symmetrical three- or five-bay facade—began in Georgian architecture of the late colonial period, especially the central-hall plan. Although remaining popular until 1860 at least, the house style changed in important ways during the nineteenth century. Often, a one-story "L-wing" would be added to the rear of the house for additional bedrooms or for attaching the kitchen and a dining area to the house. Then, during the Greek Revival period, builders would update the dwelling's architectural appearance by adding a two-story classical portico. By the 1850s and 1860s, the portico could become even more flamboyant with the addition of Victorian-inspired detailing and tracery. The Rogers-Miller House (1860) in Dandridge (see photo of the Rogers-Miller House below) shares all of these characteristics and serves as an outstanding example of the enduring popularity of late Georgian architectural forms in antebellum Tennessee.

Rogers-Miller House, Dandridge. New Victorian design ideas combined with the traditional I-house form to produce this wonderfully flamboyant portico and facade.

kets, and industry. In the late nineteenth century, progressive agriculturalists, railroad promoters, and New South businessmen urged southern farmers to exchange their past dependence on corn, wheat, and livestock for a new agricultural world that produced foodstuffs and vegetables for urban consumers. In 1898 Anna Stokely, her two sons James and John—who had learned the latest in agricultural theory while away at college—and a wealthy neighbor invested thirty-nine hundred dollars in the initial Stokely canning venture. Tomatoes were their first canned products, and for the next five years the family continued to reinvest its profits and build up the physical plant and capital of the firm. Soon, the Stokelys were canning a variety of fruits and vegetables, including string beans, berries, apples, peaches, and sweet potatoes. By 1905, having outgrown their extended operations along the French Broad, they moved to the railroad town of Newport, eight miles to the east, and built a large warehouse, a modern canning factory, and a central office building.

By that time Newport had already experienced the boom-and-bust cycle that characterized life and economic development in many Appalachian towns during the industrial revolution. First settlement dated from the early 1800s when the town of New Port was established as the seat of government for Cocke County along the French Broad River. This village site is visible today by traveling on U.S. Highway

321 one mile east of Newport. The bridge over the French Broad provides a view of the **Gilleland-O'Dell House** (1814), a Tennessee Federal house that marks the location of the original county seat (private, no access).

From the bridge is a beautiful view of French Broad as it looked in the days of the great livestock drives from East Tennessee over the Appalachian Mountains to marketplaces in North and South Carolina. A third type of farmer found in Tennessee during the antebellum era was the livestock drover, but compared to planters and yeoman farmers, little has been written about their way of life and contribution to southern agriculture. In the area of the French Broad between Dandridge and Newport, these largely Scotch-Irish drovers dominated the agrarian landscape. One hundred and fifty years ago, according to historian Edmund C. Burnett, twenty to thirty thousands hogs—or about one thousand hogs per mile—were fattened along the road between Dandridge and Newport. From this road, the hogs, sometimes numbering as many as a hundred and fifty thousand to a hundred and sixty thousand in a season, were driven overland every fall along the French Broad River to the stock markets at Asheville. Stockmen could only expect to drive hogs about eight to ten miles a day, so all along the present route of U.S. 70 were hog "hotels" that gave the drovers a place to put up their stock at night and to get a bite to eat and a decent night of sleep for themselves. Of course, driving the hogs overland required an immense amount of feed for the animals. Consequently, cornfields were another part of the agrarian landscape of the route along present-day U.S. 70. Farmers along the route typically sold twenty-five thousand bushels of corn to the drovers each year. While traveling along the beautiful and scenic section of U.S. 70 from Dandridge to the North Carolina line today, it is hard to imagine the days when rows of corn, hog hotels, and muddy paths greeted travelers rather than the gas stations, minimarts, and fast asphalt roads of today.

The great hog drives ended with the development of the regional railroad system in the post–Civil War decades. Once the railroad reached Newport—creating an entirely new town plan on the plateau overlooking the river—its days as a small, agrarian county seat and trade center (its population was only 347 in 1880) were numbered. Capitalists during the industrial revolution were drawn to mountain towns in East Tennessee because land and labor were cheap and new railroad construction meant that natural resources, including water power, coal, timber, and other precious minerals and metals, were ripe for the picking. Land use in the region changed drastically as resource mining—lumber, coal, or iron—replaced small-scale farming and raising livestock. During the mid-1880s, Newport developed as the industrial dream of Scottish, British, Canadian, and American capitalists led by Alexander A. Arthur. As the general manager of the Scottish Carolina Timber and Land Company, Ltd., Arthur planned to strip the surrounding Cocke County forests of the virgin timber, including cherry, ash, pine, oak, and lots of yellow poplar. He came armed with a new city plan as well, setting aside land for "Villa sites," factories, public buildings, and a college. The new town would represent the latest in Victorian urban planning, in jarring contrast to the first New Port, which had developed in a vernacular way without formal plans along the riverbanks.

At first, Arthur's company reshaped Newport as it desired; in 1884, for example, the county seat was moved from the older New Port to the new, industrial town. Two years later, however, nature intervened in the capitalists' great plans as a vicious flood washed away the timber, lumber booms, and sawmills of the Scottish Company. Arthur abandoned Newport and immediately shifted his attention northward to the historic town of Cumberland Gap, Tennessee, and Middlesboro, Kentucky, where he again led foreign investors in an ambitious attempt to build an industrial empire out of the hills of Appalachia.

Newport today has much to remind the visitor of its start and of its eventual development as an Appalachian industrial town. Victorian houses built high on hills overlooking the downtown, such as **Elm Hill** (1890), a wonderful Queen Anne dwelling constructed by local banker Benjamin D. Jones at 206 West Riverview Street, identify entrepreneurs who were captivated by Alexander Arthur's vision of a modern, industrial Newport. From the hills, it is possible to see how Newport's planners designed their town, with tightly packed streets facing the railroad tracks, which served as the commercial lifeline of the city until the development of modern highways in the last thirty years. Indeed, the railroad passes immediately in front of the Cocke County Courthouse (1930), which features a Colonial Revival design by Knoxville architects Manley and Young. This arrangement of urban space, different from any other Tennessee county seat, speaks volumes about the historic prominence and power of the railroad in comparison to the local government.

Route B: The Nolichucky River

To reach the heart of the Nolichucky River country, the visitor should leave Newport and travel northeast on U.S. Highway 321. Six miles later is the rural village of Parrottsville, initially settled in the 1780s by German immigrants. On Main Street (U.S. 321) stands the **Yett-Ellison House** (1857), built by Hamilton Yett, the son of German immigrant farmers. His dwelling is a late statement of Tennessee Federal style, symbolizing the Yett family's assimilation of English architectural taste (private, no access).

Another three miles east is an important pioneer landmark, the **Swaggerty Blockhouse**, identified by a state historical marker that stands adjacent to the building (private, limited access). Built by James Swaggerty between 1785 and 1790, the blockhouse is one of the few remaining in Tennessee and was used originally to protect settlers from potential Native-American attacks. The two-hundred-year-old fort has a unique cantilevered log design, with the third floor overhanging the second floor.

About six miles farther east, U.S. Highway 321 crosses the Nolichucky River. The route of U.S. 321 from here to Jonesborough lies parallel to the river, traversing an early settlement landscape. This section of road shows clearly the qualities that attracted the pioneers: good access to water, well-drained land, plenty of timber, and productive soil. In Greene County, this route passes through some of the region's best farmland. Today patches of burley tobacco, herds of beef cattle, and hay fields make up a modern farming landscape. Greeneville is the region's largest tobacco market, and in the early twentieth century many farmers turned to cultivating the plant on the advice of agricultural experts. The University of Tennessee Extension Service operates a burley tobacco experiment station just south of the U.S. 321 and Tennessee 70 junction. Burley tobacco became a popular cash crop because it was the preferred tobacco type for cigarette manufacturers. The weed is air-cured in tall, rectangular barns that are almost everywhere in Greene County. In the fall the leaves can be seen hanging in the open barns, drying to the desired consistency, and turning brown in color. Of the thirty-six historic family farms located in Greene County, for example, twenty-nine raised burley tobacco.

Established in 1783, Greeneville has prospered for two hundred years as an agricultural trade center. Although buffeted by the winds of the Civil War—one skirmish left a cannonball in the front facade of the local **Cumberland Presbyterian Church**—several historic neighborhoods provide an opportunity to explore the town's commercial and architectural evolution from the late 1700s to the early 1900s.

Main Street is the focal point of downtown Greeneville, with residential neighborhoods at both ends, commercial and religious buildings closer to the center, and the county courthouse and other public buildings grouped together at the center on top of a small hill overlooking the entire street. Greeneville, like many other early East Tennessee county seats, does not have the characteristic town square found in other areas of the South. Rather, the town is linear in nature, like those of the Shenandoah Valley. In the first two decades of Tennessee settlement, town founders brought a clear Virginia preference to the way they planned their new villages.

Greeneville was home for Andrew Johnson, who was president from 1865 to 1869. The **Andrew Johnson National Historic Site** includes properties associated with the career of this controversial Democratic Unionist, who became president of the United States after the assassination of Abraham Lincoln in 1865. Johnson was the only president ever impeached by the House of Representatives, but the United States Senate, by a single vote, refused to confirm the impeachment charges, and Johnson was never removed from office. A good place to begin an exploration of Johnson's life in Greeneville is the South Main house that was his sometime residence from 1851 until his death in 1875. During these years, Johnson was governor of Tennessee, vice president of the United States, president of the United States, and lastly a United States senator.

Across the street from the Johnson house are two significant dwellings: the **Clawson-McDowell House** (1810, 1840s) and the **Sevier-Lowry House** (1790s), a five-bay Tennessee Federal design that is considered the oldest home in Greeneville. The next two blocks, between Summer and Church Streets, are the commercial and political heart of the community. Most buildings date from the late nineteenth century when Greeneville, according to a 1887 history of Tennessee, "increased rapidly in both population and wealth." Tobacco was the key to this newfound prosperity as "the manufacture and shipment of tobacco" emerged as a leading industry (Goodspeed, 889). The Eastlake–style cast-iron cornice of **Snapp's 5&10** documents the architectural pretensions that accompanied the town's rapid expansion. An important entrepreneur was Col. John H. Doughty, who in 1884 built the four-story **Hotel Brumley** at 109 North Main and added the Victorian-designed **Doughty-Stevens Furniture Company** at 124 North Main before the decade was over.

At the corner of Depot and Main is the Classical Revival **Greene County Courthouse** (1916) designed by Thomas S. Brown; behind it stands the **Greene County Stone Jail** (1838, 1882). A block east at Depot and College Streets are two additional properties associated with President Andrew Johnson: his original tailor shop (a historic site even in Johnson's time) and his Greeneville home from 1838 to 1851, years when Johnson was an ardent defender of Jacksonian Democracy.

The corner of Main and Church Streets is the center of Greeneville's religious life. The **First Presbyterian Church** (1848, 1828) at 110 North Main features an exquisite Greek Revival facade; the **Cumberland Presbyterian Church** (1860s) at 201 North Main makes a similar classical statement, but with a mix of Italianate elements that indicate its later date of construction. At 105 North Church is one of the region's earliest examples of Gothic Revival architecture, the **St. James Episcopal Church** (1848), designed by George M. Spencer.

The next block of Main Street, between Church and Spencer Streets, experienced many changes in the last one hundred years, leaving only a few antebellum dwellings, but after Spencer Street there is

Former Hotel Brumley, Greeneville. There are several other examples of highly stylized cornices, like that of Hotel Brumley, in the late Victorian commercial architecture of Greeneville.

another historic neighborhood. The **Ripley House** (1868) and the **E. B. Miller House** (1856) are late examples of residential Greek Revival architecture while the **Harmony House** was an even more dated architectural statement when this austere Federal home was constructed in 1851 (all private, no access). Another significant early-nineteenth-century house is the **Dickson-Williams House** (1815–21), built by Irish craftsmen Thomas Battersby and John Hoy. Located at the corner of Irish and Church Streets, this house is currently being restored as a museum.

These houses help to underline the general conservatism of Greeneville's domestic architecture. For example, when a group of Irish immigrants moved here during the 1840s, the homes they built on the 200 block of Irish Street were not the stylish Gothic or Italianate of that decade, but simply variations on the Georgian I-house theme. In many southern towns, the arrival of railroads brought along new Victorian styles during the 1850s. Two Gothic cottages survive near the railroad depot, and the impressive Queen Anne–style Jeffers Mortuary is downtown. Yet, early American architectural traditions remained popular for Greeneville homes even after the arrival of the East Tennessee and Virginia Railroad. Only in the downtown commercial district does a strong Victorian presence exist.

As part of the Southern Railway empire, Greeneville witnessed commercial and industrial growth, again grounded in the tobacco industry, in the early 1900s. The historic Southern Railway passenger station, west of Main Street on Depot Street, marks this expansion, as do the many warehouses and small factories along the railroad tracks.

This industrial corridor initially developed throughout the region during the 1850s when the East Tennessee and Virginia Railroad connected the small towns in Greene and Washington Counties. The best way to explore this old railroad route is along the remaining sections of the original U.S. Highway 321/11E—part of the Lee Highway—east from Greeneville to Jonesborough. The four-lane, divided access highway that is now marked at U.S. 321/11E allows traffic to move much faster, but it largely cuts across open farmland and provides few glimpses of historic towns or places.

The older highway route begins at the north city limits of Greeneville where a monument to the early years of the Lee Highway still stands. In 1926 the local garden club built an entrance gate, called the Ye Olde Town Gate, over the highway to welcome visitors to Greeneville. About a mile northeast is the village of Tusculum, home to **Tusculum College** (1794). The historic **Samuel Doak House** (1818) and the **Old College** building (1841) mark Tusculum's antebellum era, but the historic core of campus dates from about one hundred years ago when Nettie Fowler McCormick, wife of industrialist Cyrus McCormick, donated funds for the construction of new buildings. **McCormick Hall** (1887), at the center of campus, was named in the family's honor, but the most important building in terms of Tennessee architecture is **Virginia Hall** (1901–2), designed by the world-renowned American architect Louis H. Sullivan. Virginia Hall is the only building Sullivan ever designed in Tennessee and one of the few he ever designed in the South.

Four miles east is the village of Chuckey, which is a good place to leave the modern highway and follow the old road into Jonesborough. Unlike most other upper East Tennessee villages, Chuckey retains its historic **Southern Railway Depot,** a combination passenger and freight station built in 1908. One mile east of the depot is the historic Elmwood Farm (1777), located on both banks of the Nolichucky River.

As the road enters Washington County, it stays close to the original roadbed of the East Tennessee and Virginia Railroad until it reaches Jonesborough, the county seat. The railroad, in turn, had generally followed a historic turnpike that connected Jonesborough to Knoxville. Consequently, there are places where dwellings of early settlers exist side by side with the steel rails of the railroad—where the vernacular landscape of the frontier age met the engineered landscape of the industrial revolution. Rather than the wide and expansive transportation corridor represented by today's interstate, this much older transportation route is narrow, with historic farms, stores, churches, and homes facing both sides of the highway.

Limestone is a railroad town created in the 1850s and first named Kleppers Depot for the German farmer who donated land for the townsite. On the west side of the tracks, a symmetrical line of stores faces the railroad. On the east side, oriented in a different direction than the stores, is the **Gillespie Stone House,** now abandoned and in poor repair. An early settler along the Nolichucky, George Gillespie fought at the Battle of King's Mountain in addition to agitating for the creation of the state of Franklin. His impressive house, built in about 1792 by Pennsylvania mason Seth Smith, has three first-floor rooms with no central hallway, an arrangement common in colonial Pennsylvania that recent Tennessee architectural historians call the Penn plan (private, no access). With its central chimney, the floor plan was similar to those used by German farmers on the Pennsylvania frontier and later on the Virginia frontier.

East of Limestone on the banks of the Nolichucky River, a state park marks the birthplace of one of Tennessee's most famous sons, Davy Crockett (1786–1836). Highway markers guide visitors to the park. A reconstructed one-room log cabin and a monument honor Crockett, who later gained fame as a congressman from West Tennessee and for his defense of the Alamo in San Antonio, Texas, where he died.

About one mile east of Limestone is Washington College, the first private academy in the Nolichucky Valley. The school began as the state's first private Presbyterian academy and church, established by Rev. Samuel Doak in 1780. The academy had a checkered history for the next one hundred years. Debt almost closed it before the Civil War, and as Rebel and Yankee armies traveled on the adjacent road they damaged several campus buildings. After the war, the school became the Washington Female Academy for about ten years before becoming a private academy for both sexes. Most buildings today date from the late nineteenth and early twentieth centuries. Nettie Fowler McCormick also aided this Presbyterian institution, and in 1894 she donated money for the construction of a new **Salem Presbyterian Church.** The design of A. Paige Brown, an architect who worked both in Chicago and on the West Coast, is a clever composition of Romanesque and Arts-and-Crafts architecture.

Like Limestone, Telford documents both the early pioneer and later industrial history of Washington County. Just south of town, and west of old U.S. 321/11E on Walker's Mill Road, is the **Embree Stone House** (circa 1780s), another example of the masonry skills of Seth Smith (private, no access). Mose Embree II was a pioneer industrialist who operated the region's first iron forge and owned a sawmill and hominy mill. His son Thomas Embree followed in his father's footsteps, establishing an iron-ore mine at a place northeast of Telford called Embreeville. He later opened Thomasville Iron Works and the E&E Embree nail factory, which stood along the Holston River. The Embree Iron Company plant at Embreeville was established by his brother Elijah Embree in 1831. Sixty years later British capitalists took over the old mines at Embreeville and attempted to establish a planned industrial town. This venture failed during the depression of 1893–96, but later investors turned the Embree Iron Company into a successful producer of zinc and manganese.

The Embrees were Quakers who also led the early fight for the abolition of slavery in Tennessee. In 1819 Elihu Embree began the weekly *Manumission Intelligencer,* which historians now consider the first American newspaper devoted to the abolition of slavery. The following year, Embree changed the newspaper to a monthly named the *Emancipator,* but publication ceased after Embree died in December. In 1822 Ohio abolitionist Benjamin Lundy acquired the paper, moved to Greeneville,

Eureka Roller Mills, Telford. The relationship of this mill to the nearby bridge and railroad tracks emphasizes how transportation and industry shaped the landscape one hundred years ago.

and resumed publication as *The Genius of Universal Emancipation* from 1822 to 1824.

After the tracks of the East Tennessee and Virginia pushed through Telford in the mid-1850s, they left behind a symmetrically designed town, with the commercial district on the west side of the tracks and a residential neighborhood on the east. The tracks also paved the way for a new chapter in local industrial history. In 1876 the Telford Agricultural Manufacturing Company was established in a three-story frame building that still stands between the tracks and a creek. In 1894 W. A. Maloney turned the factory into the Eureka Roller Mills.

Founded in 1779, **Jonesborough** is the oldest town in Tennessee. Its many nineteenth-century historic buildings and dwellings are justly celebrated as part of a National Register historic district. At its history museum and visitor center north of town, there are walking tour brochures that will indicate the most significant historic places.

Much of the history written about Jonesborough focuses on its early years, when it served as the capitol of the state of Franklin. In 1784 leaders of this extralegal association of three Tennessee counties formed a new "state" in reaction to the 1783 North Carolina "Land Grab Act," which sold almost four million acres of land to speculators, including then North Carolina resident William Blount. The following year, delegates met at Jonesborough and elected a reluctant John Sevier as governor and Landon Carter as secretary of state. The central government in Philadelphia, however, never recognized this new "state," and by the fall of 1788 the state of Franklin had disbanded.

Few buildings in Jonesborough remain from the late 1700s. The oldest is the **Chester Inn** (circa 1798 with an Italianate-like porch added in circa 1880) that welcomed passengers on the Great Stage Road from Nashville to Washington. The inn is now headquarters for the National Storytelling Festival that occurs every October. In the 1970s, the **Christopher Taylor House** (circa 1778) was moved from its countryside location to the center of town to preserve this significant two-story log house where Andrew Jackson once boarded. The linear town plan of Jonesborough, best viewed from the hill on North Main Street, also dates to the early settlement years.

Most of historic Jonesborough was built between the 1820s and the 1880s when agricultural prosperity and later railroad development brought wealth and prestige. Positioned as it was on the major stage road linking Philadelphia and the Southeast, Jonesborough was quite a trade center in its early days. In 1802 F. A. Michaux observed that the local "tradespeople get their provisions by land from Philadelphia, Baltimore and Richmond in Virginia, and they send, by the same way, the produce of the country" (Fink, 162). The **Green-Dillow House** on Woodrow Avenue, a block northeast of the courthouse, along with **Blair House** and **"Sisters Row"** on Main Street, a block south of the courthouse, represent the early antebellum era. The Green-Dillow House (circa 1825) is a five-bay, Tennessee Federal dwelling, with a double Greek Revival–style portico patterned after Palladian traditions. Blair House (1830) features stepped gables, an architectural detail especially prominent in early Jonesborough. "Sisters Row" (1819–22) is a row house built in the Tennessee Federal style by Elijah and Elihu Embree, with John Smith as mason.

Community growth and prosperity during the middle decades of the nineteenth century are represented by two historic churches, built at approximately the same time on Main Street and in a similar architectural style. The **Methodist Church** (1845–47) is an interesting regional statement of the Greek Revival–temple style, with Ionic order columns, topped by a colonial-style cupola. Diagonally across Main Street is the **Presbyterian Church** (1845–47), designed by Sullivan County architect W. H. Clyce in the Greek Revival–temple style. Due to its well-executed architectural details, historian James Patrick has called it "one of Tennessee's outstanding Greek Revival buildings" (129).

By the time the two churches opened for public services, more than renewed religious fervor gripped the residents of Jonesborough—railroad fever had claimed almost every businessman. Jonesborough residents supplied much capital and emotional support for the East Tennessee and Virginia Railroad, designed to link Knoxville to Wytheville, Virginia. As market networks had developed in the antebellum South, Jonesborough merchants and area farmers found themselves more and more isolated from the mainstream of southern commerce. Local investors hoped to end this isolation with a railroad.

The new railroad was headquartered in Jonesborough, with local physician and investor Samuel B. Cunningham as president. The **Cunningham House** (circa 1840) stands off Main Street near the courthouse, with the railroad line passing directly behind the dwelling. In 1855 his neighbor, George W. Willett, built a five-bay, stepped-gable house as the railroad was nearing completion (both homes are private, no access). The front facade of the **Willett House,** however, faces the tracks rather than Main Street, symbolizing the railroad's impact on future economic development and settlement patterns. Indeed, when the tracks reached town in 1857, according to historian Paul Fink, "naturally there was a great excitement and rejoicing in the town over the event, and the citizenry of the county for miles around, most of whom had never seen a locomotive or train, came to town in swarms to catch a glimpse of this new marvel" (175).

Most of the town's historic stores and shops around the **Washington County Courthouse,** designed by Baumann and Baumann of Knoxville in 1913, belong to the decades when the East Tennessee and Virginia Railroad—which became the East Tennessee, Virginia, and Georgia in 1869—dominated regional transportation. Another key

local institution—the **Holston Baptist Female Institute** (1853–55) on North Main Street, overlooking the entire town—operated as a girls' school until the Civil War. Afterwards, the Freeman's Bureau turned it into a school for newly freed African-American slaves (private, limited access).

Soon after exiting Jonesborough, the visitor enters Johnson City, the largest city in Washington County. Before the industrial revolution arrived in the late 1800s and early 1900s, however, the town was dwarfed in its commercial and political importance by its neighbor to the south. U.S. Highway 321 serves as Main Street through downtown Johnson City, and about one mile east on South Roan Street (U.S. Highway 19/23) is the **Tipton-Haynes Farm** (1783–1840), near the intersection of the federal highway and Buffalo Road. The property first belonged to John Tipton, an opponent of the state of Franklin. David Haynes bought the farm in 1838 and gave it to his son Landon. In about 1840 Landon added a Greek Revival portico to the farmhouse and designed a Greek Revival temple-style law office. The farm also has an intact antebellum slave dwelling together with other period buildings. Another two-hundred-year-old farm is northeast of Johnson City on the Watauga Road (Tennessee Highway 400). The **Dungan-St. John Farm** has belonged to the St. John family since 1866. Jeremiah Dungan, an immigrant from Bucks County, Pennsylvania, established the farm in 1778. He was a master craftsman who built a two-story limestone house

Dungan's Mill and Farmhouse, Watauga. The physical relationship between the flowing water, mill complex, and the adjacent farmhouse has not changed in two hundred years.

in about 1792. His gristmill, although altered and enlarged over the years, has been in business ever since.

From Dungan Mill it is possible to return to U.S. Highway 321 by merely following Watauga Road east to its junction with the federal highway near Elizabethton, the seat of government for Carter County. Like others in the region, this county seat has a distinctive place in the early settlement history of Tennessee, but much of what is visible today dates from more recent decades and is associated with the industrialization of Appalachia.

At the southeast city limits, clearly visible to the east from the U.S. Highway 321 overpass, is **Sabine Hill** (circa 1816–18), a superb example of Tennessee Federal architecture built for the family of Gen. Nathaniel Taylor (private, no access). About a mile away on U.S. 321, adjacent to the Watauga River, is the **Sycamore Shoals State Historic Area**. The shoals lay at the center of a local trail network that connected places like **Rocky Mount,** Fort Patrick Henry, and Sapling Grove (present-day Bristol). The park is a National Historic Landmark where the extralegal Watauga Association formed in 1772. Three years later, Richard Henderson negotiated the infamous Transylvania Purchase, which acquired over twenty million acres of land from the Cherokees for two thousand English pounds sterling and another eight thousand English pounds worth of goods. In 1776 settlers built Fort Caswell for protection against periodic Cherokee attacks led by Old Abram of Chilhowee. A reconstructed fort, called Fort Watauga, stands about

*Fort Watauga, Elizabethton.
Without clear documentation of the
fort's original appearance, those
who reconstructed Fort Watauga
during the 1970s chose to depict the
different types of log construction
found on the frontier.*

one mile west of the original location. Its log notching shows the
different types of log construction traditions that existed on the Tennessee frontier. Sycamore Shoals had its last significant moment in
American history when the Overmountain Men mustered here on September 25, 1780, before they crossed the Appalachians into South
Carolina for the decisive Revolutionary War Battle of King's Mountain
on October 7, 1780.

Three miles northeast on present-day East Broad Street is a third
important frontier site, the **John and Landon Carter Mansion,** believed
to have been constructed prior to 1781 as the home of John Carter, one
of the leaders of the Watauga Association. This two-story frame "mansion"—which James Patrick calls "among the most important witnesses
to the persistence of good architectural tradition on the Tennessee frontier" (65)—is now a historic house museum. The first floor is paneled
and has rare over mantle paintings, while the carpentry throughout the
house is superb. Its three-room floor plan reflects the influence of colonial Pennsylvania house plans.

The waters of the Watauga River attracted early pioneers and later
served as a powerful lure to twentieth-century capitalists. From the
river banks at Sycamore Shoals, the tall smokestacks of the huge
Bemberg and Glanzstoff rayon factories, which began operations in
1925, are visible. The factories even had their own railroad depot,
called Port Rayon, to handle the thousands of laborers who reported for
work every day. The overwhelming presence of the factories on the land-

Carter Mansion, Elizabethton. An example of architectural grandeur on the Tennessee frontier.

scape made the place appear almost alien to the normal scale of life in Carter County. Adding to the sense of disorientation, the chemistry of producing rayon was an unnatural process to many workers; nor did they like taking orders from their German supervisors. In general, Appalachian people, who had been accustomed to the rhythms of an agricultural life, found the regimentation of industrial life difficult to swallow. In March 1929, three thousand workers at the rayon plants went on strike. Most city and county officials strongly supported the owners. Soon, court injunctions forbade picketing. The national guard arrived to "enforce law and order"; soldiers barricaded the factories and escorted scab workers into the factories. Local businessmen also turned to vicious repression as a group of self-appointed vigilantes kidnapped union leaders and threw them out of the state. One company spy counted eight hundred state police, seven hundred business and professional men, and the state and city government as allied against the workers.

For the next three months, the supporters and opponents of the strike waged battle. "The contest in Elizabethton was an unequal one," a recent history by Jacquelyn Dowd Hall and others has concluded, "but it was not so unequal in contemporary eyes as hindsight would have it"

(213). For support and sustenance, many of the strikers could return to families who had stayed in the mountains. The surrounding countryside backed the strikers, even if local businesses in Elizabethton refused to serve them. Consequently, the strikers—many of whom were young women—aggressively worked for a union shop. During March and April 1929, travelers on U.S. 321 between the factories and downtown Elizabethton would have found "hundreds of girls," according to one account cited by Jacquelyn Dowd Hall, "in buses and taxis, shouting and laughing at people who watched them." The women defied court injunctions, forming human chains to block roads and railroad tracks, and one time they marched down the highway "draped in the American flag and carrying the colors" in order to force national guard soldiers to present arms as they passed (229).

On May 26, 1929, the union signed an agreement that ignored worker demands and the most activist strikers were immediately blacklisted. "I knew I wasn't going to get to go back," recalled Bessie Edens. "I wrote them a letter and told them I didn't care whether they took me back or not. I didn't! If I'd starved I wouldn't of cared, because I knew what I was a'doing when I helped to pull it. And I've never regretted it in any way. It did help the people, and it's helped the town and the country" (Hall, 233). To avoid future confrontations, the companies soon raised wages a bit, shortened hours, and recalled a particularly unpopular manager. Bessie Edens was right: labor relations were never perfect, but Elizabethton never again experienced such a divisive, violent strike.

From the rayon plants, U.S. 321 turns into Elk Avenue and becomes the heart of downtown Elizabethton. The Doe River divides the town into two sections, and a city park around the river is a good place to view local urban growth. The park contains the **Covered Bridge** (1882), one of only four such historic bridges in the state. Built by Dr. E. E. Hunter, the 134-foot-long wooden bridge survived the great Doe River flood of 1901 and still handles light automobile traffic today.

East of the bridge is the older section of Elizabethton. The most eye-catching landmark is the Soldier's Monument, a tall, white shaft that honors Mary Patton's role in the Battle of King's Mountain. Between the Carter County Courthouse and East Street is the **Alfred M. Carter House** (1819), an excellent example of a Tennessee Federal house, with a refined two-story Palladian portico (private, no access). Across the street, and now home to the county agricultural extension service, is the **Folsom House** (1861). Its Tennessee Federal facade indicates how traditional architectural forms remained popular here even into the second half of the nineteenth century.

The historic commercial district is located on both sides of the Doe River. On North Sycamore is the **Elizabethton Post Office** (1931), a Classical Revival design by James A. Wetmore. Another building in the same style is the **Bonnie Kate Theater**. Most buildings are from the early twentieth century when the town experienced its greatest period of growth, especially after the rayon factories opened their doors in 1925.

To connect to the next historic route, leave Elizabethton on U.S. Highway 19E and travel north toward Bristol, exiting the combined federal route of 11E/19E at its junction with Tennessee 37. This approximately eight-mile drive goes through the historic county seat of Blountville, home of the architecturally significant **Deery Inn** and **Dulaney House** (also see Interstate Highway 81 section, chapter 1), before connecting to U.S. 11W east of Kingsport.

Route C: The Holston River

The ninety miles of U.S. Highway 11W between Kingsport and Knoxville traverse another early pioneer landscape of Tennessee history. The Holston River was a popular transportation route, and many settlers established farms, taverns, stores, churches, and towns on fertile river bottomlands. The highway itself, like U.S. 11E, generally follows early-nineteenth-century routes and places travelers in close proximity to many significant places from the first decades of settlement.

The **Long Island of the Holston River,** a National Historic Landmark located in downtown Kingsport, was the river's base of operations two hundred years ago. The best direct access to this historic area is to leave U.S. Highway 11W at the Netherland Inn Road near the western city limits. The western tip of the island is a heritage park that interprets the events of the late eighteenth and early nineteenth centuries. From the park, the natural resources, the flowing river, and the broad riverbanks that made the island an excellent point of debarkation are apparent. After the Treaty of Long Island in 1777, permanent settlement began when Joseph Martin, Indian agent to the Cherokees, and his Cherokee wife, Betsy Ward, established a trading post. Over the next generation, Long Island evolved into a jumping-off point for new settlers where they would build rafts or flatboats to float down river.

In 1802 entrepreneur William King, who owned a large salt mine at the nearby town of Saltville, Virginia, established a boat yard to build

rafts for his business. It stood at the newly created town of Christianville, on the north bank of the Holston River across from the western end of Long Island. Although King died in 1808, the salt mines and boat yard stayed in business for another two decades. In about 1818, as evidence gathered from historical archaeology and period records seems to suggest, Richard Netherland took an earlier existing boardinghouse and transformed it into a three-story inn to serve those doing business at the boat yard as well as those traveling the stage road to Virginia and Washington, D.C. The restored **Netherland Inn** is a historic house museum that focuses on the lives of Richard and Margaret Netherland, who operated it until 1841. Its vernacular architectural style reflects a central-hall plan that has the kitchen wing attached in a T-wing (in the middle of the house) rather than the more common L-wing (to the side of the house). Between the inn and the Holston River, a walking path follows the route of the late-eighteenth-century stage road, providing visitors with a glimpse of what this countryside was like when the Long Island was a transportation crossroads.

Warriors' Path State Park, southeast of town along the banks of Fort Patrick Henry Lake, is also associated with the early settlement era. Established in the late 1700s, Childress Town stood at the Childress Ferry, one of the more popular ferry crossings over the South Fork of the Holston River. All that remains of the village today, however, are archaeological ruins, especially the stone walls that once supported a gristmill. On the Fall Creek Road entrance to the park is an intact gristmill, the **Roller-Pettyjohn Mill** (1903), built some one hundred years after the heyday of Childress Town. From 1833 to 1955, different entrepreneurs have operated mills at this place on Fall Creek (private, no access).

Southwest of Kingsport, U.S. Highway 11W is a divided, four-lane highway for the next forty-four miles to its junction with U.S. 25E. The road passes through Hawkins County, one of the state's oldest counties. To find its early settlement places requires leaving the modern U.S. 11W and following the older two-lane federal highway route.

Eleven miles west of Kingsport, for instance, is the junction with Tennessee 346, which is the older highway route into Surgoinsville where the road becomes Main Street. Incorporated in 1815, the town was a historic trade stop for stagecoaches and for boats floating down the adjacent Holston River. On the eastern outskirts of town is the historic **Fudge Farm** (private, no access). The farmhouse is a five-bay I-house, built by slaves in about 1851. The family still uses several historic log farm buildings, including the stock barn, granary, smokehouse, and wellhouse. In town is one of the rare southern examples of a Lustron house, a prefabricated dwelling of steel developed in Ohio during the late 1940s as an ill-fated attempt to solve the post–World War II shortage of housing (private, no access).

Tennessee 346 returns to U.S. Highway 11W five miles east of Rogersville, the seat of government for Hawkins County. At the east city limits, the highway junctions with Tennessee 70, which to the south leads to Main Street in Rogersville. Before exploring the downtown, however, it may be a good idea to take a brief side trip to an old former mountain retirement village and school north of Rogersville that used to be owned and operated by a labor union. Access to this village can be gained by taking Tennessee 70 north for five and a half miles to its junction with Tennessee 94. Turning to the west, the road passes through a beautiful mountain valley and encounters a place now called "Camelot" on local maps. Once it was known as the **Pressmen's Home,** a grand retirement home and trade-school complex for the International Printing Pressmen and Assistants' Union of North America.

The original golf course is in operation, but most of Pressmen's Home is abandoned and in varying stages of deterioration (private, no access). Sixty years ago, however, these buildings and the surrounding twenty-seven-hundred-acre estate hummed with activity. The union operated a retirement home, a trade school for training apprentice press-

men, and a sanitarium for the care of union members with tuberculosis. Union head George L. Berry chose the site after a 1909 visit to Hawkins County, where he had lived as a boy.

Construction of Pressmen's Home began in October 1910. The Home for the Superannuated Members was one of the first buildings completed, but the isolation of Pressmen's Home never lured many members to retire there. In time, mostly staff members and students occupied the building. A hotel for visiting members, the five-story and 165-room Hotel Pressauna, proved very popular after its construction in 1926. It featured big band concerts and continental cuisine from European-trained chefs. In that same year, a classically styled chapel, designed by John J. Sheridan, was added to the complex. The first training-school building dates from 1910–11, designed by the Chicago architectural firm of Holabird and Roach in the Colonial Revival style. In 1948 the union opened a second building, a four-story modernist structure of concrete, steel, and glass that was the "largest printing technical trade school in the world" (Mooney, 117) at that time. Although the peak enrollment reached only 233 students in 1963, tens of thousands of union members took correspondence courses from Pressmen's Home. The sanitarium complex dates from 1916, and the original building was designed by Asheville architects Smith and Carrier. It remained in operation until 1961 when its final thirteen patients were transferred to private care and the building was immediately dismantled.

Six years later, the union closed Pressmen's Home and moved its headquarters to Washington, D.C. Some buildings remain in use today, but most of the complex lies open to the wind and elements, an eerie monument to the era of trade union power in the United States.

Farther west of Pressmen's Home on Tennessee 66 are the isolated Clinch River Valley residents of Hancock County. Some identify with the Melungeons, a dark-skinned people found only in isolated pockets of Appalachian settlement. Sneedville is the county seat and its Hancock County Courthouse, designed by Knoxville architect Allen Dryden in 1931, is a charming statement of late Classical Revival architecture.

If the side trip to rural Hancock County is not taken, the visitor can return to Rogersville by retracing the original drive to Pressmen's Home or by remaining on Tennessee 94 until it junctions with Tennessee 66 and then returns to Rogersville.

Established in the late 1780s, Rogersville is the most intact historic town along the Holston River. Together with its original linear town plan, several residential, public, and commercial buildings document the initial generations of settlement. The best place to view its evolution is at the **Hawkins County Courthouse** (1836), designed by architect John Dameron. Although altered somewhat in 1929, the building remains a marvelous blend of the Greek Revival–temple style, with the earlier period of American classicism represented by its Federal-style doorway and Palladian windows. To the west of the courthouse is another Greek Revival building, the **Shelburne Law Office** (circa 1837), which is attached to an earlier five-bay Tennessee Federal dwelling known as the **Waterson House** (private, no access). Next door is the **Hale Springs Inn** (1824), a restored three-story Federal stagecoach inn that in the past welcomed such guests as former presidents James K. Polk and Andrew Johnson (private, limited access). Directly across the street from the courthouse is another important Greek Revival building, the former **Bank of Tennessee** (1839), designed by Thomas Jones. It is now Overton Lodge #5, F.&A.M., the oldest Masonic lodge in continuous operation in the state (private, no access).

Next to the courthouse is a three-block commercial district. The historic buildings date mainly between the 1860s and 1890s. The resi-

Hawkins County Courthouse, Rogersville. A Greek Revival landmark in East Tennessee.

dential neighborhoods of Rogersville lie to either side of the courthouse and business district. The west side contains the oldest dwellings. At 205 South Rogers Street, for instance, is **Rogers Tavern** (1786), a log and stone structure now covered with clapboard. Next door at 207 South Rogers is the **Pettibone Double House** (circa 1786), a log saddlebag house also covered with clapboard. On Rogan Street is an antebellum cemetery, where the town founder Joseph Rogers is buried in addition to the grandparents of Davy Crockett.

Three homes on the 300 block of West Main show the town's architectural evolution in the nineteenth century. The **Rogers-Walker House** at 317 West Main dates from 1836, while on either side are Victorian dwellings including the **Armstrong House** (circa 1839, 1890) and the **Kirkpatrick House** (circa 1891).

The east side of Rogersville has three different homes associated with the antebellum merchant and attorney John A. McKinney. The **Clay-Kenner House** (circa 1835) at 403 East Main was a wedding gift from McKinney to his son John. The cross gable and brackets on the front are reminiscent of Virgina dwellings from the same period. At the corner of East Main and Colonial is another McKinney wedding gift, **Rosemont** (1842), this time to his daughter Susan. The five-bay Tennessee Federal architecture of Rosemont was conservative, since the more fashionable Greek Revival courthouse and state bank already stood downtown. McKinney's own home, **Three Oaks** (1815), has a strong Virginian influence, especially in its prominent cross gable and central-hall plan.

Downtown Rogersville has a built environment seemingly frozen in the agrarian world of the nineteenth century. But surrounding the town are several reminders of how the industrial revolution also shaped local fortunes. The local built environment has a chronological pattern to it, a pattern similar to the way the rings of a tree show the tree's age. Around the courthouse and the town center are the antebellum buildings of Rogersville. A mere two blocks north, on Depot Street, is the starting point for the next period of town development and expansion, the former **Southern Railway Depot**, built after the railroad giant gained control of the Knoxville, Virginia, and Georgia Railroad in 1894. Several blocks farther away from the courthouse on old U.S. 11W (Main Street) is an early-twentieth-century factory, which brought even more of the regimentation of industrial life to generations of Hawkins County residents. Tennessee 66 follows the Rogersville spur to the Southern's main line at Bulls Gap. Spanning the Holston River is a stone-supported

Hale Springs Inn, Rogersville. The dignified Federal-style facade reflects the graciousness and simplicity of the restored interior.

railroad bridge, finished after the Civil War in the late 1860s. Northeast of the bridge is the John Sevier Steam Plant, a more modern artifact of industrialism constructed about one hundred years later by the Tennessee Valley Authority. Along the city limits are most of the recently established industrial and commercial institutions shaping the future of Rogersville.

Sixteen miles southwest of Rogersville on U.S. Highway 11W is Bean's Station, a key crossroads for over two hundred years. Goodspeed's 1887 history of Tennessee called Bean's Station "one of the best known places in Tennessee, for more than half a century prior to the advent of railroads" (853). For the pioneers, it was the intersection of the Wilderness Road and the Great Indian Warpath, a place where taverns and other resting places were located. Looking at the same intersection today, however, produces almost no connection to its distinguished past. A modern landscape meets the eye, as artifacts of automobile travel—restaurants, gas stations, and motels—cluster around the junction, now represented by U.S. Highways 11W and U.S. 25E. This place is like every other highway junction in the state.

One way to recapture the frontier landscape is to take a brief side trip along U.S. 25E for thirty miles to **Cumberland Gap National Historical Park,** where the states of Tennessee, Virginia, and Kentucky meet. Here the National Park Service is rerouting the modern highway through mountain tunnels so that the original path of the Wilderness Road can be restored to its late-eighteenth-century appearance. In this case, the park service is creating a modern engineered landscape so that a much earlier vernacular landscape can be better interpreted and understood, even though the surrounding towns of Middlesboro, Kentucky, and Cumberland Gap, Tennessee, are strongly associated with the industrial revolution of the late nineteenth century. Also on this side trip, in Harrogate, is the Abraham Lincoln Museum at Lincoln Memorial University. This museum has an eclectic but interesting collection of artifacts associated with the former president.

Returning south to U.S. 11W, Tate Springs is three miles southwest of the highway junction at Bean's Station. The resort and vacation activity that once surrounded this place has now shifted to Cherokee Lake and the many recreational facilities constructed by the Tennessee Valley Authority along this section of the dammed Holston River. But in the late nineteenth century, few places in East Tennessee rivaled the popularity of Tate Springs. During the late 1870s and early 1880s, entrepreneur Capt. Thomas Tomlinson promoted the mineral springs as a

tourist mecca. He built a large hotel, extensively landscaped his property, and began to bottle mineral water for mail-order sales across the
country. Tate Springs especially prospered from 1890 to 1919 when the
Knoxville and Bristol Railroad—known locally as "the Peavine"—operated between Morristown and Corryton, connecting the Knoxville, Virginia, and Georgia Railroad to the Knoxville, Cumberland Gap and Louisville Railroad. A Victorian **springhouse** marks the resort site.

South of Tate Springs, commercial and recreational properties
largely disappear and the countryside becomes more pastoral in quality. The resources that made this land valuable for farming—rich, rolling grasslands, timber, several creeks—are readily apparent. Eight miles
southwest on U.S. Highway 11W and one-fifth of a mile south of the
highway is the **William Cocke House** (private, no access). Built in
1850, this Greek Revival dwelling belonged to one of the most politically prominent families in Grainger County history. Democrat William
Cocke served in both the county and state governments and was elected
to the state house of representatives and the state senate.

Three miles away is Rutledge (1801), the seat of Grainger County.
"Its population has never been large," observed the Goodspeed history
in 1887, "and in this respect, perhaps, no other village in the State has
remained so nearly stationary for so long a time" (855). That changed
somewhat three years later when the Morristown and Cumberland
Gap Railroad, a precursor of the Knoxville and Bristol, built from
Morristown to Bean Station and then headed south parallel with
Richland Creek to Rutledge and on to Blaine. The tracks are gone today,

but Water Street follows the original route through Rutledge. The small size of the town's commercial district is still evident, and the empty spaces around the courthouse mean that the town lacks the feel of a true courthouse square. The historic **Grainger County Jail** (1848) is the only public building in town that dates from the antebellum period. The courthouse is a rather plain modern design, constructed in 1949.

The Knoxville and Bristol Railroad, in the context of regional rail development, was a short branch line that facilitated traffic between the major urban areas of the Upper South. But farms along the railroad line also benefited from this urban intrusion into their agrarian landscape. Six miles southwest of Rutledge on U.S. Highway 11W at the Joppa community is the historic Rolling Acres Farm (private, no access). Established by William Kinsland on 249 acres in 1866, the farm was typical for its time, with fields of cotton and hay and lots of cattle, hogs, and horses. But when the Peavine built through the farm, the founder's daughter Carrie Kinsland and her husband, A. C. Hickle, took advantage of the new market opportunities to sell lumber, livestock, milk, and other crops and vegetables. They also opened a general store that served as the local post office.

The Peavine railroad changed Blaine from another small turnpike village of the nineteenth century to a railroad town of the early twentieth century. Just north of town at the hamlet of Lea Springs is the **Cynthia Lea House** (private, no access). The dwelling is immediately north of U.S. 11W, and its steeply pitched, cross-gable-and-Gothic styling makes it easy to see from the highway. According to family tradition, Cynthia Lea was an independent woman who shocked her family by considering becoming a missionary in Africa. Certainly her choice of the Gothic Revival style spoke of her independent streak; no other such stylish Gothic cottages stood in Grainger County. Blaine is also the location of **Shields' Tavern,** another landmark of the old stagecoach era (private, no access). The date of first construction is not clear from the historical records, but by the mid-1830s, Dr. Samuel Shields had acquired the property and had turned it into a combination tavern, store, and post office. Shields' Station remained an important stage stop until the decade of the Civil War.

From Blaine, the Peavine railroad climbed over Clinch Mountain to junction with another branch of the Southern Railway at Corryton. To keep the small line from its competitors, the Southern Railway acquired control of the Peavine in late 1903. The line remained open for another twenty-five years until the combination of rising costs of operation and damaging floods closed the line from Corryton to the Morristown Steam Plant. Despite its brief existence, the Peavine "was a major link to the outside world for the residents of Richland Valley," emphasizes archaeologist Charles H. Faulkner. "The railroad, too, relied on local traffic for its lifeblood, and so a special bond developed between the crew and residents along the line" (51).

Nine miles southwest of Blaine are the John Sevier Railroad Yards, now operated by Norfolk Southern but originally built by the Southern Railway in 1925. Railroad expansion in the late nineteenth century severely diminished the commercial trade along the old stage roads, leading to the economic stagnation of rural communities such as Maynardville, the seat of government of Union County, that lacked a rail connection, while places like Corryton and Luttrell became small commercial outlets. This entire area of southern Grainger and Union Counties, along with the northern border of Knox County, has experienced little economic growth in decades. The railroads that once eclipsed the stage roads have now, in turn, been eclipsed by interstate highways. And these towns, no matter whether a railroad exists or not, are isolated from the mainstream of American transportation.

Landscape 6: Industrial Appalachia

In looking at the southern landscape of the early twentieth century, social critic H. L. Mencken observed, "The mills and factories are there to stay, and they must be faced. Nothing can be done to help the farmers who struggle on, beset by worn-out soils, archaic methods, and insufficient capital. They are doomed to become proletarians and the sooner the change is effected the less painful it will be" (Cobb, 34). Most intellectuals and policy makers of the early twentieth century shared this rather brutal and shortsighted assessment. But part of Mencken's observation was true: industrialism was reordering the southern world. It had already transformed many Tennessee towns and rural communities by the time the Southern Agrarians issued their impassioned defense of agrarianism, *I'll Take My Stand,* in 1930.

The industrial landscape is an inescapable part of the countryside. The earlier vernacular landscape that had evolved from traditional use, preferences, and agriculture was replaced by a modern landscape where the lay of the land was predetermined by engineers and architects using site plans, maps, and heavy construction machinery. But its presence does not automatically mean that communities accepted the changes brought by the railroads, mills, mine shafts, and hydroelectric dams. As already documented in Knoxville, Newport, and Elizabethton, industrialization represented an abrupt change in social relations, working conditions, and the basic rhythms of everyday life. It transformed the people and the landscape of Appalachian Tennessee perhaps more than any other event in history.

East Tennessee has many places that owe their appearance and mere existence to the industrial dreams of capitalists who came to take advantage of the abundant raw materials, especially coal, iron, and timber, and to the mountain people who provided the cheap and plentiful labor that ran the entire system. Typically, whenever the investors arrived to proclaim the location for their industrial visions, they found plenty of local businessmen, civic leaders, and politicians eager to provide whatever assistance was necessary—tax breaks, brutal suppression of labor unions, and nonexistent pollution controls—to lure the new development to their town or county. "In the South," concluded Marshall Frady, "the land of Canaan came to consist of a horizon of smokestacks. Industrialization—the devout acquisition of factories—became a kind of second religion there: the secular fundamentalism" to counter the religious fundamentalism of the countryside (Cobb, 2).

The industrialization of Appalachian Tennessee began before the Civil War, at places like the iron mines and forges at Embreeville in Washington County, the copper mines at Ducktown in Polk County, and the cotton mills at Lenoir City. But it exploded across the region in the post-Reconstruction period, especially from 1880 to 1920, due to the networking of local railroads into regional, even national transportation empires, the discovery of the region's vast natural resources, and the availability of outside capital—millions upon millions of dollars—for investment. Land companies and industrialists banded together to create instant cities to serve as commercial and manufacturing crossroads in a new industrial landscape that ran down the entire backbone of Appalachia. Bristol, for example, developed as a rail link for concerns in Tennessee, North Carolina, Kentucky, and Virginia. "Bristol has more commerce, more banking capital and a better location than any other point," bragged a promoter in a pamphlet published in 1889, "making it the commercial and manufacturing center of the territory." Other towns, like Oneida in Scott County and LaFollette in Campbell County, were much smaller industrial way stations along railroad corridors that connected northern factories to southern raw materials. Established in 1897 by Harvey and Grant LaFollette, who were coal-mine investors from Indiana, LaFollette still retains the look and feel of a turn-of-the-century Appalachian coal town.

Twentieth-century industrial villages, however, often tried to escape the look and the stigma associated with the earlier coal, iron, and timber towns. Progressive urban planning called for more paternalistic environments with better housing and more civic amenities. "Desire for control over workers was a primary reason for sponsoring housing," according to historian Gwendolyn Wright. "Advertisements for skilled workers stressed the benefits for a man's wife and children in a model town with company-built housing. In exchange, the family would be dependent on the company for their improved way of life" (184–85). Alcoa (1913), a company town established by the Aluminum Corporation of America north of Maryville on U.S. Highway 129, was a quite different place from LaFollette. The only raw materials Tennessee supplied were cheap labor and abundant hydroelectric power produced by the company's own dams, especially the huge Calderwood Dam on the Little Tennessee River. For its first generation, Alcoa was considered a model industrial community, divided into four neighborhoods that were designed, in part, to segregate the company's many African-American workers from its white laborers. But during the mid-1930s, the employees began to demand more rights and attempted to affiliate with the American Federation of Labor, then with the Congress of Industrial Organizations. After World War II, the company slowly divested itself of its control over Alcoa, selling company housing to employees in the early 1950s, then selling its electric utilities in 1955 and its waterworks five years later.

This chapter cannot introduce all of the industrial villages of Appalachia Tennessee. Travelers, however, can look for the basic elements that made up industrial Appalachia: railroad lines and likely a rail crossroads; nearby supplies of timber and seams of coal; proximity to hydroelectric stations; and a lack of good quality land that made farming unprofitable for most residents, leaving them little alternative but to commute to the factories. Two different routes best document the diversity of landscapes created by modern industry over the last 125 years. Interstate 181 is a regional expressway that connects Kingsport, Johnson City, and Erwin, three places that reflect a combination of unfettered industrialization and model urban planning that represented the most progressive elements of economic development in the early twentieth century. Then, in the middle decades of this century came the new landscapes of steel and concrete associated with the federal government and military. During the Great Depression and World War II, a strikingly modern landscape—deliberately different from what had come before—emerged along the connected routes of Tennessee Highways 61 and 95 between Norris and Oak Ridge.

Route A: The Clinchfield Railroad

The route of the Clinchfield Railroad between Kingsport and Erwin can be traced by following Interstate Highway 181, which parallels the old railroad corridor. The Carolina, Clinchfield, and Ohio Railroad—best known as the Clinchfield Railroad—was established during the early 1900s to link coal mines in eastern Kentucky and southwestern Virginia with mill towns in the South Carolina Piedmont. Led by George L. Carter and funded by northern capitalists, the Clinchfield tied regional resources together in such a way that investors looking for new areas to exploit needed to look no farther than Appalachia. Due to the high construction costs—estimated at forty million dollars—the company planned to recoup its investment in part by developing industrial towns along the line. In Tennessee, the three primary town sites were Kingsport, Johnson City, and Erwin.

Kingsport was the Clinchfield's first major venture in the state. In 1905 it acquired land north of the Holston, and by the next year it had established a city plan. Little more happened until 1908–9, when the company laid tracks into town and built the large Clinchfield Passenger Station, designed by New York architect Clinton Mackenzie, that still stands at the head of town on Main Street. Kingsport began as a small industrial town, with four factories, until 1915, when John B. Dennis and J. Fred Johnson joined talents to create a model industrial city under the patient eye of the Kingsport Improvement Company (KIC). It was a perfect partnership: Dennis supplied the money while Johnson brought vision and tireless boosterism to the dream of a model industrial city.

By 1916 a large chemical plant and wood pulp factory had joined the earlier enterprises, and Kingsport soon took on the appearance of a ramshackle boom town, with shacks and tents lining the streets. Dennis and Johnson knew that this situation would discourage the type of investors they wanted to attract, so they turned to the office of landscape architect and urban planner John Nolen of Cambridge, Massachusetts, for a properly progressive town plan. With Philip W. Foster serving as the primary designer, Nolen's plan incorporated the earlier

Tennessee Eastman, circa 1947. Later technological developments and plant expansions by Tennessee Eastman replaced the working-class community of Long Island, located in the foreground of this photograph. (Courtesy of Tennessee State Library, Tennessee Department of Conservation Collection)

1905–6 plan—which combined a traditional commercial district grid with semicircular grids for **Church Circle** and residential areas—into an expanded urban environment, complete with a golf course, parks, industrial zones, a cemetery, and a separate section for African Americans.

From Church Circle the boldness of the original plan is still visible. The circle serves as the physical and symbolic center of town, surrounded by four Colonial Revival–style churches. The seven-story bank that stands at the southeast corner of the circle was originally the location of the Kingsport Inn. Due south of the circle is the town's primary commercial district while the head of town is defined by the tall tower of the **Clinchfield depot**. The railroad tracks divided the commercial and residential areas from the early industrial concerns of 1910 to 1915 and separated the town from the Holston River, which ran south of the depot and tracks. The Kingsport plan, according to historian Margaret Ripley Wolfe, "represented a coherent expression of the principles of town planning in early twentieth century America," especially the ideas of the city efficient movement. "Any city planning that is worthy of the name," architect Nolen explained, "is concerned primarily with use and only incidentally with beauty," but he added that any good plan embraced beauty and efficiency (Wolfe, 53–54).

Kingsport's industrial future, however, was not secured until 1920 when J. Fred Johnson convinced the Eastman Kodak Company of Rochester, New York, to locate a huge new chemical factory—named Tennessee Eastman—on land facing the Long Island of the Holston. By entering the town on Tennessee 126 (South Wilcox Drive) and turning northwest on Tennessee 355 (Industrial Drive), travelers have a perfect view of the Eastman works, along with other industrial concerns recruited in the middle decades of the century. Few other drives in Tennessee convey so well the impact of industry on the natural landscape. Despite a slow start, the pollution associated with its products, and a terrible explosion in 1960 that took fifteen lives, Eastman has been the city's major employer and civic benefactor for over seventy years. Its first product was methanol for film, then plastic and textile yarn from cellulose acetate. During World War II, Eastman branched into explosives, while more recent ventures have included coal gasification.

In 1942 the presence of Tennessee Eastman and its technical expertise encouraged the federal government to establish the Holston Ordnance Works, a massive ammunition and explosives plant of over six thousand acres located along the Holston River southwest of town. Operated by Tennessee Eastman, the complex produced a powerful explosive that mixed RDX and TNT. U.S. Highway 11W passes along the northern border of the ordnance works, but the factories are closed to the public.

The Tennessee Eastman complex, the downtown district, and the Holston Ordnance Works are merely the largest elements of Kingsport's industrial landscape that tie the present to the past dreams of John Dennis and J. Fred Johnson. At 1322 Watauga Avenue is the **J. Fred Johnson House,** a Colonial Revival dwelling built between 1915 and 1917. Also on Watauga Street is the Tudor Revival **Stone-Penn House** (1916–17), designed by KIC architect Clinton Mackenzie and the residence of the first president of Tennessee Eastman. At the north end of Long Island are the remains of the working-class community of Long Island that developed within the shadows of the smokestacks of industrialism during the mid-1900s. In the last twenty-five years, Tennessee Eastman has acquired much of the old village property and demolished many homes for its expansion into the industry of coal gasification.

Twenty-three miles southeast on I-181 is Johnson City. An older route between the two cities is Tennessee 36. First known as Blue Plum Station, the place became Johnson City during the 1850s when the East Tennessee and Virginia Railroad built through the county and established the basic town design that visitors encounter today. By entering Johnson City via exit 32 of I-181, it is possible to see the close relationship between the railroad tracks and the historic downtown business district. State of Franklin Road, in particular, introduces the old industrial and warehouse core of the railroad corridor. Johnson City became an established trade center in the mid-1880s when the East Tennessee and Western North Carolina Railroad built east, connecting Johnson City to Elizabethton. During this decade, a Victorian neighborhood expanded on the hills north of the railroad tracks. On South Roan Street is the Queen Anne–style **Robin's Roost** (circa 1890), designed by William Graham (private, no access). This dwelling was later home to two of Tennessee's most colorful governors, brothers Bob and Alf Taylor, who actually ran against each other for governor in the famous "War of the Roses" in 1886.

In 1894 the Southern Railway acquired the old Knoxville and Virginia line, introducing a fifteen-year period of change that substantially altered the local urban landscape. In 1903 the federal government established the U.S. Soldier's Home (later known as Mountain Home), a retirement home and medical center for former Union soldiers of the Civil War. This 447-acre complex of thirty-six beautiful Renaissance Revival buildings, most of which were designed by New York architect J. H. Freelander, became a branch of the Veterans' Administration in 1930. It lies at the southern outskirts of town at the intersection of West Market Street (U.S. 11E/321) and State of Franklin Road. With a capacity of at least thirty-five-hundred patients, the hospital and retirement complex created many new jobs and bought tons of foodstuffs from the surrounding countryside. The WPA writer who visited the home in the late 1930s called Mountain Home "a city within a city" with a post office, "its own fire and police departments, waterworks, and telephone system" (*WPA Guide,* 323). As Johnson City has expanded around Mountain Home, this once rural retreat became an urban oasis for those who walk and jog among its beautiful buildings and landscaped grounds. The Medical School of East Tennessee State University is also located at Mountain Home.

The construction of the Clinchfield Railroad through town in 1908–9 continued the transformation of Johnson City into an Appalachian industrial center. Railroad shops provided more jobs, while factories located here to take advantage of the accessibility of raw materials via the Clinchfield system and the ability to ship their products via the Southern Railway. As a key railroad junction, Johnson City had the necessary transportation infrastructure to sustain long-term industrial and commercial growth. The city even had its own resident capitalist, the Clinchfield Railroad's George L. Carter, who built a home in the new Southside neighborhood in 1909. An investor in local industry, commerce, and real estate, Carter kept his business office in Johnson City until the early 1920s.

Prairie-style house, 714 Locust, Johnson City. The neighborhood adjacent to the new East Tennessee Normal School had several homes featuring the latest styles in domestic architecture.

At the same time the Clinchfield arrived in town, the new campus of the East Tennessee State Normal School was under construction on land south of the tracks donated by local businessmen and George L. Carter. Established by the General Education Act of 1909, the normal school opened its doors in 1911. A generation later, it became East Tennessee State Teachers College, and during the 1960s the school acquired the status of a full-fledged university. The well-maintained and landscaped historic core of campus reflects Classical Revival architecture, which was popular among college buildings in Tennessee constructed in the 1910s and 1920s. Of particular note are Alexander Hall, Lamb Hall, the Administration Building, and the B. Carroll Reece Museum, which interprets regional history and fine arts.

Directly east of campus, bounded by West Maple Street, Roan Street, and University Parkway, is the Southside neighborhood, which contains an excellent sampling of domestic architectural styles popular fifty to eighty years ago. The layout of the neighborhood, first known as the Southwest Addition, has been attributed to Clinchfield company architects, since the circular nature of the plan has much in common with the railroad's town plan for Kingsport. Representative homes include an American Four-Square house at 600 West Pine together with a very popular variation of Colonial Revival style at 614 West Pine. At 714 West Locust is a rare Tennessee example of the Prairie style, an archi-

TENNESSEE'S HISTORIC LANDSCAPE

tectural movement influenced by the work of Frank Lloyd Wright. The **Montrose Apartments** (1922), designed by architect D. B. Beeson Sr. in the Tudor Revival style, are at 701 West Locust. Bungalows abound throughout the neighborhood, while at 1107 Southwest Avenue stands a strikingly modernist design that combines elements of both International and Art Moderne architecture (all houses are private, no access).

Erwin, fourteen miles south on Interstate Highway 181, is the last of the major Clinchfield towns in Tennessee. The railroad shaped life here more so than at Kingsport and Johnson City. Erwin was a major division point for the Clinchfield, and even today the CSX Railroad uses the old Clinchfield yards for sorting out traffic before it crosses the Appalachian Mountains. Erwin's **Clinchfield Depot** (1925) is a combination of Craftsman and Classical Revival styles. Adjacent is the former Clinchfield central office (1925, with third story added in circa 1940). There are also the railroad shops, roundhouses, and support buildings characteristic of a large division point (private, no access).

Clinchfield officials dreamed of creating a model industrial village in the Appalachian Mountains. In 1916 they established a land company named the Holston Corporation and hired New York architect Grosvenor Atterbury to develop a Garden City–like residential town plan, complete with designs for model homes. Like Nolen in Kingsport, Atterbury blended his curving streets and irregularly shaped lots into the street grid that already existed, creating a unique small-town environment. He also designed four basic house plans from which approximately fifty homes were constructed. In his 1919 Holston Company pamphlet about the new town plan, Lawrence Veiller, secretary of the National Housing Association, concluded that "this development at Erwin is especially significant as showing the possibilities of well-ordered, harmonious and attractive designing in the development of what is ordinarily so sordid a thing as a new railroad shop settlement." But the railroad's experiment in model housing only lasted for a brief time. The Holston Corporation sold thirty-seven houses of the Atterbury development to Southern Potteries, Inc., for use as company housing in September 1920. The 600 block of Holston Place, together with the 300, 500, and 600 blocks of Ohio Avenue, provide good examples of Atterbury's work (all houses are private, no access).

In the history of Erwin, Southern Potteries played a role similar to that of Tennessee Eastman in Kingsport. For forty years, the company was the town's primary industry—employing as many as one thousand workers—until closing its doors in 1957. The company specialized in producing hand-painted chinaware; most of the work was done by women, following a process developed by Charles W. Foreman, who had purchased the factory in 1922. Its most popular product was its "Blue Ridge" dinnerware, which was sold throughout the country. North of Erwin, at the National Fish Hatchery, is the former **Superintendent's House** (circa 1892), now home to the Unicoi County Heritage Museum. Here the Blue Ridge Pottery Club displays a representative collection of the different items created by Southern Potteries.

The next section of our visit to industrial Appalachia begins at Norris, almost due west of Erwin. The best route is to go west on I-181 for twenty-eight miles to its junction with I-81. The interstate runs south for fifty-seven miles where it meets I-40, which continues for thirty-six miles to Knoxville. After turning north on I-75, drive twenty-four miles to the exit for Norris.

Route B: The Engineered Landscape

This route begins at Norris on U.S. 441 and on Tennessee Highway 61 and continues to Oak Ridge on Tennessee Highways 61/95.

Upper East Tennessee is the administrative—and many would say the spiritual—heart of the Tennessee Valley Authority. A small program within the context of Franklin D. Roosevelt's New Deal, TVA has reordered the Tennessee landscape as has no other act of the federal government since early Indian treaties that opened land for settlement. As historian Dewey Grantham pointed out, the agency created a new "landscape of well-designed dams and buildings, improved agriculture, and scenic value based on a chain of lakes with clear blue water and large areas of green forest" (Hargrove and Conkin, 330).

That new landscape began at Norris Dam, located twenty-five miles north of Knoxville on U.S. Highway 441, which TVA also built as the Norris Parkway, a modern scenic highway that connected its two administrative centers. The dam complex features several scenic overlooks and a visitor center. Designed from original plans from the federal Bureau of Reclamation, as adapted by TVA's chief designer, Roland Wank, the Norris Dam site "set an example of coordinated expression that was never again equaled," concluded historian Walter Creese (169). The dam and powerhouse complex (1934–36) proclaimed functionality wherever one looked but did so in a modernist fashion that also conveyed a sense of monumentality rarely achieved in American public architecture. To intellectuals of that time, the new TVA landscape spoke directly to future of America. The economist Stuart Chase wrote:

> To look at the clean, strong walls of Norris Dam between the hills of pine, to feel the will of achievement, the deep integrity of a thousand young-minded men and women, schooled in the disciplines of science, free from the dreary business of chiseling competitors and advertising soap; to realize that resources are building rather than declining and that the continent is being refreshed; to know that, over the whole great valley from the Smokies to the Ohio, men's faces turn to a common purpose and a common goal—intoxicates the imagination. Here, struggling in embryo, is perhaps the promise of what all America will someday be. (Creese, 178)

The promise of the engineered landscape intoxicated many Americans during the middle decades of this century. Besides the dam, powerhouse, parkway, and recreation areas, the Norris landscape included a village designed to house the project's many temporary workers in addition to residents who stayed after the dam was finished. The town site, designed by Tracy B. Auger and his staff, embraced some forty-two hundred acres, and only about one-fourth of that amount was used for homes and related community buildings. Central to the village plan was a two-story Colonial Revival school, staffed by TVA personnel, that proved to be one of the project's lasting institutions. TVA strove to maintain a rustic setting for its modern village by maintaining reserved greenbelt areas to the north and south of town and by keeping as many original trees on individual lots as possible. The initial houses expressed the contradiction of introducing modernity into the agrarian world of Clinch Valley. Simple shingle cottages conveyed a rustic quality at the same time that 130 cinderblock houses spoke to the technological experiment embodied in the TVA project.

When it was completed in the spring of 1935, architects and planners proclaimed the many virtues of Norris Village: its all-electric buildings, its varied community facilities, and its natural rural setting that evoked the best ideas of Garden City planning. But the village had cost twice what TVA had originally estimated. And it pandered to southern racism by not allowing African Americans to reside there, even though the races often lived side by side throughout the region. Eventually it

Norris Dam, before and after construction, 1937. TVA transformed the East Tennessee landscape with its series of huge dams and reservoirs. (Photograph by June Dorman)

evolved into little more than a TVA suburb for agency employees; it became more of a demonstration town than the model village its planners had envisioned.

By 1948 the federal government finally balked at the annual subsidy given to the village. TVA was given little choice but to get out of the town-planning business, and on June 15, 1948, it sold the village to a private company. The agency surrendered, according to historians Michael McDonald and John Muldowney, "another opportunity to formulate, coordinate, and execute a workable grass-roots policy which would have truly benefited residents of the Norris Basin" (235).

Norris represented a composite of what was perceived as America's best in architecture, engineering, and landscape architecture. But it proved to be a model that few other TVA projects ever came close to matching, perhaps because the idealism and hope of the initial New Deal years quickly dissolved into a bureaucratic mind-set that emphasized power and efficiency over the ideas of reform and renewal that had initially propelled the agency into action.

To many people in the Clinch River Valley, of course, TVA was more an agent of destruction than an accepted prophet of modernism. As TVA condemned their land and demolished their towns, it stripped away the physical environment that gave residents their very identity. Many farmers fought back the best way they could. Perhaps the most famous act of defiance came from William H. Hawkins, who owned the actual site for Norris Dam. When TVA officials came to speak to him, he lit a circle of brush around his house and burned it to the ground. TVA dams did more than destroy the homeplaces of Clinch residents; they destroyed the fabric of community by demolishing or relocating local churches and cemeteries. Those dispossessed of their land, especially the older residents of the valley, often had difficulty sustaining a sense of family and community in their new homes. The power and importance of one's sense of place was never understood by the engineers, social experts, and architects that created the engineered landscape.

Twenty miles southwest of Norris on Tennessee Highways 61/95 is Oak Ridge, another government attempt to establish an instant town to house workers for a technologically advanced federal project. Between the two modern towns is the historic trade center of Clinton, the seat of government for Anderson County. Downtown Clinton has a historic railroad depot and the Ritz Theater, a striking Art Moderne building that stands across from the Anderson County Courthouse (1967). In 1956 the effort to desegregate the state public school system began in

K-25 plant, Oak Ridge. The largest building of this huge engineering complex to create an atomic bomb. (Courtesy of Tennessee State Library and Archives, Beard Papers, Tennessee Historical Society Collection)

earnest in Clinton, and the following year Bobby Cain became the first African American to graduate from a white public high school in Tennessee. Unfortunately, in October 1958, segregationists blew up the local high school, a terrorist action that only managed to impede the integration of local schools.

Although linked by their early reliance on the federal government, the history of **Oak Ridge** differs from that of Norris in many ways. Oak Ridge was much larger, with eighty thousand people at its peak; its dwellings, apartments, and shopping centers embraced modernist designs from the firm of Skidmore, Ownings, and Merrill; its function was purely military—to produce fuel for an atomic bomb—with not a tint of reform; and it was a secret place. As the "city behind a fence," dignitaries and journalists were not invited to come to Oak Ridge and praise its virtues until well after World War II. Even today visitors cannot freely drive around many of the industrial properties; security checkpoints are everywhere. But the American Museum of Science and Energy at 300 South Tulane in downtown Oak Ridge, the Graphite Reactor historic site, and the interpretive overlooks at the major facilities allow the visitor to grasp the size and complexity of this engineered landscape.

In the fall of 1942, military officials sealed off the Oak Ridge Army

Reservation—fifty-six thousand acres, including most of the Bethel Valley north of the Clinch River—from unauthorized contact from the outside world. Here would take place some of the key experiments behind the ultra top-secret "Manhattan Project" to build an atomic bomb. Even TVA leaders knew little about Oak Ridge, except that suddenly an entity called the Clinton Engineering Works was requesting huge amounts of electricity from TVA hydroelectric dams. The first facility completed at Oak Ridge—named K-25—was the plant where uranium could be processed by gaseous diffusion, and it was located at the northwest corner of the military reservation. Tennessee Highway 58, twelve miles south of Oak Ridge, has an interpretive overlook of the plant. K-25 was bigger than any building ever conceived in Tennessee. Covering 44 acres, its U-shape was 2,450 feet long, about the length of eight football fields placed end to end. Designed by the Kellex Corporation of New York City, the building had no style, but it was a monument to expediency and ruthless technological efficiency. These same qualities characterized the electromagnetic plant—or Y-12—where 170 different buildings were scattered over a factory complex of more than 500 acres along Bear Creek Road. The thermal diffusion plant—called S-50—was another mammoth complex of buildings, pipes, and electrical wires. It had 160 buildings located on 150 acres, but it was not operational in time to contribute much to the effort of building the atomic bomb.

The smallest facility, however, was the most important. **X-10** stood for the Graphite Reactor, the world's oldest nuclear reactor, which is among Tennessee's initial National Historic Landmarks. In early 1944, scientists produced the world's first grams of plutonium, the enriched uranium used to make atomic bombs, at X-10. After the war, it was used for nuclear experiments, produced isotopes for medical research, and paved the way for nuclear-powered electricity plants. Weekday tours of the reactor, which has been decommissioned since 1963, are available at the Oak Ridge National Laboratory on Bethel Valley Road.

The different plants for enriching uranium were only one part of the Clinton Engineering Works. Mammoth factories required tens of thousands of workers, who in turn required thousands of others to provide necessary services and security. Building an atomic bomb demanded an "atomic city" as quickly as possible. "Not since the days of our pioneering forefathers has a group of people had within their grasp an opportunity such as is offered the residents of Oak Ridge," challenged town manager Capt. P. E. O'Meara in 1943. "Most of us have never before, or will never again be in a position to build our own community—

to our own specifications. Most of us have never been confronted with such responsibility" (Johnson and Jackson, 35).

The government acquired its first land in the fall of 1942, and by February 1943 it had accepted the town plan prepared by the Boston architectural firm of Skidmore, Ownings, and Merrill. Oak Ridge was the firm's first major commission, and from this beginning SOM, as it is known in architectural circles, evolved into the world's largest architectural firm. With John Merrill as primary designer, SOM's town plan was unlike those typically found at military bases. It utilized the natural contours of the Clinch River uplands; its curved streets and hillside terraces created a town that, on paper at least, could be an appealing urban landscape.

The initial homes at Oak Ridge were quite consciously unlike those at earlier federal projects like Norris or Cumberland Homesteads. They were definitely modern—some would say unadorned—following the precepts of the "International school" of architecture rather than the rustic-vernacular styles found at Norris and Cumberland Homesteads. The different design was due, in part, to SOM's own leaning toward modern architecture and, in part, to the cost ceiling per unit placed on all military housing. Perhaps the most crucial factor was time: these homes were needed immediately, so the architects turned to new ideas about the relationship between mass production, design, and materials. A rustic cottage that demanded considerable labor and time was really out of the question.

In the first months of Oak Ridge's development—when military planners envisioned a town of only thirteen thousand—Skidmore, Ownings, and Merrill experimented with new building materials. The best homes were single-family homes of varying sizes built with cemesto, a fiberboard material that had cement and asbestos bonded to each side for insulation and fire protection. Some people were housed in trailers, while others lived in the most rudimentary dwellings, which were called "hutments"—sixteen-foot-square buildings where four to six people could live. These were often the few places where African Americans could find space to live at the Clinton Engineering Works. Still more workers lived in dormitories or apartments. Today the historic neighborhoods of Oak Ridge are between Tennessee Avenue and Outer Avenue to the north, and north-south streets connect the two avenues.

The well-laid plans of the architects and the corps of engineers, however, came apart as the nonstop demand for more and more workers overwhelmed the town plan. For example, in the original SOM plan the major commercial center of Oak Ridge was to be "Towncenter," later known as Jackson Square, with fifteen to twenty stores and a guest house, known as Alexander Inn (private, open access). But by 1945, 165 retail stores were operating within the complex. That spring, military officials estimated that eighty thousand lived in or worked at Oak Ridge. To meet the unrelenting demand for more housing, officials turned first to "flattops"—prefab houses made of plywood glued to a wooden frame with a canvas roof—a portable housing type perfected by TVA at some of its construction camps. Next came the TDU, or temporary dwelling unit, that had been moved from other federal projects as far away as LaPonte, Indiana. Finally, there were "Victory cottages," little more than plywood shacks with roll roofing that were expected to survive the elements as long as the war and no more.

Oak Ridge remained under military control until 1947 when it was placed under the newly established Atomic Energy Commission. Two years later, its fences and gates came down. Oak Ridge was no longer the city behind the fence, but it remained closely tied to nuclear and other scientific experiments that occurred at the massive plants. In the 1950s the Atomic Energy Commission slowly divested itself of control over the city's destiny; June 4, 1960, was the official independence day. Yet, twenty years later, historians Charles W. Johnson and Charles O. Jackson discovered that "Oak Ridge has not become a typical community . . . because residents have refused to define it as such." They "have continued to understand the town as somehow a very different and exceptional place in which to live" (206). There remains no other landscape like it in Tennessee.

To get to the next landscape in this chapter, take Tennessee 62 from Oak Ridge for twenty-five miles to Knoxville to U.S. Highway 129 and go south for seventeen miles to Maryville.

Landscape 7: The Conservation Landscape

Great Smoky Mountains National Park

> *Always enwrapped in the illusory mists, always touching the evasive clouds, the peaks of the Great Smoky Mountains are like some barren ideal, that has bartered for the vague isolations of a higher atmosphere the material values of the warm world below. Upon these mighty and*

majestic domes no tree strikes root, no hearth is alight;
humanity is an alien thing, and utility set at naught. Below,
dense forests cover the massive, precipitous slopes of the
range, and in the midst of the wilderness a clearing shows,
here and there, and the roof of a humble log cabin; in the
valley, far, far lower still, a red spark at dusk may have
suggested a home, nestling in the cove.

Charles Egbert Craddock
(pen name of Mary Noailles Murfree), 1885

The Great Smoky Mountains National Park, with its forests, mountains, and wildlife, is a prized Appalachian landscape, adored for its preservation of a natural and cultural world once thought lost. Tennessee has two popular approaches to the park. U.S. 129 south of Knoxville goes to Maryville, where it intersects U.S. 321 and continues to Townsend. U.S. 441, accessible from Interstate 40 at exit 407 via Tennessee 66, passes through Sevierville before entering the park at its most popular Tennessee gateway, the town of Gatlinburg.

The Great Smoky Mountains constitute a conservation landscape, one deliberately created in the late 1920s and early 1930s to save the forests from the voracious appetite of the timber industry. At the same time, the creation of this landscape established a recreational playground for those who wanted to experience life in the backwoods and produced new economic opportunities through tourism.

Only seventy years ago, two-thirds of the Great Smokies were devastated, logged-out mountain land. The best way to explore the impact of the logging industry is to approach the national park on U.S. 321 between Maryville and Townsend. Signs mark U.S. 321 as the Lamar Alexander Parkway. Alexander, a native of Maryville, was governor of Tennessee from 1979 to 1987. He later served as president of the University of Tennessee and as U.S. Secretary of Education.

In 1900 Maryville was the medium-sized, prosperous seat of government of Blount County. It was home to **Maryville College** (1819), a well-respected private institution that was among the first southern schools to open its doors to African Americans, Native Americans, and women. Most of its historic campus was built 75 to 125 years ago, including such notable buildings as the Second Empire–style **Anderson Hall** (built with funds from northern capitalists and the Freedman's

Bureau in 1869), the Georgian Revival **Carnegie Hall** (1917), and the Romanesque-style **Fayerweather Science Hall** (1898).

Then, in 1901, a group of Pennsylvania capitalists formed the Little River Lumber Company and chartered a new railroad spur line to run from Maryville into the Great Smokies where they could exploit the great virgin forests with the latest in modern technology. U.S. 321 follows the old railroad route along the Little River from Maryville to the park's eastern boundary. The company created a new town called Townsend, named for general manager W. B. Townsend, where it erected a huge sawmill complex, which could easily handle thirty thousand board feet every day. Halfway between Maryville and Townsend stood the railroad town of Walland, the future home of the Schlosser Leather Company, a large tannery that processed raw hides shipped from South America.

As the rail junction for these new industries, Maryville prospered as never before. The Blount County Courthouse (1906) is a grand Classical Revival building, designed by Baumann and Baumann of Knoxville, that overlooks the town. It is a monument to these years of rapid growth. Other remnants of the town's early-twentieth-century boom are the **Indiana Avenue historic district** and the **Southern Railroad Freight Depot** between U.S. 411 and Washington Avenue.

The amount of lumber carved out of the mountains over the next three decades was stupendous. In May 1905, for example, the Townsend mills shipped out two million board feet. Three years later, the company had extended its railroad eighteen miles into the mountains from Townsend; by 1923 the accessible timber along the once virgin forests of the East Prong of the Little River was gone. As the company shifted its attention to the river's Middle Prong, production rarely slacked at the Townsend mills, with an average of twenty-two million board feet produced annually. The Great Smoky Mountains Natural History Association has established a marked auto tour of some of the Middle Prong logging sites that ends at the location of the old company town of Tremont; the tour pamphlet can be obtained at the community museum in Townsend or at park visitor centers.

By the late 1920s, the easily exploitable and valuable timber in the Great Smokies had nearly disappeared. Lumber company officials struck an agreement with conservation groups and regional businessmen who wanted to carve a national park out of the mountains. In exchange for selling its vast landholdings within the proposed park, the company could continue cutting timber for fifteen years. In 1939 the

Oliver Cabin, Cades Cove. Single-pen log cabins were once common-place elements of Tennessee's agrarian landscape.

Little River Lumber Company ceased operations after taking an esti-mated 560 million board feet of largely virgin timber out of the moun-tains. Others have estimated that the Little River Lumber Company, to-gether with smaller companies, took at least one billion board feet from the Great Smokies. Since logging during this period almost always in-volved clear-cutting, many of the beautiful trees that can now be seen in the southern half of the Great Smokies are second-growth trees—a product, like the park itself, of the twentieth century.

The old lumber town of Townsend is the best entrance to the ru-ral community of **Cades Cove,** one of the most interesting historic landscapes in the southern Appalachians. Cades Cove purports to pre-serve and interpret a nineteenth-century rural landscape before indus-trialization and modernization forever changed life in the Appalachians. Yet, Cades Cove too is a landscape of the mid-twentieth century: in pre-serving the farmsteads, the National Park Service sometimes moved and grouped buildings together, as at Cable Mill, that originally stood miles apart. It reconstructed others, including the often-photographed canti-lever barn at Tipton Place, and tore down box-construction outbuild-ings and frame dwellings that did not reflect the log architecture theme that the park service considered worthy of preservation.

Ironically, the first cabin the traveler encounters along this route to the park once belonged to descendants of John Oliver, who fought tenaciously to keep the National Park Service from claiming Cades Coves. Oliver was like many in the Cove: he wanted conservation and was not adverse to creating a national park, but he saw no reason why the financial benefits of tourism and road development should not accrue to the historic residents of the place. In late 1926 and early 1927, Knoxville businessmen, politicians, and conservation activists reassured Cades Cove residents that the national park would never take their homes, even though these leaders knew otherwise. The provisions of the Tennessee park bill set aside $1.5 million for land acquisition and granted the park commission the power of eminent domain to seize the property of those unwilling to sell, as long as owners were given "fair value" for their land.

After a Rockefeller family foundation donated $5 million for land acquisition in 1928, pressure on Cove residents to sell their land increased. Some succumbed and sold; others became more determined to stay. John Oliver discovered that it was "extremely difficult to articulate to outsiders the importance of place in the lives of ordinary cove people" (Dunn, 248). In 1929 he decided to fight eminent domain through the courts, but three years of trials and appeals amounted to nothing except a settlement of $10,650 for his property.

In December 1935 only twenty-five families remained at Cades Cove, and that month they received notice to leave no later than January 1, 1936. Park officials tore down unwanted dwellings, and once carefully nurtured fields soon turned to wilderness. John Oliver, however, stayed until Christmas Day 1937, leaving behind an almost alien place in light of all the missing homes, farm buildings, fences, and families. "The single guiding principle" to the so-called preservation of Cades Cove, concluded historian Durwood Dunn, "was that anything which might remotely suggest progress or advancement beyond the most primitive stages should be destroyed. A sort of pioneer primitivism alone survived in the cove structures left standing" (256).

This landscape of twentieth-century conservation, however, serves as one way of identifying types of vernacular buildings that once dominated the rural Tennessee landscape (see sidebar entitled "Common House Plans," Landscape 5, this chapter). Good examples of log dwellings, cribs, barns, fences, and other structures exist throughout Cades Cove. As the recent research of geographer John Morgan has demonstrated, the tradition of log architecture remained strong in Blount County until 1880. After 1880 the availability of portable, steam-powered circular sawmills, combined with the accessibility of new building materials from the railroads and the new techniques of balloon-frame construction, led to the rapid abandonment of log architecture. It became faster, easier, and more stylish to build frame houses. The Henry Whitehead place at Cades Cove, however, shows how refined log construction remained popular here as late as 1898.

The farmhouse is only one part of the vernacular landscape. At Cades Cove, both Tipton Place and Cable Mill have cantilever, or forebay, barns. A huge overhanging loft, usually resting on two log cribs, defines the structure. Representing an original American form of log construction, cantilever barns, according to Marian Moffett and Lawrence Wodehouse, "stand out as original vernacular forms, dramatic and unexpectedly elegant, particularly when their rough-hewn material and very basic construction techniques are considered" (xv). A recent survey located 316 cantilever barns still standing, most of them in Blount and Sevier Counties adjacent to the national park.

More common, however, are the single-crib barn (often used as a corn crib) and the double-pen barn, in which the two cribs are connected with a common gable roof. Again, the farmstead at Cable Mill has a good example of the double-pen barn. The four-crib barn is the largest log outbuilding found in the region. These structures have a log crib at each corner, with a huge gable roof that creates a large hay loft. Log smokehouses and springhouses are also common on Tennessee farms that date from the nineteenth century. The smokehouse is typically immediately behind the dwelling; the springhouse is located over the nearest source of water and was used for the cooling of milk and other foods as well as for a water supply (see sidebar entitled "Common Farm Outbuildings," Landscape 13, chapter 5).

Fences and fields are also part of the vernacular landscape. Today wire fences are found everywhere, but in Cades Cove and other sections of the park, along with the Blue Ridge Parkway, there are such nineteenth-century log fence types as the "snake," the post-and-rail, and the buck or reindeer fence. Stone fences are also found in this region, but are more common in Middle Tennessee. Irregular is the best way to define the shape of most fields in Tennessee. "As land was claimed, surveyed, and settled," explains geographer John Reheder, "the result was a complex pattern that appeared much like a crazy-quilt blanketing the surface. The nineteenth-century landscape was characterized by property boundaries marked by fences and tree lines, irregular shapes of agricultural fields, and a network of trails and secondary roads that linked the holdings" (101). The secondary roads of Tennessee still reveal the settlement patterns of our forefathers.

The second and certainly most popular approach to the Great Smoky Mountains National Park is from Sevierville via U.S. Highway 441. In its downtown historic district and courthouse, Sevierville retains the appearance of a late-nineteenth-century county seat. The **Sevier County Courthouse** (1895–96), designed by the McDonald Brothers architectural firm of Louisville, is one of the best examples in the state of late Victorian eclecticism. Another area that documents the town's late Victorian growth is Cedar Street. The **Trotter-Waters House** (1895) at 217 Cedar is a restored Queen Anne dwelling (private, limited access). Dr. A. W. Trotter, the original home owner, was instrumental in the creation of Murphy College, a private school that operated from 1890 until the Depression. Its Eastlake-influenced brick building (1890) stands across the street. Next door is the town's 1930s Colonial Revival public school.

Closer to the park on U.S. Highway 441, visitors are literally inundated with tourist attractions. Pigeon Forge was once a small mountain community. The **Pigeon Forge Mill** (1830) marks those early years. Little more, however, has survived the onslaught of chain motels, restaurants, gas stations, and theme parks. The popularity of "Dollywood," owned by Sevier County's own Dolly Parton, is rivaled by the many outlet malls. Both places are probably as popular as the park itself. The many shops and stores—perhaps a dream come true for those who love to study roadside architecture—continue to Gatlinburg, the western gateway to the Great Smokies. This landscape of American commercialism at its best (or at its worst, depending on the visitor's point of view) would have shocked the conservationists who wanted the national park seventy years ago, but it is exactly what the other half of the park's supporters—the politicians and East Tennessee businessmen—wanted as they agitated for the national park.

The creation of the Great Smoky Mountains National Park was like other reform initiatives of the 1920s: conservation progressives pushed it according to one agenda of change and reform while business progressives lobbied for it according to a quite different view of the future. Businessmen, and their political allies in state and local government, saw the park and the later Blue Ridge Parkway as ideal ways of improving the region's standard of living through tourism and new road development. Gatlinburg in the late 1930s, for example, had only three hotels and three museums. Moreover, Gatlinburg featured such institutions as the Arrowmont School, sponsored by Pi Beta Phi sorority for over seventy years as a way of encouraging traditional handicrafts and folk art. The Arrowmont School of Arts and Crafts still displays and sells regional crafts on U.S. 441 in downtown Gatlinburg. But since the dedication of the national park in September 1940, once tiny towns, including Townsend, Gatlinburg, and Pigeon Forge, have changed drastically to meet the needs of the millions of tourists who visit the region every year.

From Gatlinburg, U.S. 441 divides the park in two as it crosses the Appalachian Mountains. The park headquarters is at Sugarlands, two miles from Gatlinburg. The park headquarters provides information about the many natural and historic landscapes within the Great Smokies. The highway then scales the mountains, crossing the Appalachian Trail at Newfound Gap (5,048 feet high) where the visitor may travel along the spine of the Appalachians to Clingman's Dome, the highest point in Tennessee at 6,643 feet. Another area of the Tennessee side of the Smokies worth exploring is the Roaring Fork Motor Natural Trail (outside of Gatlinburg) where a historic district preserves several historic farms and buildings associated with the old **Roaring Fork community.**

The landscapes described in the next chapter begin about sixty-five miles to the southwest at the town of Vonore. Return to Maryville on U.S. Highway 321 and then take U.S. 411 southwest for twenty miles to Vonore.

CHAPTER FOUR

The Great Valley of Tennessee

The Tennessee River, observed the Southern Agrarian writer Donald Davidson, was once "provokingly beautiful and powerful, yet stubbornly unwilling to bear man's yoke and carry his burdens." But modern times "decided that this untamed river creature should become, of all the rivers of the world, the one most deftly chained, the one most thoroughly subdued to man's designing will." The locks, dams, and reservoirs of modern engineering changed the river into a "civil and obliging stream. One flick of a switch by the tenderest human finger, and the Tennessee is any man's obedient slave, though he be a thousand miles away" (Davidson, 15, 17). As it flows from Knoxville southward to its Great Bend at Chattanooga, the Tennessee River—except for a brief section between Watts Bar Dam and the mouth of the Hiwassee River—is an engineered landscape of dams and reservoirs as much as it is a natural landscape of flowing water, riverbanks, and islands. Humans have redesigned its major tributaries, the Little Tennessee, Clinch, and Hiwassee Rivers, to be part of this engineered landscape. Engineers did not "tame" nature; rather, they destroyed it and then replaced it with a technological system they could actually control.

Rivers and mountains set the boundaries for the great fertile land mass we know as the Great Valley of Tennessee. This chapter concerns the southern half of the valley, roughly between Knoxville and Chattanooga. In this region, the Tennessee River defines the western border and rugged Appalachian peaks define the east. To the north is the Little Tennessee River and its confluence with the Tennessee, while the torturous course of the Ocoee River Gorge and the Great Bend of the Tennessee lie to the south. In between these natural boundaries is a wide, fertile valley where the most productive farmland of antebellum East Tennessee could be found. McMinn County, in fact, was a prosperous cotton-producing area before the Civil War.

For centuries, people have lived, thrived, and died in this valley. Seven hundred years ago at Hiwassee Island, where the Tennessee and Hiwassee Rivers meet in southern Meigs County, stood a great village of the Mississippian culture. Rebuilt at least eight times to serve the different needs of its residents, the ceremonial buildings arranged on mounds overlooking a central plaza created a place of mystery, renewal, and commerce.

At the time of the fur trade between the Cherokees and the English colonists on the East Coast, the Little Tennessee River was the physical and spiritual heart of the Cherokee nation. The Cherokees remained in control of large sections of the southern Tennessee River Valley until treaties in 1819 and 1835 eventually forced their removal from Tennessee soil. The infamous Trail of Tears overland trek to the Indian Territory of present-day Oklahoma began in the state's southeast corner. Once the Cherokees—the first farmers of the region—were pushed out, white settlers eagerly grabbed the land for their own farms. Further, they divided the land into a new political landscape defined by county lines and rectangular town grids.

Railroads and then copper mining added an industrial overlay to the valley landscape during the mid-1800s. The East Tennessee and Georgia Railroad passed through the center of the valley. Copper mines began to reshape the very look of the land at Ducktown and Copperhill. At the turn of the century came the tracks of the Louisville and Nashville Railroad to define a second valley railroad corridor within the shadows of the Appalachian Mountains. At the same time, the timber industry came to exploit the rich timberland of the Unaka Mountain range. Thirty years later, the Tennessee Valley Authority transformed the rivers as only modern technology could: it built dams at Fort Loudoun, Tellico, and Chickamauga and then added the huge concrete cooling towers of nuclear power plants at Watts Bar Dam and Sequoyah.

These different landscapes—built by Native Americans, early settlers, gilded-age industrialists, and modern social and civil engineers—still define the sense of place and history in the southern valley of the Tennessee.

Landscape 8: The Land of the Cherokees

The Cherokees, or *Ani-Yunwiya*—the Principal People—never occupied more than small areas in East Tennessee, but no Native-American tribe exercised more influence on Tennessee history than the group known as the Overhill Cherokees who lived along the region's river valleys. Three hundred years ago, small groups of Overhill Cherokee lived along the Hiwassee and Tellico Rivers, but most resided in the Little Tennessee River Valley, east of present-day Vonore. Here was beautiful country, rich in game with fertile land for corn and other vegetable crops. Today, however, the Cherokee landscape of the Little Tennessee Valley can be experienced in only an indirect way. In 1979 the Tennessee Valley Authority closed the gates on its Tellico Dam, flooding most of the ancient Cherokee places. At historic sites such as Fort Loudoun, Tellico Blockhouse, Sequoyah Birthplace Museum, and the paved two-lane drive from Fort Loudoun east along the reservoir, there are still deer and other wild game, the river routes, and the scenic beauty that brought the Cherokees here hundreds of years ago.

Route A: The Little Tennessee River Valley

Immediately east of U.S. Highway 411 at Vonroe, on the Citico Road, are three historic sites—**Fort Loudoun, Tellico Blockhouse,** and the Sequoyah Birthplace Museum—that document in different ways the intimate relationship between the Cherokee Indians and the Little Tennessee Valley.

Although the first contacts date from at least 1673, regular trade between the Cherokees and colonial fur traders did not begin in earnest until the early 1700s. By 1707 the colony of South Carolina approved formal trade regulations, and four years later the first colonial trader to reside among the Cherokees, Eleazar Wiggan, had settled at the village of Tanassee. Wiggan came primarily in search of deer skins—used then for military uniforms—and exchanged firearms, iron axes, knives, beads, mirrors, and rum for the prepared furs. The acquisition of firearms had an immediate impact on Cherokee culture as the new technology steadily increased the number of animals killed for the fur trade.

In 1725 Col. George Chicken, the superintendent of Indian Trade for South Carolina, visited the Overhill villages eager to convince the Cherokees to join hands with the British rather than the French. Within

Fort Loudoun, Monroe County. From this reconstructed fort, the visitor may see the abundant natural resources that attracted both Native Americans and white traders to this point on the Little Tennessee River.

the next five years, an English-Cherokee alliance became a reality, and the colonists recognized Moytoy of Great Tellico (at present-day Tellico Plains) as the primary Cherokee leader. The alliance held together through the next generation of the fur trade, although by the 1750s the center of Cherokee political life shifted northward, from Tellico Plains to the village of **Chota,** led by Old Hop, on the Little Tennessee River.

In order to secure their political and commercial dominance within the Cherokee tribe as a whole, the Overhill Cherokees as early as 1747 had asked British officials to build a permanent trading post or a fort in their territory. Nothing happened until the great rivalry between the British and French over the control of the North American empire evolved into the French and Indian War (or the Seven Years' War) of 1756 to 1763. In 1756 Virginia governor Francis Dinwiddie arranged a swap of a permanent Overhill fort for the assistance of six hundred Cherokee warriors on the Virginia frontier. This first post was a 105-foot square, with a four-foot-wide and two-foot-high earthen wall topped by a seven-foot-high log palisade. The colonists never garrisoned the post, and once they returned to Virginia the Cherokees soon burned the abandoned fort.

South Carolina officials built another fort later that year. Designed by engineer John William G. DeBrahm, the new post—named Fort Loudoun in honor of the Earl of Loudoun, who was then commander-in-chief of the British forces in North America—stood on the south side of the Little Tennessee River near its confluence with the Tellico River.

But DeBrahm and Capt. Raymond Demere, the commander of the South Carolina troops, soon clashed over almost every aspect of the fort's construction, from its location to its design. Demere sarcastically reported to South Carolina governor William Lyttelton that the Cherokees "call it the Fort to put Horses, Cows, and Hogs in, but I differ in opinion with them for it would not be sufficient" (Kelly, 80). DeBrahm had already left for Charleston when Demere and his soldiers first moved into the fort in early January 1757; not until late July would Demere consider the fort complete.

The reconstructed fort at Fort Loudoun today is based upon historical and archaeological research about the post that was occupied by the colonists in the summer of 1757. Inside the large log palisade were a row of barracks, a powder magazine, a blacksmith shop (that also served as a meeting house or chapel), two corn houses, a guardroom, and various storehouses. Officers usually had private dwellings built for themselves and their families. Early relations between the Cherokees and the soldiers were cordial. Cherokee women, for example, would exchange very desirable food items, such as fish, berries, and vegetables, for trade goods. The Native Americans also liked to visit with the soldiers, and they considered the outpost as much their territory as that of the English.

But by 1760 these friendly relations had given way to mutual suspicion and distrust. That spring, the Cherokees laid siege to Fort Loudoun and cut off outside supplies. On June 10, rations at the fort were reduced to a mere quart of corn for every three men; a month later, the last bread was eaten. As the heat of the summer overwhelmed the fort in early August 1760, a number of soldiers abandoned the fort, leaving the officers little choice but to surrender. On August 8, one hundred and sixty soldiers, with sixty women and children, abandoned Fort Loudoun and began the long overland march to South Carolina. A day later, near Tellico Plains, seven hundred Cherokee warriors launched a surprise attack on the retreating soldiers and their families, killing three officers, twenty-three soldiers, and three women. The rest were captured and whisked away to Cherokee villages, where a few were murdered but most were ransomed to either Virginia or South Carolina. The occupation of Fort Loudoun came to a brutal end. Today, a historical marker on Tennessee 39 records the area at Tellico Plains where the Cherokee attack took place.

Although the garrison and fort were lost in 1760, by that time Fort Loudoun had served its military mission of keeping the Cherokees from supporting the French in the early, decisive years of the war. Due to the area's strategic importance, the new United States government returned in 1794 to the confluence of the Little Tennessee and Tellico Rivers and established **Tellico Blockhouse** across from the site of Fort Loudoun. Tellico Lake left the blockhouse site untouched, and the Tennessee Valley Authority has developed the property into a historic archaeology park, with interpretation focused on the year 1799.

For protection from aggressive settlers, the dwindling number of Cherokees of the Little Tennessee Valley wanted to re-establish an alliance with the government. National government officials in Philadelphia, on the other hand, wanted a series of posts to "control" the Native Americans. In 1794 territorial governor William Blount agreed to Hanging Maw's request for a new federal post. Tellico Blockhouse, however, soon became more than a military fort. When Congress passed the Factory Act of 1795, it enacted an administration plan to "civilize" the Cherokees by maintaining federally controlled trading posts—or factories—where the Indians would receive fair exchange for their furs as well as learn agricultural techniques and mechanical skills needed in American culture.

The Tellico Blockhouse was one of two places where the government implemented the Factory Act, and this policy demanded close and at least open relations between the soldiers and the Cherokees. John McKee was the first Indian agent at Tellico; a later agent, Silas Dinsmoor, provided cotton cards, spinning wheels, looms, and cottonseed and taught the Cherokees how to spin and produce their own cloth. In return, the Indians provided food, furs, and other valuable items. In 1799 the Duke of Orleans (who would later become King Louis Philippe of France) remarked that the Cherokees "continually supply Tellico with game, eggs, fruits in season, etc. so that the Tellico market is always well stocked, and is certainly one of the best forts in the region. The availability of women makes it very pleasant for the soldiers. Just now there is an abundance of strawberries, which the women and girls bring in and sell at ninepence the gallon" (Tellico Blockhouse pamphlet, n.p.).

In 1805 federal officials and the Overhill Cherokee negotiated a new treaty at Tellico Blockhouse. The agreement, however, moved the federal agency south to the mouth of the Hiwassee River. In 1807 the government abandoned Tellico Blockhouse and moved its trading operations to the new center of the Cherokee nation.

Fort Loudoun and Tellico Blockhouse, of course, were places where colonists and later government employees came to shape the history of the Little Tennessee Valley. Another perspective on the early period of this land is presented at the adjacent Sequoyah Birthplace Museum, which is also on Citico Road east of U.S. Highway 411 at Vonroe. Named for Sequoyah (1776–1843), the creator of the Cherokee syllabary, the museum features artifacts from the salvage archaeological investigation of the Little Tennessee Valley and includes displays about Cherokee oral history and legends. The adjacent Cherokee Memorial holds the remains of eighteenth-century Cherokees who were excavated from villages sites before the gates closed on Tellico Dam in 1979.

From the museum, highway signs indicate a two-lane, paved road to the monuments for the old Cherokee villages of **Tanasi** and **Chota**. The road first passes the **Icehouse Bottom** site, where people first lived some eight thousand years ago and continued to return to this spot until recent times. Archaeologists found artifacts here dating from the early Archaic period (8000–6000 B.C.). The village site stood near rock outcroppings that contained easily accessible nodules of chert, perfect for making stone tools. Icehouse Bottom residents of the early Archaic period probably lived in simple shelters roofed with animal skins, tree bark, or cane matting, all locally available resources. Thousands of years later, residents during the Woodland period planted the first corn in the Little Tennessee Valley at about A.D. 400. They lived in larger homes, typically covered with cane matting, and cultivated sunflowers, squash, and marsh elder.

The road then passes the village sites of **Tomotley** and **Toqua**. Nine hundred years ago along the Little Tennessee River, residents had adapted to the way of life associated with the Mississippian period (A.D. 900 to 1600). According to anthropologist Jefferson Chapman, their villages featured earthen platform mounds—where temples, homes of the elites, and council buildings stood—arranged around open plazas. Common houses typically measured sixteen-by-sixteen feet; they were built of cut saplings placed in foundation trenches and then pulled over to form stable roofs. Walls were made of waddle and daub (a mixture of interlaced sticks, mud, and other natural binding agents), and the roof was covered with grass or bark. There were no interior walls and little furniture as we understand that word today. Rather, the Indians built sleeping benches around a central, rock-lined hearth.

Toqua was the location of one of the largest Mississippian villages, and before its destruction by the Tellico Reservoir, archaeologists excavated key areas within the village. The early-twentieth-century Toqua school stands near the old village site (private, no access). Scholars have focused on life at Toqua during the late Mississippian period (circa A.D. 1400–1500), or at about the time Columbus sailed to the New World. In 1400 Toqua covered 4.8 acres and had 250 to 300 permanent residents. A palisade with bastions spaced every 60 feet surrounded the village, while a large earthen mound dominated the interior. Constructed over a period of 250 to 300 years, the mound at its peak was 25 feet high and 154 feet wide. On top probably stood a large council building and a smaller residence for the chief. Members of the chief's family and other important tribal leaders were buried in tombs within the mound.

A somber monument to the different branches of the Cherokee tribe marks the approximate location of **Chota,** a key Overhill Cherokee town in the mid-1700s. Here, concluded Jefferson Chapman, "all social, political, and ceremonial life focused on the townhouse, summer pavilion, and plaza." The townhouse was perhaps the most important building because major tribal decisions and debates took place within its walls. Lt. Henry Timberlake, who visited the Cherokees in 1761–62, described the townhouse as shaped like "a sugar loaf," which was "raised with wood, and covered over with earth," giving it "the appearance of a small mountain at a little distance." Its extremely dark interior was like "an ancient amphitheatre" with a fire in the center where the head warriors were seated. (Chapman, 110, 115). The forty-eight-by-twenty-three-foot summer pavilion was a roofed open shed with benches; around the plaza stood the homes of the average tribal residents. Researchers have identified four types of Cherokee domestic architecture; the winter house was the most common. This single-post construction house could measure up to thirty feet in diameter and had waddle-and-daub walls, a central hearth, and a conical roof covered with grass or bark. As contacts between the English colonists and the Cherokee became more frequent, however, Cherokee domestic architecture changed to reflect the log construction techniques of the colonial fur traders and later settlers.

Route B: The Trail of Tears

There are reconstructed examples of Cherokee log buildings at **Red Clay State Historical Area,** which is twelve miles south of Cleveland on a side road off Tennessee Highway 60, just above the Tennessee-Georgia state line. Easy-to-see signs direct visitors to the park. From 1832 to 1838, Red Clay served as the center of Cherokee government.

Council House, Red Clay State Historical Area, Bradley County. The reconstructed village at Council Springs marks the beginning of the Trail of Tears in Tennessee.

Around the great Council Spring met the committee and council of the nation, as well as the Cherokee supreme court. Eleven general councils, some attended by five thousand Cherokees, gathered at this quiet, bucolic spot. Red Clay was the last eastern capital of the Cherokees before their forced removal on the Trail of Tears to Indian Territory in present-day Oklahoma. The historical area includes a museum, a reconstructed Cherokee farmstead and sleeping huts, and a reconstructed council house. The Council Spring still produces over four hundred thousand gallons of water every day.

The Trail of Tears—a National Historic Trail—begins here. In 1838 federal troops under the command of Gen. Winfield Scott began to gather Cherokee families for the westward trek, first forcing them into thirty-one stockades before transferring them to eleven internment camps, ten of which stood in Tennessee. Most of these were concentrated around the Hiwassee River town of Charleston, which is twenty-three miles north of Red Clay on U.S. Highway 11 at the northern end of Bradley County. Here stood the army headquarters, named Fort Cass, and seven internment camps that housed more than forty-eight hundred Cherokees in rather deplorable conditions.

Among the approximately thirteen thousand Cherokees forced westward, about twenty-eight hundred traveled by way of the Tennessee, Ohio, Mississippi, and Arkansas Rivers, beginning at **Ross's Landing** in present-day Chattanooga. But the rest traveled overland, crossing the Hiwassee to the village of Calhoun. Then they crossed Middle

Tennessee diagonally and headed for a Mississippi River crossing at Cape Girardeau, Missouri. A recent study of the trail concluded that "road conditions, illness, and the distress of winter, particularly in southern Illinois while detachments waited to cross the ice-choked Mississippi, made death a daily occurrence" (National Park Service, 10–11). As many as eight thousand Cherokees died on the overland trip, and they called the route *nunahi-dunda-dlo-hilu-i,* the trail where they cried.

In Tennessee, the northern overland route can be roughly followed today by taking Tennessee Highway 60 from Cleveland to its crossing of the Tennessee River at historic **Blythe Ferry** and continuing to Dayton. At Dayton, take the scenic route of Tennessee Highway 30 for sixty-three miles west to McMinnville. Next, get on U.S. Highway 70S, which closely follows segments of the original trail—especially in the Woodbury area, where a group of Cherokees once camped along the creek in front of the **Houston House**—until it reaches Murfreesboro. On U.S. Highway 41 south of town, some detachments camped at the historic Black Fox Camp Springs, an early Cherokee trade site now managed as a protected wetlands area. From here, it is possible to travel northwest on U.S. Highway 41 through Nashville to the **Port Royal State Historical Area** southeast of Clarksville where the trail crossed the Red River and headed into Kentucky.

Several historic properties, along with recently placed historical signs, mark the primary northern route from Charleston to Port Royal, Tennessee. Such key points as Red Clay, Fort Cass, Blythe Ferry, the Houston House, Black Fox Camp Springs, and Port Royal have already been identified or will be discussed later in this book. Perhaps the single most important place is Charleston, the site of Fort Cass: on Market Street stands the Lewis Ross Home, once the residence of a key Cherokee leader, and the deteriorating **Henegar House**, a dwelling associated with Henry B. Henegar, a former secretary and quartermaster to Chief John Ross, who lived there in the 1850s. A later period in Charleston's history is documented by the **Cumberland Presbyterian Church,** on Railroad Street, which is an excellent example of a vernacular interpretation of Greek Revival architecture, surrounded by a historic cemetery.

To explore the Ocoee River country of Landscape 9, turn south from Charleston on U.S. Highway 11 for ten miles to the city of Cleveland, where U.S. Highway 64 heads east for eight miles to the village of Ocoee.

Black Fox Camp Springs, Rutherford County. Natural springs were important landmarks in the Native-American landscape.

Landscape 9: The Ocoee River Country

The Ocoee River is a rough and rugged river, considered one hundred years ago to be an excellent potential source for hydroelectric power and now recognized as one of the great white-water recreation areas in the South. Indeed, the rafting competitions for the 1996 Olympics at Atlanta will be held along the Ocoee River.

The Ocoee emerges from the southern Appalachians and flows through almost the entire length of Polk County before it meets the Hiwassee River northwest of the county seat of Benton. As it passes into the southeastern tip of Tennessee, the river is sometimes no more than a mere sliver of water. In 1941–43, about four miles west of Ducktown, the Tennessee Valley Authority constructed Ocoee Dam No. 3, which diverted the river through a mountain tunnel to a powerhouse three miles away. Historian R. E. Barclay observed that the "Ocoee Gorge, which was at one time a thing of scenic grandeur, now presents nothing more awe-inspiring than a dry river bed and some silent, mysterious-looking powerhouses" (3). Once again, modern engineers did not "tame" nature; rather, they replaced it with a machine-driven system they could manipulate.

Yet, travelers of the twenty-four miles of U.S. Highway 64 between the small recreational village of Ocoee and the old copper-mining center of Ducktown may still experience the beauty of the natural landscape as the highway hugs the riverbank and crosses the hills and mountains. They also see how the hand of progress has mistreated this landscape over the last 150 years.

The Rogers Farm, four miles east of Ocoee, documents the agrarian landscape of the nineteenth century (private, no access). Established by Jesse Rymer along the Ocoee River in 1861, the farm stood on what was then known as the Old Copper Road (now U.S. 64). During the next three decades, besides raising corn, wheat, rye, sugar cane, fruit trees, and even cotton—crops that prove the fertile quality of the Ocoee Valley in those years—Rymer also managed a freighting business to carry copper and goods between Ducktown, Ocoee, and Cleveland.

Just to the east is **Ocoee Dam No. 1,** also called the Parksville Dam, which marks the beginning of the hydroelectric power industry along the Ocoee River. Completed in 1912 by the Eastern Tennessee Power Company and designed by W. P. Creager in conjunction with the White Engineering Company of New York, the dam and power plant supplied electrical power to Chattanooga and other regional cities. The

Ocoee No. 2 Powerhouse, Polk County. Most electricity generated here went north to the new aluminum factories at Alcoa.

dam also promoted flood control and contained the first artificial lake in Tennessee. Since 1939 the Tennessee Valley Authority has operated the property.

About twelve miles east on U.S. 64 is **Ocoee Dam No. 2**—or the "Caney Creek Plant"—which began production of electric power in 1913. An engineering landmark in its time, the dam complex featured a four-and-a-half-mile-long wooden flume (replaced in 1990 by a metal flume that is still visible high on the south side of the gorge) that diverted water from the Ocoee to the powerhouse. W. P. Creager and the White Engineering Company also designed this structure for the Tennessee Power Company. Like Ocoee No. 1, it supplied some power to regional cities, but most of its output went north to the new reduction plant of the Aluminum Company of America (ALCOA) at the company town of Alcoa in Blount County. The power company also built a village adjacent to the dam called "Caney Creek," which had bungalows, a small hotel, a school, concrete sidewalks, and a tennis court for its employees. Residents could only cross the Ocoee by boat or by a 150-foot suspended bridge, and an electric-powered trolley took them to work. After acquiring Caney Creek with the dam in 1939, the Tennessee Valley Authority removed the village.

The final hydroelectric complex along U.S. Highway 64 is Ocoee Dam No. 3 (1941–43), built by the Tennessee Valley Authority as part of its efforts to meet the country's electricity needs during World War II. When it went into production, a War department official praised the agency for having "driven home another blow to the Axis. . . . Electricity from this station will help turn out the weapons and materials of war to defeat our enemies" (Tennessee Overhill Experience pamphlet, 19).

The three Ocoee hydroelectric plants represent the region's engineered and industrial landscape of the early twentieth century. Four miles farther east on U.S. 64, however, is an earlier industrial landscape. Copper was first discovered at Ducktown in 1843, and within four years mule teams were carrying casks of ore south to a forge at Dalton, Georgia. Marking these early days is the reconstructed smelter stack of the Hiwassee Mine (circa 1850), visible on the west side of Tennessee Highway 68 in Ducktown.

Sustained development of the Copper Basin began in the late 1850s after transportation improvements and company consolidation. First, a wagon road was completed through the Ocoee River Gorge that went from Ducktown to the new railroad town of Cleveland. Next, Julius E. Raht combined many individual mining claims into the Union Consolidated Mining Company and became superintendent of both the Polk County Copper Country and the Burra Burra Copper Company.

The German-born Raht served as the power broker for the Copper Basin's economic development for the next fifteen years. The Civil War halted mining at Ducktown in 1863, but production resumed quickly once the war was over. To fuel the smelters, miles upon miles of timberland were cut. By 1876 timber was so scarce in the Copper Basin that lumber was floated from Fannin County, Georgia, down the Toccoa-Ocoee River. From 1865 to 1878, twenty-four million pounds of copper had been taken from the underground mines, and fifty square miles of the Copper Basin had been stripped of its timber to fuel smelters and build mines.

From 1878 to 1890—due to new copper discoveries in Michigan and Montana—Ducktown copper lost its competitive edge and the mines closed. But in 1890 a railroad spur from the Marietta and North Georgia Railroad arrived, allowing companies to drastically lower transportation costs. Mining and smelting began once again, with activity reaching new heights in 1899 when the newly formed Tennessee Copper Company sunk the giant shaft at the **Burra Burra Mine** and built a

Burra Burra mine and Ducktown, circa 1910. The valiant attempts of families to maintain green yards and trees are surrounded by hundred of acres of stripped vegetation, the result of toxic wastes produced by nearby mines and smelters. (Courtesy of Tennessee State Library and Archives)

new smelter at Copperhill. Most of the lasting environmental damage to the area came from the open-roasting process of removing copper from raw ore, especially in the years from 1891 to 1904. Not only were tons of lumber required, but also the process released sulfuric acid that killed vegetation and left the landscape open to devastating erosion. Soon a barren moonscape of red hills surrounded Ducktown and Copperhill. A photograph of worker houses standing on this stark wasteland became one of the most famous illustrations in the WPA's guidebook for Tennessee. The writer observed that "all through this area, and particularly around the smelting towns are barren denuded hills, a result of early smelting operations, which carried the sulphur fumes high into the air" (474).

During the early 1900s, the Tennessee Copper Company controlled mining and smelting in the Copper Basin. In 1901 the company produced the first pig copper, and six years later it made sulfuric acid by recapturing sulfuric gases from the copper furnaces. By the late twenties, the company was even producing iron sinter and zinc concentrate from the local ore.

The **Ducktown Basin Museum,** located at the old Burra Burra mine works overlooking the town, preserves and interprets the industrial archaeology associated with copper mining. When Burra Burra finally closed in 1959, over 15.6 million tons of copper ore had been extracted.

Copperhill smelter, 1920, Polk County. The smelter complex remains a dominating element of the Copper Hill landscape. (Courtesy of Tennessee State Library and Archives)

Burra Burra mine site, 1992. Efforts at reforestation are slowly returning life to this once scarred wasteland.

The museum also interprets the only remaining **mine headframe,** visible on the east side of Tennessee 68 between Ducktown and Copperhill.

In addition to the museum, several **historic districts** of commercial buildings and worker housing in both Ducktown and Copperhill help to document the lives of those who worked the copper mines. Main Street in Ducktown has several stores, banks, and offices from the early twentieth century. Copperhill's business district is much livelier. From the historic iron bridge over the Ocoee (which serves as the boundary between Tennessee and Georgia), the dominating presence of the smelter works looming over the town is unmistakable. The residential neighborhoods in both towns have examples of the vernacular types of housing that were often provided to the southern working class of eighty years ago. Many are unadorned, pyramid-roofed cottages, while others are small bungalow cottages. The small lots, narrow streets, and plain buildings are characteristic of Appalachian mining towns. The most architecturally distinctive building in the Copper Basin is the historic **Kimsey Junior College** (1932), now the Ducktown Elementary School, on Tennessee Highway 68. Designed by the Chattanooga firm of Reuben H. Hunt, the school is an excellent example of Collegiate Gothic architecture in a small-town setting.

The most compelling elements of the Copper Basin landscape, however, are neither its buildings nor mines; rather, they are the remaining examples of waste and regeneration. North of Copperhill, at the smelter, is a huge man-made mountain of slag—the wastes produced by the smelting process—that travelers on Tennessee 68 pass by every day. The Ducktown Basin Museum provides a high vantage point to overlook the entire area. From this spot, the rebirth of the Copper Basin's forests intermixed with the cuts and pits left behind by past human attempts to extract wealth from beneath the ground can be observed. Reforestation efforts date from the 1920s, but the Civilian Conservation Corps and the Tennessee Valley Authority made the first major efforts between 1939 and 1944. Forty years later, over fourteen million new trees had been planted and the landscape had started to recover from decades of damage from mining and smelting. Today, from the Burra Burra Mine it is possible to see a landscape that nature is slowly reclaiming from past efforts that almost destroyed it. Two miles west, in Isabella, is a view of what most of this area looked like before serious reforestation efforts took place. The landscape is blasted, eroded, and filled with abandoned buildings, machines, and the crushed aspirations of a community once nurtured by the mines.

To begin the next landscape, retrace U.S. Highway 64 to the town of Ocoee.

Landscape 10: The East Tennessee Corridor of the Louisville and Nashville Railroad

The fifty miles of U.S. Highway 411 between Ocoee north to Greenback pass through an industrial landscape that developed eighty to one hundred years ago within the shadow of the Appalachian Mountains. Much of this territory was once home to the Cherokees, but after the forced removal of the Indians during the late 1830s, this became a sparsely settled area of farmsteads and small county seats, such as Benton (Polk County) and Madisonville (Monroe County).

The early Cherokee presence is marked by two sites in Benton, which is four miles north of Ocoee on U.S. 411. About three miles north on U.S. 411 is the roadside park for the **tomb of Nancy Ward,** a Cherokee woman named Nanye'hi who played an important role in the settlement history of Tennessee. Born between 1735 and 1738 at Chota, she married a Cherokee named Kingfisher when she was about nineteen, according to a recently published essay. When her husband died at the Battle of Taliwa in 1755, Ward picked up his weapons and fought in his place. In honor of her bravery, the Cherokees placed her on the council of chiefs as the "Beloved Woman," a position of great honor among the Cherokees. Soon thereafter, she married a colonial trader named Brian Ward and took the English name of Nancy Ward.

Ward again asserted her independence during the American Revolution, when she disagreed with plans by her uncle Atta-kulla-kulla and her cousin Dragging Canoe to attack English settlements. In one celebrated incident, she sent two traders north to warn Watauga settlers of an impending Cherokee attack. She is credited for rescuing Lydia Bean at Toqua and returning the captive woman to her family.

After the war Ward adapted many ways of American culture, learning to make cheese and butter and cook common English meals. In 1819 the Hiwassee Purchase gave Cherokee lands north of the Hiwassee to the settlers. Ward moved from Chota to the Ocoee River, where she operated an inn at the Womankiller Ford about one mile south of present-day Benton. Owner of 649 acres, she used slaves to help operate the inn and farm until her death in 1822.

A second place associated with Cherokee history—a bastion from Fort Marr—is located adjacent to the Polk County Jail on the southern outskirts of Benton. The bastion is visible on the east side of U.S. 411. This log building has been moved, but tradition identifies it as part of an internment stockade before the Cherokees began the Trail of Tears in 1838. The town square of Benton is dominated by the **Polk County Courthouse,** built as a Public Works Administration relief project and designed by R. H. Hunt and Company in 1937. It is a good small-town example of the PWA Modern style of architecture associated with the New Deal projects of the 1930s.

The New Deal Built Environment

Agencies and projects associated with the first two terms of the presidency of Franklin D. Roosevelt profoundly influenced the Tennessee landscape. "We are definitely in an era of building," Roosevelt stressed; "the best kind of building—the building of great public projects for the benefit of the public and with the definite objective of building human happiness" (Cutler, frontpiece). Particularly important was the legacy of five New Deal agencies: the Tennessee Valley Authority, the Public Works Administration, the Civilian Conservation Corps, the Works Progress Administration, and the National Youth Administration.

The Tennessee Valley Authority, established by Congress in 1933, was designed to improve the region's "general social and economic welfare." To meet this mandate, the agency began to construct a massive system of dams, reservoirs, and power plants, while instituting projects in conservation, progressive agriculture, economic diversification, and urban revitalization. Norris Dam on the Clinch River was TVA's first dam. Within a generation, TVA facilities covered the state, from Douglas Dam near Dandridge to Pickwick Dam near Savannah. During the late 1940s and 1950s, coal-powered steam plants were built at several river locations, including New Johnsonville, Kingston, Rogersville, and Gallatin. By the 1980s, nuclear power plants, such as Chickamauga and Watts Bar, were part of the TVA empire. Throughout the Tennessee Valley, the agency has assisted local governments in seeking and designing new environments for tourism, economic development, recreation, and urban renewal. "Those dramatic TVA building and landscape effects in concert," as historian Walter Creese has observed, "sounded a call for the arts of engineering, architecture, and landscape planning to reconcile extant differences among the various social, and more hidden economic, forces" shaping the Tennessee Valley (34).

The Public Works Administration (PWA) was part of the National Industrial Recovery Act of 1933, like TVA part of the relief-minded legislative initiative of Roosevelt's first "Hundred Days." The agency existed from 1933 to 1939, and under the guidance of its methodical administrator, Harold Ickes, the PWA developed a reputation for carefully choosing, developing, and supervising its construction projects. Its Tennessee buildings included Madison County Courthouse in Jackson, Hyde Park School in Memphis, and Caryville School in Campbell County.

The Civilian Conservation Corps (CCC), established by Congress in 1933, was a favorite of President Roosevelt. Organized in military fashion, the CCC addressed Roosevelt's concern for "conservation and planned land use. On this he never equivocated and compromised only when he had to," concluded historian Paul Conkin (*New Deal,* 47). In Tennessee, CCC camps are credited with reclaiming forests and eroded land and creating parks. Standing Stone State Park, T. O. Fuller State Park, and Pickett State Park are among the state parks partially created by CCC workers.

The Works Progress Administration (WPA) grew out of the earlier Civil Works Administration and the Federal Emergency Relief Administration. Established by Congress in 1935 as part of Roosevelt's second Hundred Days of reform, the Works Progress Administration eschewed the PWA's tradition of choosing only well-defined projects. The WPA took on almost any public program that would put unemployed Americans back to work. Its projects included community gardens to provide food for rural people (one such garden stood at the crossroads of U.S. 70S and Tennessee 281 in Cannon County), schools, courthouses, post offices, athletic fields, gymnasiums, parks, and outdoor theaters. But the agency's philosophy of finding a project where a need existed—even if nothing permanent resulted—led to charges of "make-work" and waste. "We Piddle Around" or "We Piddle Allday" was how many Tennesseans sarcastically referred to the WPA.

The National Youth Administration (NYA), another second Hundred Days agency established in 1935, aimed to put young men and women to work and provide financial assistance to students so they would stay in school. In Tennessee, the agency completed many public works projects. For instance, the NYA built schools and the Dunlap community center in Sequatchie County, erected a community center-theater in Murfreesboro, and constructed a library in Trenton.

Louisville and Nashville Railroad Depot, Etowah. (Courtesy of Tennessee State Library and Archives)

North of Benton on U.S. Highway 411 is a historic landscape that took shape as railroads built new Appalachian routes in the late 1800s. The Marietta and North Georgia Railroad entered the southeastern corner of Tennessee in 1890, but within a year the line was in bankruptcy court, not to emerge as the reorganized Atlantic, Knoxville, and Northern Railroad Construction Company until 1895. By the 1890s the entire American railroad system was experiencing a major period of consolidation that left a few railroad magnates and financiers in control of a dwindling number of large interstate lines. In East Tennessee, the Louisville and Nashville competed with the Southern Railway for regional dominance. By the mid-1890s, the Southern had taken control of a number of smaller lines to establish a new route between Atlanta and Cincinnati (now paralleled by U.S. Highway 27) that threatened the L&N's traditional hegemony in the Mid-South. In 1902 the L&N answered with plans to build its own line between the two rail centers. After acquiring the Atlantic, Knoxville, and Northern, the L&N then announced that a new line would be constructed between present-day Etowah to Tennga at the Georgia state line.

Etowah, fifteen miles north of Benton on U.S. Highway 411, became the administrative center of the L&N's new "Atlanta division" in 1908. Nothing had stood here four years earlier when the railroad began construction of a large complex of railroad shops and roundhouses. Etowah became a major division point on the line between Knoxville and Chattanooga and the most important industrial town in McMinn

County. Its plat was similar to those of other L&N-dominated towns of the early twentieth century. All commercial businesses lay on the west side of the tracks along a street named Tennessee Avenue that faced the railroad's right-of-way. A strip of land separated the businesses from the depot (1906) around which railroad engineers designed a pleasant, park-like environment. On the east side of the tracks were the railroad shops and roundhouses; any access was controlled by the railroad. To most visitors, Etowah appeared to be a one-sided town. The town design still conveys the railroad's overwhelming presence in the local built environment. Historian Michael McDonald concluded that "Etowah was an L&N town. When the railroad waxed, it waxed. When the railroad waned, it waned. It was a creation of the railroad" (Caldwell, 59).

The restored **L&N Depot and company offices** on Tennessee Avenue, built by L&N master carpenter Nathan York, have an excellent permanent exhibit on the L&N's impact on the community. Etowah grew rapidly due to constant railroad investment. Cheap, easily accessible timber made Etowah a perfect place to repair wooden boxcars, and, as demand increased, the railroad continued to expand its works. In 1924, for example, L&N built a new two-hundred-and-fifty-thousand-dollar machine shop, and employment at its works in 1927 reached twenty-one hundred, a number that represented 90 percent of the families in town. An account in 1923 described Etowah as having "the most remarkable growth of any town in the state" (Foster, 28). But in 1930 the company decided to stop building wooden cars in favor of steel gondolas. This news combined with the expanding misery of the Great Depression to immediately halt local economic expansion. The next year, L&N moved the division headquarters from Etowah to Knoxville. The town was never the same again.

Englewood, six miles to the north on U.S. Highway 411, also developed quickly once the railroad tracks arrived. In 1907 the Brient family, led by Mortimer Brient, moved its Eureka Cotton Mills from the family farm to Englewood and substantially expanded operations. Workers at the cotton mill were mostly women, who had to adjust quickly to the rigors of industrial work. The Brients were never interested in the railroad business at nearby Etowah because they did not want any competition for their local labor force, nor did they want the baneful influence of railroad workers in their village. In 1908 the Brients opened a company store, which stayed in business through the Depression. Family businesses dominated everything in town for the next two generations.

Monroe County Courthouse, Madisonville. New railroad construction often encouraged county governments to build new and appropriately stylish courthouses.

Another eight miles north on U.S. 411 is Madisonville, the seat of government for Monroe County, first settled in 1822. The **Cannon-Stickley House** (1846), about two blocks west of the courthouse square, remains from the town's early years. Designed by Thomas Blanchard, the dwelling is an excellent example of Tennessee Federal architecture, featuring a double Greek Revival–style portico (private, no access). On the outskirts of town, near the modern intersection of Tennessee 68 and U.S. 411, is the Cooke-Kefauver residence (private, no access). This home was often visited by former U.S. Senator Estes Kefauver, an important Tennessee politician of the 1950s who was the Democratic nominee for vice-president in 1956.

Madisonville's historic town square belongs to the antebellum period, but most buildings date to the 1890s or later, when the tracks of modern transportation, first represented by the Atlantic, Knoxville, and Northern Railroad then by the Louisville and Nashville, began to re-shape Madisonville. The most imposing new addition to the built environment was the Monroe County Courthouse (1897), a rather eclectic and bombastic statement of Italianate and Classical Revival styles, designed by Baumann and Baumann of Knoxville. The railroad also brought New South industrialization. In 1903 the Madisonville Knitting Mill, for example, began to recruit child labor from local farms. Still, the county seat remained small; in 1920 a mere 850 people lived there. Madisonville's industries were dwarfed by those in neighboring towns, such as Englewood, Sweetwater, and Etowah.

Railroads created the first modern transportation corridor from Benton to Madisonville, but just as noticeable as the tracks, roadbeds, signals, depots, and warehouses of the railroad days are buildings associated with the next generation of transportation: the creation of U.S. Highway 411 in the 1920s and 1930s. At Delano stand abandoned and forgotten Art Moderne–style motel cottages from the 1940s. Just up the road at Wetmore is an excellent vernacular adaptation of the standardized Gulf Oil station, along with an intact row of modernist motel cottages from the same time. Madisonville has a quite interesting array of roadside architecture, especially an exquisite A&W drive-in restaurant. These structures naturally emphasize functional trends in architecture, for they had to be designed to serve the motoring public. But their catchy signs and modernist styling also represent an American vernacular of the middle decades of the twentieth century that has influenced our perception of modern design ever since.

The next sixteen miles of U.S. Highway 441 north of Madisonville parallel the railroad tracks until the junction for Tennessee 95, where the highway continues to bear east toward Maryville while the tracks head west to Knoxville. The highway passes through the once rural countryside of the Little Tennessee Valley, transformed by the closing of Tellico Dam in 1979 into a recreational landscape. Ironically, long before the Tellico Reservoir, fishermen considered the Little Tennessee to be one of the best places in the country for trout fishing. That sport was replaced by the more grandiose goals of modern recreation and by TVA's hope to develop a model lakeside community called Timberlake.

Tennessee Highway 95 passes along the north side of the Tellico Reservoir to the confluence of the Little Tennessee and Tennessee Rivers via U.S. Highway 321 at Lenoir City. On the north side of the Tellico Reservoir, near the old railroad town of Greenback, is the historic **Griffitts House** (circa 1854), a vernacular central-hall I-house associated with a Quaker community that was established in this valley during the early 1800s. The house probably served as a stop on the Underground Railroad, which allowed escaped slaves to find freedom in northern states. Nearby, a half mile east of Jackson's Ferry, is the **National Campground,** where local churches banded together in the early 1870s to host religious meetings designed to unify whites and African Americans and Confederates and Unionists. Annual meetings are still held there every summer.

To gain access to the next historic landscape, U.S. Highway 11 at Lenoir City, continue on Tennessee 95 to its junction with U.S. Highway 321 and go five miles west to Lenoir City.

Landscape 11: The Lee Highway

U.S. Highway 11—locally known as Lee Highway in honor of Confederate general Robert E. Lee—runs through the heart of the Great Valley of the Tennessee, beginning at the confluence of the Tennessee and Little Tennessee Rivers and exiting the state near the Great Bend of the Tennessee at Chattanooga. It was part of an amazingly roundabout transcontinental route that connected New York City with San Francisco by passing through seven southern states. The highway in the South first followed the tracks of the Southern Railway to New Orleans, where it then picked up the route of the Southern Pacific Railroad to California. More important to the South, it connected the Shenandoah Valley of Virginia to New Orleans, passing through the most unreconstructed parts of the old Confederacy. Commercial, industrial, and residential development soon centered around the highway, abandoning the railroad corridor that had created most towns some seventy years earlier.

Since U.S. Highway 11 also followed earlier wagon and stage roads, the highway cuts through a landscape of great historical depth, and homes, churches, schools, businesses, cemeteries, and public buildings record significant events and people in agriculture, settlement, industrialization, town building, and the impact of the Tennessee Valley Authority. These places do not fall within any neat chronological order within the landscape, but are interwoven into the land itself, creating a record of change over time that goes a long way to explaining how and why this region looks the way it does.

Lenoir City is one of the best places to assess the impact of the Tennessee Valley Authority on the Tennessee Valley (see sidebar entitled "The New Deal Built Environment," Landscape 9, this chapter). East of town, on U.S. 321, is Fort Loudoun Dam on the Tennessee River, a hydroelectric and flood-control project completed by TVA in 1943, while to the northwest on U.S. 321 there is Melton Hill Dam on the Clinch River. Immediately south of town on the Little Tennessee River is Tellico Dam, a TVA project finished in 1979. By visiting the dams and their respective visitor centers, the similarities and differences between the projects can be seen, allowing the visitor to better understand how TVA changed its design philosophy, its approach to environmental issues, and its responsibilities in local economic development and electric power production over a forty-year period.

Within Lenoir City itself is another important interpretation of the meaning of the Tennessee Valley Authority. At the local post office (1938), constructed by the Works Progress Administration following a restrained Colonial Revival design by architect Louis A. Simon, is the mural *Electrification* executed by federally sponsored artist David S. Martin in 1940. The mural powerfully expresses the themes of progress and change represented by the new TVA power lines, which showed citizens beforehand what would quickly become a common element of the local landscape.

Lenoir City residents were already accustomed to the changing technology of modern industrialization. Prior to 1837 William B. Lenoir developed the area's first industry by establishing on present-day Depot Street an innovative cotton mill, which expanded in size and production throughout the century. Unfortunately, the **Lenoir Cotton Mill** burned in the 1980s; current plans call for stabilizing the ruins and providing a historical interpretation of this early industrial landmark.

The Lenoir family operated the mill until 1890, when the mill and most of the original family estate became the basis for the new Lenoir City, established by the Lenoir City Company. As a company town developed primarily by capitalists from New York City and nearby Knoxville, the city itself is a landmark of New South economic development. These investors believed that a new town standing at the confluence of the Tennessee and Little Tennessee Rivers—as well as being connected to the East Tennessee, Virginia, and Georgia Railway—was perfectly situated to take advantage of both river and rail traffic along with the expanding coal mining and timber industries in the immediate region. The original **Lenoir City Company Office** is at the center of the town square, symbolizing the company's role in the community. Designed by Baumann and Baumann of Knoxville in the Shingle style, the building served as the company's office for one hundred years.

Much of the success of Lenoir City can be attributed to the consolidation of the nation's railroads, especially its association with the Southern Railway, following the depression of 1893–94. The Southern immediately expanded and improved its works, building new branch lines and updating facilities. A local beneficiary was the Lenoir City Car Works, which built freight cars. The Southern gave Lenoir City the expanded transportation network it needed to become a mid-sized industrial center, typical of many New South industrial towns. What sets Lenoir City apart from other similar railroad towns in Tennessee is the later impact of TVA, which added a third chapter to its history of industrial development during the middle decades of the twentieth century.

Across the Tennessee River on U.S. Highway 11 is a quite different town, with its history firmly rooted in the nineteenth century. Loudon is a classic Tennessee River town, centered around historic Blair's Ferry. The first steamboat passed by in 1828, but steamboat traffic did not become commonplace until about 1835. The port for Blair's Ferry was located approximately where the southern end of U.S. 11 bridge now stands. Nearby on Hackberry Street and Main Street are four places from the early history of the town. The Carmichael Inn (circa 1800) is a two-story log tavern where travelers could rest, eat, and drink before taking the ferry over the Tennessee. The relocated building is now a local history museum and visitor center. Next door on Hackberry Street is the **Orme Wilson and Company Storehouse**

Blair's Ferry Storehouse, Loudon.
A lonely reminder of the decades
when river traffic dominated the
Tennessee Valley.

(circa 1850), a warehouse that features unusual decorative brickwork (private, no access). The mason used six steps to make the bricks in six designs and then laid them in unique patterns to create a picturesque facade.

At 800 Main Street, facing the river, is **Blair's Ferry Storehouse,** a circa 1835 steamboat warehouse (private, no access). The Main Street city park overlooks the Tennessee River, the original Blair's Ferry, the later railroad bridge, and the modern highway bridge, representing three different periods in the transportation history of the Tennessee Valley. How the different modes of transportation, and their reliance on quite different stages of technological and engineering development, shaped the town of Loudon in distinctive ways is quite apparent from this spot.

After leaving the riverfront area, travelers meet the street grid, tracks, and buildings of a wholly different town that evolved over a thirty-year period around the corridor of the East Tennessee and Georgia Railroad. **Mason Place** (1865), at 600 Commerce Street, stood on the west side of the tracks and was just one of several fine homes built along Commerce Street in the post–Civil War era (private, limited access). Designed by local craftsman William H. Cassada, this framed Greek Revival–style I-house was the home of Thomas Mason, who served as the state railroad tax assessor for East Tennessee from 1878 to 1880. On the east side of the tracks on College Street stood another railroad-associated institution, the **Cumberland Presbyterian Church,** which first formed after the arrival of the East Tennessee and Georgia in the mid-1850s. Local builder J. W. Clark of Sweetwater designed the 1882 church in a vernacular Victorian Gothic style. Loudon's historic passenger depot also stands off College Street.

Between the riverfront and the railroad tracks is the county courthouse and the commercial district that surrounded it after the creation of Loudon County in 1870. A. C. Bruce designed the **Loudon County Courthouse** in an Italianate style. Sweetwater contractor J. W. Clark and Bro. constructed it for $14,200 in 1871–72.

The next three towns on U.S. Highway 11—Philadelphia, Sweetwater, and Niota—relied heavily on the transportation network of the East Tennessee and Georgia Railroad. Each town bears the railroad's distinctive imprint of a symmetrical town plan, with the tracks, warehouses, and industrial concerns defining one side of the town, while on the other side stands the greatest concentration of commercial and public buildings along with churches, schools, and residential neighborhoods (see sidebar entitled "Common Railroad Town Plans," Landscape 20, chapter 7).

Philadelphia, six miles south of Loudon, has several historic buildings and a mill complex dating from its years as a cotton-processing center for farmers in Loudon and Monroe Counties. First platted by two Quakers named William Knox and Jacob Pearson during the 1820s, the railroad imposed a new symmetrical town design when it arrived in the early 1850s. The twin water towers of the Philadelphia Hosiery Mills, along with the abandoned textile building itself, mark the primary industry for most of the twentieth century.

Due to its highway and railroad connections, Sweetwater developed into the largest town in Monroe County, although it is not the county seat. Education institutions and industrial concerns have additionally contributed to its growth. At the north city limits stands the former Tennessee Military Institute, now a private school for teaching Japanese children. Established as Sweetwater College in 1874 by the Rev. John Lynn Bachman, TMI evolved into a well-regarded military preparatory school at the turn of the century. Its castellated Gothic–style administration building (1909) stands on a hill overlooking the entire campus. As military schools fell out of favor during the turbulent years of the late 1960s and early 1970s, TMI tried to stay solvent by shedding its military trappings to become the TMI Academy in 1975. Enrollment continued to decrease while the costs of maintaining its large physical plant and campus continued to increase. The school closed and has only recently reopened its doors as the Tennessee Meiji Gakwin private school.

On both the east and west sides of the tracks in Sweetwater stand operating textile mills and small factories, many using buildings that were constructed in the early 1900s. By 1920 the town had a barite mill, flour mill, planing mill, and woolen mills. Twenty years later, Sweetwater industries included cheese, hosiery, and dress factories. Most of these factories are in long, rectangular one-story brick buildings of purely functional design. At the center of town is a former station for the Southern Railway and across the street are two- and three-story brick commercial blocks from the late nineteenth and early twentieth centuries. The corbeled brickwork and Italianate-influenced window moldings of the three-story Masonic building (circa 1875) are especially noteworthy. The many early-twentieth-century homes in the residential neighborhoods also date from Sweetwater's period of greatest prosperity. Mayes Street has an especially good collection of domestic architecture; 306 Mayes is one of the best examples of a Craftsman bungalow found in any small to medium-sized Tennessee town (private, no access).

The most important public building is the Colonial Revival post office (1940), designed by federal architect Louis A. Simon and built by the Works Progress Administration. Its interior features a federally sponsored mural, titled *Wild Boar Hunt,* painted by Thelma Martin in 1942.

From Sweetwater U.S. Highway 11 enters the rich agricultural land of south Monroe and north McMinn Counties, where several historic family farms stand along both sides of the highway. Two miles south of Sweetwater is the Brookside Farm, founded by John and Elizabeth Lotspeich Browder in 1859 (private, no access). Descendents of the founders still live in the original nine-room farmhouse, and they farm over 300 acres of the original 480-acre farmstead, raising tobacco, corn, grain, and cattle, which are typical agricultural products in the Tennessee Valley. The nearby Homestead Farm, which is three miles south of Sweetwater, was established by David and Rachel Dickey Browder in about 1865 (private, no access). Many families established new farms during the years immediately following the Civil War, but few were as successful as the Browder family's farm. The second-generation owner, Charles O. Browder, was one of McMinn County's most innovative and progressive farmers. He experimented successfully with purebred cattle, specializing in Angus and Jersey cattle. His son Charles Jr., who inherited the place in 1939, was still operating the farm in the late 1980s. He lived in a late antebellum farmhouse, but little else he did reflected the agrarian ways of old. Browder expanded the family farm to twenty-four hundred acres with a registered Jersey herd of four hundred and thirty cattle as well as raising a hundred head of Angus beef cattle. The family also cultivated thirty-five acres of tobacco, four hundred acres of corn, and four hundred acres of small grains like barley, oats, and wheat. The silos visible from the highway mark well this prosperous, modern dairy farm.

Within the city limits of Niota, a railroad town seven miles south of Sweetwater, is historic Big Spring Farm, important both in Tennessee agriculture and architecture. First settled in the 1810s by Charles and Lucy Lawrence Cate, the farm now yields cattle and hay and supports a tree nursery. The second-generation owner, Elijah Cate, expanded the property by over five hundred acres between 1831 and 1873. He also built a magnificent Tennessee Federal dwelling, designed by local craftsman Samuel Cleague and probably assisted by son-in-law Thomas Crutchfield. The **Cate House** has distinctive stepped gables and a balanced five-bay facade (private, no access). Just south of the Niota city limits, near the junction of the four-lane highway bypass to Athens, is Samuel Cleague's own home (1826). The facade of the **Cleague House** reflects a two-thirds Georgian plan with, again, Cleague's distinctive mark of stepped gables. Unfortunately, this significant example of Tennessee domestic architecture, noted in the WPA guidebook to the state, stands in a dilapidated condition, open to the elements.

Niota is the only town along the Lee Highway that has its original **East Tennessee and Georgia Railroad Depot** (1855). Now considered to be the oldest extant depot in the state, the brick depot remained in use until 1972. The city of Niota then acquired the property for use as an office building.

Athens is about seven miles south of Niota on U.S. Highway 11; Tennessee 305 enters the historic downtown. Established in 1822–23, Athens retains the look of an antebellum county seat, especially around its historic town square. The neo-Colonial Revival style of the McMinn County Courthouse, designed by the firm of Galloway and Guthrey in 1967, reinforces the point that Athens is one of the region's earliest settlements. As a rural trade center, it consistently grew throughout the 1830s and 1840s, especially once a branch of the state-supported Bank of Tennessee was located here in 1838. Cotton production was very important in this period of the county's history. Displays on antebellum and nineteenth-century history are located at the McMinn County Living Heritage Museum at 522 West Madison Avenue.

Like in most other towns on the Lee Highway, the rails of the East Tennessee and Georgia indelibly shaped the history and the built environment of Athens. A historian writing one hundred years ago observed that "during the [eighteen] fifties Athens was at the height of its prosperity" (Goodspeed, 813). The railroad expanded local commercial and agricultural markets, especially the export of cotton.

Three key buildings help to document this era of growth. A historic marker on the outside wall of a house built by Samuel Cleague on North Jackson Street identifies the place where the Hiwassee Railroad, the first in East Tennessee, had its offices in 1836 (private, limited access). Financial difficulties associated with the depression of 1837 stopped the Hiwassee project in its tracks, with little construction completed, and local businessmen and planters waited fifteen years for another railroad to come to Athens.

One of the most eager for a railroad was Alexander H. Keith, who farmed hundreds of acres on the southern outskirts of Athens as well as investing in different commercial ventures in the county. In 1858 he hired the well-regarded craftsman Thomas Crutchfield to design the **Keith House,** a grand Greek Revival mansion, which still stands at 110 Keith Lane (private, no access).

In downtown Athens is another institution from the 1850s, the original three-story brick **Old College** (circa 1852), now part of Tennessee Wesleyan College (1925) and surrounded by Colonial Revival buildings from the 1920s and 1930s. The local Old Fellows lodge constructed the building for a female college, but the venture soon went into debt and the college building was acquired by the Methodist Episcopal Church South, which operated it until the Civil War. In 1867 the Methodist Church rechartered the school as the East Tennessee Wesleyan College. In 1885 it became known as Grant Memorial University and was considered one of the best private schools in East Tennessee.

By this time, Athens was booming as never before. In 1887 capitalists established the Athens Mining and Manufacturing Company, an interesting utopian scheme to create a model industrial community, which lasted only two years. But according to historians Bruce Wheeler and Michael McDonald, the venture "was the harbinger of things to come" ("Communities of East Tennessee," 16). In the 1890s, following the creation of the Southern Railway, Athens gained a flour mill, several cotton mills, and a woolen mill. But its proximity to the industrial power of Chattanooga impeded Athens's growth, and, within a decade of its creation by the L&N Railroad in 1904–6, Etowah replaced Athens as the county's industrial center. In the 1920s, for instance, Athens had a roller mill, hosiery mills, a concrete tile plant, and a table and chair factory, but nothing in Athens could match the size of the L&N works at Etowah. "Athens is a true courthouse town, and the shady square is filled to overflowing with country people on Saturdays," wrote a writer who visited Athens in the late 1930s. "They come on horseback, in mule-drawn wagons, and in cars spattered with red clay. When their trading is done the men lounge around the courthouse square, swapping gossip and political views while their women-folk attended the movies" (*WPA Guide,* 306).

This image of small-town life quickly changed after World War II when Athens diversified its economy with more industry and new commercial enterprises. A four-lane bypass was built for U.S. 11, and the proximity of Interstate 75 produced new suburban and commercial growth west of the historic square. This maze of new roads, shopping centers, strip development, and tract houses is the economic heartbeat of Athens today.

The next twenty-five miles of U.S. Highway 11 pass through three antebellum villages—Riceville, Calhoun, and Charleston—before the highway reaches Cleveland, the next county seat. Calhoun was actually the first settlement in McMinn County; it was established in 1820 and named for Secretary of War John C. Calhoun. Located on the Hiwassee River, the town marked the southern edge of legal white settlement in this region until the forced removal of the Cherokees in 1838 opened the land south of the Hiwassee. The role of Charleston, on the south side of the river, in the Cherokee removal and the Trail of Tears has already been detailed earlier in this chapter.

As the Lee Highway enters Cleveland and heads south to the county courthouse, its original route (Tennessee 74 or Ocoee Street) passes through several generations of domestic architecture, from the Colonial Revival and Tudor Revival of the 1920s and 1930s to the bungalow and Craftsman styles of the early twentieth century and to the Italianate, Second Empire, and Classical Revival architecture of the late Victorian decade. At Eighth Street, the highway divides at a triangular,

Craigmiles Hall, Cleveland. Second Empire architecture often enhanced the commercial aspirations of New South boosters.

landscaped median, complete with a Civil War monument, into north and south one-way routes that allow the visitor to explore the historic business district and square.

Railroads and industry have always played a major role in Cleveland's history. Although established after the Treaty of New Echota, the town did not have a bank or even much in the way of commercial services until the East Tennessee and Georgia Railroad was finished in 1855. Much of its trade came from the copper mines at Ducktown. The New South transformation of Cleveland dates to 1879 when Christopher Hardwick and his sons Joseph H. and John M. established Hardwick Stove Works, followed a year later by the Hardwick Woolen Mills. These two companies remained the county's primary employers for many years. In 1980, for example, Hardwick Stove had more than a thousand employees and had produced 9.7 million stoves over its first hundred years of production.

Another influential figure was local booster and banker John H. Craigmiles, who established the Cleveland Life Mutual Insurance Company in 1885. The Craigmiles family made many other contributions to the city, and today three downtown properties document the family's role in local history. In 1866 P. M. Craigmiles, the brother of John H., announced the beginning of post–Civil War recovery in Cleveland with the construction of his Italian Villa home at 833 Ocoee Street NW. Today the **Craigmiles House** is home to a local history center. P. M. Craigmiles's son Walter built the ornate Second Empire–style **Craigmiles Hall** on the town square in 1878. In 1880 John Craigmiles acquired an old two-story brick building on Ocoee Street and updated it with a new cast-iron facade. In 1891 the building became a saloon, and in 1909 C. J. Wilson bought the building and operated a mercantile business until 1949. The old **Wilson store** is now the law office of Dietrich and Dietrich.

The town's post–Civil War prosperity is reflected by more than fancy Victorian homes and commercial buildings. **St. Luke's Episcopal Church,** located two blocks north of the square at Ocoee and Central Streets, was the church of choice for Cleveland's expanding professional and entrepreneurial class. In 1877, the congregation hired architect Peter J. Williamson of Nashville to design a new church, which remains one of the best Gothic expressions in the region.

Local initiatives and outside investment sustained a steady rate of growth in the early 1900s. Cleveland developed a strong industrial base, benefiting from both its excellent rail connections as well as its place in the new federal highway system as the junction of U.S. 11 and U.S. 64. Whereas 580 manufacturing workers lived in Bradley County at the turn of the century, 1,287 such workers resided there twenty years later. Two companies were of particular significance. The Cleveland (Hardwick) Woolen Mills was, by 1925, the largest mill in the world producing ready-to-wear clothes from raw material. Its downtown factory stayed in business until 1973, when the company moved to a new forty-two-acre site north of town. In 1917 investors created Dixie Foundry, known now as Magic Chef Corporation. Sixty years later, this company employed eighteen hundred workers at its modern Cleveland factory. These large industries meant a great deal to the economic well-being of local residents. A standard-of-living index in 1925 measured the county well below the national average, but in Tennessee the county ranked eleventh out of ninety-five counties. Even after the worst of the Depression, in the late 1930s, Cleveland still had thirty factories, ranging from the massive Hardwick Woolen Mills to lumber plants.

Cleveland's built environment along Ocoee Street and the railroad tracks still reflects its dependence on industrial development from 1880 to 1930. West of the Tennessee River, the same processes of railroad expansion and industrial growth were transforming the once agrarian landscape of Rhea County. A twenty-six-mile drive on Tennessee Highway 60 connects Cleveland with Dayton, the seat of government for

St. Luke's Episcopal Church, Cleveland. The town reveals many examples of how Cleveland citizens transformed their town with new industries, buildings, and neighborhoods in the late nineteenth century.

Rhea County. When Highway 60 crosses the Tennessee River via the **Blythe Ferry**, it does so at the same place the Cherokees first crossed the Tennessee on the Trail of Tears to their new western homeland.

Landscape 12: The Cincinnati Southern Railroad

West of the Tennessee River, from its confluence with the Clinch River to its junction with the Hiwassee River, is a narrow valley between the river and the Cumberland Plateau. This is a beautiful spot in autumn as the foliage on the mountains turns bright and colorful. A particularly spectacular view is along Tennessee Highway 68 as it descends the plateau southeast of Crossville and enters the valley at Spring City. Settlement came early to the valley bottomlands once the Cherokees relinquished any claim to the land in 1805. Two years later, Rhea County was established, and after exploring several different locations in the valley, county commissioners in 1812 finally selected a place called Washington (now known as Old Washington), near a ferry crossing of the Tennessee River eight miles northeast of Dayton, to build the county seat.

By 1833 Washington was a typical county seat of its time, centered around a new courthouse designed by craftsman Thomas Crutchfield. For the next fifty years, it was the focus of political life in Rhea County and served as a marketplace for local farmers. Then, in the mid-1880s, northern capitalists built the Cincinnati Southern Railway, connecting Cincinnati to Atlanta, along the west side of the Tennessee River. Travelers may see a very interesting section of this rail corridor by driving U.S. Highway 27 for thirty-three miles between Dayton and Rockwood. The new railroad totally bypassed the county seat. "The building of the Cincinnati Southern Railroad," prophesied a historian writing in 1887, "has sealed [Washington's] fate, and doubtless before many years have elapsed it will have entirely disappeared" (Goodspeed, 820). The prophecy proved correct: Old Washington remains on the map, but little marks its former prominence as county seat. The courthouse is gone as well as most of the buildings that once surrounded it; the old square plan is almost impossible to discern. What is left today is little more than a little country village. The fate of Washington is one of the most striking examples of how railroads reorganized the late-nineteenth-century Tennessee landscape.

Rhea County farmer William C. Gardenhire immediately recognized the potential of the railroad. He divided his farm into a town site called Dayton and began to recruit industry. Between 1884 and 1887,

Dayton emerged as the primary industrial town on the Cincinnati Southern line between Rockwood and Chattanooga, exploding virtually overnight, as had few other places in East Tennessee, to become an important manufacturing center. In 1884 English capitalists led by Sir Titus Salts established the Dayton Iron and Coal Company and made plans to construct large blast furnaces, spur lines, mines, and industrial works to exploit nearby deposits of coal, iron, and limestone. The company turned out its first pig iron in early 1886; within a year, a second furnace was in operation and production reached one hundred tons of pig iron a day.

The sizeable investments of the railroad and Dayton Iron and Coal naturally encouraged others to rush there. Within three years, the Dayton Roller Mills, the Allen and Keith Flour Mill, the Burchard and Galbraith Broom Factory, the Ferguson Foundry and Machine Shop, and various sawmills were in business; soon, they were followed by the Dayton Veneer and Lumber Mills, the Dayton Hosiery Mill, the Spivey Hosiery Mills, and the Robinson Manufacturing Company. In 1887 the town's population was an estimated three thousand whereas before only a few dozen lived around a place called Smith's Crossroads. Dayton's continued growth was insured in 1895 when the Cincinnati Southern became part of the new Southern Railway empire. The line, in fact, is still an important link in the railroad's network and is now part of the Norfolk Southern system, one of the largest railroads in the eastern United States. In October visitors may take excursion trains from the Tennessee Valley Railroad Museum in Chattanooga and travel the old route of the Cincinnati Southern in Tennessee from Chattanooga to Oneida.

In 1890 Dayton's industrial power brought it political power when county officials moved the seat of government from Washington to Dayton. The courthouse square was located immediately east of the tracks, with the railroad depot located only a short block away. In 1891 town leaders and boosters provided funds for a splendid late Victorian courthouse, symbolic of Dayton's new role in the future growth of Rhea County. Designed by W. Chamberlin and Co. of Knoxville, the **Rhea County Courthouse** is a National Historic Landmark because in 1925 the famous Scopes Monkey trial, recognized as one of the most important events in American intellectual and cultural history, took place here.

In 1925 the Tennessee General Assembly passed the General Education Act, which transferred control of public education from local authorities to state experts. At the same time, it approved the Butler Act, which outlawed the teaching of the theory of evolution in the state's

Rhea County Courthouse, Dayton. This National Historic Landmark has changed little since the heated debates between Darrow and Bryan over the theory of evolution in 1925.

public schools. Reaction against the loss of control over public education at the local level combined with fears about what values and ideas the state "experts" would place in the local curriculum to produce the intellectual environment that led to the Monkey trial. Since the school session was already over, Dayton teacher John Scopes tested the constitutionality of the law by teaching evolution to a group of students. His indictment focused national attention on Dayton in the summer of 1925.

The trial was a media circus, covered by newsreel cameras and every major newspaper and magazine in the country. The prosecution called upon former three-time presidential candidate and Secretary of State William Jennings Bryan for assistance, while Scopes's defense was assisted by the noted defense attorney Clarence Darrow. Bryan argued eloquently and passionately for a fundamentalist interpretation of the Bible; Darrow just as persuasively pointed out that interpreting the Bible as the literal truth flew in the face of scientific fact and rationality. Although commentators then, and historians later, concluded that Darrow won the great debate, Bryan won the case. His appeal to fundamentalism meant much more to local jurors than Darrow's methodical rationalism. Scopes was convicted and fined one hundred dollars (his conviction was later overturned on appeal).

The trial left a lasting mark on Dayton. The courthouse became a landmark; today a museum in the basement interprets the history and meaning of the Scopes Monkey trial. East of town, on a hill overlooking the town, is William Jennings Bryan College, founded in honor of the "Great Commoner," who died in Dayton just five days after the trial was over. Beginning with a donation of twenty-five thousand dollars from businessman George Washburn, the college first opened its doors in the old Dayton high school in 1930. Financial difficulties during the Great Depression almost closed the school, but in the mid-1930s its flashy Art Deco–style Administration and Classroom Building was at least habitable, although work continued for several more years. The college is devoted to the traditional values and understanding of the Bible that Bryan had defended at the courthouse. It has expanded over the last twenty years, and several interesting buildings have been constructed, especially the 1970s modernist-style chapel near the campus entrance.

The passions that engulfed Dayton during the Scopes trial should be kept in mind while traveling north on U.S. Highway 27. Railroad tracks parallel the highway, which is dotted here and there by small businesses or abandoned small factories. The industrial landscape created by the Cincinnati Southern, and later enhanced by the Southern Railway, brought the values of modern industrial society to formerly rural and agrarian communities. The region's older residents may have accepted the railroad and may have taken jobs in the mines and factories, but they would not shed the beliefs and values of agrarian society so readily. Historian John Stilgoe has written about a "metropolitan corridor" that American railroads created between 1880 and 1930 to link together the emerging urban areas of modern America. Connecting the New South capital of Atlanta to Cincinnati, the Cincinnati Southern Railroad was certainly a good example of a metropolitan corridor, but its tracks did not automatically introduce modern values to this agrarian countryside. That transformation has taken decades to accomplish, and in some places the change still has not happened.

Spring City, sixteen miles north of Dayton on U.S. Highway 27, was another instant city created by the Cincinnati Southern Railroad over one hundred years ago. The highway follows the tracks closely through the center of town; the primary commercial and residential areas are west of the tracks, and a secondary residential area and African-American neighborhood lie east of the tracks. An important black history landmark is the Claiborn Calloway School, which became a community center with the end of segregation in the local schools in 1966.

Spring City is the only town between Rockwood and Chattanooga that still has its historic passenger depot (1909), built at the same time the Southern Railway was updating its facilities in Chattanooga with the massive Southern Railway Terminal. The community is now in the process of acquiring this brick building of eclectic Classical Revival design and hopes to convert it into a local history museum and visitor center.

Most secondary railroad towns in East Tennessee grew little after 1930. Spring City is an obvious exception to this tendency due to the impact of the Watts Bar Dam and Nuclear Steam Plant, a huge TVA com-

Passenger Station, Spring City. As the tracks divide the town in half, the Spring City Depot is a reminder of how railroads reordered the late-nineteenth-century landscape.

Watts Bar Dam, Rhea and Meigs Counties. The output from this hydroelectric facility is now dwarfed by the adjacent but not operating nuclear power plant.

plex that lies about nine miles east of town on Tennessee Highway 68. A visitor center and scenic overlooks are easy to find. From those vantage points, the modern technological tools—the concrete dam, the highway bridge, nuclear cooling towers, gates, and powerhouse—humans have used to harness the water and power from this portion of the Tennessee River are readily visible. Watts Bar began as a hydroelectric project; during World II, TVA added a steam-powered (from coal) electric plant to fuel the seemingly insatiable appetite of the atomic facilities at Oak Ridge. The demand for more power for defense installations continued into the 1950s and 1960s. Searching for a cheaper and a more environmentally sensitive alternative to coal, TVA turned to nuclear power. The giant cooling towers on the Tennessee River are concrete and steel monuments to our continuing search for the perfect energy source. A more somber reminder of that same search are the highway signs along Tennessee 68 and 58, which mark the evacuation routes in case of a nuclear accident at Watts Bar.

Rockwood is just north of the junction of U.S. Highways 27 and 70, thirteen miles north of Spring City. Here, in the Reconstruction years, the region's modern industrial history began. In 1867 northern investors Abram Hewitt, John T. Wilder, and Hiram S. Chamberlain founded the Roane Iron Company, which used coke to smelt iron ore for the first time south of the Ohio River. The factory grew steadily over the next decade, with production reaching sixty tons of pig iron a day by 1878. Ten years later, the plant included the foundry and 180 coke ovens that employed hundreds of workers. Over three thousand people lived in Rockwood at that time. The economic power of the Roane Iron Company made Rockwood a virtual company town, with the sharp divisions between the managers and the workers reflected in the range of domestic architecture along the old route of U.S. 70 (Kingston Pike) in downtown Rockwood. At the center of town are two- and three-story homes of late Victorian or Classical Revival architecture for company officials or prominent local merchants and professionals who depended on the company's patronage and presence for their livelihoods. The farther away from the center, however, the more one encounters homes of the working class, including pyramid cottages, small bungalows, and tract houses of the 1950s.

Six miles north of Rockwood on U.S. Highway 27 is Harriman, another industrial town of the late 1800s. Established in 1889 by devoted temperance advocate Walter E. Harriman, the town was once called the "Utopia of Temperance" because all land deeds sold by the East Tennessee Land Company forbade the selling, storing, or making of liquor (Siler, 38). Still standing on Roane Street (U.S. 27) is the Romanesque-style **Temperance Hall,** the original offices for the land company, before it became home to the American Temperance University and other private schools and later served as the city hall. Commercial and residential historic districts preserve other significant parts of town. At the corner of Walden and Trenton Streets is a Classical Revival **Carnegie Library,** one of the few extant libraries funded by the Carnegie Foundation in East Tennessee. Like other structures of industrial towns of the region, Harriman's buildings generally date from 1900 to 1930. During this period, the city was an important transportation and processing center for the coal industry on the Cumberland Plateau. The Harriman and Northwestern Railroad, for example, connected the city to the state-owned and prisoner-worked mines around Brushy Mountain in southern Morgan County. Today Norfolk Southern still operates several coal trains daily along this section of the line. A couple of miles north of Harriman, on Tennessee 328 at the village of Oakdale, the railroad maintains a large dormitory for its railroad crews (private, no access).

Industries and railroad connections combined to make Harriman and Rockwood the largest cities in Roane County, totally dwarfing in size and importance the much earlier county seat of Kingston, which is about four miles east of Harriman at the junction of the Clinch and Tennessee Rivers. Established in 1799, Kingston stood adjacent to **Fort Southwest Point,** founded by John Sevier in 1792. Located on a high hill at the junction of the two rivers, the fort gave settlers a good view of the surrounding countryside and offered some security from Native-American attacks. Within a decade, however, the fort became the head-quarters for the Federal Cherokee Indian Agency, headed by Return Jonathan Meigs. It remained a federal agency until the establishment of the Hiwassee Garrison in 1807.

Kingston's other nineteenth-century landmarks include the Greek Revival–style **Roane County Courthouse** (circa 1856) and the adjacent **Gideon Morgan House** (circa 1810) (private, no access).

To begin exploring the historic landscapes of the next chapter, the Cumberland Plateau, return to U.S. Highway 70 or Interstate Highway 40 and travel west for about thirty-eight miles to Crossville.

CHAPTER FIVE

The Cumberland Plateau

The Cumberland Plateau is a vast range of deep forests, steep valleys, winding rivers, and mineral-laden land that forms a considerable geographical boundary between East and Middle Tennessee. Geologist Edward T. Luther described the plateau as a "Great Wall of China" that is "a hundred times higher and fifty miles across"—a natural barrier to western migration until railroad and highway engineers mastered its difficulties in the late nineteenth and early twentieth centuries (54). This diverse and beautiful region runs from the northern border counties of Clay and Pickett through Cumberland and Putnam Counties to the almost mountainous terrain of Grundy and Marion Counties. In this chapter the northern reaches of the plateau will be limited to those counties that lie within the central time zone, but the southern half of the plateau will be broadened to include two other geologic areas: the Eastern Highland Rim and the Sequatchie Valley.

The Cumberland Plateau, according to Edward Luther, has two very different edges. The eastern edge is an "abrupt escarpment" only slightly carved by creeks and rivers; the western edge, on the other hand, is "very ragged and deeply incised" by several major rivers, including the Cumberland, Duck, and Elk (55). In between are large and sometimes untouched forests, deposits of coal, waterfalls, rivers with extensive tributaries, and good bottomland intermixed with barren, broken land poorly suited for cultivation.

The east half of the Eastern Highland Rim is a farther extension of the plateau and belongs to the larger Highland Rim geologic region that surrounds the Central Basin of Middle Tennessee. Sections here contain excellent rolling farmland, with soil based in St. Louis limestone. The pure limestone, which is highly soluble in acidic groundwater, helps to explain the region's many caves, including the cave system near McMinnville called Cumberland Caverns, which has the second-largest number of underground passageways in the country.

The Sequatchie Valley divides the southern section of the Cumberland Plateau into the plateau proper on the west and Walden Ridge on the east. High at the northern end of the Sequatchie country lie the Crab Orchard Mountains, source for the beautiful Crab Orchard stone that became a very popular regional building material in the early twentieth century.

The diverse topography and complex geology of the Cumberland Plateau have created a beautiful natural landscape. Little wonder that so many state parks and natural areas are here. Near Cookeville is the 130-foot-high Burgess Falls State Natural Area, while south of Sparta is the Virgin Falls State Natural Area. East of Spencer lies the highest falls in the eastern United States, the spectacular 256-foot-high Fall Creek Falls. This area was once devastated farmland and abused forests, but during the 1930s it became a federal recreational demonstration area. With the assistance of the Farm Security Administration, the National Park Service, and the Civilian Conservation Corps, it was reclaimed and eventually developed into Fall Creek Falls State Park. What was once a wasteland for Tennesseans became an oasis for recreation and leisure.

Other parks preserve the stark, forbidding wilderness of the plateau. Listed as a National Natural Landmark, the Savage Gulf State Natural Area in Grundy County is perhaps the most isolated place in the state. Another wilderness area is preserved by **Pickett State Park,** northeast of Jamestown, which the National Park Service and the Civilian Conservation Corps developed jointly during the 1930s. The **Cumberland Mountain State Park,** initially part of the federal Resettlement Administration's Homesteads project at Crossville, and **Standing Stone State Park** at Livingston were later CCC and WPA projects.

These parks mark more than the New Deal landscape created by federal agencies during the Great Depression (see sidebar entitled "The New Deal Built Environment," Landscape 9, chapter 4). Despite the wildness of the country and challenging terrain, most of these protected "natural areas" also have historic places where human hands have shaped the landscape over the centuries. The wildflowers, waterfalls, steep gorges, and mountain peaks today lure those who seek isolation and beauty in the Tennessee backcountry. These features meant less to past Tennesseans than the minerals underground, the timber on top, and the farmland, properly stripped of its vegetation. These, too, are places where miners dug coal in the most brutal of conditions, where farmers grew corn and tobacco and raised livestock, where reformers looked to create a new world, and where capitalists sought their big chance.

Landscape 13: The Cumberland Plateau

Crossville, the seat of Cumberland County, is the hub for our exploration of the Cumberland Plateau. All three landscapes in this chapter either begin or end at Crossville. Since the antebellum years, Crossville has been a plateau crossroads for trade and transportation as the place where the Nashville and Knoxville stage road met the stock road between Chattanooga and Kentucky. Today the four major federal roads of this region—Interstate 40, U.S. 70, U.S. 70N, and U.S. 127—converge at this spot in Cumberland County.

One of the best ways to first explore natural and historical features of the plateau is in a west to southwest direction, from Crossville to the end of the Eastern Highland Rim at Woodbury along U.S. Highway 70/70S. A second route uses Tennessee 56 to go in a north-south direction from Smithville to Tracy City and then takes U.S. 41 on to Monteagle.

Route A: The Memphis-to-Bristol Highway

> *Hordes of autos now remind us*
> > *We should build our roads to stay;*
> *And departing leave behind us*
> > *The kinds that rains don't wash away.*
> *So when our children pay the mortgage*
> > *We fathers made to haul our load,*
> *They'll not have to ask the question,*
> > *"Here's the bond but where's the road?"*
> Tennessee Highway and Public Works, April 1922

Throughout the first two decades of the twentieth century, farmers, businessmen, and travelers demanded that the state government take responsibility for building well-engineered, well-constructed, and maintained roadways. Progressives saw new roads as pathways of reform that would lift rural Tennesseans out of their poverty and ignorance. Businessmen wanted better access for their products and to use modern roads as a lure to recruit new industries. In 1913 the state approved a bond issue for the construction of the highway from Memphis to Bristol. Only during the mid-1920s, however, did Tennesseans take their first steps toward a comprehensive system of state roads. In 1922 citizens and officials created the Tennessee Good Roads Association, which promoted the state road system at county court meetings, fairs, and parades. The State Highway Act of 1923 established a reorganized state department of highways and public works, which was given total authority over state-funded highways projects and maintenance in Tennessee. These new initiatives, together with the designation of most of the highway route as U.S. 70 in 1925, spurred the construction of the Memphis-to-Bristol Highway to its completion in 1930.

U.S. 70/70S, from Crossville to Woodbury, is a seventy-six-mile stretch of highway that either passes over or parallels the original route of the Memphis-to-Bristol Highway between the Cumberland Plateau and the edge of the Eastern Highland Rim. As it crosses the rural landscape, the highway passes through several historic towns, sites, and villages that are largely unchanged from the days when the Memphis-to-Bristol Highway was the major east-west road in Tennessee.

Downtown Crossville is one such place. Its town square is dominated by the **Cumberland County Courthouse** (1905), designed by W. Chamberlin and Company of Birmingham in an eclectic Romanesque style. To the immediate east are two other important public buildings. J. F. Baumann of Knoxville was the architect of the **first county courthouse** (1886–87), which was built of local Crab Orchard stone. After a fire destroyed the interior and roof in 1905, the county renovated the old courthouse into the first county high school, which operated from 1908 to 1929. The building then became county offices and storage until recently, when the Cumberland County Historical Society acquired the property as a museum. Next door is the town's former 1937 Colonial Revival post office, but rather than the traditional red brick, this building is faced with Crab Orchard stone, making it a singular WPA design.

Indeed, since the construction of the first courthouse and city sidewalks in 1887, Crab Orchard stone has been popular with many local builders. Then, in 1925, Nashville architect Henry Hibbs used the distinctive stone for his designs at Scarritt College, bringing it national notoriety that was only multiplied when CCC and WPA designers used

Palace Theatre, Crossville. There are several other buildings in downtown Crossville that were covered with Crab Orchard stone in the middle decades of the twentieth century.

it extensively at the Cumberland Homesteads project in the mid-1930s. Many buildings in downtown Crossville added Crab Orchard stone facades during these years. For example, the architecturally significant **Palace Theatre** (1936–37) is a creative blending of Art Deco design and Crab Orchard stone by architect Eston Smith

The tracks of the Tennessee Central Railroad also have shaped downtown Crossville. The former passenger depot, built in the 1920s, is a block north of the square. The tracks cut diagonally across Main Street, creating oddly shaped commercial buildings. Across the street from the depot is the Motel Taylor, a rare surviving railroad hotel from the early twentieth century.

From Crossville, the next twenty-nine miles of the highway pass along the very top of the plateau. One writer, who traveled the old Memphis-to-Bristol Highway soon after its completion, recalled "distant views of wall-like mountains, and valleys with green pasture lands" and hills "covered with dense growths of trees, shrubs, and wild flowers" (*WPA Guide,* 464). One hundred years ago, life here was hard, as even the most creative farmer found it difficult to scratch a living out of the thin soil and challenging terrain. By the 1930s, many farmers made their cash money by cutting crossties for railroads, by picking berries during the summer, and by skinning squirrels, raccoons, opossums, and rabbits. Hunting was so important for subsistence and trade that only the poorest families lacked a pack of coon dogs.

The community of Pleasant Hill, about eleven miles east of Crossville, was an oasis of education and opportunity for plateau folk. To enter the village, leave present U.S. Highway 70 at the historical marker for Pleasant Hill and follow an original section of the Memphis-to-Bristol Highway to **Pioneer Hall** (1887–89), which is now a local history museum. Originally it was the main classroom and dormitory of the Pleasant Hill Academy, founded in 1884 by the American Missionary Association of the Congregational Church as a low-cost subscription school for plateau children. It remained the only local school until 1947, when the county school system assumed control of the facility.

At Pleasant Hill Academy, most students paid their tuition by working at the school or by raising food in nearby fields and gardens. The northern missionaries taught music, art, and foreign languages as well as the basic "three R's." In 1917 Dr. May Cravath Wharton established a medical mission at Pleasant Hill where she discovered that "everywhere, it seemed, there was work for a doctor woman to do." The poverty she encountered in the forests or along the steep hillsides shocked her. "It was poverty more complete than I had seen it even in the slums of Cleveland. . . . In so many respects they had simply nothing." But Dr. Wharton also discovered a rare strength of character among plateau folk. She found "courage, loyalty, kindness, and courtesy to old and young and strangers" as well as "a stoicism, independence and philosophizing mind." Yet, she and other reformers at Pleasant Hill were sensitive to the fact that local residents had a "temper on a trigger" and were determined "not to be dictated to" (Tretter, 19–20). Their sensitivity helps to explain why the academy met with greater acceptance and success than other reform efforts by outsiders. In her study of the Upper Cumberland, historian Jeanette Keith concluded that in general local residents "took from reformed institutions what seemed useful for the maintenance of traditional culture, and ignored those items of progress deemed irrelevant" (12).

In 1922 Dr. Wharton established a small hospital at Pleasant Hill. Five years later, after the Memphis-to-Bristol Highway had been paved through the county, she and her staff began community outreach programs, teaching "Homemade Chautauquas" at local schools. They demonstrated the latest in canning, cooking, public health, nutrition, and farming techniques. A 1932 fund-raising trip allowed Wharton to expand the hospital, and, during the Depression decade, the outreach programs augmented their scope and topics to include the general agenda of the rural reform movement. In 1950 the medical program moved to a more central location in Crossville; with federal, state, and private funding, the Cumberland Medical Center opened its doors and still serves plateau people today. At Pleasant Hill stands Wharton's last project, a retirement center called Uplands, Inc.

The road in front of Pleasant Hill Academy continues west to junction with current U.S. Highway 70. About four miles west, in White County, are small villages with a much different history. On county roads off either side of the highway are the sites of the early-twentieth-century coal towns of Eastland, Ravenscroft, and Clifty, while the highway passes through the villages of DeRossett and Bon Air. These coal mines employed thousands of workers from the 1880s until they closed in the Great Depression, leaving busted dreams, scarred workers, abandoned towns, and few physical remains of the mines themselves, save for the place names. Those who remain today call their community BonDeCroft, a combined reference to Bon Air, DeRossett, and Ravenscroft.

The first coalfield was at Bon Air, established in 1882 by Sparta resident Gen. George Dibrell, who owned fifteen thousand acres in White County. However, the real economic power behind the venture was probably the Nashville, Chattanooga, and St. Louis Railroad; its president, E. W. Cole, also served as the chairman of the coal company's executive committee. The mine was an immediate success, and by 1884 the NC&St.L extended a spur line from McMinnville to Sparta. Three years later, the spur line was extended to Bon Air, leaving Sparta on present-day Gaines Street and winding its way up the plateau. By 1905 the Bon Air branch reached the mines at Clifty and Ravenscroft.

Between 1888 and 1904, Bon Air Coal Company and the Clifty Creek Coal and Coke Company established four towns on the plateau overlooking Sparta. The Bon Air Coal Company owned at least thirty-eight thousand acres and employed six hundred men from both White and Cumberland Counties. Over the next two decades, the mines reached new peaks in production, and by 1917 they came under the consolidated control of William J. Cummins and other investors who would later create the Tennessee Products Corporation. Its headquarters was at Ravenscroft, where it operated the state's only coal shaft mine, along with a coal-distillation plant that produced acetic acid, vinegar, and alcohol until both the mine and plant closed in 1936. The coal-mining history of White County—which had ranked sixth in statewide production as late as 1920—came to an abrupt end. Considering

Rock House, White County.

the number of people who once worked the mines and the investments made by the companies, it is eerie today to travel through these hills and find so little evidence of the old coal-mining days. The people, money, and machinery were brought together for the intensive exploitation of a natural resource; once that was gone, there was nothing left to keep them here. The coal towns of White County became ghost towns.

From Bon Air, U.S. Highway 70 descends the Cumberland Plateau quickly. On the north side of the road, there is a scenic overlook that allows the visitor to scan the landscape of northern White County. This can be a spectacular view in the fall. At the foot of the plateau, on the south side, there is a historic sign pointing out the **Rock House,** a stone tollhouse built by Barlow Fiske between 1835 and 1839, that once served travelers on the Knoxville-to-Nashville turnpike. Fiske later operated a store in this building during the 1850s, and the toll gate was still in business as late as 1857. The building is open by appointment with the local DAR chapter.

From Rock House, there are two different routes to travel the three miles west to Sparta. The fastest is the present U.S. Highway 70. The more historic is the paved, yet narrower route that lies in front of Rock House. This road is a remnant of the Memphis-to-Bristol Highway where engineers used the old roadbed of the Sparta to Bon Air railroad

Hill House, Sparta. An eclectic yet delightful statement of early-twentieth-century domestic architecture in Sparta's residential historic district.

for the highway right-of-way. This road reconnects with U.S. 70 in downtown Sparta via Gaines Street, which has an interesting mix of early-twentieth-century housing. The neighborhood was originally platted as the Eastland subdivision, and new business, professional, and political leaders built homes here during the 1920s. The most important was the yellow poplar log bungalow at 403 Gaines (private, no access), designed and built in 1928 by local master carpenter John Reece Green for John Welch. An attorney, Welch also was a real estate developer, president of the local school board, a house builder, and president of Cumberland Lumber Company. He also controlled the considerable timber business in White County.

Lumber was a second natural resource taken in vast amounts from White County during the early twentieth century. The Sparta Spoke Factory was one of the region's largest, and, during World War I, White County walnut was in great demand for gun stocks, which were ordered first by Allied nations and then by the federal government once the United States entered the war in 1917. To handle the increased traffic in timber and coal, officials of the Nashville, Chattanooga, and St. Louis Railroad built a new brick combination **passenger and freight station** in 1917, just off U.S. 70 on Depot Street (private, no access).

This depot is listed in the National Register, as is the town's oldest neighborhood, a residential area along Main, College, and Church Streets directly north of the town square. Reflecting a cross section of American domestic architecture during the early twentieth century—

the years of Sparta's coal-and-timber boom—these dwellings include Queen Anne, bungalow, American Four-Square, and Classical Revival designs. The **Turner House** (circa 1915) at 115 North Main is an extremely late example of the vernacular Piano Box form, a house that has two gable wings connected by a long center section where the front door is located. Just up the street at 137 North Main is the **Crosslin House** (circa 1915), one of the region's best examples of the American Four-Square house, built by John Welch. A late example of Victorian style is the Queen Anne–influenced **Howell House** (circa 1908) at 137 North Church. The **Hill House** (1880, 1900), an eclectic combination of turn-of-the-century designs, stands at 105 College (all houses are private, no access). Early-twentieth-century buildings, such as the Classical Revival American Legion Hall and the Art Moderne **Oldham Theater** (1935, 1942), surround the town square. The White County Courthouse (1975) is a mix of late-twentieth-century Classical Revival design ideas by architect M. J. Lide.

To continue on the original route of the Memphis-to-Bristol Highway, leave U.S. Highway 70 at Sparta and instead take U.S. Highway 70S to the southwest. From Doyle to Rock Island, the road closely follows the NC&St.L spur line from McMinnville to Sparta through an agrarian countryside marked with small railroad-associated towns. The tiny village of Quebeck still has its original board-and-batten railroad depot, complete with pronounced Victorian-style brackets (private, no access). Rock Island has an even smaller historic depot (also private, no access), but the story here is much more about electric power than railroads. Inside Rock Island State Park, near the confluence of the Collins and Caney Fork Rivers, is the historic **Great Falls Hydroelectric Plant,** which first went into operation on January 1, 1917. Established by a private company to power new industry in White and Warren Counties, the complex stretches eight hundred feet across the Collins River. The Tennessee Electric Power Company (TEPCO) acquired the property in 1922 and managed it until the Tennessee Valley Authority bought the plant in 1939.

Also within park boundaries, on the Caney Fork River, is the **Great Falls Cotton Mill,** a three-story brick building that represented the first major industrial development of this natural landscape. In 1892 Clay Faulkner, H. L. Walling, and Jesse Walling established the textile mill with thirty thousand dollars in capital; before the year was out, the mill was producing four thousand yards of cotton sheeting every day.

The owners also built the mill village of Fall City where workers lived in cramped quarters for the next ten years until the mill, already damaged by a flood, was sold along with the townsite to the Great Falls Power Company in 1902. Another historic structure at the park is the 656-foot-long Rock Island Bridge (1889, 1924), which spans the Collins River.

Once the highway leaves Rock Island, it soon meets a divided four-lane highway that continues to McMinnville. The old Memphis-to-Bristol route is either bypassed or incorporated into the new highway until it reaches downtown McMinnville. Cotton mills and electric power are also important themes here. Just north of town, at the community of Faulkner Springs, was the cotton-mill empire of Asa Faulkner, the leading industrialist of nineteenth-century Warren County. His home, **Falconhurst** (1850), documents the transition from Federal to Greek Revival architecture in the late antebellum period (private, limited access). This place also was the boyhood home of noted composer and folk music scholar Charles Faulkner Bryan.

Incorporated in 1826, McMinnville has several landmarks from its early history. In 1825 Jesse Coffee built the **Black House,** a brick Federal-style house at 301 West Main. The house name dates from the residence of Dr. Thomas Black, a local physician (public, limited access). Also along Main Street are two splendid Victorian Gothic churches, the First United Methodist Church (1889) and the First Presbyterian Church (1878). Although it has lost its clock tower, the red-brick Warren County Courthouse (1897) interprets Romanesque style in a restrained manner.

These nineteenth-century buildings mix well with early-twentieth-century properties. Clearly the town enjoyed a minor revival in public architecture after the Memphis-to-Bristol Highway improved the city's transportation ties to the outside world. Across from the courthouse is the **McMinnville Post Office** (1931), designed in Colonial Revival style by James A. Wetmore. On the east route of U.S. 70S is another 1930s building, the McMinnville City Electric Building, that is a dazzling blend of Art Deco and classical elements. A third architectural style is represented by the **Magness Community House and Library** (1931) on Main Street. Designed by Nashville architect George D. Waller, this Classical Revival building was as much a community center as it was a library. It even had showers in its basement to serve both county residents who used the new road to come to town and travelers passing through.

About nine miles west of McMinnville on U.S. Highway 70S is the old country town of Centertown, once a trade and processing center for farmers in eastern Warren County. Besides the feed mills, churches, and local school, there is an interesting 1919 brick town bank that faces the highway. Many country towns had local banks, invariably located on the village's most prominent corner, before the Great Depression shut their doors for good.

From Centertown, the Memphis-to-Bristol Highway continued west toward the edge of the Highland Rim. In the community of Bluewing, at the junction of Tennessee 281 and U.S. 70S adjacent to the East Side Elementary School, stands the ranch-style home and historic farm of Cling West (private, no access). This former sheriff and road commissioner in Cannon County began his career as a road builder working on the construction of the Memphis-to-Bristol Highway. When his great grandfather William West established the family farm in about 1830, only two farms stood in this highland area between McMinnville and Woodbury.

Two miles west, U.S. Highway 70S descends the eastern face of the Rim to Woodbury, the seat of government for Cannon County. At the junction of U.S. 70S and Tennessee 53 is **"Beaver Dam,"** the historic home of Congressman William C. Houston, who served in the United States Congress from 1905 to 1919 (private, no access). Sections of the first floor date from Sam McFerrin's Indian trading post of circa 1810. In 1838 one group of Cherokees camped overnight in front of the house during their infamous Trail of Tears trek. When Houston acquired the home in 1873, it had evolved into a two-story central-hall house, with an understated Greek Revival portico. Over the next three decades, as his political and economic fortunes improved, Houston added new rooms and wings to the dwelling, turning it into one of the county's finest by the time of his election to Congress in 1904. While still in politics, Houston became an agricultural leader in Cannon County by building the area's first silo in 1916. He also brought the latest of technology to his home, being the first in Woodbury to have indoor plumbing, a telephone, and electricity. From his retirement in 1918 to his death in 1931, Houston's "Beaver Dam" continued as a social and political center, visited by such Democratic allies as John Nance Garner and Sam Rayburn. One obituary remarked that Houston's "home was an open house and many were the friends whom he entertained. . . . He lived beside the Memphis to Bristol highway, which is the main highway from Washington to the Southwest, and many of his

Houston House, Woodbury. A historic landmark in Cannon County for over 150 years.

old Congressional friends still often visited en route to or from Washington" (National Register nomination).

Dominating the Woodbury square is the **Cannon County Courthouse** (1936), a well-executed Colonial Revival design by Nashville architect George D. Waller. The courthouse is only one of two built in that style in Tennessee during the 1930s. But its red-brick, symmetrical facade, complete with pilasters and cupola, was typical of Colonial Revival public buildings of that decade.

Adjacent to the southwest corner of the square, and also facing the original Memphis-to-Bristol Highway, is a more understated Colonial Revival building, the Good Samaritan Hospital (now the county board of education offices), established in 1933–34 by Dr. Jesse F. Adams and designed by local craftsman Henry Hoover. Adams was involved in many different Woodbury enterprises, from banks to the town's first factories. He lived for forty years on nearby College Street in a two-story brick home, a masterful blending of Greek Revival and Italianate styles built between 1857 and 1859 by local craftsman William Wharton. The **Adams House** was originally used as a dormitory for the Baptist Female College in Woodbury (private, no access).

The next route follows Tennessee 53 north of Woodbury for about fifteen miles to the rural village of Liberty. This two-lane road provides a fascinating vernacular landscape of stone fences, hills, pastureland, and one-hundred-year-old frame houses. Ownership of land has historically been in small parcels in this area so the countryside has a crazy-quilt mixture of fence types, sizes of fields, types of homes, and different outbuildings. First settled in 1807, Liberty has served as a rural trade center and community ever since. The **Liberty historic district**

Common Farm Outbuildings

Houses mark the emotional and administrative center of individual farmsteads, but the farm work itself took place in the surrounding outbuildings and fields. The size and function of the barns, sheds, and cribs also record a farm's change from subsistence to market-driven agriculture.

Around the dwelling, there is a variety of outbuildings where women usually either accomplished or supervised most of the work. Privies—or outhouses—usually stood at one corner of the yard. On the opposite end of the yard, ideally, stood the springhouse, which provided fresh water and a cool place to store perishables. Between the two were chicken coops, storage places like potato houses, and a laundry. Many farms also had a smokehouse for smoking hams and bacon.

Outside of this domestic complex, usually set aside by fences and gates, were barns, sheds, and cribs to house the equipment, animals, and crops that produced goods for market. Flue-cured tobacco barns were tall and square in shape, with sheds flanking each side of the building. Most of the long, rectangular, and well-ventilated burley tobacco barns were built in the last one hundred years. Log corncribs, or log outbuildings of any type, more likely date from the mid-1800s, perhaps even earlier. From 1910 forward, livestock barns often followed standardized plans and designs provided by the University of Tennessee Agricultural Extension Service. Extension agents also handed out plans for equipment sheds, "hog parlors," garages, and other specialized buildings designed for the modern agricultural market. Local and community builders would take these plans and alter them during construction to make work easier and faster to accomplish.

During the early twentieth century, the dairy industry rapidly expanded throughout Tennessee. The tall silo dominates the dairy farm. Early-twentieth-century silos usually are built of concrete and cement. In the late 1940s, the A. O. Smith Co. developed the metal and fiberglass Harvestore silo; its bright blue enamel exterior quickly became a symbol of the prosperous dairy farmer. The silo draws the observer's attention to the large livestock barn, where hay, feed, and cattle are stored. Adjacent is the concrete milk house, where the milking machinery is kept in addition to the refrigerators that keep the milk at fifty degrees until trucks can pick it up.

Family cemeteries also exist on many Tennessee farms. These usually stand at a distance from the house, perhaps near the road or on a nearby hill overlooking the farm. There is rarely a sadder sight on the country roads of Tennessee than an abandoned family cemetery, overgrown and barely visible. In too many cases, it is the only remnant remaining from a once-proud family farm.

has vernacular interpretations of Greek Revival, Gothic, and Queen Anne architecture, as well as compelling local churches, a cemetery, and a very interesting early-twentieth-century school complex where a local history room is located. From Liberty, the route leads east on U.S. Highway 70 for twelve miles to Smithville.

Route B: Farming and Mining in the Southern Cumberland

To follow this route, take Tennessee Highway 56 from Smithville to Tracy City and then U.S. Highway 41 from Tracy City to Monteagle.

Tennessee Highway 56 passes through a wonderfully diverse landscape along the Eastern Highland Rim. From Smithville to McMinnville is an agricultural landscape that parallels the Caney Fork River (now Center Hill Lake) to the east. South of McMinnville, the highway closely follows the Collins River through the region's nursery business. After the community of Irving College, however, the highway ascends the escarpment of the Cumberland Plateau to the historic resort of Beersheba Springs in Grundy County. To the south in this rugged and forbidding country are the South Cumberland coalfields and the mining towns of Coalmont and Tracy City.

Farming, resorts, and mining have dominated this region's history, and these human efforts at extracting a living from the rugged terrain have left a lasting mark on the landscape, ranging from county seats to tobacco barns, from coke ovens to colorful resort architecture.

Established in 1838, Smithville is the seat of DeKalb County and the southern gateway to the Center Hill Lake recreation area. The courthouse square still looks like an early-twentieth-century town, complete with an old Texaco gas station, even though the courthouse is fairly modern. It was designed by the firm of Maffett, Howland, and Associates and built in 1970–71 with funds from the federal "Model Cities" program. Smithville received the coveted federal money because of the power wielded by its local congressman, Joe L. Evins, who served in the U.S. Congress from 1947 to 1977, the longest period of continuous service for any Tennessee representative. Due to his seniority, Evins gained enormous power and made sure that federal money flowed to projects in his Congressional district.

Joe L. Evins was the son of Edgar Evins, who did more than any other businessman to reshape the fortunes of Smithville in the early 1900s. The elder Evins organized, owned, and served as president of the local Consolidated Bus Lines and the Consolidated Oil Company.

He chaired the board of directors of both the Alexandria Bank and Trust Company and the Liberty Savings Bank. Evins leveraged his control over local capital investment into a successful building contracting company, which constructed the city hall, fire hall, high school gym, Van Hooser hospital-clinic, and a thirty-room private hotel. He also accepted commissions for smaller business blocks, stores, private dwellings, and club buildings, like the local Masonic hall. His **Evins Block** at 101–3 North Fourth Street is representative of his company's work.

Edgar Evins, in other words, not only reshaped Smithville in an economic sense; he also reshaped the town's very physical appearance. He typifies an early-twentieth-century phenomenon that social historians have dubbed "civic capitalists." Evins was an aggressive local businessman who operated several different companies while, at the same time, he controlled the levers of local capital by sitting on the boards of the county's banks. He was politically prominent and served fifteen years as town mayor and nineteen years on the county court before he was elected to the state senate in 1935. Evins, like other "civic capitalists" across the country, lived in the town where his investments were made and demonstrated a willingness to work with other business owners for their mutually shared interests in seeing the community prosper.

The Evins family home, "Cumberland House," is at 300 East Main Street (private, limited access). Originally built by Andrew Jackson Goodson in 1890, Edgar Evins bought the home in 1907 and turned its traditional late Georgian facade into the town's best example of the Colonial Revival, adding both a two-story classical portico and one-story pergolas to the front facade. After acquiring the home in 1960, Joe L. Evins modernized its interior and added a new bedroom and office. Thus, the house documents the tastes and needs of both Edgar and Joe L. Evins, the most significant individuals in Smithville's twentieth-century history.

From Smithville, the next eighteen miles of Tennessee 56 parallels the Caney Fork River, which the U.S. Army Corps of Engineers dammed in 1948 to create Center Hill Lake. Before the dam was closed, the Smithsonian Institution sponsored hurried salvage excavations of significant Native-American sites along the river. Prehistoric inhabitants had hunted, lived, and worshiped along this river valley for probably ten thousand years. Archaeologists located twenty-eight village sites as well as several ceremonial mounds that provided evidence about different Indian cultures. Some of the best evidence concerned Mississippian peoples who lived in the Caney Fork country from about A.D. 900 to 1450.

They lived in villages of thatched huts, built ceremonial mounds, and raised vegetables such as corn and beans for their own use and for trade.

Important sites documenting the lives of early Native-American inhabitants from Archaic, Woodland, and Mississippian cultures also can be found near Tennessee 56 south of McMinnville as the highway closely follows the path of the Collins River. These people were the first farmers of Tennessee, and agriculture has dominated the lives of those who live here ever since. The well-watered fertile land along this road has lured both Native Americans and white settlers. In the twentieth century, nursery farms—producing shade and ornamental trees, fruit trees, shrubs, evergreens, and other landscaping plants—have evolved into a big agricultural business. In the mid-1980s, over three hundred certified growers, with over three thousand acres in plants, were established in Warren County. Many nurseries are located along Tennessee 56 south of McMinnville, and most are open to the public.

This road also includes the community institutions of a rural society. Several country stores are still in business. The white-frame Fairview community center is an excellent example of the standardized architecture typical of rural schools built in the 1920s. The school at Irving College, by comparison, is a modern brick building, standing where both private and public schools have served local farm families for generations. To the southwest is the **Northcutts Cove Latter Day Saints Chapel** (1901), which marks an early Mormon settlement in south-central Tennessee. It served as the church's East Tennessee conference headquarters.

From Irving College, Tennessee Highway 56 soon begins its ascent up the Cumberland Plateau to the resort community of **Beersheba Springs**. Over one hundred years ago, the rugged landscape of Grundy County attracted entrepreneurs who wanted to exploit the minerals underground and the timber on top, as well as entrepreneurs who wanted a respite from their industrialized towns and cities to breath fresh mountain air and enjoy the plateau's breathtaking scenery.

In 1839 George R. Smartt and Dr. Alfred Paine established Beersheba Springs' first resort, where wealthy southerners could take advantage of the scenery and also bathe in the "therapeutic" waters from a nearby chalybeate spring. Fifteen years later, John Armfield purchased the property and greatly improved its grounds and housing, building a large hotel, with a two-story Doric portico, for his guests. He further provided individual cottages for such prominent patrons as the Episcopal bishops Leonidas Polk and James Otey.

Beersheba Springs Inn, Grundy County. This inspiring Greek Revival portico sits high on the Cumberland Plateau overlooking the Collins River Valley.

Beersheba Springs reached its height of popularity and prosperity during Armfield's ownership. Four hundred guests could visit at a time, and, although liquor and gambling were prohibited, they could dance, play games, sing, or bathe at the spring. After the Civil War, the village entered into a period of decline, especially after the 1880s when

Monteagle Assembly attracted some of the same clientele that once visited Beersheba Springs. The cottages came under private ownership, and the hotel complex changed owners several times until 1941 when the Tennessee Methodist Conference purchased the site as a retreat. The conference continues to maintain the hotel complex, which is open to the public to a limited degree.

The blending of log-and-frame construction, along with the mix of classical and Victorian styles, make the resort architecturally significant. In addition to the hotel, there is a scenic walk along Armfield Avenue, which includes homes such as the **Armfield Cottage** (1833–39) and the **Bass Cottage** (1856–58) (private, no access).

This landscape of leisure and recreation changes quickly to the south. Five miles south on Tennessee 56 is Altamont, a tiny county seat that has seen most of its commercial concerns close their doors. The **Northcutt House** (1885) is a good local example of vernacular Italianate architecture, and the property also has a circa 1840 log building that is believed to be the first courthouse in Grundy County (private, no access).

The road becomes more curvy and slow as Tennessee 56 winds for another five miles to its junction with Tennessee 108. Here it is possible to take a brief side trip for three miles east to Gruetli, an old Swiss agricultural colony established in 1869. The word *Gruetli* in Swiss means "to root out or clear away," and certainly the colonists found much clearing to do as they prepared the rugged and heavily forested land for cultivation. Knoxville businessman Peter Staub had lured overseas colonists with an advertising pamphlet that portrayed Gruetli as a virtual wilderness paradise, but the first colonists found miles of dense forest rather than open meadows. Most had no choice but to make the best of their new homes in America, and by 1874 about sixty emigrants lived here. Almost one hundred Swiss families eventually came; each received a surveyed lot of one hundred acres. Farming the thin topsoil was exceedingly difficult at first, but the colonists experimented with new crops, natural fertilizers, and cultivation techniques. Soon their prosperous properties produced beef, dairy products (especially Swiss cheese), fruits, cider, and wine. Their new landscape of organized and prosperous farms replaced the wildness of nature that had greeted the first colonists.

For thirty years, the Gruetli colonists preserved their cultural heritage, keeping their German language, German Reformed faith, music, and traditional crafts. In 1920 a second Swiss colony named Laager was established just to the east. Like many rural communities, Gruetli

Coalmont Bank Building, Grundy County. Once a place symbolizing the company's domination of town life, this old company office and bank is now a local library and community center.

and Laager began to steadily lose population and cultural cohesion during the mid-twentieth century. Farms once abandoned soon returned to nature. In 1981 the two communities formally combined to create the town of Gruetli-Laager. Today only a few of the original Swiss dwellings, such as the **Suter House** (1885), the **Stoker-Stampfli House** (1870), and the **Scholer Farm** (1870), mark the original settlement landscape.

After returning to Tennessee 56, the route leaves an agricultural landscape to encounter the history of coal mining in the southern Cumberland Plateau. In 1903 the Sewanee Coal, Coke, and Land Company established Coalmont as a company town, where it operated several mines and a battery of coke ovens. Soon the hills around Coalmont were stripped of their timber to feed the voracious appetites of the ovens that operated until 1944. Where travelers now see forested hills, a virtual moonscape greeted visitors sixty years ago. In 1908 the coal company reorganized itself as the Sewanee Fuel and Iron Company and operated the complex for the next forty years. Representing the link between the town and company is the Craftsman-style **Coalmont Bank Building** (1921). The first floor housed a post office and local bank, while the second floor had company offices.

Coalmont also features company houses ranging from one-story frame dwellings with side-gable roofs to pyramidal cottages that feature a central chimney. A few coke oven ruins remain too. African-American laborers once worked the ovens, and a tiny neighborhood of about twelve houses and a black school stood nearby. Racial violence during the 1920s caused the African Americans to quit Coalmont for good.

Tracy City, about seven miles south on Tennessee 56, lies at the heart of the Southern Cumberland coalfields. Entrepreneurs established wagon mines here in the 1840s, but large-scale development was delayed until the Nashville and Chattanooga Railroad reached Tracy City in 1858. The Sewanee Mining Company, created in 1852 by a group of mostly northern investors—including Samuel Tracy, for whom Tracy City is named—held early dominance. In 1860, however, the mines passed into the hands of Tennessee investors, headed by Arthur S. Colyar of the Tennessee Coal and Railroad Company.

After the Civil War, Colyar's company quickly expanded production, relying mostly on convict labor (the company paid the state forty cents a day per convict) to operate its coke ovens and mines. As Colyar later explained, convict laborers gave the company "an effective club to hold over the heads of free laborers" (Jones, 6); in other words, free labor had little choice but to accept low pay or risk being replaced by convict labor. By the mid-1870s, the company had 120 coke ovens in and around Tracy City and owned thousands of acres of land. In 1882 John H. Inman reorganized the company into the Tennessee Coal, Iron, and Railroad Company, which in time would become the largest industrial concern in the Mid-South. Tennessee Coal and Iron hired even more convict laborers, who continued to strip local forests for fuel to fire its coke ovens. By 1883 another complex of 130 ovens stood at Lone Rock, northeast of Tracy City.

The remaining free miners struck back in 1892. They commandeered trains and railroaded the convict laborers out of the county. Tennessee Coal and Iron retaliated and shipped in new convicts. Finally, after four years of struggle and violence, the company agreed to stop hiring convict labor. Yet, by this time, the company had already exhausted the most lucrative coal seams. In less than a decade, the company closed its Tracy City works and moved to Birmingham, Alabama, which was emerging as the steel capital of the New South.

The new owner of the Tracy City mines was Tennessee Consolidated Coal Company, which took a hard line with local United Mine Workers members. The early 1900s witnessed the great coal boom in southern history, and Tennessee Consolidated had no intention of letting union concerns slow production. In 1905 violence between union miners and company employees led to the murder of two miners. Gov. John Cox used the murders as a pretext to send in national guard troops to end the bloodshed and to force the miners back to work. This incident began a series of periodic conflicts between miners and the company that were not resolved until a bitter twenty-seven month strike in the mid-1920s, which eventually left the union bankrupt and broken.

The Great Depression finished what was left of the mining industry of Grundy County. At one time, 72 percent of the county's workers were on relief. In reaction to the depth of poverty and the lack of opportunity in the corporate-controlled small towns, in 1932 social workers and CIO union organizers Myles Horton and Don West established Highlander Folk School, about four miles west of Tracy City along U.S. Highway 41. Here Horton and his colleagues discussed new ways to protect worker rights as well as to offer support to community values, traditions, and identity. Local residents put on plays, held dances, and enjoyed other recreational and educational programs at the school. Resisting CIO pressure to become more conformist in the cold war years, Highlander later nurtured a generation of men and women, like Rosa Parks of Birmingham, who played important roles in the civil rights movement. Throughout the middle decades of the century, concludes historian John Egerton, Highlander proved to be "an effective voice for unionism, integration, and the rights of the poor" (*Shades,* 59). Yet, its principled stand against racism eventually brought organized governmental pressure to close the school. A raid in 1959 led to the arrest and the trial of Myles Horton and others. Two years later, the state closed Highlander and confiscated its property. Rather than contest these arbitrary seizures, the staff moved its headquarters and projects to East Tennessee.

Highlander school, like many properties once associated with the coal-mining era in Grundy County, is gone today, nothing more than a modern-day archaeological site. Many of the mines and coal-processing areas, of course, were designed to last only a few years; others were dismantled for scrap or moved to other locations. As the mines closed, small coal towns disappeared as their transitory houses and stores were moved elsewhere. However, in and around Tracy City, several places still document the mining past. One mile east of Tennessee 56 is Grundy Lakes State Park. First developed as a CCC reclamation project from 1938 to 1939, its **Grundy Lakes historic district** has remains of beehive coke ovens built as part of the Lone Rock works in the early 1880s.

Coke Oven ruins, Grundy Lakes State Park. Diligent efforts from CCC workers transformed these circa 1880s coke ovens and the surrounding devastated landscape into the Grundy Lake State Park. Different actions by different people at different times and for different motives combined to create this unique historical place.

The layers of history represented by this landscape are interesting to consider. The first man-made landscape was one of environmental and human degradation as convict labor worked in brutal conditions, stripping the countryside of its timber to fuel the insatiable appetites of the coke ovens. A generation later, a group of young men found their way through the Great Depression as part of the federal CCC program and erased most of the foul environmental destruction. They built a lake and a small recreational park, leaving only the ruins of the coke ovens to remind the future of what this place was once like.

On Jasper Road in Tracy City is **Miner's Hall** (1902), which served members of the United Mine Workers Local #510. At the corner of Depot and Montgomery Streets is the **Shook-Boyd House,** the Second Empire mansion of Col. A. M. Shook, who was the general manager of the coal company during the 1880s. Next door is the **Hampton-Baggenstoss House,** at the corner of Depot and Oak Streets, where E. L. Hampton lived when he organized the Tennessee Consolidated Coal Company in 1904 (both homes are private, no access).

Monteagle is seven miles west of Tracy City on U.S. Highway 41. This village is a popular vacation spot, with places available in the state parks and private resorts of the Southern Cumberlands. On U.S. 41 is the South Cumberland Visitor Center, a state park facility that intro-

Shook-Boyd House, Tracy City.

duces travelers to the region's scenic and natural beauty. Within the town is a wonderful man-made landscape, the original Chautauqua village of **Monteagle Assembly,** which has been a summer resort for elite southern families for over one hundred years. The village is private and not open to the public, but **Edgeworth Inn** is a bed-and-breakfast open year-round that allows nonresidents an opportunity to experience the village's delightful Victorian architecture.

The Monteagle Sunday School Assembly contains ninety-six acres and almost two hundred buildings, mostly in the picturesque Victorian styles of Carpenter Gothic and Queen Anne associated with the Chautauqua villages of the late nineteenth century. Community events center at the village mall, around which stand **Warren's Chapel,** an auditorium, gazebo, the **Pilcher Memorial Arch**, and **Nashville House,** one of the original village rooming houses. The landscape reflects an 1883 design by William Webster, who had already planned other northern Chautauqua villages, as adapted and expanded by Nashville landscape engineer F. A. Butler in 1907. Butler eliminated the village lake and much of the highly ornamental landscaping, choosing instead a much more rustic, naturalistic approach in keeping with the local topography and spirit of the Craftsman movement of that decade. Indeed, several cottages built in the early 1900s are excellent examples of Craftsman bungalow and Rustic styles of architecture.

Monteagle Assembly is the only historic Chautauqua village remaining in the South. The Chautauqua movement began in New York State as an attempt to better educate Sunday school teachers, both in religion and in the broader aspects of American culture. Here at Monteagle, Sunday school training was the initial goal, but as the Chautauqua movement had done nationwide, the village soon branched out to more secular concerns and hosted lectures on a wide variety of topics. The assembly became a place to nurture music, art, and literature, and from 1901 to 1913 the progressive Peabody College of Nashville held summer classes at Monteagle, with as many as thirty-one instructors.

The family of Southern Agrarian writer Andrew Nelson Lytle had a rustic cabin at the assembly. Here Lytle first heard the southern writer and teacher John Crowe Ransom, who later taught English at Vanderbilt and produced such notable students as Donald Davidson, Allen Tate, and Robert Penn Warren. These writers and others, including Peter Taylor, Eleanor Ross, and Madison Jones, came to the assembly for intellectual and spiritual nourishment. "All along," Lytle remarked, "this place has been congenial for artists. They work well here, in season or out." Monteagle's history, he concluded, "admonishes the present to continue to be a place to promulgate and cultivate the arts" (Waldrop, 318, 320). Since those days, the summer programs at Monteagle (which are often open to the public who pay an admission fee) have maintained standards of excellence and creativity that stand in sharp contrast to the legacy of exploitation and violence documented elsewhere in the southern Cumberland Plateau.

Landscape 14: The Sequatchie Valley

The Sequatchie Valley is a unique place within the Tennessee landscape. As an English travel writer noted more than one hundred years ago, the valley begins wide and fertile. The road the Englishman traveled back then was like "a country lane, with green fields, and venerable trees in the fencerows, with mountain slopes of all heights up to eighteen hundred feet, and close at hand." This terrain, he thought, "would suggest Switzerland, but the chestnut rails have a national individuality not European." As he continued north of Pikeville, the landscape changed: "the scene becomes wilder, the fields disappear, and steep ridges take their place. There is no room for fields now. Soon there is no room for our road, which is crowded into the gravels of the Sequachee [sic] River, here a clear brook." He was now traveling back up the wall of the Cumberland Plateau where "steeper grows the ridges until even the soil has no abiding place on them. . . . Still on we go, crossing the creek a dozen or so times in half a mile until we have run the gauntlet of the ridges, and are near the end of our journey." This was the stark land where Cumberland Homesteads would be established about fifty years later (Raulston, 18–19).

This chapter generally follows the Englishman's path. It begins at South Pittsburg, just south of the confluence of the Sequatchie and Tennessee Rivers. From here to Jasper and then to Dunlap is a largely industrial landscape, one of railroads, cement plants, and coal mines. At Dunlap, however, the railroad tracks stop, and the agricultural landscape of the Sequatchie Valley begins: prosperous farms line both sides of the river until the road begins to climb the Cumberland Plateau to reach one of the most fascinating social experiments in Tennessee history, the New Deal landscape of Cumberland Homesteads.

Route A: Mining in the Sequatchie Valley

To reach South Pittsburg from Monteagle, return to Interstate Highway 24 and drive seventeen miles east to exit 152. South Pittsburg is to the southeast, along U.S. Highway 72. This exploration of mining in the Sequatchie Valley begins on U.S. Highway 72 from South Pittsburg to Jasper and takes old Tennessee Highway 28 from Jasper to Dunlap.

The name "South Pittsburg" conveys the hopes that industrialists once placed in this community near the confluence of the Sequatchie and Tennessee Rivers. Headed by James Bowron, the Southern States Coal, Iron, and Land Company established the town in about 1873. The financial panic of that year, however, delayed the construction of company machine shops, iron foundries, furnaces, houses, and town streets until 1876.

Engineer F. P. Clute divided the townsite into distinct business, residential, and industrial zones. His still intact plan gives visual coherence to the urban landscape. The historic residential neighborhood includes the Gothic-style **Christ Episcopal Church** (1882–84) at the corner of West Third and Holly Streets.

In 1886 the assets of the townsite were reorganized into the South Pittsburg City Company, which immediately launched an aggressive campaign to attract new business and industry. In 1887 capitalists formed the **First National Bank** (now the city hall) at 204 West Third;

it is the town's most distinctive example of Victorian commercial architecture. By 1890 South Pittsburg had pencil factories, hosiery mills, brick mills, and lumber mills to accompany the large iron works of the Tennessee Coal, Iron, and Railroad Corporation.

But the bright promise of the Gay Nineties soon dimmed in the early 1900s when Tennessee Coal and Iron announced plans to relocate its works to Birmingham. To the rescue came industrialist Richard Hardy, who looked at the region's abundant limestone resources and decided that here would be the perfect place for his new Dixie Portland Cement Company. In 1907 Hardy opened his state-of-the-art factory in the new town of Richard City, directly adjacent to South Pittsburg on U.S. Highway 72. From 1907 to 1911, his large factory was the only producer of portland cement in Tennessee. It employed over six hundred workers and shipped an average of fifty railroad cars full of cement every day. Remnants of the old factory complex still stand directly north of Richard City (private, no access).

In 1926 Dixie Portland Cement merged into the Penn-Dixie Cement Company, and two years later its Richard City works were modernized with the latest in technology. Over the next two decades, the plant continued to modernize, but every change brought less demand for workers. What once had been a powerful economic fulcrum in Marion County became just another factory that impacted the lives of only a hundred families rather than the lives of hundreds of families. In 1982 Penn-Dixie sold the factory to Florida Mining and Materials, which later that year became part of Moore McCormick Resources. The new owners wanted local workers to drop their union affiliation; when the employees refused, the corporation abruptly closed the factory. By 1985 Richard City was no longer a viable town and was annexed by South Pittsburg.

The original **Richard City townsite,** designed by Lee Hunt Engineering, documents the high hopes Hardy once had for his empire. The design reflects the typical functional street grid of that time. But by walking through the neighborhood, travelers may notice several distinctive elements that connect Richard City to its roots as a cement factory company town. A cement-covered road leads from the town to the factory. Many cement stucco homes that Dixie Portland Cement built for factory workers remain as residences. Most are either in the Pyramid Cottage vernacular style or have a rectangular cottage form called the "Dixie cottage." A few remaining cement fences also separate individual yards from the street. The most impressive remnant of Hardy's town is

Hardy Memorial School, Richard City. The monumental classicism of the Hardy Memorial School reflected the paternalistic goals of the builders of Richard City.

the **Richard Hardy Memorial School** (1926), a grand neoclassical building built of cement at 1620 Hamilton Avenue. Designed by Chattanooga architect Charles E. Bearden, the school's library and huge auditorium served as community centers for Hardy's workers. Originally named the Dixie Portland Memorial School, officials changed the name to Hardy Memorial after Richard Hardy died in 1927.

Jasper, the seat of government for Marion County, is seven miles northeast of South Pittsburg on U.S. Highway 72. Although established in 1817 with a forty-acre donation by a Cherokee woman named Betsy Pack, Jasper experienced its first industrial boom some fifty years later in 1867, when the Nashville and Chattanooga completed a branch line between Bridgeport and Jasper. On Besty Pack Drive stands the historic **McKendree United Methodist Church** (circa 1875, 1889, 1911), one of the town's few historic buildings that dates from the Reconstruction years. Another community building from roughly the same period is the Greek Revival temple–style Masonic hall, which is one block east of the square (private, no access). Once known as Sam Houston Academy, it was finished the year the railroad arrived in 1867 by an African-American carpenter named Alfred White.

From the late 1870s to 1891, Jasper experienced a second railroad-induced spurt of growth when the Sequatchie Valley Railroad Company, and later the Nashville, Chattanooga, and St. Louis, extended

Ketner's Mill, Marion County. Construction of the railroad encouraged a local farmer to build a new brick gristmill along the banks of the Sequatchie River.

the Jasper spur to Victoria, then to Dunlap, and finally to Pikeville. The town emerged as a regional crossroads. Its historic NC&St.L depot, just south of the square on U.S. 41, marks the railroad's influence (private, limited access). The town square also is the junction for U.S. Highways 41, 64, and 72, and the amount of truck traffic around the Marion County Courthouse (1925) on any business day is a constant reminder of the importance of transportation to the local economy.

Old Tennessee Highway 28 in Jasper passes through the Sequatchie Valley. About seven and a half miles to the north is Victoria, a village established in 1878 along the original rail line of the Sequatchie Valley Railroad. About two and a half miles to the east, along the Sequatchie River, is **Ketner's Mill,** built by Alexander K. Ketner at about the time the rails reached Victoria (private, limited access). As one of the few nineteenth-century mills left standing in Tennessee, it records the earlier industrial history of the valley when entrepreneurs relied on the natural force of the river for power rather than on the coal and coke that powered the machines of the industrial revolution. Across the road is the Ketner House, a nineteenth-century dwelling at the heart of the historic Ketner family farm.

Three miles north of Victoria is the town of Whitwell. An early

Coke Oven ruins, Dunlap Coke Ovens Historic Site. The heavy foliage surrounding the coke ovens obscures the environmental damage caused by the constant oven fires during the first quarter of the twentieth century.

1800s settlement originally called Cheekville, the name was changed in 1887 to Whitwell in honor of Thomas Whitwell, the former English president of the Southern States Corporation. The town was once known as the Coal City of the Sequatchie because its mines were the most lucrative properties of the Tennessee Coal, Iron, and Railroad Company. Coal miners kept working here until 1928.

Dunlap, the seat of government for Sequatchie County, is about fifteen miles farther north on Tennessee Highway 28. Its **Dunlap Coke Ovens historic site** is the best place to explore the mining history of the Sequatchie Valley. Once the county garbage dump, the park contains long rows of beehive ovens, used in the early 1900s to turn locally mined coal into coke for the iron furnaces and factories at South Pittsburg and Chattanooga. The first ovens were built in 1902; by the time operations ceased in 1928, some 268 coke ovens had been constructed. The ovens, according to local historian Carson Camp, "were built in double rows with each separate oven touching those on either side. Railroad tracks ran along the top of each row. Coke was fed into the top of the ovens from rail cars. Each oven held six tons of coal, which made three tons of coke. After 72 hours in the oven they would spray it down with water, pull the coke out with long rakes, and load it onto railroad cars for shipment to Chattanooga" (Murfreesboro *Daily News Journal,* Sept. 2, 1987).

Today large trees and dense vegetation surround the ovens; in fact, nature has been busy reclaiming the site for the last sixty years. But, as historian Camp explained in the newspaper interview cited above, "The heat alone made any growing thing impossible when the ovens were operating," and the landscape here was once as barren and alien as any moonscape. The park visitor center, a re-creation of the original company store, has exhibits about the site as well as interpretive maps for walking tours of this significant industrial complex.

Most of Dunlap's urban buildings date from between 1902 and 1927, the years when the coke ovens were in operation. Established as the county seat in 1858, Dunlap's **Sequatchie County Courthouse** (1911) is a two-story Classical Revival design by the Chattanooga architectural firm of W. K. Brown and Brothers. At the corner of Cherry Avenue and U.S. Highway 127 stand two other noteworthy buildings, the two-story Sequatchie Valley Bank (1908) and the **Dunlap Community Center** (now library), built in 1939 by the National Youth Administration. (See sidebar entitled "The New Deal Built Environment," Landscape 9, chapter 4.) The Great Depression had devastated Dunlap, and the new community center at the heart of the downtown business district symbolized the community pride and hope of those who remained.

Route B: Farming in the Sequatchie Valley

To view the agricultural landscape of the Sequatchie Valley, this route follows U.S. Highway 127 from Dunlap to Crossville.

North of Dunlap on U.S. Highway 127, beginning in general at the Sequatchie/Bledsoe county line, the traveler will encounter a more rural and traditional landscape, dotted here and there by assorted grain, dairy, and cattle farms. U.S. 127 is the direct route to Pikeville; an alternate road is the older route of state highway 28 that parallels U.S. 127 to the immediate west. It is a slow and bumpy road at places, but this older state road puts the visitor into closer touch with local farms and dwellings.

This is a good place to look at barns and silos typically found on Tennessee farms. The transverse-frame barn is a two-story frame rectangle, with a gable roof of tin, that has entrances at the gable ends. The first floor was used for livestock, while the second was reserved for hay storage, with the hay commonly stored "loose." Some of these barns were constructed from standardized plans introduced by agriculture extension agents in the early twentieth century. A second type is the three-portal barn, another two-story design, which features three different aisles and a steeply gabled roof, again with the entrances situated on the gable ends. This barn type gained popularity during the early 1900s. The third barn type, the pole barn, is of more recent vintage, as it became popular after World War II. It is a one-story building with a low gable roof that has a framework of upright poles set into the ground. Typically, steel-girder trusses provide roof support. This barn is reserved almost solely for livestock and machine storage since new buildings and technology have eliminated the need for second-floor hay storage. As geographer Allen G. Noble has observed, "The pole barn represents the introduction of industrial architecture into American agriculture" (Noble, 2: 47).

Another artifact of industrial architecture is the tall, bright blue Harvestore silo, first developed in Wisconsin during the late 1940s. These standardized metal-and-fiberglass structures, usually about sixty feet high and twenty feet wide, differed from earlier silos of wood or concrete. Their airtight design effectively ended decomposition of the stored silage. The fiberglass lining kept silage from freezing during cold weather. Moreover, the silo had machinery to unload silage from the bottom. Farmers loved this last feature; it eliminated the difficult and dangerous task of climbing the silo and pitching a load off the top.

Silos and barns are conspicuous elements of the rural Sequatchie landscape. The recent trend of storing the annual hay crop not in barns or sheds but in large, machine-produced rolls of hay can be noted. Spoilage can be considerable using this method, but farmers prefer it because it eliminates the need to move hay back and forth between the barn and the fields and because the amount of spoilage is less costly than constructing a new hay barn.

The roadside along U.S. Highway 127 reveals these common buildings of the agricultural landscape (also see sidebar entitled "Common Farm Outbuildings," Landscape 13, this chapter). Specific historic farms, however, allow the visitor to place a human face on the sometimes abstract patterns of the landscape. About sixteen miles north of Dunlap, near the old railroad community of Lee's Station, is the Kelly Farm, established by James J. Kelly in 1874 (private, no access). The farm began with three hundred acres devoted to raising Hereford and Jersey cattle as well as corn, wheat, and small grains. Family members recall that "corn was harvested by cutting with a long steel knife, put into shocks until dried, and then each ear pulled from the stalks and thrown into the wagon." Wheat was hand-harvested at first, using "a homemade cradle, with long prongs and long steel blade, [to] cut the wheat, [which was then] tied into bundles ready for threshing" (West, 131). Due to his success as a farmer and as an entrepreneur in Pikeville—especially his role as a founder of the First National Bank of Pikeville—Kelly expanded his farm to almost one thousand acres. After his death in 1922, three of his children continued operating over three hundred acres of family land as a Grade A dairy business. This farm has been a profitable and popular enterprise in Bledsoe County throughout this century.

About two miles to the north is the McReynolds-Shelton Farm (private, no access). Established during the Civil War by Samuel M. McReynolds, the farm was similar to its nineteenth-century neighbors in that it produced many different crops and types of livestock for market. Like his neighbor Kelly, McReynolds also ran profitable businesses in Pikeville. In 1910 Charles L. McReynolds inherited the farm and continued producing the same traditional crops as his father. When Samuel McReynolds's grandson Charles Ernest McReynolds inherited 307 acres in 1926, however, he transformed it into a modern dairy farm. A student at the College of William and Mary in Williamsburg, Virginia, McReynolds adopted progressive farming methods, and profits from his new dairy business, recalled family members, allowed them to acquire electricity "before most of their neighbors" (West, 132). McReynolds, in turn, took the technology and further modernized his dairy business. Later family farm owners closed the dairy operation in favor of raising cattle, swine, corn, hay, small grains, and soybeans, which are all crops, save for the soybeans, that one could have found on the farm of Samuel McReynolds some 120 years ago.

Pikeville is a trade and supply center for the farmers of Bledsoe County. With lumber, hosiery, and stove mills, it was a minor industrial center during the early twentieth century. Only 488 people lived there in 1920. The downtown has changed little since then, and a residential area is part of the **South Main historic district.** The **Bledsoe County Courthouse** (1909) is another neoclassical design from the firm of W. K. Brown and Brothers of Chattanooga. These architects also designed the Classical Revival Methodist Church and the Gothic Revival Church of Christ, both on Main Street. Unlike many town squares, homes still stand around the Pikeville courthouse. The most important is the **John Bridgeman House** (circa 1820), an excellent example of a two-story Tennessee Federal dwelling, constructed just after Pikeville became the county seat in 1819.

A WPA writer who visited Pikeville during the 1930s fondly recalled how the town square bustled with activity on Saturday afternoons. "Between visits to the stores," the writer observed, "the hill people wander over to the courthouse lawn where there are almost continuous arguments on social, political, and religious questions, usually settled by old-timers whose opinions are highly respected. There is much gossiping, too, about cooking, ailments, crops, courtships, marriages, births, and deaths. Children of all ages run in and out of the crowd, and family dogs scamper and fight. Tobacco chewing and snuff dipping are popular diversions" (*WPA Guide,* 503). Pikeville's historic one- and two-story commercial buildings, together with the brick churches, courthouse, and nineteenth-century homes, help visitors to imagine this scene of traditions long since forgotten.

A small frame school on the north end of town, on old state highway 28 but visible from the modern road, documents the other side of life in Pikeville during the mid-twentieth century. The **Lincoln School** is a historic African-American school and community center, constructed with support from the Julius Rosenwald Fund in 1925–26 (for more on the Rosenwald program, see Landscape 21, chapter 7). It is an excellent example of standardized school architecture and features a unique pressed tin floor-to-ceiling interior. The school cost $5,336; the Rosenwald Fund donated $900 while the state added $3,236, and the local African-American community raised the final $1,200. Local residents remember having fish frys to raise the money. Like most Rosenwald schools, Lincoln served as a place for community meetings, political rallies, and as a black voting precinct.

North of Lincoln School, the rural landscape of the Sequatchie Valley emerges once more. The Stephens Dairy Farm (circa 1816–19) is the oldest family farm in the county. Founded by Isaac Stephens, who was the first Bledsoe representative in the Tennessee General Assembly, the farm initially yielded livestock, corn, and small grains. It remained devoted to these crops until Sam S. Stephens turned it into a prosperous dairy farm during the 1920s.

From the Stephens Farm, eight miles north on U.S. Highway 127 the road reaches the intersection with Ninemile Cross Road. To see an interesting rural cemetery, turn east here, crossing old state highway 28, then passing through the tiny hamlet of Ninemile. Then take the bridge over the Sequatchie River, which soon intersects with the paved county road known as East Valley Road. Turn north at this intersection

Swafford Chapel Cemetery, Bledsoe County. The limestone-covered graves mark the final resting places of the locally prominent Swafford family.

and then look for the sign to the Swafford Chapel Church. The cemetery behind the church has several early graves of the Swafford family, which played an important role in Bledsoe County history for nearly two hundred years. These graves are covered with hand-laid limestone blocks, a tradition rarely documented in Tennessee. The cemetery also provides a splendid view of the northern Sequatchie Valley landscape, which shows clearly how two centuries of farming have shaped and tamed the wilderness.

About fifteen miles north of the Ninemile Road junction on U.S. Highway 127 is the mid-twentieth-century world of **Cumberland Homesteads,** high on the Cumberland Plateau in Cumberland County. As part of its relief effort during the Great Depression, the federal government in 1933 established the Division of Subsistence Homesteads, which was merged two years later into a new agency called the Resettlement Administration. These federal programs aimed to create modern, well-planned rural environments that would uplift and bring meaningful economic employment to poor, devastated rural communities. The projects were described as "subsistence homesteads" because reformers assumed that the best working environment in these depressed rural areas was one in which a family had enough land to produce a garden and have some livestock for food. Working at local factories, or ideally at cooperatives, would then earn cash money. Cumberland Homesteads was a perfect place to test these reform ideas because the coal bust in

CCC stone bridge, Cumberland Mountain State Park. This state park was initially established as the recreational center of Cumberland Homesteads.

White, Cumberland, Fentress, Morgan, and Putnam Counties had put many miners and lumbermen out of work, an unemployment problem only compounded by the number of dirt-poor farmers in the region.

Made up of 262 units, Cumberland Homesteads was to be a model rural community. As consulting planner John Nolen commented, "The subsistence homestead is a combination of several things which are usually separate, for example, in industry and gardening or farming; part-time industrial employment and desirable provision for food and shelter; work and better use of leisure time" (Cutler, 119). This landscape is still basically intact today. For the project, workers from the Civilian Conservation Corps, together with local residents, cleared almost twenty thousand acres of land, setting aside a new recreation park (now Cumberland Mountain State Park) where they constructed a stone bridge that is the largest single CCC structure in Tennessee. They also built a lighthouse-like **Administration Building** (now a museum) with Crab Orchard stone, a local road system, schools (which still operate), and factories (mostly closed now). The most conspicuous part of the landscape were the individual fifteen- to twenty-acre homesteads, most of which were built of Crab Orchard stone in a restrained Tudor Cottage style. The original homes each came with a poultry house, smokehouse, privy, and a two-story barn, which the family built first so they could live there while the dwelling was constructed. The homes can still be seen along U.S. Highway 127, Tennessee Highway 68, and U.S. Highway 70 to the east.

The planning for Cumberland Homesteads interjected standardization into the landscape where little had existed before. For example, the stone dwellings reflected standardized architectural plans by William Macy Stanton. They had setbacks of about seventy-five to one hundred feet, with uniform forty-foot frontages. Plateau folk found that a seemingly endless stream of visitors, government experts, and inspectors compromised their privacy. Some resented the different rules of the project and regretted the loss of individual initiative.

Agriculture was not the primary focus of life at Cumberland Homesteads. But with a captive population, country life reformers took every opportunity to teach plateau residents about the crops and techniques of modern agriculture. Programs at the local school encouraged experimentation on the small family plots. Residents were taught new methods for producing potatoes, strawberries, and soybeans along with raising goats for market and soil conservation and land-clearance techniques. Once introduced at Cumberland, these lessons had long-term benefits for the greater plateau region because the crops had some money-making potential.

Cumberland Homesteads never produced the miracle that reformers such as Eleanor Roosevelt had prophesied. The factories had difficulty staying in business; the homes were cold until TVA electricity came in the late 1930s; and workers complained about being shortchanged on their work credits toward purchasing their homes. But most residents stayed. "Life was not easy but we were all working for the same goal and it was a good community," recalls Elizabeth Peavyhouse. "We were young . . . it was a challenge and we didn't mind" (*Crossville Chronicle,* July 1, 1988). Historian Paul K. Conkin concluded that "even though the new communities were not at all like heaven, they apparently were better than anything else available" (*Tomorrow a New World,* 213).

Landscape 15: The Upper Cumberland

The Cumberland River is a thread of life that connects the people of Smith, Clay, and Jackson Counties. The first century of settlement focused on the Cumberland River, creating classic Tennessee river towns such as Carthage, Granville, and Celina. Steamboats and log rafts once crowded the river, but now a series of dams have transformed much of

York Mill, Pall Mall, Fentress County. Part of a state historic park recognizing Sgt. Alvin York's contributions to Fentress County.

the Cumberland into recreational lakes between Carthage and Celina. Pleasure boats ply the waters, and the logging industry has moved inland and away from the river.

The Upper Cumberland refers to more than the upper reaches of the Cumberland River in Tennessee. It is also the land east of the river, the rugged terrain of the Upper Cumberland Plateau, along the bottoms of the Obey and Wolf Rivers in Pickett, Overton, Fentress, and Putnam Counties. Railroads, especially the Tennessee Central, have shaped this landscape, so stories about mines, lumber camps, and CCC projects, familiar themes found earlier in this chapter, are found here as well. The route also encounters the larger-than-life story of Alvin C. York, a World War I hero who returned to make his own stamp on his homeland.

The Upper Cumberland is therefore a composite: in part a nineteenth-century landscape focused on rivers and in part a twentieth-century landscape centered in the plateau. Both parts share in common, however, a history of exploitation of timber, minerals, and farmland, the successes and failures of which still mark the countryside. Exploration of this landscape begins at Crossville, the transportation crossroads of the Cumberland Plateau.

Route A: Overland Transportation in the Cumberland Plateau

From Crossville to Carthage, U.S. Highway 70N basically parallels the route of Walton Road, one of the early east-west roads in Tennessee and the first overland route in the Upper Cumberland. Completed in 1802, this crude wagon road linked Kingston on the Clinch River to Carthage on the Cumberland River. At Monterey, eighteen miles west of Crossville, the next generation of transportation appears: the historic right-of-way of the Tennessee Central Railroad, the most important link between Nashville and the Upper Plateau until the mid-twentieth century. U.S. Highway 70N also follows this route westward to Baxter, where the road stays its course to Carthage while the tracks slip southward, headed for Lebanon. The interstate highway, of course, represents the region's most recent chapter in overland transportation. Opened in the early 1970s, it is the fastest way from Crossville to Carthage, but it avoids most of the historic towns and places of the Upper Cumberland.

Eighteen miles west of Crossville on U.S. 70N is Monterey, established in 1893 as a processing and trade town for the mines in southern Overton and Fentress Counties. The Cumberland Mountain Coal Company platted the town and immediately began plans to link the settlement to the Cincinnati Southern lines at Harriman. This railroad link was completed in 1900, and Monterey boomed not only as a trade center but also as a manufacturing center. An important house associated with this period of rapid change is the Wilder-Woolbright House at 208 Holly Street (private, no access). This upright-and-wing vernacular dwelling was the home of industrialist John T. Wilder from about 1902 to 1909. A major investor in the region's coal mines and industry, as well as the owner of the town's Imperial Hotel, Wilder was a former founder and vice-president of the Cincinnati Southern Railway and the Charleston Cincinnati and Chicago Railway (later known as the Clinchfield). In 1894 he invested in his first coal mine near Monterey. Eight years later, after the railroad extended a spur line into southern Overton County (a route now followed by Tennessee 164), Wilder established the Fentress Coal Company in neighboring Fentress County where the coal town of Wilder was named in his honor. His house on Holly Street remained his headquarters until 1909 when he moved his office to his newly opened Imperial Hotel, directly adjacent to the railroad tracks. The hotel is one of the few railroad hotels left in the Cumberland Plateau.

Cookeville, the seat of government for Putnam County and home to Tennessee Tech University, is about fourteen miles west on U.S. Highway 70N. Although established as a county seat in 1854, Cookeville was still a small country town thirty years later. It stood directly in the middle of a "neutral zone" of potential railroad development. No one seemed interested in investing the millions of dollars necessary to build a line through the demanding terrain of the plateau.

In 1884 one northern capitalist, Alexander Crawford, decided to take that risk in order to reach potentially vast coalfields and virgin stands of timber in northern Cumberland and southern Fentress, Overton, and Morgan Counties. Crawford established the Nashville and Knoxville Railroad, which began at Lebanon and arrived at Cookeville in 1890. The railroad created a new commercial district on the west end of town by locating its depot at the corner of Broad and Cedar Streets. The company sold lots around the tracks as well as to the east along both sides of Broad Street. Cookeville has since developed an urban look different from that of other Upper Cumberland county seats. The town has two historic business districts: the square around the Putnam County Courthouse (1900)—featuring the **Arcade Building** of 1913—and another area adjacent to the passenger station. Connecting the two districts are several civic buildings on Broad Street, of which the Renaissance Revival–style U.S. Post Office and Courthouse (1916) is of particular interest. The middle section of Broad Street thus serves as a public link between two separate commercial areas.

In 1902 Nashville capitalist Jere Baxter purchased the Nashville and Knoxville Railroad for his Tennessee Central line. He immediately began to improve local rail facilities, and his company extended market opportunities for all Cookeville businessmen. In 1909 Tennessee Central built a new passenger station, albeit in a late Victorian design, at the corner of Broad and Cedar Streets. The **Tennessee Central Depot** is now a museum about the railway's role in Cookeville history. The company declared bankruptcy in 1912, and it took ten years to emerge from receivership. The last passenger train left the station in 1955, but Tennessee Central kept its freight business until a final bankruptcy closed the line for good in 1968.

In 1912, when bankruptcy closed the Tennessee Central, another important Cookeville institution—Dixie College, soon to become Tennessee Tech—opened its doors to the public. Initially established in 1909 by the Church of Christ with the assistance of local business leaders like Jere Whitson, Dixie College finally opened in 1912 as the city's

Tennessee Central Railroad Depot, Cookeville.

new high school. Two years later, it merged with the Putnam County High School, and in 1916 its campus along the railroad lines north of town became the setting for the new state-supported Tennessee Polytechnic Institute. The school had classes on the collegiate and high school levels, reflecting an assumption of state educational leaders that the Upper Cumberland needed both. Tennessee Tech remained largely a technical high school until 1924, when the state board of education allowed the school to offer a four-year college program. It gained university status in 1965.

The historic quadrangle of Tennessee Tech follows in general the original plans for Dixie College, conceived by William D. Ittner in about 1910. The buildings feature a Colonial Revival theme, boldly stated by the main administration building, Derryberry Hall. Georgian Revival style is reflected in **Henderson Hall** (1931), the first engineering school building designed by Benjamin F. Hunt of the architectural firm of R. H. Hunt in Chattanooga.

West of Cookeville, U.S. Highway 70N closely parallels the tracks of the Tennessee Central Railway for eight miles to the town of Baxter, named in honor of company president Jere Baxter. The railroad created several new towns like Baxter along its line, and eventually a region once accustomed to river transportation came to rely on the railroad because it was a dependable and faster connection.

From Baxter, it is another twenty-three miles on U.S. 70N to the town of Carthage. The drive is picturesque as the road rides along hills and narrow ridges and passes through small villages like Chestnut Mound and Elmwood. This land lies between the Caney Fork River to the south and the Cumberland River to the north. In Smith County several historic family farms are located along the highway. About twelve miles west of Baxter is the Beasley Farm (1870), where family members as late as the 1980s still lived in the original two-story vernacular farmhouse (private, no access). This farm, like many in Smith County, produces corn, hay, and cattle. Five miles farther east on U.S. Highway 70N is the Neal Hollow Farm (1865), which was established at the end of the Civil War by John and Martha Allgier. Its recent yields of corn, tobacco, and timber are typical for farms in this region (private, no access). Two miles east of Carthage is the Gore Farm, noted for its production of livestock. This place is also famous in Tennessee political history as the home of former U.S. Senator Albert Gore Sr. His son Albert Gore Jr., another former U.S. senator and current vice-president of the United States, keeps his in-state residence in a ranch-style house on an adjacent farm (both private, no access). The town of Carthage marks the end of this early transportation route.

Route B: The Upper Cumberland River

There is a beautiful and historic stretch of the Cumberland River along U.S. Highway 70N east of Carthage, which junctions after nine miles with Tennessee 53 at Chestnut Mound. Tennessee 53 goes along the banks of the Cumberland River for the next thirty-eight miles, providing scenic views of the river as well as encountering the historic river towns of Granville, Gainesboro, and Celina.

For well over one hundred years, Carthage was a center for the Upper Cumberland River trade. Crossing either of two bridges over the Cumberland affords a brief view of the old river wharfs where steamboats and lumber rafts once passed on their journey to Nashville. Established in 1804, Carthage was "a flourishing post town" by the 1830s, with a population of seven hundred with plenty of professionals, merchants, tradesmen, and "an extensive steam mill for sawing and grinding" (Morris, 127). New prosperity came in post–Civil War years as Carthage emerged as a key crosstie shipping point, a business that knew no end in those heady days of railroad building. A monument to those days of economic recovery—the **Smith County Courthouse**—dominates the town square. This impressive local example of Second Empire style dates from 1875.

The construction of the new courthouse also coincided with the timber boom that shaped regional history and landscape until the mid-1900s. "The importance of logging and rafting activities to the people of the Upper Cumberland cannot be overstated," concludes folklorist Lynwood Montell (*Kettle Creek,* 84). Millions of dollars eventually exchanged hands for virgin hardwoods of the region, and during particularly busy seasons rafted logs would line the banks of the Cumberland River for twenty-five miles east of Nashville.

By 1874 Nashville was a lumber-processing center, and an amazing 22.5 million board feet of sawn lumber came from the Upper Cumberland in just that one year. The farmers who lived near the river north of Carthage relied on logging for their yearly cash income. One Upper Cumberland raft pilot recalled, "That's all there was to do around here. There wasn't no factories; there wasn't nothing to do and that's the only way anybody had of getting any money. There was logging, rafting, and running the river. And that was the only sale we had for timber at that time" (Montell, *Kettle Creek,* 85).

Most farmers hauled their logs to the riverbanks with teams of mules or oxen. They then prepared a "chute"—a cleared path ranging from fifty to one hundred yards wide from the bank to the river—that made rolling the logs into the river much easier. As the logs floated downstream, they would be trapped and held by log booms at Carthage, Gainesboro, and Celina. A log boom included a "log trail, which was the narrow platform or catwalk extending along the stream bank . . . and a swing, which was a floating log rope with one end permanently anchored to the opposite bank. When looped across the river and secured to the trail, the free end ensnared the logs floating downstream" (Montell, *Kettle Creek,* 96). The company of Liberman, Loveman, and O'Brien operated the Celina log boom about three-fourths of a mile up the mouth of the Obey River. It could collect about three thousand logs before the load would be rafted to Nashville.

Rafters put together their loads by alternating what they called "floater" logs, lightweight timber such as poplar and ash, with "sinker" logs, such hardwoods as walnut and oak. The larger logs were placed at the front, with the smaller logs placed according to their descending size. Using homemade oars, two to six men would guide the rafts downstream. One Clay County resident fondly remembered that "it was a thrill to hear their voices come down the stream, watch the raft pass by slowly, and then float around the bend of the river" (Montell, *Kettle Creek,* 100).

Six miles north of Chestnut Mound on Tennessee 53 is Granville, where several properties mark the village's prosperity during the logging years: the brick Presbyterian church; the solemn vernacular Gothic of the Methodist Church; and the now abandoned and rusting storefronts along Clover Street, including the shotgun-shaped office of Doctor Luther Freeman, who provided medical care to people along the Cumberland for most of this century.

Eight miles farther north is a junction with a county road that leads west to the Fort Blount Ferry. An archaeological site near the ferry documents the earliest days of settlement in Jackson County; only the road, sloping riverbank, and the current of the Cumberland allow visitors to envision the crude transportation crossing represented by the old ferry (private, no access). Established in 1794, **Fort Blount** stood on the east bank of the Cumberland and protected the new Nashville-to-Knoxville road that crossed the Cumberland River at this point. Soon after its creation, the county court granted a license to William Gillespie to operate a ferry and tavern there. He charged twelve and a half cents to take one person and a horse across the river while a wagon and four horses cost one dollar and each quart of corn took another four cents. Dinner at the tavern cost a quarter, which was the same amount charged for a half pint of brandy. Whiskey was comparatively cheap: only twelve and a half cents for a half pint.

Gainesboro is five miles north of the ferry road junction. Established in 1817, Gainesboro became the second county seat in Jackson County. Most of the buildings found in its courthouse square historic district, however, date to the town's years as a key rafting center. The architecture of the **Jackson County Courthouse** (1927), designed by the Nashville firm of Tisdale, Pinson, and Stone, is typical of the buildings here; it reflects only some elements of style, in this case the Colonial Revival, in what is otherwise a vernacular building. About 350 people lived in Gainesboro at the time of its construction.

The Cumberland River runs free of any modern dams for the next nineteen miles of Tennessee 53. Celina, which is near the confluence of the Obey and Cumberland Rivers, was a town created at the very beginning of the logging boom in 1870. Its **Clay County Courthouse** (1872–73) was built by local craftsman D. L. Dow. Celina was an important stop in both the logging and steamboat trade. The Kyle family operated a rafting business, for example, that employed about one hundred men from Clay, Overton, and Pickett Counties. On average, a rafting trip to Nashville took seven days. Rafters considered Celina a fair and considerate place. One remembered that Celina folks treated rafters "as nice as if we was home" (Montell, *Kettle Creek,* 114). The New Central Hotel and the Riverside Hotel were favorite places to spend the night. Logging remained important in Celina until 1931 when the Kyles closed their family operation. Within ten years, log rafting had become a thing of the past on the Upper Cumberland.

Celina's steamboat days also belong to the early 1900s. Then steamboats came to Celina regularly to haul away chickens, lumber, and other resources. With a trade monopoly for two miles up and down the Cumberland River from Celina, Hugh Kyle operated a large franchised warehouse that supplied goods to towns as far east as Byrdstown and Jamestown. But the expansion of trucking after World War I and state programs to improve highways during the 1920s spelled an end to the steamboat trade. Some companies mounted excursion boats up and down the river during the 1920s, but by the Great Depression, that too had ended.

Today one can only imagine the era when steamboats puffed up and down the river since recent hydroelectric development has turned the river into a lake for pleasure boats.

Route C: The Reformers' Upper Cumberland

Cutting across the northern Cumberland Plateau from Celina to Rugby is Tennessee 52, perhaps the most scenic road in the region. At places it certainly is one of the most winding and hilly roads, and it is not a route for someone in a hurry. But there is no better landscape to discuss how dreamers and reformers sought a new and better life in the rugged countryside of the plateau. Some hopes were realized; others were dashed. But in such places as Free Hill, Alpine, and Rugby, it is still possible to see the places where adventurous and committed souls left a lasting mark on the people and landscape of the Upper Cumberland.

To begin this route, take Tennessee Highway 53 north of Celina to a paved county road marked Neely Creek Road. Turn west for about a half mile and then climb up the bluffs overlooking the Cumberland River by way of the Free Hill Road. Free Hill is a unique place. Few African Americans live in the Upper Cumberland today, and those who try to move into the region often face unrelenting hostility. But Free Hill is an African-American community that has existed since before

Free Hill Community Center, Celina. This community symbol was supported with money from the Rosenwald Fund in 1921.

the Civil War—perhaps as early as 1830—built on four hundred acres of land given to four newly freed slaves by a local landowner known only as Mrs. Hill. The four freed blacks dreamed of their own community, located away from the prejudice of the river communities, and they established the place known as "Free Hill." The continuing vitality of the community is documented by its historic cemetery and its community center, which was originally a public school built with assistance from the Rosenwald Fund in 1921. Craftsman Robert "Bud" Garrett recalled the legends of the community's origin: "You know, way back in the olden days I heard it talked by my father and my older folks that they placed all the black folks up in Free Hill on that rock so they couldn't grow nothing, hopin' they'd starve 'em out. But they finally made it, most of 'em did and lived to a ripe old age" (Peterson and Rankin, 4). Garrett was famous throughout the region for making flint marbles, used by blacks and whites alike to play the popular local game of rolly hole marbles. During the 1940s, he made and sold enough marbles to purchase an old school bus and shuttle community residents from their hilltop homes to jobs in Celina. The game of rolly hole remains popular today, and a national championship is held annually at

Standing Stone State Park. Throughout Clay and Overton County, players of the game can be recognized by the distinctive forty-by-twenty-four-feet-wide, hard-packed clay playing surfaces located adjacent to their homes.

Those who settled at Free Hill blended their dream community into the landscape. Nearby, a different group of visionaries in the twentieth century destroyed the landscape in order to fulfill their dreams for the future. For decades, engineers had envisioned a series of dams to stop the periodic floods that devastated the Upper Cumberland. In 1943 the U.S. Army Corps of Engineers built the first one, damming the Obey River just before it met the Cumberland and creating the huge Dale Hollow Reservoir, which stretches eastward into Pickett County and southern Kentucky. This began the systematic control of the Upper Cumberland and its tributaries, turning what had been a wild river into a predictable resource for power generation and recreation. The Dale Hollow Dam and Reservoir is less than a mile from the Free Hill turnoff on Tennessee Highway 53. A visitor center provides tours and has a small museum.

The engineers' dream, however, was a nightmare for the farmers who lived in the Obey and Wolf River Valleys. Pickett County lost most of its best land, and one of four residents were moved to make way for the reservoir. The community of Willow Grove disappeared completely, compelling one former resident to lament:

> A lovely little village nestled at
>   the foot of the mountains,
> With friendship flowing every-
>   where, like bubbling fountains.
> It was loved by all who dwelt
>   thereabouts—young and old,
> The Dale Hollow Dam drove
>   them out in the rain and cold.
>   (Montell, *Kettle Creek,* 186)

After Free Hill and Dale Hollow Dam, return to Celina and take Tennessee 52 eastward for ten miles to the Standing Stone State Park. During the Great Depression, the federal government transformed this formerly devastated landscape into a new recreational park for residents in the Cumberland Plateau. By 1930 loggers had clear-cut most of the timberland in northern Overton County, leaving a barren, eroding landscape. Standing Stone State Park reflected the dream of reforestation—that proper conservation could reclaim land once left abandoned and abused by human hands. The federal Department of Agriculture and U.S. Forest Service worked with CCC, state, and local officials to establish the park. Most of the land was set aside for conservation purposes, but between 1938 and 1942 the Works Progress Administration also constructed a rustic-style lodge, headquarters, and guest cabins, centered around a sixty-nine-acre man-made lake. Most of these WPA buildings, preserved as the **Standing Stone Rustic Park historic district,** remain as artifacts of New Deal ideas about conservation, recreation, and architecture (see sidebar entitled "The New Deal Built Environment," Landscape 9, chapter 4).

Ten miles east of Standing Stone is Livingston, the seat of government for Overton County. Livingston has long been a trade crossroads for the Upper Cumberland, and shops around the town square are still busy throughout the week. The **Overton County Courthouse**, built by Joe Copeland in 1868–69, is the oldest in the region. Another famous institution is the Livingston Academy, established by the Christian Women's Board of Missions of the Disciples of Christ in 1909. These reformers believed that education was the best way to lift local people out of their backwardness and poverty. Livingston Academy became the physical embodiment of their dreams to build a new future for the Upper Cumberland.

At first, Livingston businessmen and civic leaders eagerly sought the new mission school. They offered free land and a faculty residence. Local attorney (and future governor) A. H. Roberts personally presented the town's case to the mission's board in Indianapolis. To honor his contribution, the **Roberts Law Office** stands at a corner of the school grounds. But once the prize was theirs and the school was in operation, some residents wondered if outside assistance was worth the cost. The academy principal hired mostly northern teachers, and tax monies were spent on an institution where little local control could be exercised.

Despite local doubts, the missionaries stayed at the task, hoping that "their students would be the yeast that would uplift a backward, ignorant rural area," observes historian Jeanette Keith. Indeed, "creating a constituency that would support good schools and roads was part of the reason the mission schools existed" (176). The irony was that the better-educated students soon left the community in search of opportunities unavailable in Overton County.

Alpine Presbyterian Church, Overton County. This beautiful stone Gothic church is the only active part of the old Alpine Institute campus.

Another historic mission school in Overton County is located eight miles east of Livingston on Tennessee 52 at the village of Alpine. Unlike Livingston Academy, which became a public elementary and high school in 1947, Alpine Institute has closed its school doors and now only maintains its Presbyterian church. But it was the first of the county's mission schools, established in 1821 by John Dillard as a Cumberland Presbyterian mission. The school was destroyed during the Civil War and rebuilt after hostilities ceased. But then the Ku Klux Klan burned it a second time; after this arson, the school did not reopen until 1880.

The early checkered history of Alpine Institute left few physical traces. The buildings today date from the 1910s to the 1930s, after northern Presbyterians took control of the institute in 1906 and operated it until 1947 as a self-help school, where students worked on the institute's one-hundred-acre farm to pay their tuition. The well-conceived and well-constructed Presbyterian church (1934) is in Gothic style. The WPA also built a gymnasium here in 1939. Since most buildings were constructed with beautiful native stone, what remains of the campus evokes both the rustic nature of the landscape and the dreams of educational reformers.

Twenty-one miles to the east, after a trip up an extremely curvy and hilly road, is a third important educational institute in the history

York Institute, Jamestown. The understated classicism of York Institute reflects the personality and character of its founder and administrator, Sgt. Alvin C. York.

of the Cumberland Plateau. The **York Institute** at Jamestown was Alvin C. York's gift to his fellow citizens in Fentress County. A world-famous war hero who had captured 132 German soldiers during the Battle of Argonne in World War I, York shunned the national spotlight to return to his home at Pall Mall. Over the next two decades, he donated money for the construction of several public projects. To build a public school in Jamestown that could improve the quality of life in Fentress County, York enlisted the support of local residents, outside acquaintances, and state officials. Classes began in 1926, and for the next eleven years York operated the school under the guidance of the state board of education. When illness prevented York from continuing in 1937, the state legislature accepted responsibility. It is the only state-run and state-supported local school in Tennessee. The campus includes the original administration and agricultural buildings, along with a dormitory (1915), first used as the county poor farm and now housing local crafts.

Another monument to the legacy of Alvin C. York stands about nine miles to the north of Jamestown along U.S. Highway 127. The **Sergeant York State Historical Area** preserves places and buildings associated with York's life. A gristmill he owned from 1943 to 1950 is open to the public. Dating from 1880, the mill was successfully operated by the locally prominent Pile family from 1890 to 1943. Across the road is York's home, a two-story Craftsman Four-Square design built in 1922, as well as a general store and post office (1920) that York built after returning to Tennessee. Other significant places in Pall Mall include the abandoned York Bible School (1941–43), the York Chapel (1922–23), and York's grave at the Wolf River Methodist Church. The cemetery that surrounds the church is a significant artifact of local folk culture containing frame and limestone gravehouses as well as a stunning view of the surrounding countryside. State officials are now planning the restoration of the old Bible school into a visitor center and museum and hope to open the York home for tours.

After returning to Jamestown on U.S. Highway 127, again turn east on Tennessee 52. This time the route leaves behind the dreams of education reformers for a landscape settled by colonists who came to build a new world in Fentress and Morgan Counties during the late nineteenth century. Five miles east of Jamestown is Allardt, a German colony established by Bruno Gernt in 1881. Gernt was a land agent for Cyrus and James N. Clarke, two Nebraska speculators who controlled thousands of acres in Fentress County. Gernt sold their land in parcels between twenty-five and one hundred acres, mostly to Germans immigrants. Like any good land agent, Gernt made the hard land of Fentress County sound like an agricultural paradise; by 1885, about seventy-five families lived there and twelve thousand acres had been sold. By the following year, the colony was well established, with several businesses and light industrial concerns complementing the community's agricultural trade.

Unlike neighboring Rugby, Allardt survived its first difficult years of settlement, and it became the second-largest town in Fentress County. Much of the credit for its stability and longevity has been attributed to Bruno Gernt, who was willing to recruit families with the skills and experience needed to build a new village where nothing had stood before. **Gernt's home and office** are listed in the National Register (private, limited access) as are other early properties, including the **Allardt School** (1910), associated with the settlement and development of this German colony. The **Bruno, Hugo, and Arthur Gernt dwellings** (private, no access) are important examples of German-influenced vernacular architecture; all of them were probably built by local carpenter Max Colditz.

Twelve miles farther east on Tennessee 52, near the border between Fentress and Morgan Counties, the dense forest suddenly opens up to the cleared lots of **Rugby,** the most famous utopian community in Tennessee. Novelist, politician, and social reformer Thomas Hughes of England established Rugby in 1880 as an ambitious experiment to dem-

Rugby Free Library, Morgan County.

onstrate that the arts-and-crafts philosophy of returning to the land and learning the basic skills of life could invigorate the rather worthless "second sons" of England's upper class as well as those of the middle-class who sought new opportunities. "Our aim and hope are to plant on these highlands," promised Hughes, "a society in which the humblest members, who live by the labour of their own hands, will be of such strain and culture that they will be able to meet princes in the gate, should any such strange persons ever present themselves before the gate tower of Rugby in the New World" (Egerton, 51–52). Under the Board of Aid to Land Ownership, which had acquired some sev-

Christ Church Episcopal, Rugby. A striking combination of Carpenter Gothic style and English Arts-and-Crafts sensibilities.

enty-five thousand acres of land, Hughes and his English partners sold parcels to investors during the fall of 1880, and, by the next summer, some three hundred residents had moved to the colony. Although a sizeable percentage was made up of English immigrants, most colonists were Americans.

The architectural style of the colony reflected the British taste for the Gothic, built simply of board-and-batten construction. Consequently, the remaining historic buildings represent the state's best collection of Carpenter Gothic architecture. Among the earliest buildings were dwellings such as **Pioneer Cottage** (1880), **Walton Court** (1880), **The Lindens** (1880), **Adena Cottage** (1881), and **Uffington House** (1881–87), where Hughes's mother and niece lived for six years. Historic Rugby, Inc., has also reconstructed three early commercial buildings: the vernacular Second Empire–style boardinghouse known as Newbury House, the Rugby Commissary, and the offices for the Board of Aid to Land Ownership.

The second year proved almost fatal to the colony. Planned cooperative ventures had not worked. Typhoid fever broke out at Tabard Inn, claiming six lives, and the hotel was closed. Residents not accustomed to the demands of farming the thin soil of Morgan County were easily discouraged. By the end of 1881, only sixty people remained at Rugby. But a new infusion of capital and colonists arrived the following spring, and the years of 1882 to 1887 were the best of times at Rugby. New institutions, such as the marvelous **Hughes Free Library** (1882), which boasted one of the best collections of Victorian literature in the country, gave the colonists a chance to escape their frustrations by reading a new book. The library, together with the neighboring tennis courts, symbolized the tension that existed between the practical and the idealistic in the colony. By 1884 the village had around four hundred and fifty residents and sixty-five buildings, including a tomato-canning factory (although the crop was ill-suited for cultivation in Morgan County). A sawmill, printing office, and blacksmith shops had either been completed or were under construction. Prospects for future growth looked good.

The next three years were a mixed success. The canning factory, the newspaper, and the private Arnold School failed, but a larger Tabard Inn and a new **Christ Church Episcopal** both opened in 1887. Yet, by that time a slow but sure death had settled in at Rugby. In 1892 the Rugby Tennessee Company Limited took over the Board of Aid to Land Ownership, but the new money was too little, too late. The colony's patron, Thomas Hughes, died four years later, and then in 1899 a fire destroyed Tabard Inn. American investors established the Rugby Land Company and bought the remaining property. Most colonists left, and the dream of Rugby—what Hughes had called "this lovely corner of God's earth"—crumbled away. Historian Robert S. Fogarty concluded that Rugby "was a grand experiment that was well financed, well publicized, and, like most utopian ventures, well intentioned. It led to the construction of some impressive buildings and focused attention on the condition of the young gentry. What resulted was simply a parody of Victorian life on the American frontier, a sort of stage set for young people to play out a portion of their youth" (120).

To end this tour of the Upper Cumberland, retrace the route on Tennessee 52 back to Jamestown and then take U.S. Highway 127 south to Crossville.

CHAPTER SIX

Middle Tennessee

Middle Tennessee is a land of many distinct places, grouped under two large geologic areas: the "barrens" of the Highland Rim and the "garden" of the Central Basin. The previous chapter surveyed most of the Eastern Highland Rim; in this chapter the western half of the rim, with its rolling uplands of forests, tobacco fields, and mineral deposits of iron-producing limonite, will be examined. The Central Basin, however, dominates the geography of Middle Tennessee. For two hundred years, here is where most Middle Tennesseans established farms, built businesses, and made their homes. Running north to south, this rich agricultural region is carved from a bed of solid limestone and is located in a slight depression of six hundred feet that is about fifty miles wide.

Both the Highland Rim and the Central Basin document thousands of years of human history. The **Old Stone Fort State Park** on U.S. Highway 41 at Manchester preserves a large walled ceremonial enclosure from the Middle Woodland Period of about fifteen hundred years ago. Near the narrows of the Harpeth River, on U.S. Highway 70 in Cheatham County, Mississippian peoples built a spectacular two-part temple mound village at a place now known as **Mound Bottom** (private, no access). On high ground overlooking the river, the villagers leveled a hilltop to create a terraced plaza that is about one thousand feet long and five hundred feet wide. Standing nearby were at least three other temple mounds. Less than a mile away stood the second part of the village on river bottomland. It too featured a large plaza with a huge temple mound. The size of the Harpeth River complex indicates that well-drained land adjacent to rivers throughout the Central Basin was home to large numbers of Native Americans during the Mississippian period. The Western Highland Rim also had its share of prehistoric inhabitants, and one group was located near the confluence of the Duck and Tennessee Rivers, south of New Johnsonville on U.S. Highway 70. Cultural remains at the **Dover Flint quarries,** about thirty miles to the north, represent the earliest history of mining on the Western Highland Rim (private, no access). Prehistoric peoples along the Tennessee and Duck Rivers carved ceremonial and military items from beautiful brown-and-blue-speckled flint taken from these rock quarries.

During the 1700s, long before American independence, French-Canadian fur traders and English long hunters encountered the abundant resources of Middle Tennessee. After establishing Nashville during the winter of 1779–80, settlers soon created more permanent farms and villages along the Cumberland and its tributaries. From these settlements, other explorers ventured out to build even more villages and county seats. During the first half of the nineteenth century, Middle Tennessee blossomed as a land of enormous agricultural potential. By mid-century the railroads came to reap the benefits of the agrarian largesse and to introduce the different work rhythms of industrialization at cotton mills, sawmills, and the great iron furnaces of the Western Highland Rim.

But the extensive rail network of Middle Tennessee also brought vast armies of destruction during the Civil War. Travelers of the region's federal highways will find a great number of roadside historical markers documenting troop movements, skirmishes, and major battles of the Civil War; in fact, there are many more historical markers on this theme than any other period in Tennessee history. While this preponderance of markers tells us that the war meant much to those who erected the markers, it also reflects how the war touched almost every town. Some, such as Murfreesboro and Franklin, still show the marks the armies left behind.

The biggest alterations in the Middle Tennessee landscape, however, came between the postwar recovery and the early twentieth century. Railroad expansion, industrialization, mining, the struggles of the newly freed African Americans, and commercial agriculture reshaped towns and countryside. This process of change multiplied in the twentieth century as new national highways linked local towns to Miami and Chicago, public schools and colleges were constructed, larger corporations replaced smaller factories, and expensive dam projects from the

Tennessee Valley Authority and the U.S. Army Corps of Engineers altered the very nature of the landscape itself.

To encounter this rich historic tapestry of Middle Tennessee, the traveler may choose from two thematic landscapes—which focus on agriculture or transportation—or two geographical themes—the Cumberland River country of northern Middle Tennessee or the Western Highland Rim.

Landscape 16: The Cumberland River Country

Northern Middle Tennessee, especially the many historic communities between the Cumberland River and the Kentucky border, may also be described as the Cumberland River Country. The Cumberland was a vital lifeline for the early settlers who established some of the region's first towns at Nashville (1784), Clarksville (1785), Gallatin (1802), Dover (1805), and Carthage (1804). Since the river carried steamboats linking northern merchants and southern raw materials, it was of considerable economic importance throughout the nineteenth century. Its value as a transportation network also made the river strategically important during the Civil War. The decisive Union victory at Fort Donelson launched the career of Gen. U. S. Grant. Engineers took over the river in the twentieth century, turning much of the historic Cumberland into modern reservoirs and recreational wonderlands. Old Hickory Dam, built by the U.S. Army Corps of Engineers during the 1950s, tamed the waters from Nashville east to Hartsville. To the west, the corps's Lake Barkley joined the earlier Kentucky Lake that the TVA created to transform the northern half of Stewart County into the national recreation area known as the Land Between the Lakes. This modern, yet traditional landscape at the northwest corner of Middle Tennessee is where this chapter begins.

Route A: Land Between the Lakes to Clarksville

U.S. Highway 79 cuts through the middle of Stewart County, and its tall bridges on the Tennessee and Cumberland Rivers link the western third of Tennessee to its middle third. The countryside is uneven, rolling more than hilly, and woods and undergrowth cover much of the land. Signs along the highway, however, make clear that this region is a recreational wonderland, full of places to camp, fish, or merely relax. However, this perspective of the land and its value was not one shared by the initial generations who settled Stewart County; this section will introduce their different way of looking at the landscape as a resource.

Three miles west of Dover, on U.S. Highway 79, is "the Trace," the roadway entrance to Land Between the Lakes, a national recreation area of a hundred and seventy thousand acres of rolling fields and woodlands developed by the Tennessee Valley Authority in the mid-1960s. The federal government owned sixty-seven thousand acres of the project, but TVA had to settle with hundreds of private property owners for the remaining one hundred and three thousand acres. The agency eventually moved nine hundred families from their land, and the Tennessee villages of Model, Blue Spring, Hays, and Mint Spring ceased to exist.

Land Between the Lakes was a major departure for the TVA; here the TVA was reshaping the land into new uses rather than covering it with reservoir water. Agency officials hoped that the project would improve their reputation in land conservation and environmental protection as it also served a recreational purpose and stimulated a depressed local economy with tourism dollars. After removing the native population, the agency had at its disposal a largely vacant landscape, similar in ways to the early national parks in the West, where no one lived but anyone could visit.

TVA replaced the living artifacts of the area's history and culture with a new landscape of picnic areas, bird sanctuaries, campgrounds, restored historic sites, and, especially, a re-created nineteenth-century village called "The Homeplace—1850," which is just south of the Kentucky border. Historian Walter Creese views the Homeplace as resuscitating TVA's "original arcadian dream of landscape innocence and purity" (134). This 250-acre complex of log dwellings and outbuildings was designed to convey the region's mid-nineteenth-century landscape. The vernacular buildings, interestingly, were once the type TVA could not wait to demolish as it constructed its major Appalachian projects of the 1930s and early 1940s. But by the mid-1960s, understanding America's vernacular log tradition was important in the study of architecture, folklore, and geography so the buildings became interpretive assets rather than shacks to be torn down.

Certainly the building types reflect a common landscape of the late antebellum period (see sidebar entitled "Common House Plans," Landscape 5, chapter 3, and sidebar entitled "Common Farm Outbuildings," Landscape 13, chapter 5). The main dwelling is a log dogtrot house. A picket fence separates the house and its outbuildings from the

rest of the farm. Nearest the dwelling are three areas—the springhouse, orchard, and garden—closely related to the domestic production of the farm. Farm women used these areas to produce vegetables, fruits, and eggs for everyday meals. They often traded surpluses for valued commercial items from peddlers or the local general store. Nineteenth-century farm women, in this way, contributed significantly to the farm's overall economic stability as well as to the living standards of their families. Beyond the immediate area of the house was the more market-oriented section of the farm. A variety of log types exist, from a tall tobacco barn to a pig pen and crib, along with separate log buildings for horses and oxen.

The Homeplace is a rare Tennessee example of a "living history" museum, where time is frozen at a particular year in history and the buildings and activities are chosen to reflect what was common during that time. In this case, the park interprets an emerging commercial farm in 1850. The fictional family produces tobacco and perhaps livestock for market, but most of its activities center around domestic production. Recent research by historian Donald L. Winters suggests that many other Tennessee farm families followed a similar mixed strategy of producing limited amounts for the market while insuring self-sufficiency and the farm's survival. Appropriately, the Homeplace is open only from the planting months of the spring, beginning in March, to the end of harvest in November.

Across the road from the Homeplace is a public reserve for buffalo, which were a more common site on the Tennessee landscape two hundred years ago. Place names on Tennessee maps show where buffalo herds could once have been located, but overhunting wiped out the herds east of the Mississippi. One way to envision the profound difference between the landscape of the Native Americans and the settlement landscape of the nineteenth century is to imagine these herds running throughout the Tennessee countryside. Settlers destroyed the wild game of Tennessee and replaced it with domesticated herds of cattle and swine.

Less than a mile south is a preserved historic site that records another significant component of the nineteenth-century landscape of Stewart County. The ruins of the **Great Western Iron Furnace** are a powerful reminder of the large number of iron works that once dotted the Western Highland Rim. Brien, Newell, and Co. of Nashville operated the furnace from 1854 to 1856, with at least eighty African-American slaves providing most of the labor. A second important iron industry site lies outside of the park, five miles east of Dover on Tennessee 49. Organized initially by Samuel Stacker and later controlled by Wood, Yeatman, and Co. of Nashville, **Bear Springs Furnace** operated from the antebellum era to 1921, producing thousands of tons of pig iron. Again, it is possible to envision a landscape entirely different from the one that is encountered today by imagining the smoke, environmental degradation, and sweat and blood of unending, repetitive labor associated with the iron industry of the nineteenth century.

These historic sites in and around Land Between the Lakes document the nature of Stewart County life at the beginning of the Civil War. However, events in the winter of 1862 dramatically altered the local economy and displaced hundreds of residents. The February 1862 Battle of **Fort Donelson** took place about three miles east of the Land Between the Lakes entrance on U.S. Highway 79. The National Park Service has preserved the fort as a national historic battlefield, and its visitor center has an informative film and exhibits.

In February 1862, a Union army commanded by Brig. Gen. Ulysses S. Grant launched a major offensive against two forts located in Stewart County. **Fort Henry** guarded the Tennessee River (outworks from this post still stand in Land Between the Lakes). Fort Donelson defended the Cumberland River. Both forts also protected the strategically important iron industry of Stewart County. If they fell, the iron industry could be destroyed and the rich heartland of Middle Tennessee would be wide open to the advancing Federal armies.

Grant's plan called for a combined overland and river attack, with new ironclad gunboats under the command of Flag Officer Andrew S.

Foote leading the way. On February 6, Foote's boats hit Fort Henry with all the firepower they could muster. And the fort's twenty-five hundred Confederate troops, under the command of Lloyd Tilghman, answered with deadly accurate counterfire. "We were struck with rifle and heavy shot and shell 30 times," Officer Foote recalled. "I had the breath, for several seconds, knocked out of me, as a shot struck opposite my chest, in the iron clad pilot house on deck." At first, it seemed, the Confederates had the advantage, but Foote pushed on—"it must be victory or death"—and the gunboat's heavy guns began to demolish the fort and demoralize the Confederates (Cooling, 103, 106). Tilghman gave up the fight, remaining with a small command of about one hundred to surrender the fort while the rest escaped to Fort Donelson.

Grant's troops did not arrive in time to take part in the battle for Fort Henry, but they played the crucial role in the contest over Fort Donelson. Built by slaves and soldiers, the fifteen-acre Confederate position stood along a bend in the Cumberland River. It was well fortified with walls ten feet high, stocked with twelve heavy guns and lighter artillery, and defended by a force of about fifteen thousand soldiers. No mere naval attack would carry this position; an overland attack was essential.

On February 14, Foote's gunboats courageously floated up the Cumberland toward Fort Donelson and engaged the Confederate batteries for about an hour and a half, but this time the boats were repulsed. That left the matter up to Grant's troops. For two days they had carefully positioned themselves around the fort and had surrounded the Confederates. In an attempt to save some of the army, Rebel commanders Gen. John Floyd and Gen. Gideon Pillow massed their troops for an attack on the Union right on February 15. The morning assault went well as the Yankees began to give ground, but just as success was almost in reach, Pillow and Floyd inexplicably decided that the counterattack had stalled and they ordered the troops to return. Later that night, Pillow and Floyd turned over the fort's command to Gen. Simon B. Buckner and then retreated to Nashville with about two thousand men in tow. Col. Nathan B. Forrest also escaped with his cavalry.

On February 16, Buckner asked Grant for his terms of surrender; the Union general replied: "No terms except an unconditional and immediate surrender can be accepted. I propose to move immediately upon your works" (Cooling, 209). Buckner had little choice but to accept. The actual surrender ceremony took place later that day at **Dover Tavern,** located adjacent to the Cumberland River in downtown Dover. From

Sevier Blockhouse, Clarksville. The thick stone walls and sparse window openings indicate the dangers faced by early settlers in western Middle Tennessee.

this spot, there is an excellent view of the river; it was control of that transportation corridor that led to the hard fighting at Forts Henry and Donelson.

The significance of the Battle of Fort Donelson was far greater than giving Gen. U. S. Grant the popular nickname of "Unconditional Surrender." Historian Thomas L. Connelly concluded that the fall of Fort Donelson, combined with the quick loss of Middle Tennessee, "was a disaster for Confederate supply. Gone were the South's chief powder mills on the Cumberland, the Great Western Iron Belt, and the abundant corn and livestock region of Middle Tennessee" (30). The South also lost Nashville, an invaluable supply and manufacturing center, not to mention the military hardware that was surrendered.

From Dover, U.S. Highway 79 crosses the Cumberland River and moves to the northeast for thirty-one miles to Clarksville, the next major historic port on the river. Nestled at the confluence of the Red and Cumberland Rivers, Clarksville was established in 1785 by John Montgomery as the westernmost outpost in the Southwest Territory. As U.S. 79 enters the western city limits, it passes by the historic community of New Providence. Historical markers direct travelers to two National Register sites connected to local river history. On Walker Street is the **Sevier Station,** the earliest dwelling still standing in Clarksville. In about 1792, Valentine Sevier Jr. moved his family from Greeneville to

TENNESSEE'S HISTORIC LANDSCAPES

this one-room limestone home overlooking the confluence of the Red and Cumberland Rivers. But the Seviers faced unrelenting hostility from Native Americans, who considered them trespassers. An attack in the fall of 1794 killed eight members of his family. Valentine Sevier Jr. died in 1800; his grave is at nearby Riverview Cemetery.

Two blocks away on "A" Street is the remarkably intact Civil War fort known as **Fort Defiance/Fort Bruce.** Confederate commanders directed a large number of local slaves to build this fortified post overlooking the river confluence. But Fort Defiance never played a significant role in defending Clarksville as local leaders surrendered without a fight soon after Fort Donelson fell in mid-February 1862. The Union army renamed the post Fort Bruce, then occupied it for the remainder of the war.

Returning to U.S. Highway 79, the route descends the river bluffs to the downtown riverfront area. The best vantage points are on U.S. Highway 41A (Riverside Drive) to the southeast. McGregor Park is probably the best place in Tennessee to see the Cumberland River and understand how it could shape a town's development. On the bluffs directly to the east lies the historic town square. Here was the initial center of commerce for Clarksville, tied directly to river traffic. Clarksville was incorporated in 1819, and by the early 1830s it could boast of twelve stores, three taverns, eleven craft shops, a cotton gin, and a wool-carding machine clustered between the riverfront and town square. Although only one pre–Civil War building remains there—the circa 1841–43 **Poston Block** at 126–30 Main Street—the square design itself is an important artifact of the city's beginnings.

To the southeast from McGregor Park, the beginnings of Clarksville's industrial history can be seen. At Commerce and Spring Streets once stood the historic Whitfield-Bates Foundry (known locally as Clarksville Foundry), part of which dated from 1853. The foundry produced Civil War artillery and ammunition until Union troops closed it in 1862. In postwar decades the **Clarksville industrial district** developed around the foundry. The export of tobacco became a major activity in the late 1850s, and several large tobacco warehouses stood along the river bluffs. One building—the Grange Warehouse— was once recognized as the world's largest tobacco warehouse, but it burned in 1977. After the Civil War, railroad transportation soon eclipsed the river in importance as the Louisville and Nashville, Tennessee Central, and Illinois Central built warehouses, repair facilities, and freight stations. A hundred years ago, this district hummed with activity because Clarksville in 1895 was the largest tobacco export center in the country, shipping up to forty thousand hogsheads a year. It was also the United States' third-largest tobacco market.

The railroads also shaped a rapidly expanding urban landscape. Since the town square was situated directly on the river bluff, downtown businesses could not expand to the west. They could build to the north or south along the riverbank or to the east toward the depots and main lines of the railroads. Most development indeed moved eastward. Rebuilt after a disastrous fire in 1878 leveled many businesses and the county courthouse, the 100 to 300 blocks of Franklin Street—the core of the downtown **Clarksville architectural district**—embody window moldings and cornices typical of Victorian commercial architecture.

During the late 1800s, the city's reputation as an industrial producer and tobacco exporter grew by leaps and bounds. On Commerce Street two new public buildings reflected the new confidence and prosperity. The **Montgomery County Courthouse** (1878, 1900), designed by S. W. Bunting and C. G. Rosenplaenter, is thoroughly eclectic in its architecture, while its distinguished neighbor across the street, the former **Federal Building and Custom House** (1897–98), is now home to the Clarksville-Montgomery County Historical Museum. Designed by federal architect William M. Aiken, the building is a flamboyant and eclectic example of French Renaissance style, jazzed up by a steep slate roof and copper American eagles perched at the corners. The museum features permanent exhibits on Clarksville history and the significance of the tobacco trade.

Just up the hill from the museum is the **Dog Hill historic district,** which evolved between 1870 to 1900 as a neighborhood for the city's emerging professional and managerial class. It has a mixture of one- and two-story frame dwellings, reflecting such popular Victorian styles as Gothic, Italianate, Eastlake, and Second Empire. G. B. Wilson, an architect and builder who owned the local Sewanee Planing and Flooring Mills, designed several dwellings. His own home stands at 422 S. First Street, built in the 1870s as a lovely folk Gothic cottage (private, no access).

Clarksville's African-American community also established itself during the post–Civil War decades. The **St. Peter African Methodist Church** at 518 Franklin was built in 1873 for a congregation that had formed seven years earlier. The Fifth Ward Baptist Church at 900 Franklin serves a congregation that was established in 1871. These two examples make Clarksville similar to other southern towns where newly freed slaves often combined with free blacks to create their own churches as soon as possible after the Civil War. Clarksville was unlike many southern towns, however, in that it continued to allow African Americans the right to vote long after Reconstruction was over. As late as 1906, African Americans had an opportunity to elect representatives to the local board of aldermen; then Jim Crow repression kept Clarksville blacks from the ballot box until the civil rights movement of the 1960s.

Madison Street (U.S. 41A), between Second and Tenth Streets, is another one-hundred-year-old neighborhood. Although modern development has eliminated some landmarks, the street has important historic churches, public buildings, and residences. At 319 Madison is the double-spired Gothic Revival **Madison Street United Methodist Church** (1882) while the former **Clarksville High School** (1907, 1916) stands at the corner of Madison and Greenwood Avenue. The school is a good example of a trend in historic preservation to convert old school buildings into apartment complexes (private, no access). Across from the school is an excellent collection of early-twentieth-century bungalows. The Louisville and Nashville passenger station (circa 1890) stands a few hundred feet north of the intersection of Madison and Tenth Streets. Old warehouses lie along the railroad corridor and across the street is a turn-of-the-century factory now owned by the American Snuff Company (private, no access). Once Clarksville became a producer as well as an exporter of tobacco products, its economic growth through the twentieth century was greatly enhanced. A 1923 account described Clarksville as "an up-to-date city with all conveniences [and] a large tobacco market" (Foster, 74).

Another key contributor during the 1920s was Austin Peay Normal School (now Austin Peay State University), created in 1927. The campus may be reached by returning to Madison Street and then taking Seventh Street north to College Street. Colonial Revival architecture characterizes the campus and is well expressed in the Independence Hall–like appearance of the administration building. The college also maintains two historic dwellings, the Italianate-style **Archwood** at 703 East College, built by local postmaster Samuel Rexinger in 1878, and the magnificent Classical Revival mansion at North Second Street known now as the **Emerald Hill Alumni Center** (both public, limited access). During the 1850s, when influential Whig political leader Gustavus A. Henry lived here, the dwelling was a good example of Tennessee Federal style. In the early twentieth century, however, owners added the overwhelming two-story portico of four massive Corinthian columns, turning the house into a Classical Revival showplace.

Route B: Clarksville to Nashville

To continue following the Cumberland River, return to Riverside Drive and follow this road (also marked as U.S. 41A Bypass) southeast to its junction with Tennessee Highway 12, an official Tennessee Scenic Route that parallels the river. Twenty-one miles to the southeast is the small village of Cheap Hill. From here, about two miles or so to the south is the confluence of the Cumberland and Harpeth Rivers. This area can't be reached by automobile, but a large prehistoric village, known to archaeologists as **Indian Town Bluff,** once existed at the confluence (private, no access). The Mississippian period site contains earthworks and evidence of at least fifteen mounds. Native Americans probably lived at this strategic river junction for centuries; now it is an abandoned and forgotten place, insignificant to a culture accustomed to traveling by roads and highways rather than rivers. In a newspaper interview, state archaeologist Nick Fielder observed that the Harpeth area Indians of the Mississippian period "were very much like the early pioneers. They lived on individual farms, in community-like hamlets and in larger towns. They built public buildings on top of earthen mounds with smaller houses surrounding them. They lived in pole construction houses plastered with mud and with grass roots. Up and down the Harpeth River you can find a whole range of homesteads, hamlets, and towns" (*Nashville Tennessean,* May 3, 1987).

Eight miles south of Cheap Hill is Ashland City, the seat of government for Cheatham County. Established in 1856 and incorporated three years later, the town has few buildings left from the river days of the nineteenth century. Its **Cheatham County Courthouse** was designed by R. E. Turbeville in 1914. About four miles north of Ashland City, on Tennessee 49, are the ruins of **Sycamore Mills,** the major industrial employer in Cheatham County from 1868 to 1904. The old mill site stands next to the golf course of the local country club (private, limited access). The natural water power of the property had attracted millers as early as 1790, and by 1844 Samuel Watson operated a gristmill, sawmill, cotton mill, and powder mill. When Cheatham County was created in 1856, the county was named for Edward Cheatham, one of the Sycamore Mills' owners. The first meeting of the Cheatham

County Court took place at the mill. Two years later, Watson, along with Edward and Robert Cheatham, reorganized the company into a gunpowder manufacturing firm, and by 1860 the gunpowder produced that year was valued at twenty-five thousand dollars.

The fall of Fort Donelson immediately closed the gunpowder works. But by 1867 the plant was back in business as the Sycamore Manufacturing Company, this time under the sole direction of Samuel Watson. A major expansion in production came in 1873 when Watson sold part interest in the factory to the Du Pont family of Delaware and invested in the old machinery of the former Confederate Powder Works at Augusta, Georgia. Once installed and repaired, the old machinery worked well and the company prospered. But Samuel Watson did not live long to enjoy this good fortune. He died in 1876, and his heirs sold his interests to the Du Pont Company.

Du Pont greatly expanded operations and established a company town near the mills. By 1886 the mill produced about ten thousand pounds of gunpowder daily and around it stood a school, a union church, a blacksmith, company store, and thirty residences. The mill remained in operation until 1904, but today only archaeological remains of housing and blast walls along with a dam hint at the noisy, dirty, and dangerous place this powder factory once was. Perhaps the most spectacular artifact is the wrought-iron, cable-stayed bridge, designed by company president and general manager E. C. Lewis in 1891. It is located directly northeast of the highway marker on Tennessee 49. According to the Historic American Engineering Record, the bridge is the only intact nineteenth-century cable-stayed bridge in America. From his start at Sycamore Mills, Lewis would go on to become a major Nashville capitalist, serving on the board of the L&N Railroad and as chairman of the board of the Nashville, Chattanooga, and St. Louis Railroad. In 1897, he directed the Tennessee Centennial Exposition and is one of those officials credited with the idea for the Parthenon.

After returning to Ashland City, the next twenty miles east on Tennessee 12 lead to Nashville, the political, commercial, and industrial heart of the Cumberland country. This route has some excellent views of the Cumberland River where it is possible to imagine the days when steamboats puffed along this stretch carrying their heavy loads of agricultural products from the Central Basin into the marketplaces of the Mississippi and Ohio river systems.

Route C: Nashville to Carthage

Once in Nashville, the Cumberland River trek to Carthage could take several different routes to reach U.S. Highway 70. The most scenic and direct way is to follow Tennessee 155 from the western outskirts of Nashville as it winds through the city—becoming, in order, White Bridge Road, Woodmont Boulevard, Thompson Lane, and finally Briley Parkway—to its junction with U.S. Highway 70 on the eastern outskirts of Nashville. This junction is south of the Cumberland River on the historic Lebanon Pike, a route as old as the state itself. In the Donelson-Hermitage area are three famous antebellum plantations: Clover Bottom, the Hermitage home of Andrew Jackson, and Tulip Grove (for more information on these houses, see Landscape 3, chapter 2). Other parts of U.S. 70 document our current demands for fast food, quick service, and easy-access parking. Largely undistinguished commercial strips are everywhere; recent suburban developments intrude all along the highway. U.S. Highway 70 shows the uneasy balance between the past and present that exists on many Tennessee roads.

North of Hermitage, on the Cumberland River, is one of the region's most interesting places associated with World War I. Having abandoned its Sycamore Mills just before the outbreak of World War I, the Du Pont Corporation in 1917 chose to build a much larger ammunition plant, this time adjacent to the river in Davidson County, to supply American and Allied armies. To reach the Du Pont plant and the company town that stood outside its gates, leave U.S. Highway 70 at Hermitage and take Tennessee 45 directly north to the town of Old Hickory. In Old Hickory Du Pont quickly built a mammoth complex in 1917 that was capable of producing seven hundred thousand pounds of smokeless gunpowder a day. But the plant only operated for eight months until the end of World War I. Du Pont then converted the plant to make cellophane and rayon. The **Old Hickory historic district** documents the architecture and original features of the adjoining neighborhood of former company housing.

The twenty miles of U.S. Highway 70 between Hermitage and Lebanon passes several historic Cumberland farms not as well known as their Nashville counterparts. Cloydland Farm, which is fourteen miles east of Nashville, is over two hundred years old (private, no access). Beginning with 220 acres in 1789, John and Margaret Scott Cloyd raised livestock, grain, cotton, and corn along the rich river bottomland. Their surviving **Cloyd House** was built in 1791. The farm's mod-

Warner Price Smith House, Wilson County. Owners are now restoring this significant example of folk architecture.

ern history is similar to many in this area as the Cloyds later switched in the twentieth century to raising special breeds of livestock, including Poland China swine, registered Polled Shorthorn cattle, and Hampshire sheep.

Outside of Mt. Juliet, twelve miles west of Lebanon, is the **Warner Price Smith House** (private, no access). In 1853 Smith purchased a circa 1820 log I-house, with a central dogtrot. By adding a two-story portico and filling in the dogtrot with a new entrance, he transformed it into a vernacular Greek Revival showplace (see sidebar entitled "Common House Plans," Landscape 5, chapter 3). Five miles west is another historic dwelling, similar in appearance to the Smith House. The **Campbell-Ruck House** was built between 1841 and 1843 by B. W. G. Winford (private, no access). As late as 1975, the property had 220 acres, but in that year all of the farmland was sold for suburban development, except for a small lot for the original dwelling. Other historic farmsteads have met with a similar fate near the major towns and cities along U.S. Highway 70 throughout Tennessee.

Thirty miles east of the state capitol, on U.S. 70, Lebanon is the seat of government for Wilson County. Located at roughly equal distances from Nashville, Gallatin, Hartsville, Carthage, and Murfreesboro, the city developed as an important early-nineteenth-century crossroads for the commerce of northern Middle Tennessee. It also enjoyed political clout during the years of heated political conflict between the Whig and Democratic parties, since it was the home of James C. "Lean

Jimmy" Jones, a popular Whig governor, later U.S. senator, and railroad promoter. Jones's antebellum two-story brick farmhouse stands about three miles north of town on U.S. Highway 231 (private, no access).

Since the Cumberland River was six miles to the north, Lebanon only indirectly benefited from river traffic; early railroads also bypassed it. The ill-fated Tennessee and Pacific managed to connect the town to Nashville by the early 1870s, but not until Alexander Crawford built the Nashville and Knoxville Railroad in the 1880s did Lebanon have a secure connection eastward. In 1893 the line reached the coal mines at Monterey and stopped, seemingly for good. To the rescue, at the turn of the century, came the tracks of the Tennessee Central Railroad. When the line's eastern section was completed in 1902, Lebanon enjoyed renewed economic prosperity based on its new transportation connection.

Another contributor to turn-of-the-century prosperity was Castle Heights Military Academy (1902) on West Main Street (U.S. Highway 70). Educators and local boosters hoped that the school's splendid 225-acre campus, complete with romantic yet masculine castellated Gothic buildings, would attract the best sons of the South for a rigorous, private education. In 1917, after its conversion to a military school, Castle Heights flourished. During the 1930s, the Classical Revival McFadden Memorial Auditorium and the Art Deco McFadden Gym (recently demolished) joined the original Gothic designs. In 1936, the school acquired the adjacent **Mitchell Mansion** (1906), a great stone Classical Revival dwelling, for use as an elementary school. But in the mid-1980s, amid howls of protest from students, alumni, and local citizens, the school closed. Although some parcels of the campus have been sold for new businesses, it is still possible to drive around the campus and enjoy the architectural diversity of its quickly deteriorating buildings. Artifacts and documents from the school are also maintained in a special room at the Cumberland University library.

West Main Street connects Castle Heights to the town square. Once this boulevard was almost purely residential, home to several grand dwellings. At 428 West Main Street stands one of the state's outstanding examples of Victorian domestic architecture, the Queen Anne–Eastlake–style **Buchanan House,** built from 1894 to 1897. Knoxville architect George F. Barber designed this picturesque eclectic design for Isaac W. Buchanan, who was a founder of and professor at Castle Heights Military Academy. The **Fessenden House** at 326 West Main is much more traditional in its antebellum-era architecture; it is now a local history museum. As automobile traffic grew along U.S. 70 during the twentieth century, however, more and more businesses moved to West Main Street. Today the street awkwardly mixes residential and commercial buildings, and several historic nineteenth-century homes have been eliminated in favor of continued commercial development.

The center for cultural life in nineteenth-century Lebanon was Cumberland University. The great tower of its **Memorial Hall** (1892–96), designed by Nashville architect William Crawford Smith, dominates the downtown skyline. The Cumberland Presbyterian Church established the school in 1842, and four years later its famous law school opened. Over the next decade, the school expanded its curriculum to include a school of engineering and a school of theology. For over one hundred years, Cumberland was famous for the number of judges, congressmen, and senators who graduated from there. Cordell Hull, secretary of state under President Franklin D. Roosevelt, is perhaps the most illustrious graduate. He recalled that his Cumberland professors were "the finest law instructors I have ever known at any institution of learning" (*Memoirs*, 1: 27).

In 1956 Cumberland became a private, nondenominational two-year junior college, and then six years later declining enrollments and funds forced it to sell the law school to Samford University in Birmingham. It entered a period of decline that was reversed in 1982 when Cumberland again became a four-year liberal arts college and later added two graduate programs.

As U.S. Highway 70 moves through the downtown and then passes through the eastern end of Lebanon, the route encounters a historic African-American neighborhood. Where U.S. 70 splits into two new routes—U.S. 70N, which follows the Cumberland River to Carthage, and U.S. 70 to the historic railroad town of Watertown—there is a third road, Tennessee 141, known locally as Trousdale Ferry Pike. After about a half mile to the east, this road leads to **Rest Hill Cemetery,** a historic place associated with the beginnings of Lebanon's black community.

Established in 1867–69, Rest Hill Cemetery is the only surviving physical remnant of Lebanon's original African-American community. Before the Civil War, Lebanon had no distinct black neighborhood, but with Reconstruction and the aid of the Freedman's Bureau from 1865 to 1872, a neighborhood formed on the town's eastern outskirts. The cemetery was an important symbol of community as well as a source of ethnic pride and identity. For African Americans, according to folklorist John M. Vlach, "The cemetery has long had special significance. Beyond its association with the fear and awe of death, which all humans share, the graveyard was, in the past, one of the few places in America where an overt black identity could be asserted and maintained" (*By the Work of Their Hands,* 109). Until 1933 Rest Hill Cemetery served as the only black burial ground in Lebanon, and locally prominent late-nineteenth- and early-twentieth-century African-American businessmen, politicians, and educators were buried there. For example, J. R. Inman, who died in 1917, led the fight for black public schools in Wilson County and helped to create the Wilson County Colored Teachers Association.

To continue south of the Cumberland River, return to U.S. Highway 70N and drive east for twenty miles to the town of Carthage. This section of highway crosses beautiful miles of farmland, mostly devoted to raising livestock, dairy products, and tobacco. About ten miles east of Lebanon, near the junction of U.S. 70N and the Hiwassee Road, is Clendennan's Branch Farm, a historic family farm established by Jonathan and Betty Lamb in 1852. From this point, the highway runs much closer to the Cumberland River. About one mile east is **Rome Ferry,** a historic crossing point on the Cumberland River that dates probably from around 1830. Confederate cavalry commander John Hunt Morgan used it in 1862 to escape from Federal troops during one of his Middle Tennessee raids. The ferry tug, the *Jere Mitchell,* is named for a Smith County soldier who died in World War II.

Carthage is another eight miles to the east. From Carthage, cross either bridge and take Tennessee Highway 25 (Main Street) to begin exploring the north side of the Cumberland River. As Main Street heads north of the square, the **United Methodist Church,** complete with a Second Empire spire, can be seen at 609 North Main. At **1004 North Main** is the Carthage residence of former U.S. Senator and Secretary of State Cordell Hull, who played a key role in American foreign relations during the administration of Franklin D. Roosevelt and was awarded the Nobel Peace Prize (private, no access).

Route D: Carthage to Springfield

Tennessee Highway 25 from Carthage west to its junction with Tennessee 49 near Springfield is one of the state's most historic and scenic roads. Not only will the sixty-eight miles along this two-lane road take the visitor through a beautiful landscape, but also it parallels the Fort Blount trail—an overland route used by early pioneers—in Smith, Trousdale, and Sumner Counties.

Dixon Springs is a tiny village about eleven miles northwest of Carthage. The county court of Smith County met for the first time in 1799 here. The first "courthouse" was the log home of Tilman Dixon, a place now known as **Dixona** (private, no access). Combining the original two-story log dwelling of Tilman Dixon with two brick Italianate-influenced wings from the mid-nineteenth century, Dixona is one of the region's most interesting vernacular structures. The mid-1800s changes turned the house into a two-story "piano-box" form, with the brick wings and log central core linked by a two-story center section with a Greek Revival portico.

This home, like many others in the immediate vicinity, is part of the **Dixon Springs historic district,** which contains several buildings typical of a nineteenth-century rural crossroads village. It includes the one-story piano-box–style Ross House (1830, circa 1900), the Georgian I-house style of Arcadia (circa 1840), the old public school (circa 1915), which is now the local Missionary Baptist Church, the Dixon Springs Union Church (1877), and other historic stores and dwellings (all private, no access).

In and near the town are historic family farms (private, no access). To the east on old State 25 is Beechwood Farm, founded by David and Elizabeth Burford in 1831. A former Democratic speaker of the state senate, Burford experimented with many types of crops and bred fine race horses and mules. In the next generation, the family introduced the area's first Jersey dairy cattle and opened businesses in Carthage. George W. Allen ran the place from 1920 until his death in 1975. A local Democratic party leader, Allen was a pharmacist, president of a Carthage bank, and member of the county court for sixty years. Graced by an elegant late Georgian–style dwelling, Point Breeze Farm is just south of Dixon Springs on the Rome Road. Founded by Nancy Cunningham Sanders in 1803, the farm has recently specialized in tobacco, hay, and cattle.

Allendale Farm (1864) is immediately west of Dixona on Tennessee Highway 25. With tobacco cultivation, river commerce, and the Tennessee Valley Authority each subtly shaping its history, Allendale Farm typifies the local agrarian experience. William Sanders, a postmaster, became known for producing an excellent dark tobacco leaf on his 267 acres. The next family owners built a vernacular upright-and-wing house that still stands, embellished by four classical columns taken from an old hotel in Red Boiling Springs. Then, in the twentieth century, the farm was operated in a typical progressive fashion but unfortunately lost about one hundred acres to TVA's Hartsville nuclear project during the mid-1970s. Recent family owners have specialized in burley tobacco along with raising corn, milo, and cattle.

About six miles west of the Smith County line is Hartsville, the seat of government for Trousdale County. At its eastern city limits, on a hill overlooking the junction of Tennessee Highways 25 and 10, is the **James DeBow House** (1854–70). This unique blend of Greek Revival and Italianate architecture is where local leaders met to set the boundary lines for Trousdale County in 1870 (private, no access). From this junction, a side trip of twenty-eight miles via Tennessee 10 and 52 to the northeast takes the visitor to the historic mineral springs resort of **Red Boiling Springs.** Charming historic hotels, including the Cloyd, Armours, and Donoho hotels, continue to entertain guests, and the intact landscape is probably the best-preserved old mineral springs resort in Tennessee.

At the entrance to Hartsville, look south for the landscaped town sign. The visitor may turn here on East Main Street to take a more historic route to downtown. Before reaching the square, there is a small historic neighborhood, especially in the 400 block of East Main, that contains a variety of interesting architectural styles, including a central-hall Gothic cottage, gracious Classical Revival homes, and Queen Anne–influenced upright-and-wing dwellings.

Although the first settlers came to the Hartsville area in the late 1780s and the town became a new county seat in 1870, the **Hartsville downtown historic district** mostly dates from the late 1890s to the 1930s. Hartsville lacked a railroad until the mid-1890s, when a spur line to Gallatin was completed. Officials of the Chesapeake and Nashville Railway Company then built the **Hartsville Depot,** which still stands on Broadway Street. In 1906 the rail line was sold to the Gallatin and Scottsville Railway, a branch of the Louisville and Nashville that operated the line until 1977. Access to regional markets via the new railroad link encouraged entrepreneurs to establish a local tobacco industry. The Hartsville Tobacco Warehouse opened along with two other processing companies, the R. C. Owens Tobacco Company and the Willard Tobacco Company. Today large tobacco warehouses remain near the railroad tracks.

The railroad developments of ninety years ago, and three fires from 1902 to 1904, spurred major downtown changes. Local businesses, banks, and even the courthouse had been initially oriented near the corner of Broadway and Main since Broadway connected the old business district to the railroad tracks. Then, in 1904, a fire destroyed the second courthouse and, shortly after a replacement building was completed, another fire demolished the third courthouse. When residents rebuilt in 1905–6, most chose brick or masonry. As an additional precaution against future disasters, county officials moved the courthouse across the street, away from the fire-prone commercial district, and isolated it in a square-like design, creating a town square where none had existed before. This 1906 courthouse stands today, while commercial activity still takes place along Main Street to Broadway.

Again traveling west on Tennessee 25, a huge man-made object dominates the landscape between Hartsville and the junction of Tennessee 25 with U.S. Highway 231. The abandoned cooling tower for the Hartsville Nuclear Reactor project is a monument to our foolhardy assumption that nuclear energy is the magic technological answer to future energy needs. Throughout the 1970s, the financial wisdom and environmental impact of the Hartsville project were questioned in many different forums. Locals strongly supported the power plant, however, since it brought needed jobs and promised future prosperity. Once construction began, no one thought that the project would stop. However, beleaguered by outside criticism, wary of the ever-increasing construction costs, and caught in a budget squeeze, TVA canceled the project in 1984. The cooling tower, along with several other major structures, were mothballed; it became a multimillion-dollar investment left to peer over the Cumberland landscape.

As Tennessee 25 crosses into Sumner County, travelers enter the tobacco belt of Sumner, Robertson, and Montgomery Counties. Tobacco has long been a mainstay of the state's agricultural economy. Two types—burley and dark-fired—are produced. The burley leaf is air-cured in large, rectangular gable-roof barns that provide for ample ventilation. One of the largest—over ninety feet in length and forty feet in height—was built by Robert Williams at the **McCauley Hill Farm** in Montgomery County. But there is also a different type of tobacco barn that is taller and more square and has smoke holes or ventilators. These barns produce "dark-fired," or smoked, tobacco, which was very popular one hundred years ago, and is still used in chewing tobacco and snuff. A 1930s description of the dark-fired process noted that the tobacco, once harvested, was placed on four-foot-long sticks and hung in tobacco barns for a traditional forty days and nights over a fire: "The finest barns have ventilators and a thermometer and hydrometer to insure the proper degree of heat and moisture during the long vigil. But

Tobacco farmer, 1951–52 Annual Report of Tennessee Department of Agriculture. The original caption read: "A 'hand' of leaf like that shown above gladdens the heart of the tobacco planter." (Courtesy of Oscar Farris Agricultural Museum, Tennessee Department of Agriculture)

the average farmer uses patience, experience, and 'horse sense,' knowing that his long summer's work may be ruined in an hour if too much dry heat 'kills' the tobacco by destroying the oils that give it pliability and flavor. When the curing has been completed the tobacco is stripped from the stalks and tied into 'hands'—convenient bundles containing five or six of the big leaves—to wait transport to the market" (*WPA Guide,* 392). Clarksville, Springfield, and Gallatin were major tobacco markets where huge warehouses are still near railroad tracks and the cries of the tobacco auctioneer can be heard every fall and winter.

Tennessee Highway 25 in eastern Sumner County is also a very good place to explore the region's early settlement landscape. Castalian Springs is about eight miles west of Hartsville. As early as A.D. 1400, Mississippian period Indians had established a village here, marked by ancient mounds, which may still be seen on the north side of the highway near the village post office. Stone box graves, made by lining the burial with thin sheets of limestone, also survive in the vicinity (private, no access). Buffalo herds came to the salt lick where their old trails crisscrossed. The animals attracted white long hunters, such as Isaac Bledsoe, who visited here in 1771 and encountered the salt lick and sulphur spring that was once known as Bledsoe's Lick, but is now called Castalian Springs. Six years later, Thomas Spencer and other hunters arrived, built crude cabins for shelter, and probably planted the region's first English crop of corn in 1778. Over the next two years, Isaac Bledsoe and other settlers built **Bledsoe's Station** as the first fort in Sumner County on a rise overlooking the springs. The post, however, was not permanently occupied until 1784 when Anthony Bledsoe, the older brother of Isaac, constructed a stockaded fort. An early settler, writing about the fort in the 1850s, recalled that it was "an oblong square, and built all around in a regular stockade except at one place, where stood a large double cabin" (National Register nomination). Today this settlement site near the Bledsoe Cemetery north of the highway has been preserved as an archaeological park.

Below the park is the entrance to **Wynnewood,** a historic log-constructed inn and dwelling. In 1828 Alfred R. Wynne, Stephen R. Roberts, and William Cage opened the property as a stagecoach inn and mineral springs resort adjacent to Bledsoe's Lick. By 1830 the inn and spring were known as Castalian Springs—and that name has stuck to the community ever since. In 1834 Wynne bought out his partners, and his family and descendents lived in the rambling log house until 1971 when the property and adjacent spring became a historic house museum and was listed as a National Historic Landmark. Wynnewood had a checkered history as a rural summer resort; its greatest popularity came at the turn of the century.

To the west on Tennessee 25 stands the grand limestone mansion called **"Cragfont,"** the home of James Winchester, a prominent politician, land speculator, and plantation owner. Built between 1798 and 1811, this excellent frontier example of late Georgian architecture contains one of the state's best examples of an early decorative interior, featuring painted and stenciled interior walls, staircases, and woodwork. According to family tradition, Winchester hired a group of Baltimore craftsmen to build the original Georgian mansion. In 1810–11, in order to entertain on a more lavish scale, Winchester directed the construction of a second-story ballroom and card room on the original T-wing of the house. The ballroom was the largest then in existence in Middle Tennessee. A second-story gallery tied the house together, letting guests move freely from the ballroom to other chambers.

Winchester was a native of Maryland, so it is not surprising that Cragfont is like many of the great plantation houses of the Chesapeake region of Virginia and Maryland. Its siting was in a prominent location, with a long ceremonial drive that allowed a commanding view of the facade at the last possible moment. Its Georgian architecture conveyed

Cragfont, circa 1950, Castalian Springs. The grand manor house before restoration. (Courtesy of Cragfont Historic House Museum)

stability and refined taste. The ballroom spoke to Winchester's role as a gracious host, providing an elegant social place for the local planter elite to gather. Then, like many of its coastal counterparts, the house was the administrative center for a huge tobacco plantation that employed well over a hundred African-American slaves as its work force. Unfortunately, none of the many slave quarters that stood outside the domestic complex remain or have been reconstructed. Family members recalled that the slave quarters were "cabins built in a long row, all joined, a chimney between each two rooms. There was a large room and a loft for each family" (Durham, *Winchester,* 89).

Continuing west on Tennessee Highway 25 toward Gallatin, the visitor begins to encounter places associated with the antebellum landscape of Sumner County. Immediately west of Castalian Springs, visible on the north side of the highway, is the **James B. Jameson House** (1844). Local craftsman John Fonville built the red-brick, five-bay Tennessee Federal home with a Greek Revival portico (private, no access). He is also credited with the similar design of **Oakland** (1850), which stands about a mile to the west at 1995 Hartsville Pike. Oakland originally belonged to Dr. Daniel Mentlo, a physician and farmer who was an important leader in the local Democratic party (private, no access).

Gallatin, four miles to the west, has several additional buildings that document the antebellum landscape of the planter era. However, its historic **town square** has mostly late-nineteenth- and early-twentieth-century commercial buildings—the Swaney-Swift Drugstore is of particular note—centered around the **Sumner County Courthouse** (1939–40). This excellent example of PWA Modern architecture, by the Nashville firm of Marr and Holman, replaced a one-hundred-year-old Greek Revival landmark. Immediately west of the square on Tennessee 25 are two early-nineteenth-century landmarks. The **First Presbyterian Church** (1837) is a Greek Revival temple–style building. **Trousdale Place** (circa 1813) is a historic house museum where the Sumner County Museum is located. Gen. William Trousdale, the fifteenth governor of Tennessee, lived here throughout the middle decades of the nineteenth century.

Tennessee Highway 109 runs south of the square, and a brief detour for two nineteenth-century homes is recommended. About two miles south of the square, on the west side of the road, is **Rosemont** (1828–35), a grand example of Greek Revival architecture (private, no access). The home's lavish classical porticos, concluded historian James Patrick, were "prophetic of the romantic classicism that became popular in Tennessee in the late forties and early fifties" (131). Its commanding presence of the landscape spoke to the prominence and power of the plantation economy in antebellum Sumner County. The famous writer and Democratic activist Judge Josephus C. Guild lived here on a five-hundred-acre plantation that Gallatin's urban growth eventually reduced to a five-acre city lot. Efforts are now underway to restore the mansion into a house museum and visitor center.

After returning north to town, again on the west side of the road at Factory Lane, the visitor encounters the Fitzgerald House (circa 1870), the Italianate villa of Henry Fitzgerald, who owned a local cotton mill. This Victorian statement of power and prestige spoke to the new industrial forces transforming the South after the Civil War. At 148 Factory Lane is a rare surviving example of nineteenth-century company housing, a two-story brick dwelling Fitzgerald built for his factory foreman.

From Gallatin, a brief twenty-two-mile round trip along U.S. Highway 31E to Hendersonville allows visitors to explore an interesting mix of early and more recent architecture that reflects different periods in regional history. Although modern suburban and highway

Rosemont, Gallatin. This significant example of the early Greek Revival movement in Tennessee architecture awaits restoration.

developments have intruded, the surviving antebellum plantation homes and later Classical Revival dwellings along this route are set back from the highway and combine with the surrounding open fields to convey a landscape of plenty and prestige that is commonly associated with the nineteenth century. But the look of the land has much to do with more recent times, especially with 1928 when the Southern Grasslands Hunt and Racing Foundation acquired and leased almost twelve thousand acres for use in fox hunting and steeplechase competitions. The foundation reshaped the rural landscape by cleaning up brush, pulling up wire fences, and adding miles of rail and stone fences, hundreds of gates, and other visible barriers for the fox hunters. It also renovated older farmhouses and built new barns and kennels. For the steeplechase, it built the four-and-a-half-mile Grassland Downs course, which was across from where Volunteer State Community College now stands. First run in 1930, the steeplechase was an immediate success and, in its second year, was described as "the most prestigious event of its kind ever held in this country" (Durham and Thomas, 37). But, by 1931, the country was mired in an ever-deepening economic depression. In March 1932, the Grasslands foundation filed for bankruptcy, leaving its consciously designed attempt to replicate the "hunt" landscape of old English and colonial lore as its only legacy.

The Grasslands investors used the historic antebellum plantation known as **Fairvue,** located four miles west of Gallatin off U.S. 31E, as their administrative and social center (private, no access). This National Historic Landmark belonged to Isaac Franklin, a slave trader who was one of the wealthiest Tennesseans of his time. Its many extant buildings document antebellum planter culture as do few other places in the state. The main house features an Ionic double portico derived from Palladian precedents designed by David Morrison, an important antebellum Tennessee architect who also designed the state penitentiary, the Davidson County Courthouse, Rachel Jackson's tomb at the Hermitage, and the Spring Street Methodist Church in Nashville. The plantation also has many period outbuildings, including such rarities as a circular icehouse, and several brick slave quarters.

Ashcrest Farm, on U.S. 31E on the eastern outskirts of Hendersonville, also dates to the early nineteenth century as it was established in 1810 (private, no access). But this historic family farm has shed most of its nineteenth-century past in exchange for new crops and methods of production. This historic family farm yielded crops typical of the region—corn, wheat, small grains, and livestock—until the turn of the century, when Clara Callender and her son Ewing began to cultivate large amounts of apples, peaches, and grapes for the growing urban population of Gallatin and Nashville. The Classical Revival–influenced farmhouse (1913) was built at this time. Throughout the twentieth century, several areas of Sumner County have specialized in fruit production. Portland, near the Kentucky border, still hosts an annual strawberry festival.

Another significant historic site in Hendersonville is **Rock Castle,** located along the banks of Old Hickory Lake (the dammed Cumberland River) two miles south of U.S. 31E. This late-eighteenth-century plantation house once belonged to frontier leader Daniel Smith, and it remains a very interesting example of frontier architectural craftsmanship and interior design. A graduate of the College of William and Mary, Daniel Smith was a well-respected surveyor, Revolutionary War captain, militia general, territorial secretary, chairman of the committee to draft the original Tennessee constitution, and a United States senator during his long and illustrious career in North Carolina and Tennessee. Smith first settled along the river in the mid-1780s and soon built a two-room stone dwelling. By 1796 his large limestone Georgian mansion was complete, incorporating the early house into a rear addition. Built by nephews Peter and Smith Hansborough, the house documents architectural skill on the Tennessee frontier. Although it strives for Georgian symmetry and balance, its two-story portico, which was added during the Greek Revival period, is not quite centered on the front facade. The interior has the common central-hall plan of the time, and the carpenters added unique fireplaces that feature central-mantel, over-mantel, and floor-to-ceiling side cabinets placed within an integrated and painted black walnut-paneled wall. Old Hickory Lake almost claimed all of the property during the 1950s, but determined efforts saved the house, family cemetery, and smokehouse. The sites of slave quarters and farm buildings are underwater, and the original 3,140-acre plantation is either covered with water or suburban homes. The mansion is open to the public; a visitor center has an informative exhibit and slide program about Smith's career.

Returning to Gallatin via U.S. Highway 31E, there is a historic log building directly north of the road near the western city limits. The **Mary Felice Ferrell House** (1928–31) may look as if it belongs to the frontier age, but it best reflects a particularly Mid-South version of the Colonial Revival movement, in which old antebellum log buildings were moved together to create a new "restored" dwelling (private, no access). The Colonial Revival period in Southern architecture, especially from the mid-1920s to the mid-1930s, was closely tied to a new interest in historic buildings, including the massive restoration project at Williamsburg, Virginia, and the emergence of colonial decorative arts as the predominant traditional furniture of the era. Architects who produced Colonial Revival designs, however, had little intention of copying images of the past. Instead, according to architectural historian David Gebhardt, they wanted to use historic images and fabric "as a point of departure for the creation of new variations on an existing theme" (110). For example, Mary Felice Farrell, a local antique dealer, decided to build her home and shop along U.S. Highway 31E at the same time that the Grasslands foundation was redesigning the countryside into a fox hunters' paradise. She moved two historic log buildings to the old log Avondale Station stage stop and created her own Colonial Revival dream house.

From Gallatin to Springfield, Tennessee Highway 25 cuts away from the Cumberland River to enter countryside drained by two tributaries, the Red River and Sulphur Fork Creek. After the intersection of Tennessee 25 and 76, the route passes into Robertson County and the northern section of the Western Highland Rim. This is the heart of dark-fired tobacco country—and the drive recalls the words of poet Robert Penn Warren in his "Boyhood in Tobacco Country" (1980):

> All I can dream tonight is an autumn sunset,
> Red as a hayrick burning. The groves,
> Not yet leafless are black against red, as though,
> Leaf by leaf, they were hammered of bronze blackened
> To timelessness. Far off, from the curing barns of tobacco,
> Blue smoke, in pale streaking, clings
> To the world's dim, undefinable bulge.

Over these fields and farms, the famous "Black Patch" tobacco war took place ninety years ago. In 1900, over 13,400 acres in Robertson County were planted in tobacco, producing some 10.4 million pounds. The crop totally dominated the local economy, and thousands of sharecroppers had no other livelihood but the annual tobacco patch. But after the turn of the century, rising production in Tennessee and Kentucky combined with the monopoly power of the newly formed American Tobacco Company and its associated foreign companies to force a steep drop in the market price for dark tobacco. By 1904 prime leafs brought only three cents at auction, and it cost farmers at least five cents a leaf to make the crop.

In the fall of 1904, farmers and plantation owners organized the Dark Tobacco District Planters' Protective Association (better known simply as the Association) to strike back at the tobacco monopoly. The strategy was to limit production, pool local tobacco resources, sell only through Association warehouses, and force the tobacco trust to raise prices. Felix Ewing of the mammoth **Glen Raven** plantation near Adams was chairman of the executive committee and was called the "Moses of the Black Patch." In most counties, between 70 and 80 percent of tobacco farmers became Association members, led by large landowners who forced their sharecroppers to join.

Many farmers, however, refused to join the Association, especially when the American Tobacco Company began to offer nine to twelve cents a leaf in order to break the Association's unity. Association members called the competing farmers "hillbillies," and soon many churches and schools were split between the two groups. Springfield became a center of conflict. Here, beginning in 1907, the Association published its own newspaper. Association members used threats, intimidation, and violence to force compliance from unwilling "hillbillies." Members formed the "Silent Brigade," and, according to historian Rick Gregory, these night riders "whipped, and in a few cases killed, hillbillies and trust buyers, scraped plantbeds, burned or dynamited tobacco barns and warehouses, and, as they became more sure of themselves and their power, staged spectacular raids that captured entire towns at night" (354–55). For example, in December 1907, 250 night riders captured Hopkinsville, Kentucky, where they dynamited two trust-owned tobacco warehouses.

Soon the state legislature passed laws designed to curb night riding and the destruction of tobacco fields, but the violence ended only in 1909 when the American Tobacco Company and other allied companies gave in to the Association and began to buy only from Association warehouses, at an average price of nine cents a leaf. The Black Patch escaped economic ruin, and dark-fired tobacco remained the foundation of the local economy for another two generations.

Five miles northeast of Springfield, Tennessee Highway 25 junctions with Tennessee Highway 49. To see several family farms associated with tobacco history in Robertson County as well as still operating tobacco warehouses and stripping rooms, drive into Springfield for five miles on Tennessee 49. This route also passes by farms and homes associated with the nineteenth-century distillery business in Robertson County.

Just west of Tennessee 49, on the Eden Corner Road three miles northeast of Springfield, is **Woodard Hall Farm** (1792), the oldest fam-

ily farm in Robertson County (private, no access). The farmhouse has an original section dating from 1792, along with later additions from circa 1800 and the 1850s. The farm prospered during the mid-1800s under the guidance of Wiley Woodard, a prominent Whig politician and business-man who was also involved in the county's flourishing distillery industry. Along with the old site of the distillery, the farm retains its historic office, outside kitchen, smokehouse, family cemetery, tobacco barns, and tenant houses, outbuildings typical of a nineteenth-century plantation. Their lo-cation within the larger farm landscape maps the social divisions between people and activities during those decades. For example, the entrance road leads first to the farm office, where visitors welcome at the home could be directed that way. Those there for business or work, however, would be directed in the opposite direction, where, hidden from the main house by topography and foliage, stood tobacco barns, stock barns, and tenant houses. As late as 1994, Jack Cook was the tenant who grew the yearly tobacco crop, and he and his wife lived in a board-and-batten tenant house typical of those constructed in the early twentieth century.

About two and a half miles northeast of Springfield, clearly vis-ible on the north side of Tennessee 49, is the Krisle and Stark Hereford Farm (private, no access). Springfield businessman and distiller John W. Stark began with 177 acres in 1876, and he built his family a brick Victorian upright-and-wing house in the 1880s. In recent years, the family continued to produce tobacco but also expanded the farm to over three hundred acres and bred registered horned Hereford cattle.

Another mile to the west along Tennessee 49, on a steep hill overlooking the highway, is **The Beeches** (1869), a grand Second Empire farmhouse with marvelous decorative interior painting, that belonged to John Woodard (private, no access). He was a local state representative, farmer, and owner of the Silver Springs Distillery, one of the largest companies in the county. Indeed, nineteenth-century Robertson County was a major whiskey producer, and at one time about seventy-five companies were in business.

After passing by several early-twentieth-century tobacco warehouses, travelers encounter the historic county seat of Springfield, which dates from 1796. Sited on a hill overlooking Sulphur Fork Creek and the busy traffic of U.S. 41 is the **Robertson County Courthouse** (1879–81 with 1930 additions), designed by Nashville architect William C. Smith in the Second Empire style. Surrounding the courthouse is a late Victorian and early-twentieth-century historic commercial district, including a Second Empire storefront, the modernistic **Tennessee Power and Light Company Office,** and the impressive 1899 **Woodard Hall.** Throughout the town, along the major roads, including Tennessee 49, U.S. Highways 41 and 431, and the tracks of the Louisville and Nashville Railroad, are rectangular tobacco warehouses of all sizes and materials. Legendary auctions happen here at the first of every year. An account from the 1930s recalled:

> The slow tempo of life in the fields and the firing barn give way to activity that moves faster than ticker tape. It revolves about the auctioneer with his rapid sing-song that is understood by no one but the ten or twelve buyers who follow him about the warehouse floor. Even the oldest resident, whose ears have rung with this sound every year of his life, cannot tell you what the auctioneer says. The farmer who raised the tobacco, though he watches anxiously from the background, cannot understand this jargon. He only knows that his whole year's crop can be sold in the time it takes him to cut a piece of chewing tobacco from the plug in his pocket. (*WPA Guide,* 394)

In 1932 local farmers established the Eastern Dark Fired Tobacco Growers Association. Its headquarters are south of the square, along the old route of U.S. 41.

Other successful local ventures—such as the Springfield Woolen Mills, which now operates as NASCO, Inc., with the original factory

Simmons Tobacco Warehouse, Springfield. With the coming of railroads, the tobacco industry of the Black Patch boomed as never before.

and later expansions on North Main Street—combined with the tobacco industry to make Springfield a prosperous twentieth-century community. Impressive homes on West Fifth Street between the courthouse square and the old high school include Gothic, Queen Anne, and American Four-Square dwellings (all private, no access). The Classical Revival Woman's Club (1906) at 303 West Fifth was originally the home of Neel Gleen, the founder of Springfield Woolen Mills. Across the street is the two-story Italianate J. E. Garner House (circa 1850s). North Main Street and Oak Street also housed fine turn-of-the-century Classical Revival, Queen Anne, and later bungalow and Spanish Revival residences. Businessmen and professionals even built two striking modern buildings: the Art Deco Coca-Cola plant on North Main Street and an Art Moderne medical office at 401 West Seventh (private, no access).

A worthwhile side trip west of Springfield uncovers two huge historic tobacco plantations. Located along Sulphur Fork Creek, **Wessyngton** and **Glen Raven** can be viewed from the roadside by taking U.S. Highway 41 northwest of Springfield to the communities of Cedar Hill and Adams (both private, no access). Wessyngton (1819, with later additions) is four miles south of Cedar Hill. Identified by a lavishly decorated cast-iron and stone entrance gate, this mammoth dark-fired tobacco plantation belonged to the Washington family, who farmed here for over 150 years. Antebellum Tennessee knew of few other plantation

Tobacco field, tenant farmer, and barn at Wessyngton, Robertson County. (Courtesy of Tennessee State Library and Archives)

families so prosperous. In 1860, for example, George A. Washington owned over 13,000 acres and his 274 slaves raised 250,000 pounds of tobacco. The plantation still retains many historic buildings from this era of wealth and prestige. After the Civil War, Joseph Washington used sharecropper arrangements to further increase the annual tobacco crop. Driving a hard bargain with his croppers, Washington forced them to turn over a half of their crop while also pledging to work for him for sixty-five cents a day when he needed their labor. Croppers further agreed to never work for anyone else without permission, to tend Washington's stables every day, to feed the field stock, to keep all fences in good repair, and to donate three days of work free each year for every male member of the family. This time was devoted to putting up the annual hay crop. A hundred years ago, travelers along this road would have seen entire families, mostly African Americans, doing the hard and dirty work of keeping the tobacco in good order. As recent studies have indicated, black tenant farmers were technically "free" compared to slaves, but their options were so limited that they lived in virtual peonage.

Compared to the Tennessee Federal facade of Wessyngton, the massively proportioned classicism of **Glen Raven Mansion** (1897–1902) is garish and overstated. Located south of Adams on Tennessee

Worker's cottage, Glen Raven, Robertson County. Glen Raven was the last attempt to create a plantation landscape in Tennessee's Black Patch.

256, the three-story house reflected the grandiose ambitions of Felix Ewing, one of the key leaders of the Black Patch tobacco war against the American Tobacco Company in the early 1900s. Ewing had already become a rich man from an Arkansas Delta cotton plantation and several Nashville businesses. Then in 1891 he married Jane Washington of Wessyngton, and they soon moved to Robertson County to start a dark-fired tobacco plantation on 865 acres Jane had inherited from her family. Glen Raven represented a return to agricultural practices of an earlier era when a plantation was like a self-supporting rural village. Glen Raven had its own church, school, post office, store, power plant, dairy, and mill. Ewing built many one-and-a-half-story board-and-batten tenant houses for his workers, and some of these can be seen along Tennessee 256, especially near the original mill and post office/store, both built in 1896. The Ewings operated the plantation until 1931, when the Metropolitan Life Insurance Company foreclosed during the Great Depression.

West of Glen Raven is the **Port Royal State Historic Area**, which features a magnificent reconstructed covered bridge at the confluence of Sulphur Fork Creek and the Red River. The annual tobacco crops from Wessyngton and Glen Raven would cross the original bridge on their way to tobacco markets at Clarksville. The state park is about four

Port Royal Covered Bridge, Robertson and Montgomery Counties. This bridge linked the great tobacco plantations of Robertson County to the state's largest tobacco market at Clarksville.

miles west of the Glen Raven estate; the best route is by way of Tennessee Highway 76, south of Adams. A historic **Masonic lodge** (1859) at the park has exhibits about river transportation in the nineteenth century.

Landscape 17: Transportation and Middle Tennessee Towns

Access and proximity to reliable transportation profoundly influenced economic development and town creation in Middle Tennessee. No matter how rich the land, farmers still had to get their crops to market. The rich planters of antebellum Maury County, in fact, built their own road from Mount Pleasant to the Tennessee River at Clifton in order to ensure their access to regional markets. The Nashville and Chattanooga Railroad, during the nineteenth century, and the Dixie Highway, in the early twentieth century, were two especially significant transportation corridors. Both influenced the regional landscape, leaving behind entire towns, reshaped communities, and specialized buildings and artifacts directly related to the demands of railroad and automobile traffic. At times, the two routes run close together, creating a maze of hotels, gas stations, warehouses, and symmetrically placed commercial blocks. In the larger cities, the twentieth-century landscape of transportation often overwhelms that of earlier decades, but in many Middle Tennessee country towns, it is possible to see towns little changed from the railroad heyday of one hundred years ago.

Route A: Nashville to Murfreesboro

The Dixie Highway is largely a forgotten road today, but during the 1910s and 1920s, its approach was eagerly awaited by businessmen and progressive reformers alike. U.S. 41 now parallels portions of the old road between Nashville and Murfreesboro. The highway was the dream of Carl G. Fisher, the owner of a car battery company and a major investor in south Florida real estate. Fisher envisioned the road as a major north-south link that would enhance the Florida tourism industry while benefiting all other points in between. He found important support from the Chattanooga Automobile Club, which sponsored the first meeting of the Dixie Highway Association in the spring of 1915. The meeting also appointed Judge M. M. Allison of Chattanooga as president and selected the Tennessee river city as its headquarters. Tennesseans, from the very beginning, played a crucial role in the development of the Dixie Highway. Some were interested solely in the road's economic benefits; others saw the highway as a way to end regional isolation and backwardness.

From 1915 to 1927, a road system of 5,706 miles was constructed. Two different branches of the Dixie Highway passed through Tennessee. The eastern branch followed U.S. 25W from Jellico to Knoxville and then followed U.S. 27 from Rockwood to Chattanooga. The western, primary road entered the state near Adams in Robertson County and passed through Nashville before following the path of the Nashville and Chattanooga Railroad to Winchester and then on to Chattanooga. Wherever highways such as the Dixie passed, according to historian Howard L. Preston, "the natural environment became so intertwined with the material culture of automobility that an entire new cultural landscape emerged to serve the needs of a people who were between one place and another" (128).

From the late 1840s to 1854, the Nashville and Chattanooga Railroad had created its own series of landmarks as it built through southern Middle Tennessee, especially in the design of new towns along the line. Railroads required a siding every six to eight miles to enable passing trains to avoid each other. At almost every siding emerged some sort of community, ranging from a hamlet to a major trade town, depending on the prosperity of the surrounding countryside and the plans of the railroad. Therefore, as the Nashville and Chattanooga built southward, it created new towns where little to nothing had stood before, places such as Smyrna, Bell Buckle, Wartrace, Tullahoma, Decherd, and Cowan. (See sidebar entitled "Common Railroad Town Plans," Landscape 20, chapter 7.)

The small community of Una, eight miles south of downtown Nashville on U.S. Highway 41, is a good place to begin a combined survey of the highway and railroad corridors. Beginning here, for the next twenty-three miles on U.S. 41 the two routes closely parallel each other. Una has two significant buildings associated with the early automobile days: the I. M. Smith and Son General Store (1880s) and the recently closed **Ellis Service Station** (1929). T. H. Ellis built this brick vernacular adaptation of a standard Gulf Oil Company design to serve Dixie Highway travelers between Murfreesboro and Nashville. His family had operated the garage ever since. Unfortunately, current local government highway plans call for the building's demolition.

The next place associated with both transportation routes is LaVergne in Rutherford County. The railroad created LaVergne in the early 1850s, but it remained a rural village for the next one hundred years, even after it was linked to the Dixie Highway. After the expansion of the original U.S. 41 into a paved four-lane highway during the late 1940s and the construction of Interstate Highway 24 some twenty-five years later, LaVergne began to grow as a bedroom community of Nashville. Spurred by industrial developments in the late 1970s and early 1980s, especially the Firestone/Bridgestone factory, the town sprawled along U.S. 41 until today it is difficult to tell where LaVergne ends and the adjacent town of Smyrna begins.

Smyrna's railroad beginnings, however, are easier to see because the four lanes of U.S. 41 pass through the heart of the earlier railroad village. To the immediate west of the highway in downtown Smyrna is the original symmetrical commercial district as well as a brick railroad depot. Nineteenth-century Smyrna was little more than a rail shipping point for crops and livestock from surrounding plantations. The Tucker-Cheney House (circa 1860) at 112 Oak Street was the grand Greek Revival and Italianate mansion of John Tucker, who managed a successful farm in the last half of the nineteenth century (private, no access). About two miles east, on the outskirts of town, is the historic **Sam Davis Home.** This antebellum I-house, with a commanding Greek Revival portico, was the boyhood home of Sam Davis, a Confederate scout who was executed by Union soldiers at Pulaski in 1863. Davis's brave last words— "If I had a thousand lives, I would lose them all here before I would betray my friends or the confidence of my informer"—made him a southern war hero. The house, its farm outbuildings, and surrounding acreage document the landscape of nineteenth- and early-twentieth-century agriculture in Middle Tennessee.

Murfreesboro is eleven miles southeast along U.S. Highway 41. However, from Smyrna the most historic approach is to leave U.S. 41 at its junction with Tennessee 102 and travel west to the stoplight intersection with the "Old Nashville Highway." This road is the original Dixie Highway, and it directly parallels the Nashville and Chattanooga for the remaining nine miles to Murfreesboro.

Along those railroad tracks in 1862 marched the Federal Army of the Cumberland, commanded by Gen. William Rosecrans, as it took its first tentative steps toward the strategic transportation center of Chattanooga. For the Federal invasion of the Deep South, the railroad was an invaluable lifeline of supplies and communication. Union commanders always planned to keep the iron rails within easy reach. Outside of Murfreesboro waited the soldiers of the Confederate Army of Tennessee, led by Gen. Braxton Bragg. They too had used the tracks to keep themselves well fed and supplied throughout the fall months. They were now spoiling for a fight.

From December 31, 1862, to January 2, 1863, the two armies fought for their lives and for control of the railroad tracks in the bloody Battle of Stones River. About eight miles south of Smyrna, on the old route of the Dixie Highway, is the entrance of the **Stones River National Battlefield,** established by Congress in 1927. The railroad was the strategic objective of the first day's relentless fighting. Bragg wanted to push the Yankees off the railroad so supplies and reinforcements could not save the Federal command. His surprise attack on New Year's Eve morning caught the Union troops at breakfast, and before mid-morning many Federal positions had been abandoned and the troops were in great disarray. By noon, the Army of the Cumberland was shaped like a great right angle: its western division had already retreated to the railroad tracks while another division held fast on the east side. Gen. George Thomas, placed squarely at the bend of the angle, held the Union line together. But his position was extremely vulnerable. Bragg could have extended his flanking attack and probably destroyed the disorganized Union position along the tracks and turnpike. But, like earlier Confederate commanders at Shiloh, Bragg decided to smash the Union center and push Thomas away.

Thomas was not a man easily moved. He held a strong defensive position in a four-acre stand of cedars and rock outcroppings known as the Round Forest. Throughout the afternoon, his soldiers repulsed wave after wave of Confederate charges, as the first bone-chilling Rebel yells soon became screams of desperation. One Union soldier recalled, "We could see their men falling like leaves, but the broken ranks were filled and they held their ground with a heroism worthy of a better cause. At last they had to yield, but they retired in good order, leaving their dead on the field" (Cozzens, 164). Nothing could break the Union center. After the battle, several soldiers of the command of Union general William Hazen built a memorial, called Hazen's Monument, to the courageous defenders of the Round Forest. It is considered to be the oldest Civil War memorial in the country.

On New Year's Day, both armies tried to make sense of the confusion from the day before. Bragg had little left to mount a successful assault; Rosecrans was too damaged and disorganized to counterattack. The following afternoon, Bragg ordered Gen. John C. Breckinridge, a former vice-president of the United States, to launch a full frontal assault on a Union position, fortified with fifty-eight artillery guns, that protected Stones River. This futile assault lasted only about a half hour, and Breckinridge lost about one-third of his command. After this costly defeat, Bragg abandoned Murfreesboro and moved toward the Duck River, guarding a more southern section of the Nashville and Chattanooga line. The Confederates lost an opportunity to destroy a Union army, but Rosecrans was so damaged that his march to Chattanooga was delayed for over six months. As the Yankees licked their wounds in Murfreesboro, they constructed **Fortress Rosecrans** as their base of operations and supply. This was one of the largest earthen-wall forts of the war; by entering Murfreesboro on the old route of the Dixie Highway, travelers will see Redoubt Brannen, one of the few extant features of this post; another section is at Old Fort Park.

About one mile south, Old Nashville Highway ends at the modern six-lane Broad Street or U.S. Highway 41. The construction of a Broad Street bypass around downtown Murfreesboro in the late 1940s and early 1950s substantially changed the town's appearance. As it passed south of the square, it replaced part of the old industrial core and a working-class, mostly African-American, neighborhood. New businesses, gas stations, restaurants, and motels moved away from downtown to the new bypass. Today the traveler may drive through Murfreesboro on U.S. 41 and find little but an endless commercial strip.

Two different routes lead to the historic downtown. One route is to turn north on Memorial Boulevard (U.S. 231/Tennessee 96) and take an immediate right on College Street to enter the downtown. The Dixie Highway came this way, and for the first three blocks a combination of old garages and gas stations that reflect the development of "gasoline alleys" in the early twentieth century is visible. Historian Daniel Vieyra identifies the gas station as "the first structure built in response to the automobile"; indeed, it became "the nucleus of the drive-in culture" (xiii, 9). Of special note is the Art Moderne–style Red Rose Creamery, which once housed a popular soda shop for local teenagers.

The second approach from Broad Street is via West Main Street, which connects the town square to the historic Queen Anne–style Nashville, Chattanooga, and St. Louis depot (1887). An interesting progression of commercial activities, from warehouses to professional offices, connects the depot to the square. The **Rutherford County Courthouse** (1858), a masterful blending of Greek Revival and Italianate elements, dominates the central business district. The square has buildings from the late 1800s and early 1900s, but today's appearance largely reflects the architectural revival styles associated with the Main Street rehabilitation programs of the 1980s.

Although the courthouse was spared, the Civil War and Union occupation of Murfreesboro from 1863 to 1865 severely damaged the town and surrounding countryside. Thirty miles in any direction from Murfreesboro, a newspaper correspondent observed in 1864, was a "womb of destruction . . . one wide, wild and dreary waste, so to speak" (Sims, 44). But not all was a wasteland. The **Childress-Ray House** on North Academy, the ancestral home of Sarah Childless Polk, wife of President James K. Polk and the grand dame of nineteenth-century Nashville society, survived the fighting, as did the Italianate-style **Baskette House**

(now Woman's Club) on College Street and the **Landsberger-Fite-Anderson House** (1855) on North Spring Street (all private, no access).

On the outskirts of town stood antebellum plantations, damaged by the war but determined to stay in business. The owners of the beautiful Italianate **Oaklands Mansion** at 901 North Maney turned the old ceremonial drive into a new addition to Murfreesboro, hoping that real estate sales would boost farm profits. The town's most important architectural monument, Oaklands is now a historic house museum about Murfreesboro's planter elite on the eve of the Civil War. Another antebellum plantation, the **Arnold-Harrell House** (1860–61) at 1710 East Main, remained an operating farm until the 1940s when it too was subdivided (private, no access). Designed by local builder Edwin Arnold, the farmhouse's portico is the town's best example of the transition between Greek Revival and Italianate architecture.

Recovery was slow to come after the war, and a great fire destroyed many businesses in 1869. Entrepreneurs, including Ingram B. Collier, tried to boost the local economy with new investments. In 1878–79 Collier constructed the three-story Second Empire **Collier-Crichlow House** at 511 East Main as a symbol of the community's new hope for the future (private, no access). The lumber industry, led by a cedar bucket factory, became important. But the 1880s were not kind to Rutherford County. The county lost population, and, by the turn-of-the-century, only 3,739 people lived in Murfreesboro.

Progressive institutions of education and reform, however, reinvigorated Murfreesboro in the early twentieth century. In 1911 Middle Tennessee State Normal School opened. The creation of a state normal school—from which would eventually emerge the seventeen-thousand-strong Middle Tennessee State University—for the training of high school teachers made education an instrument of change in the history of Murfreesboro. Two of the campus's most historic buildings are easily visible from the street. At the corner of Tennessee Boulevard and East Main Street is the President's House (1911), a Georgian Revival design by Nashville architect C. K. Colley that popularized that style for many later homes along East Main Street. Two blocks to the north on North Tennessee is the **Pittard Campus School** (1929), the college's teacher-training school, designed in Classical Revival style by the Nashville firm of Marr and Holman.

In 1918 the African-American community improved its public education facilities by working with state and city officials to build **Bradley Academy** at 415 South Academy Street. Designed by the Knoxville architecture firm of Manley and Young, the two-story brick school is clearly visible from Broad Street and is now a local African-American history museum. The school also served as a social center for musicals, dances, and community fairs. During the 1920s, it was the black public health-care center, staffed by nurse Mary Ellen Vaughan. This graduate of Tuskegee Institute became a fixture in the African-American community for the next thirty years. She established the town's first black newspaper, the *Murfreesboro Union,* which promoted community unity and progress.

But considerable poverty, particularly in adjacent rural communities, existed on the eve of the Depression. In 1925 a visiting public health expert from the Commonwealth Fund of New York observed:

> There are numbers of "just tenant houses", the big economic problem of the rural districts. [These] may be a log cabin with a cooking-eating attachment of boards; or it may be the old fashioned two-room log house, divided by the porch in the middle; or it may be the plank affair with two or three small rooms. It has not adequate light. Many use the old wooden shutter which is minus the window panes—and I have been in one house in Rutherford County where there was absolutely no window space! The walls are frequently papered with old newspapers or all sorts of advertisement; and when the winter winds are blowing, one sees practicability in this bizarre taste. . . . This tenant house is used interchangeably by the white or colored tenants.
>
> (Hoffschwelle, 373)

The Rutherford Hospital (1927) on North University Street and the **Rutherford Health Department** (1931) at 303 North Church Street reflected the progressive concern about rural public health in the early 1900s. Both were established by the Commonwealth Fund, a private philanthropic foundation based in New York, to improve the public health of what was then considered a typical rural southern community. In 1924 the fund began a child health demonstration unit in Rutherford County as one of its four national pilot programs. The first year was difficult, but within three years, the program was so pleased with its success and so assured of the need for a professional laboratory and hospital that it built the first of what would soon become a national program of hospitals for needy rural communities and small towns. Although many additions and changes have occurred at the hospital, its front facade, designed by Chicago architects Berlin and Swern, stands unchanged along North University Street.

In 1931 the Commonwealth Fund provided money for the construction of the **Rutherford Health Department** as the first permanent rural public health facility in the nation. The center is in the town's best example of Colonial Revival architecture, designed by James Gamble Rogers. Throughout the 1930s and 1940s, the building was the state's showplace for rural public health as it served as a training ground for an entire generation of southern public health officers, doctors, and nurses. It also physically documents an important chapter in the early-twentieth-century reform of American medicine, particularly the partnership between foundations, local boosters, and public agencies to improve the health and life-expectancy of rural southerners.

Route B: Murfreesboro to Tullahoma

From Murfreesboro to Tullahoma, the dual routes of the Dixie Highway and the Nashville and Chattanooga Railroad remain parallel to each other, but they verge in slightly different directions and create two different landscapes. U.S. Highway 231 follows the earlier route of the Dixie Highway to Shelbyville and then to Tullahoma on U.S. 41A. The twenty-five miles separating Murfreesboro and Shelbyville were once very pastoral and quiet after exiting the interstate interchange, but in the past decade, suburbs, a new four-lane highway, and industrial concerns have replaced many farms. The original agricultural landscape had two distinctive patterns. First, in Rutherford County, dairy farming dominated the landscape. Silos, large cattle barns, and concrete milk

Rutherford Health Department, Murfreesboro. This Colonial Revival building, designed by James Gamble Rogers, helped the Commonwealth Fund introduce public health medicine to rural Tennessee.

houses are visible along this route. In part because of the health department's effort to improve the local milk supply and new programs from the agricultural extension service designed to encourage farmers to establish dairy herds, the dairy industry of Rutherford County grew rapidly during the 1920s and 1930s. The Carnation Corporation built a milk plant in downtown Murfreesboro; its smokestack still stands at the intersection of U.S. 41 and U.S. 231.

After travelers cross into Bedford County, Tennessee walking horse training farms—with their well-appointed horse barns, landscaped grounds, and painted wood fences defining the property—run parallel to the highway. Modern walking horse barns can be differentiated from earlier livestock barns in several ways. Generally, they are much longer rectangles as every horse is provided with a separate stall. Their exteriors are typically more lavish in design and often painted bright colors. Today most horse barns lack a hayloft, while the full hayloft, with a central opening, is characteristic of the mid-twentieth-century livestock barn. The walking horse industry became prominent in Bedford County during the mid-twentieth century, and today Bedford is the heart of walking horse country. The mecca of any Tennessee walking horse fan is the grounds of the famed "Celebration," located a few blocks south of the junction of U.S. 231 and U.S. 41A in Shelbyville. The Calsonic Arena has a permanent display about the walking horse industry.

To continue on the actual route of the Dixie Highway through Shelbyville remain on U.S. 231 south to the town square. The **Bedford County Courthouse** is a late statement of the Classical Revival, designed by Nashville architects Marr and Holman in 1935. It was built after a lynch mob in 1934 burned the earlier courthouse in its frenzy to kidnap a young black man accused of assault. Threats of violence had ruled Shelbyville for several days prior to the arson. Even one hundred national guardsmen could not restore order until the accused had been taken out of the county. After his removal from the town, the gangs burned the courthouse in retaliation.

The courthouse sits in the middle of what geographers believe to be the first central courthouse square in the country (see sidebar entitled "Central Courthouse Squares," in this section). The historic **Shelbyville square** has several attractive commercial buildings from a hundred years ago, especially on the south and east sides, where Italianate and Romanesque commercial styles predominate. The west side has the Art Deco **Gunther Building** (1927). On the north side,

Central Courthouse Squares

Geographers have identified southern Middle Tennessee as the cultural hearth of the "central courthouse square" plan that has shaped hundreds of county seats west of the Tennessee River. The central courthouse square plan refers to an arrangement where the courthouse sits in a block in the center of the square with four equal sides of commercial buildings facing it. The plan was easy for surveyors to lay out and remained popular as late as 1900. Shelbyville, the seat of Bedford County, is believed to be the first central courthouse square in the country (see photo of the Bedford County Courthouse below).

Between 1810 and 1812, Shelbyville, then Fayetteville, Pulaski, and Winchester in rapid succession, became new county seats, all based on the central courthouse square plan. As geographer Edward T. Price has explained, "We must believe that local officials in these towns were exchanging ideas, perhaps through the mediation of legislators or surveyors" (135). Many similar courthouse squares were later platted in Indiana, Illinois, northern Iowa, and especially Texas. The last central courthouse square to have been built may be in New Mexico, platted in circa 1898.

The central courthouse square plan has many meanings. Once, it stood at the town's center of political, commercial, and financial power. It was where all parades ended, where political rallies could gather hundreds on the open streets and sidewalks, and where community events and festivals took place. "The square recapitulate[d] the history of the town," concluded Price. "The courthouse was its reason for being, its first central function, the seat of its creator" (142).

Today some of the largely ceremonial and cultural characteristics of the central courthouse square remain in place. But fewer people daily congregate on the square to pass the time of day or to address both their commercial and civic needs. Especially in larger cities, the square might remain as the center of town, but it is no longer the center of community, or even commercial, activity. Rather it is a place where offices for banks and professionals are concentrated. A drive downtown on a typical night or on most Saturdays illustrates the change: increasingly, fewer cars are around the square and almost no one is "hanging out." The situation around most town squares contrasts markedly with the incessant hum of activity and the many people driving along the highway strip. In too many Tennessee towns, new renovations and development plans have been unable to stem the flight of more and more commercial concerns to the strip development of outlying shopping centers and discount stores along adjacent highways. The courthouse square in Tennessee is shedding its commercial function for a more limited, but still significant, role as the bureaucratic center of local finance, law, and government.

Bedford County Courthouse, Shelbyville.

where Dominion Bank stands today, was the Dixie Hotel, which catered to travelers on the old highway for many decades.

Just north of the square is the **Bedford County Jail,** built with hand-hewn limestone rocks in 1867. On South Main Street is the former post office, now **Cooper Memorial Library** (1914), designed in a Classical Revival style by federal architect Oscar Wenderoth. A few steps farther south is the old textile factory of the Fly Manufacturing Company (1927). In the early twentieth century, Shelbyville was a thriving industrial center. A 1923 survey listed "an electric light plant, water works, cotton factory, a hub and spoke factory, foundry, saw mills, planing mills, and other manufacturing enterprises, with good banks, churches, schools, and two newspapers" (Foster, 47). On West Jackson Street near the Duck River stood the company town of Shelbyville Mills. Today the old textile complex is used as a pencil factory, but the company school, church, and three distinct generations of company housing are still visible. The pencil industry remains vitally important to the local economy. The Musgrave Pencil Company is one of the most largest pencil manufacturers in the world. Its factory grounds contain the historic Turner Institute Building, a former African-American private school designed by Nashville architect Moses McKissack.

To leave downtown by the old Dixie Highway route, take Tennessee 64 (Depot Street) east for three miles to its junction with U.S. 41A where it continues southeast for twelve miles to Tullahoma. When the Dixie Highway arrived in Tullahoma in the 1920s, it created a new commercial and residential center in an old railroad-dominated town. South Jackson Street was the Dixie's path through the city, and here the elegant Tullahoma Public School (1922) was constructed, along with stylish new bungalows and revival dwellings on the 200 and 300 blocks of the street.

Tennessee 269 is an alternative route from Murfreesboro to Tullahoma that follows closely the tracks of the Nashville and Chattanooga. The small towns and hamlets along this road were established and, in most cases, platted by the railroad company in the early 1850s. Reflecting the symmetrical town plans typically used by antebellum railroads (see sidebar entitled "Common Railroad Town Plans," Landscape 20, chapter 7), these towns are remarkably intact documents of what small railroad villages were like between 1880 and 1920.

In southern Rutherford County, about a half mile east of the junction of U.S. 231 and Tennessee 269, is the hamlet of Christiana. Facing the tracks is the Gothic Revival cottage known as the Grant-Sugg Farm (circa 1853). Railroad engineer Col. James H. Grant picked this spot for a homestead of about 150 acres and built the county's first Gothic Revival cottage. According to family tradition, Grant named the town "Christiana" after his black cook, Christiana Daniels. However, this native of Maine and staunch Unionist may have selected the name in reference to the shoot-out between black Quakers and Maryland slave owners who were determined to arrest two fugitive slaves that happened at Christiana, Pennsylvania, in 1851.

About ten miles south of Christiana on Tennessee 269 (known locally as Liberty Pike), is Bell Buckle, one of the most visited railroad towns in Middle Tennessee. The **Bell Buckle historic district** features three distinct areas. Railroad Square was constructed at the turn of the century, following a fire that destroyed most of the downtown in the early 1890s. Behind the commercial strip is a residential neighborhood that contains excellent examples of such vernacular forms as the central-hall house, the classical-influenced I-house, and the Victorian gable-front-and-wing house. Queen Anne dwellings and bungalows are also present. The campus of Webb School is largely modern, but the historic **Junior Room** (1886) and Alumni Building (1928) help to document the private school's early history. Established at Bell Buckle in 1886 by Sawney Webb, the school has been a leading preparatory institution ever since.

Clark-Roche Farmhouse, Wartrace. This stately Queen Anne farmhouse, built by Henry A. Clark, overlooks the Nashville, Chattanooga, and St. Louis tracks outside the village of Wartrace.

Wartrace is about six miles south of Bell Buckle on Tennessee 269. The **Wartrace historic district** displays most of the major elements of a railroad town. The depot is missing, but on the west side of the tracks stands the **Cunningham and Co. Mill** (1885); **Chockley Hall** (1852), an early tavern stop for travelers; a NC&St.L caboose; and the **Walking Horse Hotel** (1917) (private, limited access). This three-story brick hotel is one of the few railroad hotels remaining in Middle Tennessee. Originally called the Hotel Overall, the name changed in 1939 to the Walking Horse Hotel in honor of owner Floyd Carothers's horse, "Strolling Jim," which won the championship at the first Walking Horse National Celebration. The hotel today is a virtual museum to the Tennessee Walking Horse, and Strolling Jim is buried in the old training grounds behind the hotel.

A much smaller railroad town, Normandy, is another six miles south on Tennessee 269 near the Coffee County line. After the road and tracks cross the Duck River, follow a short country road to historic **Cortner's Mill,** which once served local grain farmers. The **Normandy historic district** is about one mile south of the mill. In 1889 the Normandy Immigration, Real Estate, and Labor Association established basically a new townsite on the other side of the tracks from the original town. Four years later, the editor of the Shelbyville newspaper remarked that the place had "an entirely different appearance altogether from that which I was familiar with several years ago. Normandy may now be considered nearly a new town, with its fine residences, churches, and large academy" (*Shelbyville Times-Gazette,* July 6, 1893). But, in the next generation, Normandy grew at a snail's pace, reaching only a peak population of 250 in 1917. It has stayed a small hamlet ever since, despite the presence of nearby Normandy Dam.

The next town on the line is Tullahoma, the original center point of the Nashville and Chattanooga Railroad. In the mid-1930s, a county historian observed that "Tullahoma is, and has always been a railroad town" (Ewell, 52). Certainly the Nashville and Chattanooga, together with its land and capital investments, laid the foundation for Tullahoma's emergence as the largest and most important commercial city in Coffee County.

In 1850 railroad company officials, including Volney S. Stephenson, Benjamin Decherd, and Gen. William Moore, established the Tullahoma Land Company with the intention of establishing a company-owned town at a place where company engineers envisioned the future development of a railroad crossroads. When construction crews neared the area eighteen months later, the land company began to sell its Tullahoma properties, largely to outside speculators who assumed that the location itself, halfway between Nashville and Chattanooga and halfway between the county seats of Shelbyville and Winchester, guaranteed the town's future. In 1855 the railroad selected Tullahoma as the hub for its Manchester-McMinnville branch line. The company also built a large passenger and freight station on Atlantic Street, which immediately became the town's focal point with both commercial and residential neighborhoods radiating from that street.

The Civil War devastated Tullahoma, and today no buildings remain from the years of 1851 to 1865. Instead, there is a perfect example of a late Victorian to early-twentieth-century railroad town. The west side of Atlantic Street is commercial and industrial. Extant historic buildings include the **Dewey-Troxler Store** (circa 1885) at 225 North Atlantic; the old **U.S. Post Office** (1927), a blending of Classical Revival and Art Deco styles by federal architect James A. Wetmore, at 201 North Atlantic; and the **Tennessee Glove Factory** (1924) at 108 South Atlantic (all private, no access). The east side of **Atlantic Street,** especially the three blocks across from the passenger station, represent a residential enclave for well-to-do merchants, professionals, and railroad managers. These large houses reflect a variety of Victorian styles, from the Second Empire of the **Smith House** (1885) at 214 North Atlantic and the Queen Anne-Eastlake of the **Raht-Couch House** (1891) at 308 North Atlantic to the vernacular Queen Anne of the **Wilkins House** (1905) at 409 North Atlantic (all private, no access).

Industrial growth, especially in the production of lumber, baseball gloves, and softballs, and then the start of the Genesco shoe company, spurred the local economy in the early 1900s. The railroad made several investments too. In 1915 it established a three-hundred-acre demonstration farm outside of Tullahoma as a way of encouraging better crop production and new immigration. The railroad still owned over four thousand acres in and around Tullahoma, and it was eager to put its property to use. In 1917 company president John P. Howe offered the army all the land—including the demonstration farm if necessary—for maneuver grounds or for an infantry school and Machine Gun school. The railroad's offer involved more economic concerns than it did patriotism. An army base located near its Tullahoma terminal would create more profitable traffic along the main line. When Washington rejected the offer, the railroad in 1918 attempted to use the land as a colony for displaced European farmers. The experiment began with five Belgian families, but the immigrants abandoned their farms even before they had repaid the railroad for its assistance.

Two years later, the NC&St.L established a division headquarters at Tullahoma, thus exerting even more influence on the local economy. The place was full of railroad workers. On the 600 block of North Washington Street, two blocks from the tracks, a local builder constructed a row of worker cottages (private, no access). The railroad land was finally put to use in 1926, when the state built Camp Peay for the Tennessee National Guard. Then, fifteen years later, after the bombing of Pearl Harbor in December 1941, railroad, state, and local officials convinced the military to convert Camp Peay into a federal induction center, renamed Camp Forrest. During the war, an estimated two hundred and fifty thousand soldiers passed through its gates, stimulating a commercial boom all along U.S. 41A. With an estimated temporary population of seventy-five thousand, Camp Forrest drastically impacted Tullahoma. Residences, offices, and schools were built as quickly as possible. Local industries supplied servicemen with everything from milk to leather jackets. But in 1946 the military closed Camp Forrest, leaving the huge tract of land empty virtually overnight. Over the next three years, local boosters lobbied the military to return, this time with a high-tech research center for testing aerodynamic and propulsion systems. In 1951 the Arnold Engineering Development Corporation Center induced another military-related boom in Tullahoma's history. The old railroad town centered around the tracks had been replaced by a military town dominated by the four-lane commercial strip of U.S. 41A. The Arnold Center is closed to the public except for a museum about its history and development.

Route C: Tullahoma to Cowan

U.S. Highway 41A follows both the Dixie Highway and the Nashville and Chattanooga Railroad closely from Tullahoma to Decherd, where the Old Dixie road veered away from the tracks, passing through the center of Winchester to junction with U.S. Highway 64. From Winchester, the Dixie traveled east up Monteagle Mountain to Tracy City where it then climbed down into the Sequatchie Valley at Jasper only to immediately turn north to Whitwell. There the Dixie Highway crossed Walden's Ridge on Tennessee 27 and headed into Chattanooga. Just outside the hamlet of Powell's Crossroads, Dixie officials erected a simple monument, in honor of Judge M. M. Allison, marking the highest point on the Dixie Highway.

Due to the challenging terrain, the Nashville and Chattanooga took a roundabout way to reach Chattanooga. The adventure began at Cowan, a symmetrically designed railroad town on present-day U.S. Highway 41A/64, twenty miles southeast of Tullahoma. Here trains would pick up "pusher engines" to help them through **Cumberland Tunnel** and down Cumberland Mountain. Designed by John E. Thompson and built mostly by slave labor, the 2,228-foot-long tunnel was one of the great feats of antebellum railroad engineering. Today at Cowan, the **NC&St.L Depot** (1904) is a museum about Cowan's railroad past. After leaving Cowan, the trains headed south to Sherwood. In 1875 the former lieutenant governor of Wisconsin, C. D. Sherwood, president of the Tennessee Immigration and Land Company, purchased a large block of land to establish a model industrial community and health resort. Nothing much came of Sherwood's plans, although later a large lime factory operated at Sherwood. Today the factory's ruins cast an eerie shadow upon the landscape. After Sherwood, the tracks cut into northern Alabama to the town of Stevenson in the Tennessee River valley. Here the trains turned northeast up the valley and entered Chattanooga.

To encounter the highways of Landscape 18, turn west at Cowan and return to Winchester for eight miles on U.S. Highway 64.

NC&St.L Depot, Cowan. Once a busy railroad office, this building is now a quiet town museum.

TENNESSEE'S HISTORIC LANDSCAPES

Landscape 18: The Agrarian Landscape of Middle Tennessee

Middle Tennessee is famous for its rich, productive farmland. The Central Basin was the heartland of Mid-South agriculture throughout the nineteenth century, and even in more modern times, the seasonal rhythms of agriculture still shape everyday life in many towns and communities. As early as 1834, chronicler Eastin Morris confidently remarked that "a large proportion of the lands in this middle section, in addition to their acknowledged fertility, lie well for cultivation" (7). Generations of writers would repeat the same observation.

The agrarian landscape of Middle Tennessee embraces tobacco fields, pastures for dairy cattle, open fields for livestock, cotton fields, cornfields, grain fields, and fruit patches. Rural architecture is almost as varied. The grandiose Greek Revival mansions of southern Maury County are among the most famous homes in the state. But farmers of more modest means also claimed status and prestige by adding classical porticoes to their folk houses, whether they were one-story central-hall cottages or the larger two-story I-houses. In the Victorian era the folk gable-front-and-wing house, perhaps with the front gable decorated with a bit of gingerbread detailing, was popular (see sidebar entitled "Common House Plans," Landscape 5, chapter 3). The new century brought more standardized forms of architecture, such as the farmhouse bungalow and the large two-story Four-Square house. These dwellings are often labeled as popular architecture because they followed standardized designs, were mass-produced, and then sold through such popular catalogs as Sears and Roebuck and Montgomery Ward. The outbuildings that surrounded these dwellings were typical of those used on Tennessee farms since the nineteenth century (see sidebar entitled "Common Farm Outbuildings," Landscape 13, chapter 5).

This landscape explores regional agricultural diversity by first passing through the Elk River Country along U.S. Highway 64 between Winchester and Pulaski. Then, visitors may travel in a rough triangle, taking U.S. Highway 31 north of Pulaski to the rich farmlands of Williamson County and retracing their steps to Columbia before traveling U.S. Highway 43 through the famous plantation country of southern Maury County and the distinctive Mennonite landscape of northern Lawrence County.

Route A: The Elk River Country

To investigate the Elk River and its surrounding lands, take U.S. Highway 64 from Winchester for sixty-two miles to Pulaski.

Winchester, Fayetteville, and Pulaski are three Middle Tennessee towns that share much in common. They benefit from the proximity of the Elk River and its tributaries. Each is a county seat established during the 1810s. Their town plans share the distinctive central courthouse square plan (see sidebar entitled "Central Courthouse Squares," Landscape 17, this chapter). Each has a local economy that was once dependent on agriculture until historic railroad connections brought modern industry and factories. The Civil War was no stranger as well; Pulaski and Winchester perhaps suffered more than Fayetteville. Finally, local citizens and government officials have turned to historic preservation to protect and enhance their communities. All three, at one time or the other, have participated in the Tennessee Main Street Project as the restored and newly painted downtown facades attest. Fayetteville and Pulaski also have architecturally significant residential neighborhoods listed in the National Register. Another apparent similarity is that each of the town squares is dominated by a properly imposing courthouse. Yet, each building embodies a different twentieth-century style of architecture, reflecting some individuality among three towns that share much in common.

Winchester has an excellent example of the ideal courthouse of the 1930s: the modern yet classic look of PWA-sponsored architecture (see sidebar entitled "The New Deal Built Environment," Landscape 9, chapter 4). Nashville architects Marr and Holman designed the **Franklin County Courthouse** in 1936–37. Although progressive in its architectural blending of neoclassical pilasters and Art Deco elements, the building also embodied the era's segregation ethos. Restrooms for African Americans, for example, were in the basement and only accessible by an outside door.

Across the street stood another architectural monument, in this case to the importance of agriculture in Franklin County. The Italian Renaissance–style **Farmers National Bank** (now Third National Bank) dates from 1899. Designed by local builder Tom Scott, the building also housed the local Masonic lodge on the third floor and the offices of H. M. Templeton, a cotton gin operator and factor, on the second floor. The bank is the tallest commercial building in downtown Winchester, but other business areas also maintain an air of propriety and distinc-

Franklin County Courthouse, Winchester. By building modern courthouses, the New Deal placed its stamp on many Tennessee communities.

tion, usually expressed by ornate, Eastlake-influenced cornices like those on Hammer's store. The Oldham Theater is the only building that reflects the courthouse's modernist styling in any meaningful way. On the western outskirts of town, on U.S. Highway 64, are the charred remains of another local architectural landmark, the Hundred Oaks Castle (1890). Local citizens hope to restore the Castellated Gothic–style mansion by the end of the decade.

Agriculture and vernacular architecture dominate the next stretch of U.S. Highway 64 west of Winchester. Five miles west is the rural community of Belvidere, founded by German and Swiss immigrants in the late 1860s. The Glaus Farm, about two miles northeast of Belvidere, dates from 1869, and its founder, Michael Glaus of Switzerland, helped to establish the German Reformed church of Belvidere (private, no access). One hallmark of German agricultural traditions is the bank barn, a two-story barn that has a raised bank allowing for direct access to the second-floor loft. On U.S. 64, there are still a few extant bank barns in the Belvidere area, such as the **Zaugg Barn**, southeast of Belvidere (private, no access).

Following the Civil War, Franklin County residents looked to the "New South" philosophy of industry and commerce with considerable interest. As early as 1856, local businessmen had operated a textile mill

near the community of Old Salem, about four miles west of Belvidere. In 1873 Robert N. Mann and Ezariah David opened the huge **Falls Mill** textile factory. To reach the mill site, turn north at the historical marker on U.S. 64 and travel for a mile. The factory employed mostly young farm women until it closed in 1906. Their lives working the machines of the industrial revolution differed substantially from the way of life on the family farm. Then the building became a cotton gin for the next three decades. The **Falls Mill historic district** includes the three-story mill building, which is now an operating gristmill, as well as the historic Robert Mann house (private, no access) and an abandoned gristmill from the turn of the century. The Rocky Springs Stagecoach Inn (1836), a two-story poplar log house built by Jacob Hamilton, was moved to the Falls Mill property in 1987.

The early agrarian community of Old Salem, south of Falls Mills on U.S. Highway 64, has largely disappeared, but here was once thriving cotton country. Peter Simmons was a prominent cotton dealer and planter. Little remains of his farm, but his two-story brick **Simmons House** still faces the highway eleven miles southwest of Winchester (private, no access). Simmons and other local dealers stored cotton at Old Salem until the nearby Elk River was high enough to float barges full of ginned cotton to New Orleans.

About fourteen miles west on U.S. Highway 64 is the railroad town of Kelso, a later version of the country trading center. After a terrible fire destroyed much of the original business district in 1893, its

Falls Mill, Franklin County. Now a gristmill, this beautiful spot was once a place of industrial drudgery when it was a textile mill in the late 1800s.

economy never fully recovered, and Kelso ever since has been a small country town. Its Victorian railroad depot of board-and-batten construction, however, is a reminder of the village's past days of prominence as a local rail center. Another reminder of earlier transportation routes is north of town: the **Kelso Bowstring Arch Truss Bridge** over the Elk River. In 1878 the King Iron Bridge Company constructed the only bowstring truss bridge in Tennessee for eight thousand dollars.

About six miles west of Kelso on U.S. 64 is Fayetteville, the seat of government for Lincoln County. Dominating its central courthouse square is a modern Colonial Revival courthouse (1971–72), designed by Morton-Carter and Associates, together with a re-created Victorian gazebo. This combination has little to do with historical accuracy, but certainly reflects the conflicting tastes for both the traditional and the picturesque during modern times. Spanning one hundred years of commercial architecture, noteworthy buildings on the square include the Art Deco–influenced Lincoln Theater, the understated Romanesque design of Pythias Hall, and the Victorian cornice of the old post office building.

After its founding in 1812, Fayetteville initially grew slowly, but as local agricultural production expanded in the 1840s and 1850s, the town emerged as a substantial county seat. Things were only better during the 1850s as Lincoln County also benefited from the statewide agricultural prosperity. For instance, the cash value of Tennessee farms in

1850 was almost $98 million; just ten years later, that amount had increased to over $271 million. A historic church and several dwellings along Mulberry Avenue (U.S. 231) north of the square date from that decade. The **First Presbyterian Church** (1854) is an excellent red-brick example of the Greek Revival–temple style. Classical porticoes also adorned the **Marshall-Woodard-Ashby House** (1853) and the **Whitaker-Fulton-Jennings House** (circa 1850). A vernacular interpretation of Gothic Revival was represented by the **McDonald-Bolner House** (1854) at 400 South Elk Avenue (all private, no access).

When the Duck River Valley Narrow Gauge Rail Road was completed to Columbia in 1882, a new world of commercial opportunities unfolded for Fayetteville entrepreneurs. Many of these new professionals and businessmen built Victorian homes beside the older classical homes on Mulberry and South Elk Avenues. The house at **311 South Elk,** for example, was built in the rare Stick style, while the **Bright-Thomison House** at 624 Mulberry reflected Queen Anne architecture. The most flamboyant was the Steamboat Gothic of the **Douglas-Wyatt House** (1894–95), designed by Nashville architects Rickman and Bills, at 301 North Elk Avenue (all private, no access). The African-American community also grew in these decades, and in 1902 black residents built the Victorian-style Mount Zion Missionary Baptist Church at 304 Maple.

Small industries came to Lincoln County in the twentieth century as its rail connections were extended and strengthened. The most important factory, however, linked industry to the county's many profitable farms. The **Borden Milk Plant** (1927) on South Main Street made the dairy industry of Lincoln County possible and profitable. By processing powdered milk and butter, the factory took advantage of new urban markets for dairy products. Borden opened four other plants simultaneously with the Fayetteville factory, but this one specialized in powdered milk, a new product of the company. At its peak production, the plant processed about one hundred thousand pounds of milk a day from over twelve hundred regional farmers and employed about seventy-five workers. The factory remained in business until 1967. Twenty years later, local citizens and county officials renovated the old factory and made it the new home of the Lincoln County Museum. The museum has an excellent collection of artifacts about local agricultural history.

A scenic side trip that reveals more of the rural landscape of Lincoln County is the fifteen-mile drive on Tennessee 50 from Fayetteville to Lynchburg. The seat of government for tiny Moore County, Lynchburg is one of Tennessee's most famous country towns due to the overwhelming presence of **Jack Daniel Distillery,** which is the oldest national registered distillery in the country (private, open for tours). On the hills above town are large warehouses where the aging whiskey is stored. The **Moore County Courthouse** (1885), a late vernacular statement of Italianate architecture, dominates the always busy town square. Many of the early-twentieth-century buildings now have businesses that cater to the tourist trade, but others still serve the needs of the local community. Surrounding the square is an amazing collection of vernacular domestic architecture. The **Mary Bobo Boarding House**—now a famous local restaurant—is an excellent example of a Greek Revival–influenced I-house, built in 1867. One-story central-hall houses, such as the Hinkle-Price House (1877) on Majors Avenue, are common, while several outstanding vernacular Gothic and Italianate dwellings are located to the east and north of the square (private, no access). The **Green-Evans-Hudgens House** (1857), at the eastern outskirts of town on Tennessee 55, is significant for its Greek Revival architecture and its interior decorative painting by Fred Swanton, who painted interiors in at least four area houses during the late 1880s (private, no access).

Nine miles west of Fayetteville on U.S. Highway 64 is the **Childress Farm,** one of the many properties that once supplied milk to local dairy plants (private, no access). Built by Reps O. Childress, the two-story brick I-house dates from 1825, and the four-columned Greek Revival portico was added in about 1840. A variety of farm outbuildings mark the 170-year evolution of a family farm to a modern dairy producer.

At mile marker 2 on U.S. Highway 64, near the Giles County line, is a large barn with a gable roof painted to urge travelers to stop at Rock City in Chattanooga. "Rock City" barns are found along the older federal highways leading into Chattanooga. At their height in 1956, Rock City signs adorned over eight hundred barns from Georgia to Texas to southern Michigan; as late as 1987, forty-four Rock City barns still stood in Tennessee. Clark Byers of Chattanooga selected and painted most of the barns. "First, we'd black 'em out, doing one half of the barn and then moving to the other," he recalled. "After that, we'd go back and begin the white lettering. I never used a stencil—we moved too fast" (Sarver, 10). Byers and his helpers repaired any holes, nailed down loose boards, and paid owners five to ten dollars. The farmer got a painted and repaired roof; Rock City got a cheap billboard on a major federal highway.

Pulaski, the seat of Giles County, is another twelve miles west on U.S. 64. Its **Giles County Courthouse** is the grandest of the notable

Giles County Courthouse, Pulaski. The massive classicism of this courthouse reflected local agricultural and industrial prosperity in the early twentieth century.

southern Middle Tennessee public buildings. Designed by Benjamin N. Smith of Alabama in the Beaux-Arts style of classicism, this 1909 building has mammoth porticoes supported by Corinthian columns defining each of its four sides and topped by a Corinthian supported cupola. At the south end of this monumental structure is a statue of Sam Davis, a Confederate scout executed by Union troops here in 1863. On a hill east of the square is Sam Davis Avenue, and a small museum is located near where the hanging took place. The historic courthouse square reflects the varied types of commercial architecture that existed from 1865 to 1935, including a Second Empire **Opera House** (1868) at 109 N. First, the Victorian Gothic **First Presbyterian Church** (circa 1895), and the Art Moderne **Hunter Furniture Company** at 138 N. Second Street.

Surrounding the town square are historic neighborhoods that reflect popular styles of southern domestic architecture from Reconstruction to the Great Depression. **Sam Davis Avenue** has central-hall houses, gable-front-and-wing dwellings, bungalows, and Four-Square homes that mirror its development from 1858 to 1920. The **West Pulaski historic district** includes the town's oldest dwellings, especially the Greek Revival–influenced townhouses on the 300 to 600 blocks of South First Street.

Giles County was a major cotton producer in the antebellum era, and by 1850 two cotton mills were in business at Pulaski. Ten years later, the Nashville and Decatur Railroad was completed, giving the town modern transportation links to the north and south (today U.S. 31 generally follows the old railroad route). After the Civil War, the railroad brought new industrial opportunities. By the mid-1880s, Pulaski had almost three thousand residents; many were employed at the cotton mills, a buggy factory, a lumber mill, and other small businesses. The **Brown-Daly House** at 301 W. Madison is an architectural metaphor for the changes industrialism brought to Pulaski. Now a local bank, it was originally the circa 1855 home of Democratic activist John C. Brown, a wealthy planter who served as Tennessee governor from 1871 to 1875. Then, in the late 1890s, local merchant and banker T. E. Daly transformed the earlier traditional dwelling into a Queen Anne showplace, with porticoes, bays, turrets, and finials. Its radically different facade mirrored the changes then taking place in the local business community (private, limited access).

Pulaski's economic diversification continued in the early 1900s. A brickyard went into operation, as well as a wood products factory, a clothes factory, and a dairy creamery. Yet, cotton remained important; in 1923, eight to ten thousand bales of cotton were being shipped annually from Pulaski. The 300 and 400 blocks of South Second and South Third Streets reflect the domestic architecture of those years in the classicism of the **Smithson-Brindley House** (1910) at 326 South Third and the **Booth-Arthur Bungalow** (1914) at 408 South Third (both private, no access).

Pulaski was also home to noted African-American architect Moses McKissack. His firm's Bridgeforth School (1927) is a restrained Colonial Revival design for the town's segregated black school; it was built with Rosenwald funds and used until 1958. It stands just north of town on U.S. Highway 31.

Route B: Agricultural Landscapes in Southern Middle Tennessee

The thirty-one miles of U.S. Highway 31 between Pulaski and Columbia show one of the most beautiful agrarian landscapes in Tennessee. The initial farms were established in the early 1800s, but this area blossomed later that century after the construction of the Nashville and Decatur Railroad, which by 1860 linked the region to the L&N and NC&St.L lines at Nashville and to the Memphis and Charleston line at Decatur. For the next one hundred years, cotton, livestock, corn, fruit, and dairy products were yielded in abundance. This section of U.S. 31 is a two-lane highway that often parallels the track as it cuts through still productive farmland. It is a route that keeps travelers in close touch with local history, as it ranges from twentieth-century demonstration farms and country towns to historic family farms.

Twelve miles north of Pulaski is the imposing gateway leading to historic **Milky Way Farm,** developed by candy magnate Frank C. Mars (private, limited access). This privately owned and operated early-twentieth-century demonstration farm was one of the largest producers of dairy cattle in the country. Mars also raised successful racehorses. In the late 1930s, the estate contained over twenty-seven hundred acres, complete with its own racetrack, clubhouse, twenty-five large stock barns, and fifty homes for employees. Many of these buildings no longer exist, but enough of the estate remains to document the lavish care and attention Mars directed on his plantation.

Lynnville, a place typical of country railroad towns of one hundred years ago, is five miles to the north, just off U.S. 31 on Tennessee 129. Platted by the Nashville and Decatur in about 1860, the town has the common symmetrical plan of the mid-1800s (see sidebar entitled "Common Railroad Town Plans," Landscape 20, chapter 7). The depot is gone, but facing the tracks is an interesting row of commercial buildings where farmers once came in steady numbers to market their crops, buy new equipment, and satisfy their consumer needs for food, clothing, and dry goods. The **McQuigg Brothers Store** (circa 1860) is an excellent example of a small-town cast-iron storefront.

Maury County, one of the richest agricultural counties in Tennessee during the mid-nineteenth century, is four miles north of Lynnville on U.S. Highway 31. Its well-watered and prosperous farmland has led contemporaries and later historians to describe the county as a garden spot in the Mid-South. But even here, small, independent farms that grew little cotton, had few slaves, and practiced mixed agriculture were the norm in the antebellum era. According to historian Stephen Ash, these more middle-class farmers lived differently than the planter elite: "the rhythms of rural life dictated a routine of tasks—barn raisings, log rollings, corn shuckings, hog killings—that brought neighbors together in toil, and a cycle of respites—after the laying-by of the crops in the summer, for example, and after harvest in the fall—that united them in leisure and diversion" (22).

Three miles north of the county line, at the hamlet of Hollywood, is a historic family farm that represents how the mixed agriculture of the nineteenth century evolved into the "progressive" specialized farm of the present age. Established by John and Sarah Walker Matthews in 1816, Tanglefoot Farm (private, no access) first yielded corn, cotton, wheat, and all types of livestock on its 215 acres. In 1855 the farm was inherited by Joseph Matthews, who expanded its boundaries by 140 acres and built a sawmill to add a bit of light industrial diversification to the farm's traditional crops. Little else changed until 1935, when burley tobacco became a major cash crop. Twelve years later the great-great-grandsons of John and Sarah Walker Matthews opened a Grade A dairy and added soybeans to the farm's tobacco, corn, and wheat fields. Agricultural improvements continued for another generation and culminated in the recognition of owner John D. Matthews as Maury County's Conservation Farmer of the Year in 1973.

Route C: The Franklin Campaign of 1864

Seven miles north on U.S. Highway 31 is Columbia, the seat of Maury County. The Civil War savagely struck this land in late 1864 as Confederate general John Bell Hood led his battered Army of Tennessee on a futile invasion of Nashville. Between Columbia and Franklin, Hood used an antebellum turnpike—which U.S. 31 follows today—as his invasion route, and many places associated with his 1864 campaign are still visible along the highway.

Watching the Confederate advance carefully was a large Federal force under the command of Gen. John Schofield, who wanted to protect the Duck River crossing at Columbia. Schofield initially considered making his stand here, and he took up headquarters at the Greek Revival temple-style mansion known as **Beechlawn** (1853–60, private, no access), located by a roadside historical marker at the southern city limits of Columbia. But once Hood arrived in force on November 27, 1864, Schofield abandoned his fortified position to move north of the Duck River. Hood promptly made Beechlawn his command center.

Two days later, the Confederate general launched a bold flanking maneuver designed to bypass Schofield at Columbia and to seize the Nashville Turnpike (present-day U.S. Highway 31 again) at Spring Hill, which is eleven miles north of Columbia on U.S. 31. But his troops and cavalry could not move fast enough. Schofield got just enough men there to protect the turnpike, and that night his command continued north for thirteen miles, inexplicably without any meaningful Confederate opposition, until it reached the town of Franklin the next afternoon. Here the Federal army settled into extensive and well-designed fortifications that stretched from one end of town to the other. "These were no ordinary earthworks," observed historian Thomas Connelly, "there were deep outside ditches, head logs atop the dirt parapets, and a menacing array of abatis and *chevaux-de-frise* to slow an enemy's advance" (91). Nothing like that remains in Franklin today, but on U.S. 31 is the **Carter House,** a National Historic Landmark where some of the most vicious fighting took place that afternoon and evening. In addition, a museum at the house has exhibits about the battle.

From his new headquarters on **Winstead Hill,** Hood ordered a direct frontal assault on Franklin, despite howls of protest from his subordinates. At four o'clock in the afternoon, a long row of eighteen Confederate brigades, with regimental colors flying and bands playing, marched forward. For the next five hours, the undermanned and exhausted Army of Tennessee valiantly tried to break the Federal line. "The booming of cannon, the bursting of bombs, the rattling of musketry, the shrieking of shells, the whizzing of bullets, the shouting of the hosts, and the falling of men in their struggle for victory," later wrote Confederate general George W. Gordon, "all made a scene of surpassing terror and awful grandeur" (Huddleston, 111). Vicious hand-to-hand fighting around the Carter House and a cotton gin across the road almost broke the Yankee line, but timely reinforcements proved too much for the weary Rebels. The fighting continued through the night until about nine o'clock when Hood ordered a withdrawal in order to prepare his troops for another assault the next morning.

But there would not be another attack. Hood's foolhardy charge had decimated the Army of Tennessee. Of the 16,000 Confederates involved in the assault, 6,200 were casualties, a staggering 38 percent. The Confederates suffered 1,750 killed, including six generals and 54 regimental commanders. Four of the generals were laid out on the back porch of **Carnton Mansion,** a Greek Revival plantation house, which is a mile southeast of Franklin on U.S. Highway 431 (public). Next to the mansion is the **Confederate Cemetery** (1866), the final resting place for 1,481 Confederates who died at the Battle of Franklin.

The ferocity of the fighting during the great battle of November 30, 1864, did not destroy the small city of Franklin (1799), and today its large fifteen-block downtown historic district helps to document the town's appearance during the war as well as during the postwar recovery and expansion. From the Carter House, continue on U.S. 31 north for about a mile to the town square. In the southwest corner is the **Williamson County Courthouse** (1858–59), built by John W. Miller at the height of local agricultural prosperity. Williamson County, in 1850, was the second-wealthiest county in Tennessee, a rank only enhanced by the arrival of the railroad later that decade. Its extensive system of turnpikes allowed farmers better access to local, statewide, and regional markets. Its proximity to Nashville meant access to a growing urban market. Its fertile land was well watered by the Harpeth River and its many tributaries. Its agricultural products were diverse; while Williamson County had its share of rich tobacco and cotton fields, its abundant foodstuffs—livestock, corn, wheat, peas, rye, and potatoes— were what truly set the county apart.

What remains of the town's pre–Civil War built environment certainly reflects this wealth and prestige. Along First, Second, and Third Avenues are several important landmarks, and most properties have

Carnton Mansion, Franklin. Carnton is significant for its Greek Revival architecture as well as for its role in the Battle of Franklin.

identifying markers in their yards. The three-story Gothic Revival–style **Hiram Masonic lodge** (1823) on Second Avenue South is a National Historic Landmark, so listed because it was the state's first three-story building, its first brick Masonic lodge, and the first home of the Protestant Episcopal church in Tennessee. A devoted Mason, President Andrew Jackson, personally led the negotiations for a new Chickasaw Treaty here in 1830. On the same street is **Clouston Hall** (1830s), designed by local craftsman Joseph Reiff. Third Avenue South has a splendid example of local Greek Revival architecture in the **John W. Miller House** (1850s) as well as the much earlier **Saunders-Marshall House** (circa 1805). The **Moran-Campbell-Pope House** (circa 1822 with later Italianate detailing from circa 1850–60s) at 120 South Third was the home of the important Tennessee cabinetmaker Charles Moran (all private, no access).

Third Avenue South has its own excellent examples of late Victorian domestic architecture, but perhaps the best way to recapture the environment of Franklin after the Civil War is to return to the square and take West Main Street or Fair Street. Between the 800 and 1000 blocks on both streets are some of Tennessee's best examples of picturesque Victorian architecture, especially the **Lillihouse Cottage** (circa 1894) at 930 West Main, and the delightful row of gable-front-and-wing houses on the 1000 block of Fair Street. This neighborhood was part of

Lilihouse Cottage, West Main Street, Franklin.

the **Hincheyville** subdivision developed for a new entrepreneurial and professional class. Franklin relied on the strength of its agricultural economy, small factories, and local banks to fuel continued growth in the late nineteenth century.

Route D: Agricultural Diversity in Middle Tennessee

The agricultural landscape of Middle Tennessee is remarkably diverse. Livestock farms can range from unglamorous pig farms to ornate walking horse plantations to cattle farms. Dairy and tobacco farms are everywhere, while some families have been cultivating row crops on their small farms for decades. Cotton has even returned to the more productive areas of the Central Basin at the same time that the acreage of tobacco farms has declined. The combined routes of U.S. 31 and 43, from Franklin to near the state line at Loretto, allow visitors to sample this agricultural diversity as they pass through nineteenth-century railroad towns, prosperous antebellum county seats, beautiful plantations, and modern farm communes.

Eight miles south of Franklin on U.S. Highway 31 is the old railroad town of Thompson Station, once a trade center for southern Williamson County farmers. At the turn of the century, entrepreneur Milton C. Hatcher established a broom factory that depended on local farmers growing enough broom corn for his use. A fire destroyed the factory, and Hatcher moved operations to Memphis, but farmers still produced broom corn to ship via rail to the new Memphis factory. The history of the nearby Moss Side Farm, just west of U.S. 31 at Thompson Station, gives another view on how shifting demand for particular crops has changed the look of the land. In the early nineteenth century, Francis and Mary White yielded corn, wheat, and cotton out of 340 acres of land. But by 1900, cotton was no longer planted in favor of tobacco and millet. Seventy years later, none of the original crops was cultivated, as the farm, like many in this area, specialized in burley tobacco and cattle. Thus, the landscape changed from being dominated by row crops and field hands to open pasture, hay fields, and scattered small tobacco plots.

The next town south is Spring Hill, which is on the border between Williamson and Maury Counties. Until 1985, when General Motors Corporation announced it was locating the Saturn automobile factory on the old Haynes Haven plantation, this was a typical southern crossroads town, with a range of nineteenth-century domestic architecture. Most of the historic properties are still there, but new stores, homes, public buildings, and roads have forever changed the atmosphere of this once rural place as the modern engineered landscape of the factory and new highways intrude into the older vernacular landscape.

On Depot Lane in Spring Hill is the **Ewell Farm,** once one of the region's great stock-breeding plantations (private, no access). Established by Lazinka Campbell Ewell and her husband, former Confederate general Richard Ewell, and later expanded by Lazinka's son, Maj. Campbell Brown, the Ewell Farm introduced some of the first Jersey cattle to the South and bred some of the first harness-racing horses in the country. Its semiannual horse races, cattle sales, and stock auctions became week-long events, attended by the rich and powerful from throughout America, including Theodore Roosevelt. The Louisville and Nashville Railroad bisected the plantation, which had its own depot and a huge warehouse along the tracks.

Two antebellum plantation seats, both owned by the Cheairs family, are nearby on U.S. Highway 31. The first dwelling, **Ferguson Hall** (1851–52), is just south of the center of Spring Hill. This gracious Greek Revival mansion became a private military school in 1905 and later an orphans' home in 1935 (private, limited access). During the Civil War, Confederate cavalry leader Earl Van Dorn was murdered here by Dr. George B. Peters, who allegedly suspected that Van Dorn was having an affair with his wife. A bit farther south, also on the east side of U.S. Highway 31 but in Maury County, is the second Cheairs family plantation, **Rippa Villa** (1855), built by Nathaniel Cheairs. Both homes are almost identical interpretations of the Greek Revival, with overbearing Corinthian porticoes. Rippa Villa now serves as a visitor center and museum for the many historic sites in Maury County.

Nine miles to the south on U.S. 31 is Columbia (1817), which was a large and well-appointed town by the time of the Civil War. Today antebellum and later Victorian and early-twentieth-century buildings are intermixed in the National Register–listed downtown business district and in historic residential neighborhoods, creating an urban landscape grounded in 150 years of agricultural evolution and success.

The grand Classical Revival architecture of the **Maury County Courthouse** (1904–6), designed by the New York firm of Carpenter and Blair, overlooks a historic square that was largely restored during the Main Street revival programs of the 1980s. To the immediate north is the **Vaught Block** (1858), designed by local builder and architect Nathan Vaught, who did much to shape the antebellum commercial and residential architecture of Maury County. The square is the heart of activities during Columbia's annual Mule Day celebration, held traditionally on the first Monday in April. The city has billed itself as "the largest street mule market in the world," and the Mule Day fair reminds visitors of the key role mules once played in southern agriculture.

Until the widespread adoption of motor-driven machinery after 1940, mules powered most farm work in Tennessee. Mules were of extraordinary value, especially to small-farm owners. A hybrid animal, mules are a mix of jackass studs and mare horses. Mules can be either males or females, but in the great majority of cases they are sterile and cannot reproduce. Thus, mules became more expensive than either workhorses or oxen, but regional farmers who cultivated cotton or tobacco preferred mules because they believed the animals were more surefooted, smarter, and stronger than horses or oxen. Moreover, farmers believed that mules rarely succumbed to disease and performed well in the hot southern summers. Although they acknowledged that mules had a complex—most would just say stubborn—personality, farmers countered that the animals had thicker skins than other work animals and could be beaten with regularity. When in the mood, mules responded to simple commands. Farmers yelled "gee" for a right turn, "haw" for a left turn, "whoa" to stop, and "come up" to start. Farmers and mules, in other words, worked together as a team to produce the family's

Mule Day Parade, 1947, Columbia. Although mules no longer play so important a role in southern agriculture, Columbia still hosts an annual Mule Day celebration. (Courtesy of Oscar Farris Agricultural Museum, Tennessee Department of Agriculture)

subsistence. Perhaps that explains why rural families became so attached to their mules, giving them names and treating them like pets.

For 150 years, West Seventh Street served as Columbia's primary commercial artery, and its first blocks linked the square to Franklin Pike (U.S. 31) before the street continued west to junction with Mount Pleasant Pike (U.S. 43) and then Hampshire Pike (U.S. 412). One block west of the square is the former **Bank of Tennessee Building** (1838–39), designed in Greek Revival–temple style by Nathan Vaught (private, no access). The state-supported bank was an important element in the Whig party's plan to reinvigorate and update the state financial system during the middle decades of the nineteenth century. Towns throughout Tennessee lobbied hard to acquire the branch banks because their presence meant that more capital would be available for local investment. From 1840 to 1860, the Columbia branch bank combined with an unparalleled boom in the local planter economy and the construction of the Nashville and Decatur Railroad to transform Columbia into the state's third-largest city by 1850 and its wealthiest county by 1860.

A six-block walk along **West Seventh Street** introduces the visitor to a historic neighborhood associated with Columbia's remarkable nineteenth-century growth. The tour might begin at the Federal-style **Samuel Polk House** (1816), which is a National Historic Landmark house museum due to its association with former President James K. Polk, who lived there as a young man in his twenties. No other Polk-owned residence exists in Tennessee so this house serves as a museum to Polk's career in local, state, and national politics. A Democratic stalwart during the era of bitter political battles between Whigs and Democrats, Polk served as speaker of the U.S. House of Representatives and as Tennessee's governor before being elected as president in 1844 and spending one term in the White House.

Next door is the Gothic Revival **St. Peter's Episcopal Church** (1860), a place of worship for the county's elite throughout these decades. Across the street, between the 300 and 400 blocks of West Seventh, is a mix of domestic styles. The **Church House** is a Second Empire design completed in about 1873, while the historic **Carmack House** (1856) has been converted into a funeral home. The **Lucius Frierson House** (1876) at 400 West Seventh is a gaudy mix of Italianate and Second Empire elements (all private, no access). One block south on Athenaeum Street is one of the state's most striking architectural statements, the former rectory of the **Columbia Athenaeum,** built in a vernacular Gothic Revival style by Drummond and Lutterloh in circa 1835. It is now managed as a historic site by the Association for the Preservation of Tennessee Antiquities.

Recent businesses mark the next two blocks, but vernacular interpretations of Victorian styles dominate the 600 block of West Seventh. The 700–900 blocks feature domestic architecture popular in the early twentieth century, including bungalows and Colonial Revival homes. The **Hart House** at 925 West Seventh is a Colonial Revival design by architects Warfield and Keeble of Nashville. Nearby are homes that once represented farms on the outskirts of Columbia. **Shadowlawn** at 917 West Seventh is a Tennessee Federal dwelling built in 1851–54. The **Pise-Parsons House** (1858) at 909 West Seventh is one of the state's best examples of Carpenter Gothic style. It followed a design in Andrew J. Downing's popular Victorian architecture pattern book *Victorian Cottage Residences* (1842). Across the street is the Greek Revival **Stratton-Douglas House,** built in 1850 (all private, no access).

Another two blocks to the west, where the street intersects the railroad tracks, is Columbia Academy, the former home of the Colum-

The Athenaeum, Columbia.

bia Military Institute and the earlier site of the **Columbia Arsenal.** Between 1890 and 1891, the federal government established Columbia arsenal on sixty-seven acres, building nine beautiful brick-and-masonry buildings as offices, officer quarters, munitions storerooms, and war magazines. Several of these buildings remain in use: the guardhouse, Main Building, Ragsdale Hall, Academy Hall, Moore Hall, and Frierson Hall. But later that decade, the government moved all munitions operations to an Indiana arsenal and turned the Columbia complex into a training headquarters during the Spanish-American War. In 1902 the arsenal was closed and was declared surplus federal property. Two years later, private investors and public officials had acquired the property and reopened it as the Columbia Military Academy, a college preparatory school for boarding students. The military academy remained open until the 1980s when it closed and a private school took over the facilities.

Halfway through the West Seventh historic district is the street's intersection with old U.S. Highway 43. A drive along this older route leading southwest from Columbia—now marked as Tennessee Highway 243—passes through the rural community of **Ashwood,** one of the best concentrations of antebellum plantation architecture and landscape in the country. "From Columbia south-westward lies one of the most beautiful bodies of land in the United States," remarked state geologist and agricultural booster Joseph B. Killebrew in the late 1800s. "Certainly none other in Tennessee surpasses it, and no other is so well known, or often spoken of by travelers. [It] contains some of the handsomest and most productive farms in the state" (831). One hundred years later, historian Richard Quin found that little had changed. The Ashwood area between Columbia and Mount Pleasant is a "remarkably intact landscape of historic farms . . . with its fields and property boundaries, roads and other features much as they were in the plantation era" (1). Today, however, developmental pressures threaten the integrity of this significant landscape of history and architecture.

The first great estate is **Clifton Place,** which sits on a hill overlooking the highway about five miles southwest of Columbia on Highway 243 (private, no access). An agricultural innovator, Democratic party activist, Mexican War hero, and Civil War flop, Gideon J. Pillow directed the construction of this Greek Revival mansion from 1838 to 1839. The house originally was an example of Tennessee Federal architecture based on a central-hall plan. In about 1852, however, Pillow added the heavy Ionic capital portico and side wings to the front of the house, turning a traditional piece of Tennessee architecture into a flamboyant Greek Revival showplace. Clifton Place was primarily a stock farm—specializing in merino sheep, Irish Grazier hogs, and Durham cattle—but it also produced cotton, corn, hemp, and fruit. The designer of Clifton Place was master craftsman Nathan Vaught, who is also credited with a second Pillow family home, **Bethel Place,** another Greek Revival mansion that stands about one mile east of Clifton Place on a county road (private, no access).

A mile and a half southwest on Tennessee 243 is **St. John's Episcopal Church** (1839–42), built under the direction of Leonidas Polk as a plantation church to serve the adjacent estates of the four Polk brothers. This magnificent achievement in rural Gothic Revival architecture was probably the last private plantation church built in the South; it is now open only for special occasions. A historic artifact in itself, the church cemetery contains several excellent examples of funerary decorative art and documents the class divisions common in antebellum plantation communities such as this one.

Less than a mile down the highway is perhaps the most important architectural statement in the Ashwood district, the dwelling known as **Hamilton Place** (1831–32), a Palladian-influenced mansion built for Lucius Polk by a crew of carpenters and workers imported from North Carolina (private, no access). Remarkable for its coherent statement of classicism in a time when Maury County was still part of the Tennessee frontier, Hamilton Place was the first of the major Ashwood plantations. Elements of its design reflect Palladio's own Villa Pisano and Brunelleschi's Hospital at Florence. Its understated and tasteful classicism is rare among the typically gaudy plantation homes of the Mid-South.

The most famous Polk plantation, **Rattle-N-Snap,** is another half mile away, and its gleaming ten-columned Corinthian portico is clearly visible from the highway (private, limited access). Built in the mid-1850s for George Washington Polk, Rattle-N-Snap is a National Historic Landmark as a nationally significant example of southern plantation architecture. It reflects the influence of the northern Greek Revival movement, especially the work of Minard Lafever, but it best represents the architecture of southern nationalism. Architectural historian James Patrick explains that this new style "was intended to express the mind and sentiments of an agrarian society" that had confidence in its social, political, and economic dominance of the countryside (181). Looking at places such as Rattle-N-Snap, one is reminded of the wise words of English historian Raymond Williams: "For look at the sites, the facades, the defining avenues and walls, the great iron gates and the guardian

St. John's Church, Maury County. The bucolic landscape of the Ashwood district is now threatened by unchecked and short-sighted development.

Hamilton Place, Maury County. An important example of Palladian classicism on the emerging plantation landscape of Middle Tennessee.

lodges. These were chosen for more than the effect from the inside out; where too many admirers, too many of them writers, have stood and shared the view, finding its prospect delightful. They were chosen, also . . . for the other effect, from the outside looking in: a visible stamp of power, of displayed wealth and command: a social disproportion which was meant to impress and overawe" (Meinig, 92–93). The current owners are considering plans to reshape Rattle-N-Snap into a modern tourist development, complete with a resort hotel, conference center, motel and restaurant, and golf courses.

In the antebellum era, while owners lived graciously inside the manor houses of the Ashwood district, slaves did the work of the plantations. The open fields on either side of the present-day highway would have been the domain of African-American stockmen, field hands, and mule drivers. In 1860 40 percent of the county's population was in slavery, and this percentage was much higher in the Ashwood area. In that year, for example, Hamilton Place's Lucius Polk owned eighty-two blacks; Gideon Pillow had eighty-one slaves at Clifton Place; and George W. Polk at Rattle-N-Snap had eighty-three slaves. The slaves not only worked fields, built fences, and tended livestock; they also were the workmen who actually constructed the great homes. At Rattle-N-Snap, recalled Caroline Polk Horton, "slaves, who were skilled stone and brick masons and carpenters" built the mansion. "There were no shortcuts, no labor saving inventions. Each workman knew the *best* was expected of him, so, loyal interest, pride, and efficiency, was their goal" (Quin, 90). The landscape of the Ashwood rural neighborhood, therefore, is a white landscape as far as its actual conception; but in its execution, it is also a black landscape, because it reflects the considerable skills and hard work of enslaved African-American farmers and craftsmen. One wonders how the envisioned modern development will impact this unique historical landscape.

The town of Mount Pleasant is another four miles southwest on the old route of U.S. Highway 43, still marked as State Highway 243. Established in about 1810, Mount Pleasant has a long history as a nineteenth-century rural village, but most of the homes and businesses date from after 1895, when phosphate was found at a nearby farm. Valuable for chemicals and especially fertilizers, phosphate was in high demand at the turn of the century, and the discovery of new deposits near Mount Pleasant unleashed a whirlwind boom. In 1890, for example, the local population was only 466, but by the end of the decade Mount Pleasant had 2,007 residents—a 400 percent increase in just ten years. Phosphate mining remained important until the middle decades of the twentieth century.

The 300 to 600 blocks of the **North Main historic district** show what happened in Mount Pleasant once the phosphate boom took off. Only the Greek Revival dwelling known as **Walnut Grove** (1857), attributed to Nathan Vaught, remains from the nineteenth century. The rest were built between 1896 and 1940 during the height of the phosphate industry in Maury County. The **Pleasant Street historic district** has a similar history. Here a new subdivision developed in 1899 around the Greek Revival plantation house known as **Manor Hall** (1859). Homes in the late Victorian, Craftsman, and Four-Square styles were built for the phosphate mine owners, managers, and entrepreneurs who moved here to take advantage of new business opportunities.

South of Mount Pleasant, U.S. Highway 43 rejoins the old road marked as Tennessee 243. For the next twenty-three miles south, U.S. Highway 43 generally follows the historic federal Military Road (1816–20), which ran from Columbia to Madisonville, Louisiana, and was built by Gen. Andrew Jackson. Highway 43 also closely follows the rail line of the Columbia, Lawrenceburg, and Florence Railroad—a branch line controlled by the Louisville and Nashville—that was constructed between Columbia and St. Joseph from 1879 to 1884.

Two quite different utopian farming communities are located along this section of the highway. About nine miles south of Mount Pleasant, near the town of Summertown, is the former counterculture commune known as "the Farm." Established in 1970 by Stephen Gaskin and others, the Farm sought an alternative way of life from what the Farm's founders perceived as the crass consumerism and suburban, individualistic life of the sixties. In the early 1970s, over eight hundred people lived on the Farm's fifteen hundred acres. These inhabitants held their property in common, practiced neither birth control nor abortion, and were vegetarians. The first years were difficult, and the commune almost starved to death. But with persistence, members learned to farm tough land, develop new communal businesses, and establish a somewhat stable community. Some members became experts in historic log architecture and have restored or built log buildings throughout the region. Other members became recognized for their abilities as midwives, especially Ina May Gaskin, who has been described as the "acknowledged foremost theoretician and practitioner" of the natural-birth movement in the United States (*Washington Post,* national weekly edition, December 28, 1992). By 1989, Farm midwives had assisted seventeen hundred births; less than 5 percent had to be taken to a hospital, and forceps were used in a mere 0.5 percent of the births.

Ethridge is south of Summertown in Lawrence County. This rural place is home to a small Mennonite farming community that has lived here since the mid-twentieth century. The Mennonite farms can often be identified by the sheer number of small frame outbuildings surrounding the farmhouse, together with the lack of cars, tractors, and trucks and the use of windmill generators. Mennonites farm in a traditional nineteenth-century manner, using draft animals, animal or wind-powered machines, and travel to town using horse-drawn buggies.

Lawrenceburg is six miles south of Ethridge, and the historic **town square** is located directly on the old Military Road. This federal road brought regular mail traffic through the tiny county seat in the early days when Tennessee legend Davy Crockett operated a gristmill where Davy Crockett State Park is now located. But little else happened until the late 1840s when a new modern turnpike between Columbia, Lawrenceburg, and Waynesboro was completed, and the town's first bank opened. In the next decade, the town's abundant water power on Shoal and Crowson Creeks attracted industrial entrepreneurs who built numerous cotton textile factories. By 1860 Lawrence County produced 20 percent of the finished cotton goods in the state, but then the Civil War and the depressed cotton market of the Reconstruction era wrecked most local industries.

Recovery began in 1870 when J. B. Juep of Cincinnati established the "German Catholic Homestead Association" to relocate German immigrants into the wilds of the Highland Rim of southern Middle Tennessee. This association eventually acquired twenty-five thousand acres, and hundreds of homesteaders moved to the county. Rev. Henry Huesser chose the land and directed the early settlements. Then in 1879–80 came the Columbia, Lawrenceburg, and Florence Railroad, which ran downtown, with the tracks passing directly behind the east side of the square. Once the railroad was completed, many of the old cotton mills were reopened, and in 1882 a group of local entrepreneurs established the Marcella Falls Woolen Mills. The textile industry was back on its feet and drove Lawrenceburg's economy into the twentieth century.

Many of the buildings around the town square are between eighty and one hundred years old. During the 1890s, new building blocks, including the Welch Building at 32–34 Public Square, were constructed. Destructive fires in 1891 and 1898 forced businesses to build again, this time in brick. And fueling this new boom was booster rhetoric that described Lawrence County as an agricultural paradise. From 1900 to 1910, the county grew proportionately more than any county in the state, a population boom that had a remarkable impact on downtown Lawrenceburg, as sixteen buildings in the downtown historic district date between 1900 and 1910.

Today the commercial buildings are there, but the historic courthouse was demolished in the 1970s, leaving an open city park with only a rare historic Mexican War monument and a 1920s statue of Davy Crockett. The new courthouse (1974) was placed west of the square on U.S. Highway 64. Designed by the Nashville firm of Hart, Freeland, and Roberts, it is a very interesting local statement of the modern architectural style called New Formalism, popularized nationally during the 1960s by architect Edward D. Stone's design of the Kennedy Center in Washington, D.C.

Eleven miles south of Lawrenceburg on U.S. Highway 43 is Loretto, a trade and religious center for the German Catholic homesteaders of the late 1800s. Local citizens have marked many historic buildings, including the Wiggerman House (1890) on Commerce Street, where the town's first telephone exchange was established, the Patt blacksmith shop (1910), and the hotel (1897) and general store (1905) operated by John Hollander. On Church Street is the **Sacred Heart of Jesus Church** (1911), a traditional blending of Gothic and Romanesque ecclesiastical designs.

Town square and Mexican War Monument, Lawrenceburg. The Military Road, built by soldiers under the command of Andrew Jackson, passes through the Lawrenceburg square.

TENNESSEE'S HISTORIC LANDSCAPES

St. Joseph, another four miles south on U.S. Highway 43, is another German Catholic homesteading settlement. Its **Church of St. Joseph** (1885) has a beautiful painted interior, which was executed by Rev. John Sliemers in the early twentieth century. The original church building, established by Rev. Henry Huesser and others in 1872, is nearby and is used now for storage.

Landscape 19: The Western Highland Rim

The Western Highland Rim is much like its eastern counterpart: it is a rough, hilly, almost mountainous land interspersed with narrow, fertile river valleys. The western rim has always been noted for its natural resources. **Bon Aqua** and **Primm Springs** in Hickman County were once famous for their natural mineral springs. The region's vast pig-iron industry was centered in such places as **Napier** in Lewis County, **Cumberland Furnace** in Dickson County, Nunnelly in Hickman County, and Erin in Houston County. Erin still has the remains of iron works at its northern city limits. Rich timber resources existed in Wayne County, with activity focused on the county seat of Waynesboro. Today the pace of mining and lumbering has slowed, and the western rim is, by and large, an economically depressed area. The towns remain small and mostly disconnected from major transportation corridors. To find the history of the western rim, the traveler must be willing to get off the interstate and drive on two-lane state and federal highways.

Route A: The Natchez Trace Parkway

The Natchez Trace Parkway, which stretches from the Mississippi River at Natchez to the Cumberland River south of Nashville, encompasses two different types of historic landscapes. The earlier landscape is the wagon-rutted overland road that developed first as a Native-American trail and then as a boatman's trail before the federal government designated it as a mail route in 1800. Most of the extant historic trail dates from the period of 1801 to 1803, when federal troops cleared the trace of obstructions and built new bridges. Travel on the historic trace declined steadily after 1815.

The Natchez Trace that can be traveled today, however, is a modern parkway landscape. The idea of a "parkway"—defined by historian

Phoebe Cutler as "a self-contained and uninterrupted stretch of road, landscaped and appointed with recreational facilities"—became popular with landscape architects and planners in the 1920s (51). Established by Congress in 1938, the Natchez Trace Parkway combined the desire for recreational roadways with the concurrent wish of Americans to be in closer touch with their frontier past. It also provided work for crews from the Civilian Conservation Corps and the Works Progress Administration (see sidebar entitled "The New Deal Built Environment," Landscape 9, chapter 4). To meet its dual goals, the parkway includes not only picnic areas and scenic vistas but also historic sites and landscapes that document earlier agrarian landscapes of the Western Highland Rim. It is a historical monument to landscape architecture and park planning during the New Deal era.

To reach the Natchez Trace from St. Joseph on U.S. Highway 43, follow Tennessee Road 227 west as it winds its way into the Western Highland Rim through old iron industry villages, such as Iron City, to its junction with Tennessee Highway 13. To the west, Tennessee 13 meets the parkway south of the old railroad town of Collinwood in Wayne County.

The parkway traverses one hundred miles of the Western Highland Rim from its junction with Tennessee 13 to its end near the village of Pasquo on Tennessee Highway 100. At mile marker 375 is the Old Trace Drive, a two-and-a-half-mile route that allows the visitor to actually drive on the historic trace and see the surrounding rural landscape as overland travelers did one hundred years ago. Six miles farther north is the old mining town of **Napier,** with a historic area interpreting the eroded landscape and environmental damage caused by open-pit iron mining. The pig-iron works at Napier first went into operation in about 1834, and by 1876 the blast furnaces were producing 207 tons of pig iron every month. During the 1890s, the company reorganized and improved its works with new machinery. A company town developed for the approximately 160 men who worked either in the mines or at the furnaces. By 1912, a hundred tons of pig iron were produced daily, and the mines operated until 1923. Another mile to the north, as the parkway crosses the Buffalo River, was the early iron furnace known as **Steele's Iron Works,** first established as the Buffalo Iron Works by John Jones, Davis Steele, and Thomas Steele in 1822.

At mile marker 385 is the parkway exit for the Meriwether Lewis National Monument, where a monument, interpretive area, and pioneer cemetery mark the place where Meriwether Lewis, famed western explorer and leader of the Lewis and Clark Expedition, met his death in 1809. Historians ever since have debated whether Lewis was murdered as he spent the night at Grinder's Stand or whether he committed suicide. This parkway exit also provides access to the town of Hohenwald, seven miles west on Tennessee Highway 20. German and Swiss immigrants established the town in the late nineteenth century, and in the last decade, residents have added Swiss architectural details to several downtown businesses and public buildings. The historic **Hohenwald Depot** was built by the Southern Iron Company in 1885.

Five miles north of the Meriwether Lewis site, at mile marker 390, is Gordonsburg, where several phosphate mines once operated at the turn of the century. East of the parkway on U.S. Highway 412 is a two-story stone **commissary building** that served the miners as a company store. Seven miles later, at mile marker 397, an original section of the Natchez Trace marks a portion of the boundary of the Chickasaw lands ceded to the United States in 1805 and 1816. The tobacco barn exhibit, at mile marker 401, details a part of the agricultural landscape created by farmers in the twentieth century. This exhibit allows the tourist a rare opportunity to walk inside a tobacco barn and see how farmers cure the crop.

At mile marker 407, the trace crosses the Duck River at the site of the **Gordon House** (1818), a rare extant tollhouse associated with early-nineteenth-century overland travel. This hall-and-parlor plan was built of brick, reflecting the owner's wealth and prestige on the Tennessee frontier. John Gordon had been a Nashville postmaster and a trusted aide to Gen. Andrew Jackson before he established his Duck River plantation at Gordon's Ferry in 1812.

From the Gordon House, the parkway continues on a hilly and curvy path along the edge of the Western Highland Rim through western Maury and Williamson Counties. Historic places, rather than individual houses or buildings, are preserved on this section of the parkway. Perhaps the most interesting is at mile marker 426, a part of the trace cleared by the U.S. Army in 1801–2. The soldiers' camp was a mile away at nearby Garrison Creek, where there is a modern dairy farm (private, no access) on the west side of the road. The parkway's present terminus is its junction with Tennessee Highway 96 west of Franklin near mile marker 438.

Gordon House, Natchez Trace Parkway. The house of John Gordon has been preserved, but little else remains to show what his prosperous farm and ferry stop looked like. It is possible only to imagine where slave quarters, farm outbuildings, and animal sheds once stood.

Route B: The Iron Industry of the Western Highland Rim

Our exploration of the Middle Tennessee landscape began with the nineteenth-century iron industry in Stewart County between the Tennessee and Cumberland Rivers. It will end by returning to Tennessee's "iron range" country. The region's industrial history began two hundred years ago in Dickson County. The ruins of one important early site— the **Laurel Furnace** owned by Richard Napier—is preserved within the Montgomery Bell State Park. This lovely and historic park is about thirty miles northwest of the Tennessee Highway 96 exit from the Natchez Trace. Travelers may take Tennessee 96 west to its junction with U.S. Highway 70 near Burns and then turn east and follow the signs on U.S. 70 to the park entrance. Developed by the Civilian Conservation Corps, the Public Works Administration, and the National Park Service as a national recreation demonstration area during the mid-1930s, the park is named for Montgomery Bell, a pioneer industrialist in Tennessee.

Born in Pennsylvania in 1769, Bell initially came to Tennessee in 1802 to operate the rudimentary Cumberland Iron Works at Cumberland Furnace. Two years later, he purchased the works outright and began developing his own iron empire. By 1850, for example, 332 slaves worked at his furnaces and forges throughout the western rim.

As the most productive iron master in the state, Bell operated two major iron works. At the **Narrows of the Harpeth State Historic Area,** about ten miles east of Montgomery Bell State Park on U.S. Highway 70, Bell owned the **Patterson Forge.** Here he designed an ingenious tunnel, built by slave labor between 1818 and 1820, that took advantage of the natural topography to create water power for his heavy machinery. Described by historian Robert E. Dalton as "the oldest extant tunnel in the United States" (7), the 290-foot tunnel through a limestone ridge separating a sharp bend in the Harpeth River is still a spectacular site today. It has been designated as a National Historic Landmark. Around the tunnel developed an early industrial company town—called Bellville—for the slaves who operated the iron works. Bell's own home once stood on a ridge above the tunnel.

His second major venture stood fourteen miles north of Dickson, on Tennessee Highway 48, at the town of **Cumberland Furnace.** To reach this spot, drive west to Dickson on U.S. Highway 70 and then take Tennessee 48 north. In 1795 Gen. James Robertson established Cumberland Iron Works as the first furnace in Middle Tennessee. Robertson, however, lacked the capital and ability to develop the mines, and by 1801 he had joined with Adam Shepard and John Jones in a new partnership to manage the mines. Success still was not forthcoming. A year later, the partners hired Montgomery Bell to operate the works, and in 1804 Bell purchased the iron works and the surrounding 640 acres for $16,000. Bell quickly turned Cumberland Furnace into a money-maker. By 1809 he was supplying federal troops with cannon balls, small-arms munitions, and gunpowder. In 1825 Bell sold Cumberland Furnace and the surrounding acres to Anthony W. Van Leer and others for $50,000.

Cumberland Furnace still has dwellings, commercial buildings, a railroad depot and industrial ruins associated with its long involvement with the mining and processing of iron. Overlooking the town is the **Drouillard House** (1868–70), the Italianate summer residence of Florence Kirkman Drouillard, who inherited the Van Leer estate in 1863, and James Pierre Drouillard, who operated the mines in the post–Civil War decades (private, no access). This family increased production dramatically during the Reconstruction years, and by 1873 the works produced an excess of three thousand tons of iron per year. A few years later, the Drouillards built **St. James Episcopal Church** (1879) for the community. On the church grounds is the **Cumberland Furnace Schoolhouse** (circa 1879) that served both as a school and as a Masonic lodge.

South of Cumberland Furnace on Tennessee Highway 48 is Charlotte, the seat of government for Dickson County. The **Dickson County Courthouse** (1833), designed by local builder Philip Murray, is the oldest remaining courthouse in Tennessee still in public use. Although named county seat in 1804, Charlotte has relatively few properties from that era because a tornado in 1830 almost totally destroyed the town. Surrounding the courthouse is a historic **town square** that reflects Charlotte's height of prosperity and influence during the 1830s and 1840s, before the railroad came to Dickson County. The most impressive building is the three-story **Leech General Merchandise Store** (1849), built by merchant Leonard L. Leech. The **Moore Law Office** is a small one-story vernacular version of a Greek Revival temple–style building (private, no access).

Route C: The Nashville and Northwestern Railroad

Seven miles south of Charlotte on Tennessee 48, Dickson was established during the construction of the Nashville and Northwestern Railroad in the Civil War. Initially this railroad was designed to connect Nashville to the Mississippi River at Hickman, Kentucky. By 1860 much of the railroad west of the Tennessee River was finished. But during the Civil War, Federal officials decided to ignore the original construction plans and used troops and contraband slaves to complete the line from Nashville to the Tennessee River at New Johnsonville (see sidebar entitled "Contrabands in the Civil War," Landscape 20, chapter 7). Today U.S. Highway 70 closely follows the railroad line.

Dickson first took the name of Sneedville in honor of one of the railroad's engineers, but in 1868 town leaders changed the name to Dickson. Four years later, the railroad line became part of the evolving Nashville, Chattanooga, and St. Louis Railroad. Dickson's town plan reflects its dependence on the railroad. The tracks bisect the downtown commercial district into two parts. The primary business district (North Main Street) is a one-way street until it meets the tracks; then once Main Street crosses the tracks, it enters a secondary business area and becomes a two-way route. Unlike most railroad towns in Tennessee, Dickson retains both a historic depot and a railroad hotel known as the **Halbrook Hotel** (1912). The railroad hotel was more than a place to stay for traveling salesmen; it also spoke of the community's sense of permanency and prospects for the future. In an economic sense, a small town without a railroad hotel appeared hopeless and inconsequential. The Halbrook Hotel was also the birthplace of Tennessee governor Frank G. Clement, who was a colorful and controversial three-term governor during the 1950s and 1960s. When Clement first became governor in 1953, according to historian Robert E. Corlew, he introduced "a new era in Tennessee politics," tackling such issues as constitutional reform, reapportionment, racial integration, and mental health reform (572). The old Dickson Post Office (1936), designed by Louis A. Simon and built by the Works Progress Administration, has a federally sponsored mural titled *People of the Soil,* by Edwin Boyd Johnson. It is the only extant Depression era mural by a Tennessee artist left in the state.

Tennessee City, about seven miles west on U.S. Highway 70, was the next town created by the builders of the Nashville and Northwestern. Today it is merely a tiny rural village, but one hundred years ago an ambitious social experiment began here. In 1894, at a time of economic depression throughout the country, utopian socialist Julius Wayland acquired two adjoining five-hundred-acre tracts at Tennessee City where he planned to build a model "cooperative commonwealth." That summer, the first colonists arrived, and they were none too impressed with the town—"a sorry collection of primitive Southern homes on a railroad track"—or with the thick forests and rocky land that they were expected to farm (Egerton, *Visions,* 67).

Wayland named his colony "Ruskin" in honor of the English social thinker and art critic John Ruskin. To comply with Tennessee law, he structured the colony as the "Ruskin Co-operative Association," which made each colonist a stockholder in all activities of the colony, save the publishing house, which Wayland reserved for himself. The colony began well: by the fall of 1894, one hundred residents lived there and over seventy-five thousand people subscribed to the newspaper, *The Coming Nation.* Within a year, however, petty disputes and internal disagreements turned the cooperative commonwealth into a nightmare for Wayland. In the summer of 1895, he left Ruskin for good.

Wayland's departure damaged but did not destroy the colony. Searching for better land than what was available at Tennessee City, the colonists in the winter of 1895–96 began to move to a new site about five miles north on Yellow Creek. This place can be reached by taking

Commonwealth House, Ruskin, Dickson County. This monument to the nineteenth-century search for communal utopias is slowly decaying.

the unpaved Gilliam Hollow Road north of Tennessee City for almost three miles to its junction with Tennessee 46 (locally known as Yellow Creek Road). Turn north on Tennessee 46 for another two miles to the Ruskin Colony site. By 1897 the move was complete, and at the center of the new village stood the three-story **Commonwealth House,** which housed the print shop, dining room, library, bookstore, nursery, lodging quarters for guests or new arrivals, and a large auditorium (private, no access).

"The first part of 1897," according to historian John Egerton, "may have been the colony's zenith" (*Visions,* 75). It owned eighteen hundred acres, possessed a successful printing business, and had over 250 residents living and working in 75 buildings. Hopes were high. Mrs. Isabel Herring remarked, "We are content with our seemingly hard lot, isolated from civilization, because we hope to establish a precedent or live out a principle which we hope to see followed by others with less hardships because of our sacrifice and the example of our combined efforts" (Fogarty, 159). But, outside of the decaying Commonwealth House and nearby **Ruskin Cave,** little is left from that beehive of activity and that reservoir of hope and good will. From 1897 to 1899, the colony tore itself apart over internal disputes concerning the role of women, education, religion, "free love," and power sharing within the cooperative. Ruskin Colony failed even though it was financially solvent.

In the summer of 1899, a court-appointed receiver sold cooperative assets at public auction, and Ruskin was no more. Since then, Ruskin has served as the grounds for a succession of institutions: a private school, a college, a resort, and a campground.

Returning to U.S. Highway 70 from Ruskin, the next railroad stop on the historic Nashville and Northwestern corridor is McEwen, about seven miles west of Tennessee City. St. Patrick's Catholic Church and School is where an "Irish Picnic" has been celebrated every spring since 1854.

Both the railroad and highway impacted the look of Waverly, the Humphries County seat that is located nine miles west of McEwen on U.S. Highway 70. East of the town square is an exquisite Art Moderne Greyhound Bus Station, now home to the local chamber of commerce. This bright blue enamel building emphasizes the importance of the old Memphis-to-Bristol Highway to small towns along U.S. 70. Towns such as McEwen, Waverly, and Camden were once on the main east-west highway in Tennessee, and their colorful gas stations, bus depots, cafes, and motels were once busy places—until the construction of Interstate

Nolan House, Waverly.

40 sixteen miles to the south totally bypassed a fifty-mile section of U.S. 70 between McEwen and Huntingdon. Today only a few commercial artifacts, including the Greyhound station in Waverly or the Spanish Revival Wismer Motel in Camden, mark their once busy thoroughfares.

On a hill north of Waverly, overlooking the railroad tracks and town square, is the **Nolan House** (private, open), home of James N. Nolan, a second lieutenant in the Federal army during the Civil War, who had first come to Waverly as part of a contingent that protected the railroad line at nearby Fort Hill. After the war, Nolan returned to Waverly, and in 1870 he built a stylish gable-front-and-wing Victorian house overlooking the tracks. In Waverly he operated a mercantile business, a railroad hotel, and a marble yard. The former mayor of Waverly, Nolan became state controller in 1881.

Protecting the Nashville and Northwestern Railroad and controlling the Tennessee River were basic strategic objectives for the Federal army throughout the Civil War. Eight miles west of Waverly on U.S. Highway 70 is the **New Johnsonville State Historic Area,** where Union troops built fortifications to protect the port and railroad bridge crossing the Tennessee River at this point. On November 4, 1864, these fortifications proved useless when Confederate troops, under the command of Gen. Nathan Bedford Forrest, launched a surprise artillery attack from the west bank of the Tennessee River. The Confederates almost totally destroyed the Union supply depot: more than thirty barges, gunboats, and transport were sunk or demolished. Railroad warehouses and other supplies were also destroyed, and federal officials estimated the damage at eight million dollars. The Confederate position can be visited by crossing the Tennessee River on U.S. Highway 70 and following the signs at Camden for the next eight miles on Tennessee 191 to Pilot Knob, the location of the Nathan Bedford Forrest State Historic Area. This location provides a great view of the Tennessee River. The park is also home to the Tennessee River Folklife Interpretive Center.

After crossing the Tennessee River, along its east bank travelers will see the giant New Johnsonville coal-fired steam plant of the Tennessee Valley Authority (public, open for tours). After two years of debate, Congress approved this steam-generated electrical power plant in 1949. It represents TVA's change in direction during the postwar years as it focused its programs and appropriations on the production of electrical power by means other than hydroelectric dams, in spite of the environmental costs of strip-mining Appalachian coalfields or the cost overruns of nuclear power plants.

CHAPTER SEVEN

The West Tennessee Plateau

Millions of years ago, the plateau counties of West Tennessee were part of a shallow sea, full of marine life. Coon Creek in McNairy County is one of many places that are famous fossil-hunting grounds. When the sea receded, it left a low plateau, ranging roughly from two hundred to three hundred feet above sea level, as a quite distinct geologic region. Native Americans chose to orient their lives and villages along the rivers that crisscrossed this plateau for hundreds of years. **Pinson Mounds** on a branch of the Forked Deer River, the **Shiloh Indian Mounds Site** on the Tennessee River, and the **Obion Mounds** near the headwaters of the Obion River document much earlier settlement patterns of Woodland and Mississippian cultures. Later, the Chickasaw Indians settled near the Mississippi River at present-day Memphis and along the Hatchie River in the southern end of the region.

After the Jackson Purchase in 1819, however, the vernacular landscape of Native Americans was replaced by the political landscape of the surveyor; then, in rapid succession came new designs on the land from town planners and railroad engineers. A vast landscape of commercial agriculture—from cotton to tobacco to fruits—dominated the countryside and left a lasting mark on the culture and economy of West Tennessee.

As crops grew in abundance and value, railroad companies expanded lines into the region to cart away the largesse of the countryside. Railroad construction in the years after the Civil War shaped the settlement landscape of the western plateau in entirely new ways, as it largely ignored the rivers and tributaries. Where railroad lines crossed, as they did at Jackson or Humboldt, regional trade centers evolved and prospered. Only three county seats in this region lack a railroad connection, and of those Savannah has long been a port on the Tennessee River. The engineered landscape of the railroad has shaped the settlement patterns of West Tennessee more than any other single force.

Landscape 20: Rails West: Railroads in West Tennessee

Almost any map of West Tennessee will show the close relationship between nineteenth-century railroad corridors, town settlement, and modern highway routes. The expansion of the railroads in the late nineteenth and early twentieth centuries created a matrix of towns and cities where most West Tennesseans live and work. This landscape of roadbeds, rails, wooden ties, steel bridges, signals, and railroad buildings imposed order and regularity on the western plateau, representing the intrusion of modern industrialism in what had been a rural and sparsely populated region.

Three rail lines were particularly important. The Memphis and Charleston ran east from Memphis and left the state in McNairy County as it headed for Corinth, Mississippi. Today U.S. Highway 72 follows the general eastern route of the railroad in Shelby County, while through Fayette, Hardeman, and McNairy Counties, Tennessee Highway 57 parallels the railroad. The Southern Railway operated this line for most of the twentieth century, and now the tracks belong to the giant railroad corporation Norfolk Southern.

The major north-south railroad corridor belonged to the Illinois Central. The main line entered the state at South Fulton in Obion County, then ran south to the important rail junction of Jackson, where it picked up the route of the Mobile and Ohio and continued south, leaving Tennessee near the tiny town of Guys in McNairy County. U.S. Highway 45 now parallels this route, and U.S. 45E follows the main line from South Fulton to Jackson while U.S. 45W follows a Mobile and Ohio branch from Jackson to Humboldt and on to Kenton at the border between Obion and Gibson Counties.

Running diagonally across the plateau were the tracks of the Louisville and Nashville Railroad. The main line entered in Henry County and headed southwest toward Memphis. U.S. Highways 70 and 79 now follow this corridor closely. The line of the Nashville, Chattanooga, and St. Louis, a company controlled by the L&N after 1880, crossed the Tennessee River at New Johnsonville and connected with L&N tracks at McKenzie in Carroll County before it continued to the northwest. Today U.S. 70A parallels these historic tracks. CSX Corporation operates the trains along both lines.

The highways along these railroads encounter the region's primary towns and cities. Interestingly, Interstate 40 follows no historic rail route as it cuts westward from the Tennessee River to Memphis. Jackson is the only city it touches, and perhaps this lack of connection to the towns and cities of West Tennessee is why this stretch of the interstate strikes so many travelers as empty and boring.

Route A: Memphis and Charleston Railroad

The historic route of the Memphis and Charleston parallels the combined U.S. Highway 72 and Tennessee 57 to the southeastern corner of Shelby County and then continues to follow Tennessee 57 to Pocahontas near the border between Hardeman and McNairy County. The route has many adjacent historic sites: Civil War fortifications; historic farms and plantations; small rural towns with Victorian commercial facades facing the tracks; and other buildings and places that document how the railroad impacted the landscape of the Wolf River country.

Chartered in 1846, the Memphis and Charleston Railroad was an ambitious attempt to link the cotton markets of the Mississippi River to those of the Atlantic Ocean. Building eastward from Memphis, the company utilized the earlier roadbed and Wolf River right-of-way of the LaGrange and Memphis Railroad, one of the first railroad projects in Tennessee. The LaGrange line began in 1835 as an effort to link Memphis to the rich cotton areas of Fayette County; a branch line was even planned from Moscow to Somerville (now paralleled by Tennessee 76). Lack of funding combined with the depression of 1837 to keep the railroad from completing its lines as quickly as promised. Under the forceful leadership of Eastin Morris of LaGrange, however, the roadbed was largely completed, and the first ten miles of rail from Memphis had been built by 1841. The following year, the first train cars were in service, but only for six miles from Memphis. The company failed later that year, and no construction occurred until the new Memphis and Charleston

Common Railroad Town Plans

Railroad corporations, and their allied or associated land companies, designed two basic types of railroad towns in Tennessee during the nineteenth century. The first, and most common, was the symmetrical plan. On one side of the tracks stood commercial establishments in a long line facing the depot. In this plan, little depth existed in the downtown business district, but there was plenty of width as each business could be surveyed by waiting drummers (traveling salesmen) and passengers on the train (see photo of the town of Henry in the Landscape 20 section of chapter 7). Behind the commercial district was a residential neighborhood. Often, little to nothing stood on the opposite side of the tracks in the smallest railroad towns. In the larger trade centers and county seats, cotton gins, warehouses, small factories, and mills faced the commercial district as the tracks ran through the middle of town. This arrangement of spaces helps to explain the old phrase "they live on the other side of the tracks." Here, on the industrial side of the corridor, stood the homes of the poorest members of the working class.

The symmetrical design appealed to the antebellum railroad engineer because it helped to separate railroad and industrial business from commercial and residential areas. It also reserved high-priced real estate—valuable because it was adjacent to the tracks—for commercial and industrial concerns. The farther away from the tracks the cheaper were land prices, so residential buyers invariably chose lots at least two blocks away from the railroad corridor.

The great majority of towns created by the railroads from 1850 to 1880 reflected the symmetrical plan. But later in the century, the "T-plan" began to become part of the Tennessee landscape. A T-town has a distinctive look. The tracks form the top of the T, with the passenger depot standing at the head of the town. Radiating from the depot was a single, primary commercial street, often named Main Street, that formed the stem of the T. Railroad engineers liked the T-plan because the top of the T separated the business of the railroad, and associated industrial activities, from everyday commerce. It further eliminated unnecessary—and dangerous—crossings over the track. The stem of the T placed the most expensive real estate closest to the depot, while lots that were farther away from the passenger station could be sold more cheaply. Consequently, the first blocks of a typical Main Street were home to commercial businesses and professional offices. The latter blocks would be residential lots and the location of churches, schools, and civic buildings.

company acquired its roadbed and right-of-way, beginning construction again in the 1850s.

James C. "Lean Jimmy" Jones, the former Whig governor of Tennessee, was the president of the Memphis and Charleston. He aggressively built up the company's capital by selling stock with somewhat extravagant promises throughout the Deep South. To New Orleans investors, for example, he emphasized how rail construction would increase cotton cultivation and the Mississippi River trade throughout Mississippi and Tennessee. At Charleston, on the other hand, he claimed that the railroad would divert commercial traffic from West Tennessee and northern Mississippi to the Atlantic Ocean. In 1857 the railroad was completed to the Nashville and Chattanooga Railroad at Stevenson, Alabama. By arranging for the use of the Nashville and Chattanooga tracks to Chattanooga, the line gave West Tennesseans access to the Atlantic trade via Georgia railroads that junctioned there.

One of the first Memphis and Charleston towns was Germantown, on U.S. Highway 72. It is now a booming city, full of new shopping centers, suburban developments, and civic and corporate offices, and it is a good place to begin exploring the Memphis and Charleston corridor. Although no trace remains today, a unique social experiment in Tennessee history began at Germantown in 1825. Nashoba, established by the radical visionary Frances Wright, was a two-thousand-acre utopian community based on the idea of racial equality. Having searched for a middle ground between slavery and abolition, Wright perceived her experiment at Nashoba as a fair solution. Once purchased from their owners, slaves would work at the colony to pay back the purchase price. While there, whites would live with and educate the blacks to prepare them for freedom. But once the debt was repaid, the African Americans were not free to go just anywhere. Wright planned for them to be resegregated in territory outside the United States.

Her plan, no matter how well meaning, was doomed to failure because of its inherent contradictions, of the difficulty of clearing and cultivating the land, and of the lack of money to keep the colony intact during the first difficult years. In 1827, after a long stay at Robert Owen's utopian community at New Harmony, Indiana, Wright decided to make Nashoba an interracial colony where all property was held in common, religion was discouraged, and open marriages were encouraged. The idea of "free love" brought heated criticism to Nashoba, and the criticism came on top of negative publicity about the colony's finances and the harsh treatment of slaves. But Wright was away from Nashoba for most of the year. When she returned in 1828, she attempted vainly to save it; after finding no easy solution, she left in July, leaving African Americans to keep the colony operating.

Wright returned one last time in 1829. She found thirty-one residents, and, despite their hard work, Wright was now convinced that because of their color blacks could never achieve equality in America. She loaded the families on a boat and took the thirteen adults and eighteen children to Haiti during the winter of 1830. Her early experiment in socialism and racial equality was abandoned, this time for good.

Nashoba, however, remained in family hands. Frances Wright died in 1852, and three years later her husband passed away, leaving all family property in America to a daughter, Sylva D'Arusmont. In 1855 D'Arusmont came to America to inspect her inheritance and decided to keep Nashoba because now the tracks of the new Memphis and Charleston passed right by the plantation. She contracted with Eugene de Lagutery (whose name was later anglicized to Guthrie) to move to Nashoba, manage the estate, and build a tourist resort for railroad passengers. By 1860 the hotel had opened, but different legal and personal entanglements eventually closed the property. In 1878 Sylva D'Arusmont Guthrie, now the widow of Eugene Guthrie, returned to Memphis to reclaim the family property. She received 1,422 acres from the courts and lived at the old colony manor house for the rest of her life. When she died in 1903, her children sold Nashoba.

There remains one last interesting footnote to the colony's history. During World War I, anti-German hysteria reached such a pitch that the leaders in Germantown chose to change the town name to Nashoba. In other words, in an era of Jim Crow segregation and terrible racism, local leaders preferred to be associated with a radical experiment in racial equality than to be associated with the Kaiser's armies. The name switch only lasted as long as the war, but it is a reminder of the historic link between the radical experiment of Frances Wright and the present railroad town along U.S. Highway 72.

Another link to Germantown's railroad past is the town depot (now offices for the chamber of commerce). Germantown's name comes from the large number of German immigrants who settled here in the mid-1830s. At about the same time, construction began on the LaGrange and Memphis Railroad, and the village became a trade center for surrounding cotton farms and plantations.

During the Civil War, the Union army occupied the village in order to protect the rail line. From 1862 to 1865, the Memphis and Charleston Railroad was a reliable supply source for the Union army; in fact, it was the best supply route for Chattanooga. The **Germantown Redoubt,** apparently built by the Forty-ninth Illinois Infantry in the summer of 1863, is an extremely well-preserved remnant of those days of occupation. It is located along the railroad tracks at Fort Germantown Park on Honey Tree Drive.

Travelers today along U.S. Highway 72 might find it difficult to envision the nineteenth-century landscape along the old Memphis and Charleston Railroad. Certainly modern development and multilane highways in Germantown obscure its historic reliance on the railroad. But about eight miles east, just after the split of U.S. 72 from Tennessee 57, lies Collierville, another historic railroad town that retains the look and feel of a rural trade center of one hundred years ago. The town is located along the original surveyed route of the LaGrange and Memphis Railroad, but since that company never reached so far east, Collierville first developed more in reaction to the construction of the Memphis and Charleston Railroad between 1852 and 1853.

Collierville was a small hamlet at the time of the Civil War, but due to its strategic rail location, over two thousand Federal troops occupied the town in 1863 and 1864. A series of skirmishes between Federal and Confederate troops also took place in the fall and winter of 1863. The conflicts and long occupation destroyed most of the original village so it was largely redesigned and relocated in the months immediately after the war.

In 1866 Dr. Virginius Leake and Harrison Irby purchased ninety acres for an adjacent but new Collierville townsite. Oddly, they designed the new Collierville in the older town square tradition, with the railroad tracks making up the southern quarter of the square. Collierville is one of the few railroad towns in Tennessee to have such a unique appearance.

The town square of Collierville developed a busy Victorian trade center, but most of the historic buildings remaining today date from the years of 1895 to 1930 when the business district was rebuilt in brick. Most of the historic homes in the surrounding residential neighborhoods date from those same years. This period coincided with the Southern Railway's acquisition and development of the old Memphis-to-Charleston line. A good example of the railroad's impact is its historic depot (1902), which originally stood in LaGrange until it was moved to Collierville in 1944. Then, during the American bicentennial,

Southern Railway Depot, Collierville. This building was the LaGrange Depot before it was moved to Collierville.

the depot was moved again to the south side of the square to serve as offices for the chamber of commerce.

Another important contributor to local growth was W. W. McGinnis, who by 1898 controlled local lumber and construction businesses, as well as a coal company. He was also active in local government, and into the next century he developed a countywide reputation as a builder and architect. In the **Collierville historic district**, examples of his work include the Methodist Church on North Rowlett, his own Tudor cottage at 120 Walnut, and a Craftsman bungalow at 126 Walnut. In its historic dwellings, churches, cemeteries, town square, railroad depot, shotgun dwellings, and 1930s high school, Collierville reflects the varied components of the small-town environment of rural West Tennessee.

East of Collierville, railroad tracks lie just to the north of the highway, providing a visible link between the agriculture of the Wolf River Valley and the national marketplace. About fourteen miles east of Collierville are two historic family farms (both private, no access). Facing both sides of the highway, the Teague Farm (1870) has produced cotton, corn, and livestock through the decades. In 1882 Rebecca Ann Wade established the nearby Burch Farm; its fields also have yielded cotton, as well as soybeans. Women as active operators of the family farms were not uncommon. At one time or another over two-thirds of the historic family farms identified in the Tennessee Century Farm program were owned by women, whether they had inherited the property from their parents or had taken control after the deaths of their husbands.

The old railroad town of Moscow (platted in 1853) is seventeen miles west of Collierville. It is possible to turn on either Memphis or Charleston Streets to reach the historic commercial area by the tracks. The town was a "register station," which meant that all trains stopped here to register and receive orders from the stationmaster. The old depot is gone, but the brief strip of commercial businesses facing the tracks—including the Moscow Mercantile Company—reflects the town's earlier days as a rural trade center. Few historic buildings exist because a fire in November 1937 decimated the downtown, claiming forty-two buildings.

Nine miles east of Moscow on Tennessee 57 is LaGrange, the original planned terminus of the LaGrange and Memphis Railroad. One of the region's oldest towns, LaGrange dates from at least 1824, and the first town plat came the following year. The town soon prospered as a cotton-processing and rural trade center. LaGrange in 1828 had "sixty houses, 240 inhabitants, four stores, two taverns, and a dozen mechanics." Incorporated in 1831, the town "bids fair to be one of the most interesting villages in that section of the state" (Morris, 189).

Situated on a low bluff overlooking the Wolf River, LaGrange stood at the site of an early Indian trading post called "Cluster of Pines." Trade with Chickasaw and Choctaw Indians occurred regularly. In 1835 a visitor observed: "A great many Indians come daily to LaGrange, dressed in their native costumes, and make a novel and good appear-

Woodlawn Mansion, LaGrange. Impressive manor houses still convey the meaning of the plantation landscape in Fayette County.

ance, but which is of course of so common everyday occurrence as to have lost all interest to the inhabitants" (Morton, 100).

Due to its early date of settlement and successful start, LaGrange has many more antebellum-period buildings than other railroad towns along Tennessee Highway 57. The **Immanuel Episcopal Church** (1843) is a handsome, red brick vernacular building that once served local plantation owners, who also lived in Greek Revival splendor at such homes as **Tiara** (1845), built by Frank Cossitt, the double-portico **Hancock Hall** (1857), and the Greek Revival–influenced **Lucy Holcombe Pickens House** (all private, no access). Lucy Holcombe Pickens was born in LaGrange and spent her childhood there. After her family moved to Texas, she married Francis W. Pickens, who served as ambassador to Russia and was then elected Confederate governor of South Carolina. During the Civil War, Lucy became just as famous as her husband since her likeness appeared on at least three series of Confederate currency.

On the eastern outskirts of town is a historical marker for **Woodlawn,** another striking Greek Revival mansion (private, no access). The original house, built by War of 1812 veteran Maj. Charles Michie, dates from 1828, and the colossal Greek Revival portico probably dates to the late 1840s or early 1850s. Local tradition states that Michie added the portico to the east entrance rather than to the original entrance because he did not want his mansion to face the new Memphis and Charleston Railroad directly. The railroad brought both Confederate and Federal troops to the doorsteps of Woodlawn during the Civil War. Union troops occupied the town from June 1862 to the end of the war, and Gen. William T. Sherman used the house as a temporary headquarters.

The Ames Plantation lies just to the east of Woodlawn along the Fayette and Hardeman county line between LaGrange and Grand Junction (private, limited access). In 1847 John Jones built the Greek Revival–style "Cedar Grove," now the manor house at Ames Plantation. He was a very wealthy planter who also owned town lots in LaGrange. After his death in 1879, the estate passed into the hands of several different family members. In 1901 the manor house and four hundred acres were sold to Hobart C. Ames, a millionaire Boston industrialist, who was an avid quail hunter and sportsman. Ames wanted this land—which he soon enhanced to twenty-five thousand acres by leasing and purchasing surrounding lands—for a world-class home for the national field trials for bird dogs. The national championships continue to be held here every February. A WPA writer described the hunt at Ames Plantation:

> Quail are hunted either afoot or on horseback. The dogs forage the sedge grass or fence rows until they sight a covey. One dog usually leads, and the others follow, running or walking at fixed intervals. When a covey is found, the dogs point or set it until the hunters arrive. On instruction from their masters, the well-trained dogs move in and cause the quail to rise. A few sportsmen shoot from horseback, but the majority dismount and tie their horses as soon as the dogs have found the birds. The dogs bring the dead and wounded birds to the hunters, and then begin hunting the ones that have escaped into thickets and brush. (492)

Ames also used his plantation for agricultural experiments. For instance, in 1912 he hired John Watson Bruce Sr. of Scotland to help supervise the breeding of black Angus cattle. Like many earlier southern planters, Ames arranged for his vast acreage to be sharecropped, and in the early twentieth century, some two hundred families lived on the plantation.

After his death in 1945, and that of his wife, Julia Colony Ames, in 1950, the estate became part of the Hobart Ames Foundation, which made much of the plantation available to the University of Tennessee's College of Agriculture. Experimental farming has taken place here ever since as a branch of the West Tennessee Experiment Station at Jackson.

The Ames History Project is now documenting the plantation's past and has already identified the location of houses, cotton gins, gristmills, cemeteries, and old roads. The property has the potential of becoming the best documented planter landscape in the state.

Grand Junction, at the Hardeman County border, was where the Memphis and Charleston met the New Orleans, Jackson, and Great Northern, a railroad that ran south to New Orleans and north through Jackson to the Ohio River. It later became an important junction between the Illinois Central and the Southern Railroads, and an abandoned depot is a reminder of the town's past significance in the southern railroad network. A faded sign on the depot notes that from Grand Junction, it is 394.17 miles to New Orleans and 517.83 miles to Chicago. During the Civil War, Grand Junction was home to one of the war's first and largest "contraband" camps. But the exact location of the camps has never been marked.

Tennessee Highway 57 continues to follow the old Memphis and Charleston route in southern Hardeman County for another eighteen miles through the small towns of Saulsbury and Middleton. Saulsbury was the birthplace of Wycliffe Rose, an important early-twentieth-century social reformer who worked with the General Education Board and the Rockefeller Sanitary Commission. Middleton is still a sizeable country village, with a historic two-story Masonic lodge that faces the tracks. At Pocahontas, the highway crosses Hatchie River and begins to veer through the southwestern corner of McNairy County to Corinth, Mississippi.

Route B: Illinois Central Railroad

U.S. 45 follows the path of the Illinois Central Railroad through the middle of West Tennessee. After entering Tennessee at South Fulton, U.S. Highway 45 branches into western and eastern routes. U.S. 45E follows the 1870s branch line from East Cairo, Kentucky, to Jackson. Then, in Jackson, the two parts of U.S. 45 merge together and follow the older route of the Mobile and Ohio branch for thirty-six miles to Selmer and then for another nineteen miles into Corinth, Mississippi.

The Illinois Central was the first federal land-grant railroad. Established in 1850, the line initially was strictly regional, connecting the river port of Cairo to Chicago and other Illinois points. Buoyed by profits from the Civil War, however, the company began an aggressive expansion campaign. In 1872 the railroad provided money to extend a

Contrabands in the Civil War

As the Civil War moved into Tennessee in 1862, thousands of slaves fled farms and plantations to seek safety from the advancing Union troops. Before the Emancipation Proclamation took effect in 1863, these escaped slaves were called "contrabands," as in contrabands of war, since they were not considered free persons under the law.

Some of the first contraband camps were established in Tennessee. According to the memoirs of U. S. Grant, "an army" of contrabands, "of all ages and both sexes" moved toward his army base at Grand Junction, Tennessee, following the Battle of Shiloh in early 1862. Under orders to protect escaped slaves, Grant believed that his advance into Mississippi would be impossible unless the mass of slaves was organized and put to work. Certainly the devastation of the West Tennessee campaign meant that much needed to be done. "The plantations were all deserted," Grant remembered. "The cotton and corn were ripe: men, women, and children above ten years of age could be employed in saving these crops."

That fall, the general placed Chaplain John Eaton in charge of the relief effort. "We together," Grant later recalled, "fixed the prices to be paid for the Negro labor, whether rendered to the government or to individuals. The cotton was to be picked from abandoned plantations, the laborers to receive the stipulated price . . . from the quartermaster, he shipping the cotton north to be sold for the benefit of the government. Citizens remaining on their plantations were allowed the privilege of having their crops saved by freedmen on the same terms. At once the freedmen became self-sustaining. The money was not paid to them directly, but was expended judiciously and for their benefit."

Grant later concluded that his Grand Junction program was "probably, where the first idea of a 'Freedman's Bureau' took its origin." (Long, 221). But the contraband camps offered only a limited definition of freedom. Basic safety was secured, but due to the low priority these camps received from the quartermaster, food, shelter, and medical services were inadequate. The escaped slaves had no direct control over their wages, and when they worked for the army they did so only in menial tasks, including chopping wood, unloading boats and trains, or doing laundry. Sometimes, commanding officers and soldiers could be as abusive as their former owners and overseers. But for thousands, life in the camps, no matter the difficulties, was preferable to slavery. African Americans eagerly came to contraband camps to begin the process of rebuilding their lives as free men and women.

Contraband camps existed throughout the state. Besides the major camp at Grand Junction, other large camps were at President's Island in Memphis and near the railroad yards in Nashville and Chattanooga. Indeed, Nashville contrabands helped to build Fort Negley and finished construction of the Nashville and Northwestern Railroad from the capital city to the Tennessee River.

line from Jackson, Tennessee, to East Cairo, Kentucky, replacing an earlier Mobile and Ohio Railroad connection. This new line allowed the Illinois Central to link its traffic to the combined New Orleans, Jackson and Great Northern and the Mississippi Central, which formed a direct route to New Orleans by way of Jackson, Tennessee. Jackson immediately became a very important rail junction, linking Deep South cotton to Midwest industries.

Hard times in wake of the Panic of 1873 sent both the northern and southern links to Jackson into receivership, and in 1874 the Illinois Central took control of both lines. On July 29, 1881, the railroad switched its southern line to standard rail gauge, allowing for more interchange of traffic. Then, eight years later, the Illinois Central opened a modern steel bridge across the Ohio River, connecting Cairo, Illinois, to East Cairo, Kentucky. The rail lines of West Tennessee became part of the rapidly expanding and profitable midwestern transportation network.

Eleven miles south of South Fulton on U.S. 45E is the railroad town of Martin, which was incorporated in 1874. An interesting way to reach the historic downtown is to ignore the U.S. 45E bypass and take Tennessee 372 (the old federal highway route). An old Illinois Central caboose stands near the post office to document the railroad's influence in local history, but a brief glance at the town plan is enough to see that Martin exemplifies the late antebellum railroad town.

The town was named for William Martin, owner of Weakley County's largest tobacco plantation. As the Nashville and Northwestern Railroad expanded toward Hickman, Kentucky, during the 1850s, the amount of tobacco Martin could guarantee for shipping convinced the railroad to run through his property. After the Civil War, his sons Marshall and George Martin donated even more family land for the construction of the Illinois Central's Jackson-to-East Cairo extension. The brothers gave the railroad a large right-of-way and donated land that later served as a city park. In exchange, they could design the town and sell lots to interested speculators. As town founders, the Martin brothers also built a sawmill and gristmill while opening a dry goods store.

In 1876 civil engineer Thomas I. Little laid out the town, placing commercial and residential areas on both sides of the tracks because George Martin owned land on the east side while his brothers Marshall and William owned land on the west side. This plan is still evident today. Between the tracks and the western commercial strip is the Weldon Memorial Library, which was once the town's Colonial Revival post office (1917), designed by James A. Wetmore. The old Martin family home, **Marshalldale,** sits at the corner of South McCombs Street and Ryan Avenue. This dwelling is an eclectic mix of Italianate (circa 1875) and Queen Anne (circa 1895) architecture that includes the family's original frame residence, which was built in about 1850.

On the northwestern outskirts of Martin, along Tennessee Highway 22, is the campus of the University of Tennessee at Martin. Established in 1927, the school was once known as the University of Tennessee Junior College with a curriculum geared to agriculture and home economics and supervised by the Agricultural Extension Department of the University of Tennessee. During the 1930s, the campus contained 285 acres, and most of the land was devoted to the college farm and an experiment station. The Knoxville firm of Barber and McMurry adopted a Colonial Revival theme for its initial buildings, including the Brehm Agricultural Hall and the Sociology Building. This architectural style has been maintained in later buildings like the 1959 Administration Building and in other classrooms built during the college's boom in the 1960s and early 1970s when Martin grew to accommodate over five thousand students.

Also in Weakley County are two other Illinois Central towns, Sharon and Greenfield. Located about eight miles south of Martin on U.S. 45E, Sharon was first named Dedham, for its early New England settlers, but in 1901 the town name was changed, according to one account, because a railroad conductor passing remarked that the beauty of the countryside recalled the "Rose of Sharon," a common flower in this area at that time. Sharon's T-town plan is different from other Illinois Central towns in Tennessee (see sidebar entitled "Common Railroad Town Plans" in this section).

Established in 1873, Greenfield is about six miles south of Sharon. It has the more common symmetrical plan of Illinois Central towns. Unfortunately, these buildings retain little of their historic appearance at present because huge sheets of metal cover several facades, turning their once playful facades into large, bland advertising signs to catch the attention of travelers along U.S. Highway 45E. The railroad once operated a "fast express" service here, for the shipping of strawberries to midwestern markets.

Continuing south on U.S. 45E, travelers cross into Gibson County and soon reach Bradford, which was incorporated in 1913. The WPA writer who visited here during the 1930s observed that Bradford was "a typical southern village. On hot summer afternoons farmers and

Davy Crockett Memorial Cabin, Rutherford. In the 1920s, long before Crockett was rediscovered by television and the movies, local citizens moved the remaining logs of Crockett's last West Tennessee home to the high school grounds of Rutherford where they reconstructed this memorial to the famous frontiersman.

easy-going townsmen play checkers in front of the stores along Main Street, sometimes interrupting the games with political discussions that rival the temperature in intensity" (*WPA Guide,* 413). But, as more and more Tennesseans have left small towns for new opportunities elsewhere, places like Bradford have lost much of the community life common two or three generations ago.

Many who left the small villages of Gibson County did so for new opportunities in Milan and Humboldt during the middle decades of the twentieth century. About twelve miles south of Bradford on U.S. 45E, Milan is at the junction of the Illinois Central and the Memphis branch of the Louisville and Nashville. An Italian Renaissance passenger depot once stood at the actual junction point in downtown Milan, and its demolition in 1993 greatly weakened the physical link between the community and its railroad past. Also downtown, to the southeast of the depot, is the **Milan Post Office,** a mid-1910s Renaissance Revival design by Oscar Wenderoth. The presence of the railroads made Milan an important shipping point for fruits and vegetables; it also brought shirt, raincoat, and cigar factories by the 1930s.

Moreover, the rail junction lured new governmental projects. On the northeastern outskirts, along the Louisville and Nashville line and

U.S. Highway 79, is the Milan Experiment Station of the University of Tennessee Extension Service. To the east and southeast, along the Illinois Central line and U.S. Highway 45E, is the huge tract of land for the Milan arsenal, established in January 1942. Eleven thousand people worked on its 28,500 acres throughout World War II. Activities focused at two separate locations: the Wolf-Creek Ordnance plant operated by the Proctor and Gamble Corporation and the Milan Ordnance depot, operated by the federal government. In 1943 these separate operations were reorganized as the Milan Ordnance Center, which operated an ammonium nitrate plant as well as producing ammunition. Parts of the complex are still in business, but are closed to the public.

About eight miles south of Milan on U.S. 45E is Medina, a tiny, forgotten place now, but in the middle decades of this century, it was a busy rail transfer point, home to the shipping sheds of the Illinois Central. Five miles farther, the two branches of U.S. 45 meet again and enter Jackson.

Located in the valley of the Forked Deer River, Jackson was settled soon after the Jackson Purchase of 1819 opened the rich land of what is now Madison County for settlement. As a midpoint between Memphis and the Tennessee River, the town was a regional commercial crossroads, with its own mills, cotton gins, and general merchandise businesses.

When railroads pushed into West Tennessee during the 1850s, the town emerged as a key rail hub, and business increased dramatically.

The first railroads arrived in 1857. The Mississippi Central and Tennessee Railroad extended its line from Grand Junction through Hickory Valley and Bolivar (generally following the present route of Tennessee Highway 18). At the same time, the Mobile and Ohio built north from Corinth, Mississippi, and generally paralleled the current route of U.S. Highway 45 to Jackson. By the following year, the Mobile and Ohio line extended far north into Kentucky, where it made a ferry connection with the Illinois Central. Three years later, Jackson stood in the middle of a crucial north-south rail corridor that ran from Chicago to Mobile and New Orleans.

No important Civil War battles occurred in Jackson or Madison County, but to control the railroads, Union troops occupied Jackson in early 1862. After the Civil War, the railroads rebuilt their damaged facilities and continued to expand to the west and north. During the 1870s, the Illinois Central took control of the lines and began to turn Jackson into one of its most important division points. New roundhouses and shops were opened in 1880 south of West Sycamore Street, and Jackson emerged as a key regional cotton market. In 1920 the company opened a new **Illinois Central office building** at 245 West Sycamore (private, limited access). It is the only significant historic Illinois Central building still standing in downtown Jackson because new highway construction and urban renewal during the 1960s and 1970s replaced many of the old railroad structures. The Casey Jones House museum at the interstate is a historic dwelling where the famous Illinois Central engineer once lived, but it has been moved from its original neighborhood.

As it became a nineteenth-century transportation hub, Jackson developed the neighborhoods, central business district, and cultural institutions typical of a medium-sized railroad city. Traveling eastward on Main Street, the traveler crosses the tracks and immediately enters the **East Main Street historic district,** a neighborhood that developed in reaction to the railroad's arrival in the late 1850s. The vernacular Greek Revival of the **Hurt House** (1857) represents the first homes of the neighborhood. Most houses date from 1875 to 1900, including the Italianate **Duke-McKinnie House** (1877) and the colorful and eclectic Queen Anne **Polk House** (1895). The neighborhood's sidewalks have been restored, and signs that date the homes can be found in most yards (all private, no access).

During Reconstruction, newly freed slaves joined with the few free blacks in Madison County to create large African-American neighborhoods in Jackson. One historic residential area is around **Lane College.** From East Main Street, the visitor may turn west to Royal Street, which roughly parallels the route of the Illinois Central through the town, and turn north to Lane Avenue. At Lane Avenue, turn east once again and cross the tracks to the college. Lane College dates from 1882, the decade when the Illinois Central improved its southern lines. Thousands of African Americans in Jackson found work with the railroad as porters and as skilled and unskilled laborers; some were able to save enough money to provide their children with a better future at Lane College. The college was one of the first in the country to be established by blacks for blacks. Bishop Isaac Lane of the Colored Methodist Episcopal Church worked throughout the 1870s to establish a church college to emphasize Christian teaching and learning. The initial four acres were purchased in 1880, and two years later the college had its first building and was known as the C.M.E. High School. The name was soon changed to Lane Institute, in honor of Bishop Lane, and by 1887 the school had graduated its first class of five students.

Ten years later, Lane Institute opened its college department, and in 1903 Rev. James A. Bray became the first African-American president. To replace earlier buildings lost to fire, Bray directed the construction of a new Administration Building—now called **Bray Hall**—in 1905. Its Classical Revival architecture, designed by Jackson architect Reuben A. Heavner, featured a commanding portico of four Corinthian columns and established the architectural theme for the rest of the campus buildings constructed in the early twentieth century, such as **Saunders Hall** (1908) and **Daniels Library** (1923). These buildings were erected during the presidency of James F. Lane, son of the school's founder, who invigorated and expanded the curriculum and public service activities. For instance, the West Tennessee Farmers Conference, an extension service program for African-American farmers and businessmen, met at the college from 1909 to 1955.

From Lane College, the city square may be reached by returning to Royal Street and traveling south. The eight-story classicism of the Great Southern Hotel is a reminder of the grand old hotels once common in most southern railroad cities. The **Madison County Courthouse** is an Art Deco design by Marr and Holman, built with Public Works Administration funds in 1936–37. From the square, about two miles south on U.S. 45 south is **Bemis,** a model mill village of the early 1900s that stands on the main line of the Illinois Central. Here is the region's most compelling artifact of how railroads, capitalists, and laborers took southern cotton and made a new industrial future.

According to the architectural historian John Linn Hopkins, Bemis "is a place with few peers as an industrial community, representing the attempts of two generations of industrialists, town planners and social designers to seek solutions to the deep problems of housing the working class in America" (National Register nomination). The town dates from 1900; it was designed for Jackson Fiber Company, a subsidiary of the Bemis Brothers Bag Company (which is still one of the nation's largest packaging companies). The company decided to built a massive plant in the heart of the West Tennessee cotton region on three hundred acres of donated land from the county. Here at Bemis, the company could purchase raw cotton directly from area farmers, gin it on site, and then spin and weave it into the finished cotton bags, which could be shipped via Jackson's excellent rail connections to almost any point in the country. By 1905 two huge mill factories had opened, processing some 8.5 million pounds of cotton annually with 56,728 ring spindles on line along with 1,570 automatic looms. Bemis had its own water supply, heating system, and powerful generators for electrical power.

While building the massive plant, the company's founder, Judson M. Bemis, and his son Albert F. Bemis also wanted to establish a model mill village, embracing the latest in Garden City planning principles. The younger Bemis, a recent graduate of the Massachusetts Institute of Technology, worked with company architects and engineers to create a compelling and diverse village landscape of stores, churches, segregated schools, public laundry and bath house, library, recreational facilities (even a six-hole golf course), and many houses. Much of this village landscape remains intact today. Indeed, the town's domestic architecture ranges from cottages with Arts-and-Crafts porches to Colonial Revival homes and bungalow cottages to the entire gamut of southern vernacular worker housing, including shotguns, pyramid cottages, and saddlebag-like duplexes.

After World War I, the Bemis Bag Company began ambitious plans to upgrade its facilities, a move that coincided with a similar investment plan by the Illinois Central. The company hired architects Arthur A. Shurtleff and Andrew H. Hepburn to design a new residential neighborhood of Colonial Revival cottages and new community improvements, including an auditorium that could seat one thousand people. By 1940 about three thousand people lived in Bemis. After World War II, the mill stayed in business, but its prominence began slowly to recede. In 1965 the company began to sell its houses to the employees on a seniority basis. Eleven years later, the city of Jackson annexed Bemis, and in 1980 the company sold the old cotton mill plant.

Bemis embodied in a physical sense the Progressive Era concept of welfare capitalism, of corporations serving as a paternalistic godfather for a community of laborers. With its elegant streetscapes, spacious homes, abundance of public facilities, medical services, and cash wages, Bemis provided a more conducive environment for worker happiness than many other southern mill towns. Yet, in a place where the company absolutely controlled time and wages, working conditions, and even the appearance of homes and streets, southern laborers found few of the freedoms once taken for granted by their forefathers. The steady work and pay of the new industrial South presented opportunities, but they came at a cost that many rural southerners had no choice but to pay.

From Bemis, U.S. Highway 45 runs southeast along the Illinois Central and Mobile and Ohio route, crossing the Chester County line and entering the county seat of Henderson, which is seventeen miles south of Jackson. Henderson too prospered initially as a railroad town, and a group of two-story brick buildings face the tracks at the western end of town. From these beginnings as a symmetrically planned town, however, Henderson developed in a quite different manner in the early twentieth century. Main Street runs perpendicular to the tracks, and the town's primary businesses and financial institutions are on Main. Also on Main Street is the **Chester County Courthouse** (1913), a Classical Revival brick building with a four-column Doric portico. A few blocks to the east is Freed-Hardeman University, a Church of Christ private college that began in 1869 as Henderson Male and Female Institute. The name changed several times in the early twentieth century until Freed-Hardeman, in honor of former college administrators A. G. Freed and N. B. Hardeman, was chosen in 1919. Historic buildings include the Romanesque-style Milan-Sitka Building and the neoclassicism of Paul Gray Hall and Old Main Administration Building.

The last county seat on the old Mobile and Ohio line is the town of Selmer, the McNairy County seat of government. It is nineteen miles south of Henderson on U.S. Highway 45. The rural village of Purdy was the first county seat, but when the Mobile and Ohio built through the

county in the late 1850s, the company routed the trains through nearby Bethel Springs and bypassed Purdy. In 1890 voters moved the county seat to Selmer because of its commercial prominence as a railroad town. Purdy soon declined into little more than a crossroads village.

Selmer is the only town on this route that retains its historic Mobile and Ohio passenger station (private, limited access). Designed by the Nashville firm of Marr and Holman, the McNairy County Courthouse at Selmer reflects the PWA Modern styling of the 1930s, even though it was built in 1948.

Route C: The Louisville and Nashville Railroad

The Louisville and Nashville Railroad was chartered in 1850 and developed over the next fifteen years as a major Mid-South system. By the end of the Civil War, the railroad had established a western link to Memphis, but owned only the first forty-six miles, stopping at the Tennessee-Kentucky border. The remainder of the route was divided between the short Memphis, Clarksville, and Louisville Railroad, which ran from the state line to Paris, and the much longer Memphis and Ohio Railroad, which operated from Paris to Memphis.

In 1867 the Louisville and Nashville leased the Memphis and Ohio branch, and purchased total control five years later. The next year, the railroad leased the route of the Memphis, Clarksville, and Louisville. Thus, even before the end of Reconstruction, the Louisville and

Nashville controlled West Tennessee's primary east-west link. The best way of exploring the impact of the L&N on West Tennessee is to drive U.S. Highway 79 from Paris to Humboldt.

During the postwar years, the competing Nashville, Chattanooga, and St. Louis Railroad also expanded its operations in West Tennessee. A related branch line, the Nashville and Northwestern, had been constructed between Hickman, Kentucky, and McKenzie, in Carroll County, by 1861. The eastern end of the branch line, however, had moved only a few miles west of Nashville. Once the Federal army had occupied Nashville in the spring of 1862, Union commanders quickly completed the route. Using escaped slaves as laborers, the army built the eastern branch to the Tennessee River at New Johnsonville (see sidebar entitled "Contrabands in the Civil War" in this section). After the war, the railroad constructed a bridge across the river and soon completed its tracks to McKenzie. In West Tennessee, U.S. Highway 70 and then Tennessee Highway 22 follow this line from the Tennessee River to McKenzie.

In 1874, the Nashville and Chattanooga Railroad took control of the Nashville and Northwestern, renaming the company the Nashville, Chattanooga, and St. Louis Railroad. The state capital had a secure link to the Georgia lines at Chattanooga, the Tennessee River at New Johnsonville, and the Mississippi River at Hickman, Kentucky. Clearly the company would now be a major competitor of the Louisville and Nashville. To forestall such an event, however, the L&N soon moved to take financial control of its competitor. By the winter of 1880, the NC&St.L still existed in name and operated its own rolling stock and offices, but control over its finances and future development was in the firm grasp of the Louisville and Nashville. Not until 1957 would the L&N finally formally merge with the NC and St.L. Ten years later, the lines became part of the Seaboard System Railroad, and in 1980 it merged into an even larger corporation, CSX Railroad, which continues to maintain the line and rail facilities today.

The first section of the L&N empire in West Tennessee is the Paris-to-Humboldt route on Highway 79. Paris is a railroad town. Established in 1823, the town was the original seat of government for Henry County. Its advantageous location near the Tennessee River amid rich farmland watered by the headwaters of the Obion River allowed frontier settlement to expand rapidly, and by the mid-1830s the town featured two small factories, ten stores, two taverns, three schools and an academy, along with a cotton gin. But Paris remained a relatively small antebellum trade town until the 1850s, when railroad construc-

Henry County Courthouse, Paris.

tion brought new investment and residents. During Reconstruction, the Louisville and Nashville took control of the two railroads that connected at the city, and in 1898 the company established a division point here, complete with machine shops and roundhouses that employed hundreds. Paris flowered as never before and became a classic example of a late Victorian railroad town. A city history published in 1900 bragged that "since about 1892 the city of Paris has experienced a most astonishing degree of expansion and prosperity. Her population has almost doubled in that period, and her general business has increased about fifty per cent. The prospects now are that the next decade will witness a more astonishing degree of progress" (Greene, 10).

Many businesses, public buildings, and dwellings still mark the city's boom of one hundred years ago. The historic town square is dominated by the massive **Henry County Courthouse** (1897), designed by famous Chattanooga architect Reuben H. Hunt in an eclectic blend of Romanesque and Renaissance Revival architecture. An interesting mix of commercial storefronts and public buildings surround the historic courthouse, while the **Paris Post Office** (1918) is a Colonial Revival design by federal architect James Knox Taylor.

One block west of the courthouse is the four-story **Courthouse Annex** (1898), once an opera house for traveling shows and vaudeville. A few steps west are the tracks of the Louisville and Nashville that pass through the heart of town. Since Paris was already an established county seat before the arrival of the railroad, the business district is not oriented to the tracks in a clearly designed manner as is common in most other West Tennessee towns.

To the immediate north is a turn-of-the-century **L&N Combination Depot,** so named because it combined the functions of passenger and freight depots. This building marks the beginning of the L&N yards that continue to the north and can be viewed from the depot. The railroad yards initially included nine major buildings: a cab and tender repair building, a boiler shop, a huge machine shop, a blacksmith shop, planing mill, oil house, dry kiln, engine-and-boiler house, and offices and storerooms. The activities at these buildings influenced local development in two ways. First, according to the railroad's Robert Gates, the yards emphasized "a tangible, pulsating fact that this is an inviting field for capital; that manufacturing may prosper here; and they will draw other enterprises as surely as the magnet attracts the steel" (Greene, 62–63). Second, the works employed about five hundred mechanics, workmen, and managers.

In response to an overwhelming demand for new housing, local builders, contractors, and architects built hundreds of new homes, many in the latest styles then popular in American domestic architecture. The neighborhoods of Paris, consequently, represent an outstanding collection of turn-of-the-century American architecture. The 600 block of North Poplar Street is the heart of the **North Poplar historic neighborhood,** which railroad officials, professionals, and businessmen called home. Here stand four good examples of Classical Revival homes, along with three brick American Four-Square houses. Designed by Brinton B. Davis, the **O. C. Barton House** (1913), at 614 North Poplar, is one of the region's best examples of Renaissance Revival architecture.

Dunlap Street also has an interesting mix of architectural styles, including some of the oldest historic dwellings in the town. With its mansard roof, 207 South Dunlap reflects Second Empire architecture. Thomas W. Crawford originally built the **Porter Mansion** at 407 South Dunlap in 1848. Gov. James D. Porter and his wife acquired the home in 1877 while Porter was serving his two terms as governor of Tennessee. Porter lived here until his death in 1912. The house has served as a historic landmark since the 1930s.

As the town's neighborhoods developed in the late Victorian era so did its public school system. The **Robert E. Lee School** (1893) was first called the Paris Public School and served the city as its elementary school for many years. On Grove Boulevard is the **E. W. Grove-Henry County High School** (1905–6), designed by Chattanooga architect Reuben H. Hunt. Like Hunt's earlier county courthouse, the school building is an eclectic statement of late Victorian architecture, with both classical and Romanesque elements. The school is named for E. W. Grove, a former Paris resident, who in 1905 gave the county an endowment of fifty thousand dollars for the school's maintenance and operation. In 1917 the state's first vocational agriculture course was established at this high school.

Along the next fifty miles of U.S. Highway 79 southwest of Paris are small railroad villages including Henry, Trezevant, Atwood, and Gibson. Trezevant, for example, was named for James Trezevant, the leader of a railroad construction party who built a switch and siding here in 1857. These small rural trade centers are symmetrically designed, with a brief block of commercial buildings facing the tracks, but all lack their historic passenger stations to document the railroad days (see sidebar entitled "Common Railroad Town Plans" in this section). Never very large, these villages perhaps lost the most when

Tennessee's—and the nation's—transportation preferences changed from railroads to automobiles in the mid-twentieth century.

Humboldt, fifty miles southwest of Paris and thirteen miles northwest of Jackson, is the next major L&N town. Its design is a classic expression of the T-plan (see sidebar entitled "Common Railroad Town Plans" in this section). Along the top of the T is the railroad line itself with the old freight depot, standing at the head of the town and representing the railroad's predominance. Along the stem of the T, or Main Street, are public and commercial buildings, including the Classical Revival city hall and the Art Deco Plaza Theater, and then residential neighborhoods and schools.

One of Humboldt's most intact historic neighborhoods is around the Colonial Revival Humboldt Elementary School at the corner of Main and North Seventeenth Street. The one hundred to three hundred blocks of North Seventeenth have significant examples of Queen Anne architecture, especially the **Dodson-Himelright House** (1894) at 119 North Seventeenth (private, no access).

Signs throughout Humboldt remind travelers of the town's importance as a strawberry market. The War Memorial Building is home to the Strawberry Museum; even the water tower overlooking the town

View of Main Street from the old depot location, Humboldt. This look up Main Street shows the distinctive pattern of the T-plan railroad town.

is decorated with a bright red strawberry. For decades, every spring Humboldt has hosted a Strawberry Festival. A 1930s account described the festival as including "vaudeville shows, circus acts, a balloon ascension, fireworks, parades, horse shows, concerts, and a beauty review" that culminated in the crowning of a festival queen (*WPA Guide*, 419). With the encouragement of railroad officials and agricultural reformers, strawberries became a major crop in West Tennessee during the early twentieth century.

From Humboldt, a brief thirteen-mile side trip south on U.S. Highway 45 to Jackson locates other significant railroad properties. The Nashville, Chattanooga, and St. Louis Railroad operated a West Tennessee branch line, originally called the Tennessee Midland, which at Jackson connected to the Illinois Central and the Mobile and Ohio. On South Royal Street in downtown Jackson are two buildings associated with the NC&St.L. At 590 South Royal is the **NC&St.L passenger station** (1907), which is now being converted into a railroad museum. Across the street, at 545 South Royal, is the **Murphy Hotel** (1911), a classic example of a railroad hotel. Its intact interior and period furnishings still convey the atmosphere of an early-twentieth-century hotel that welcomed traveling salesmen and wearied travelers for an overnight stay (private, limited access).

Murphy Hotel, Jackson. One of the few operating railroad hotels in the state.

The second section of the L&N empire in West Tennessee involves its subsidiary, the Nashville, Chattanooga, and St. Louis Railroad. U.S. Highway 70 follows a portion of the NC&St.L route, entering West Tennessee near the town of Camden, the seat of government for Benton County. Lumber was the county's major industry from 1875 to the 1950s; peanuts were an important crop during the early 1900s. Another agricultural product from Benton County found throughout Tennessee stores is sorghum. The WPA writer, who visited Camden in the 1930s, noted that "in September and October sorghum mills are busy along the roadsides. Smoke curls from wood clearings, and the lights from furnaces and lanterns glow far into the fall nights" (458). Sorghum is made from slow-cooked sugarcane, and the best is made by the older horse-powered mills that can still be found throughout Tennessee.

In Camden, a modern courthouse (1974), designed by Nashville architects Hart, Freeland, and Roberts, dominates the town square, surrounded by a block of substantial turn-of-the-century storefronts on the south side with a mix of two-story and one-story businesses along the other three sides. At the northwest corner is the **Camden Post Office,** designed in a Colonial Revival style by Louis A. Simon and constructed by the Works Progress Administration in 1936. This building is a well-preserved example of the standardized Colonial Revival design that Simon prepared for small towns throughout the South. It even includes its original federally sponsored mural, *Mail Delivery to Tranquility—The*

U.S. Post Office, Camden. Similarly designed Colonial Revival post offices, built by the WPA, are found in many West Tennessee county seats.

First Post Office in Benton County, painted by John H. Fyfe in 1938. These Colonial Revival post offices are a recurring element in the West Tennessee landscape. Lexington, for example has one, also with an intact mural, titled *Progress of Power,* by Grace Greenwood. The traditional designs of these post offices differ markedly from the PWA Modern style found in many other public buildings from that decade, including the courthouses in Dresden, Union City, Ripley, and Jackson. Taken as a group, the small-town post offices make an interesting conservative architectural statement about the presence of the New Deal and the federal government in West Tennessee.

Bruceton, about seven miles west of Camden on U.S. 70, remains closely tied to railroad activity. Here in 1922 the Nashville, Chattanooga, and St. Louis Railroad established machine shops and a switching yard. A railroad spur also connects the shops directly north to Paris. An old railroad bunkhouse stands at the head of town, near the tracks, as well as a more recent unadorned freight office and train sheds. Typical of railroad towns developed during the early twentieth century, Bruceton has a T-plan design (see sidebar entitled "Common Railroad Town Plans" in this section).

Huntingdon, which is eleven miles west of Bruceton on U.S. Highway 70, is the seat of government for Carroll County. Settled during the early 1820s, Huntingdon's town square has been the center of local business and professional activity for over 170 years. The gleaming

Classical Revival style of the Carroll County Courthouse, designed by
Hart, Freeland, and Roberts of Nashville, dates from 1931, but many of
the surrounding buildings are much earlier and represent good examples
of Victorian storefront facades. Especially notable is the cast-iron facade
of the former Bank of Huntingdon, built in 1887, which stands just east
on Main Street. During the late 1920s and early 1930s, Huntingdon's
square experienced significant changes due to the opening of the Memphis-to-Bristol Highway, which passed through the center of town. Not
only was a new courthouse built, but also older buildings were demolished to make way for a new gas station, the Court Theater, and a new
Colonial Revival post office (1931) designed by James A. Wetmore.

The commercial district of Huntingdon focuses on the courthouse
square, but residential neighborhoods are aligned to the railroad tracks.
Browning Avenue has an interesting mix of nineteenth- and early-twentieth-century domestic architecture. The street includes a Colonial Revival high school from the 1920s, a large Queen Anne house, an exquisite triple-gable Gothic Revival home, and a Tudor Revival dwelling from
the middle decades of this century (all private, no access). Several impressive dwellings from eighty to one hundred years ago also stand on
West Paris Avenue, north of the tracks and town square.

To continue following the NC&St.L line, travelers will need to
switch to Tennessee Highway 22 at Huntingdon and continue ten miles

NC&St.L Depot, McKenzie. Due to the importance of railroads in local history, this exquisite Italian Renaissance–style station deserves historic preservation.

north to McKenzie, a classic West Tennessee railroad town at the original junction of the NC&St.L and the Memphis branch of the Louisville and Nashville. The town was originally platted and organized in 1865. Like Collierville in Shelby County, which was platted at about that same time, McKenzie has a town square design with the depot and tracks one block away. Its depot is an excellent small-town example of Renaissance Revival architecture, and it has an L shape that allowed plenty of room on the platform for passengers and freight.

The business district has additional notable buildings, including the Art Deco Park Theater, the Classical Revival Bank of McKenzie, now home to the local library, and the Colonial Revival post office (1935), which has been converted into the Governor Gordon Browning Museum. Born in 1889 in Carroll County, Browning served three terms as governor and is most important for his fight, together with Estes Kefauver, to break the power of the mighty Memphis-based Crump machine over the Democratic party and state government. McKenzie is also home to Bethel College, initially founded in 1842 by the Cumberland Presbyterian Church. Its historic buildings include Campbell Hall (1924), designed by A. F. Lindsey. The Gothic Revival **First Cumberland Presbyterian Church** (1888, 1920), designed by the McDonald Brothers of Louisville, is the town's best statement of Victorian architecture.

The original Nashville and Northwestern branch of the NC&St.L
Railroad continued northwest from McKenzie to the Kentucky line, and
today Tennessee Highway 22 parallels the tracks. Six miles away is
Gleason, in Weakley County, where the tracks pass through the center
of town with the school on one side and a strip of businesses on the
other. Established in 1871, the town is known for its local clay industry. The WPA post office (1940) is interesting because Louis A. Simon's
modernistic design is quite different from the Colonial Revival style he
used for the designs of other small-town post offices in the region.

Another six miles northwest on Tennessee 22 is Dresden, the seat
of government of Weakley County. Immediately south of town, at the
junction of old Tennessee 22 and 9, is **Oakland,** a decaying Second Empire farmhouse that initially belonged to planter Alfred Gardner. Dresden
was incorporated in 1827 and evolved as a railroad trading center for
tobacco, sweet potatoes, lumber, and vegetables from neighboring
farms. Dominating the town square is the Weakley County Courthouse
(1949), an interesting late blend of classicism and Art Deco design by
the Nashville firm of Marr and Holman. In sharp contrast is the Colonial Revival post office (1936), designed by Louis A. Simon and built by

the Works Progress Administration. Gracing its interior is a federally sponsored mural about county history, titled *Retrospection* (1938), by Minetta Good.

Dresden enjoyed its greatest success from 1870 to 1920, a prosperity mirrored in several fine houses south of the courthouse. At 151 South Cedar, for example, is an eye-catching Queen Anne house (private, no access). At 321 Linden Street is **Cary Lawn** (1923), an Italian Renaissance home built as a summer residence for Rhea and Charlie Ewing Cary; it has most recently served as the Dresden residence of Ned Ray McWherter, governor of Tennessee from 1987 to 1995 (private, no access).

Landscape 21: The West Tennessee Countryside

For centuries, agriculture has dominated the way people have used the land of West Tennessee. The first farmers were Native Americans, who grew corn and other vegetable crops in the region's fertile river bottomland. After the Jackson Purchase of 1819 came white slave owners and settlers who carved out a vast landscape for agriculture by clearing tens of thousands of acres for their cotton, corn, and livestock. Cotton was king on the region's plantations. Between 1840 and 1860, cotton production tripled in West Tennessee, and by 1880 the region produced 84 percent of the state's crop.

The post–Civil War landscape differed from that of the antebellum period as emancipation and the breakup of several large plantations created hordes of new West Tennessee farmers. Fayette County in 1860, for example, had 942 farms; ten years later the county had 2,796 farms. As credit tightened in the late nineteenth century, however, many farmers found themselves slipping into tenancy and becoming sharecroppers, tied by law and tradition to the dictates of large landowners.

Tenants and sharecroppers usually had no choice but to produce cash crops, such as cotton and tobacco. At the same time, however, more independent West Tennessee farmers began to experiment with new crops, and, by the early twentieth century, the region had its pockets of extremely creative and diversified agriculture. Certainly the cotton belt of eastern Shelby, Haywood, Hardeman, Madison, and Fayette Counties concentrated on single-crop agriculture while northwestern counties, such as Henry and Weakley, still specialized in tobacco. But Gibson County became a leading fruit market, especially for strawberries. Other farmers turned to wheat and small grains, and almost every farm entered the livestock business.

Today cotton remains important to West Tennessee agriculture, but it shares the rural landscape with soybeans, sorghum, sweet potatoes, fruit, milo, corn, grains, and livestock. This diverse farming landscape can be experienced on almost any highway in the region, but the best routes begin from the junction of U.S. Highways 64 and 70 at Bartlett in Shelby County. To the east the traveler may take U.S. 64 from Bartlett to Somerville and on to Bolivar. To the northeast, the traveler may take U.S. Highway 70 from Bartlett to Brownsville then to Jackson. Two worthwhile side trips are Tennessee 76 from Brownsville to Moscow and Tennessee Highway 77 from Trenton to Milan.

Route A: The Tennessee Cotton Belt

Tennessee has its own "Cotton Belt": eastern Shelby, Fayette, and Hardeman Counties, together with the adjacent county of Haywood and western Madison County. There are two routes travelers might like to take to view Tennessee's Cotton Belt; both may begin at Bartlett in Shelby County. The first is U.S. Highway 64 for about fifty-one miles from Bartlett to Bolivar. The second is a sixty-nine-mile route on U.S. Highway 70 from Bartlett to Jackson. Here, as late as World War II, cotton cultivation dominated the landscape, and, as of 1941, African-American residents made up about 70 percent of the population in Fayette and Haywood Counties and almost 40 percent in Hardeman and Madison Counties. Many places, farms, and towns remain to record the region's history.

From Bartlett, U.S. Highway 64 winds its way eastward along an old Chickasaw Indian trail into the center of the Tennessee Cotton Belt. The recent expansion of the road to four lanes from Bartlett to Somerville, however, artificially detaches the visitor from the rural landscape and may eventually turn the small towns along the route into bedroom suburbs of the Memphis metropolitan area.

Somerville, the seat of government of Fayette County, stands at the crossroads of U.S. Highway 64 and Tennessee 76, the two roads that serve, respectively, as the east-west and north-south transportation corridors of the Tennessee Cotton Belt. For decades, the town was known as "the heart of the plantation area of West Tennessee" (*WPA Guide,* 492). Despite many changes over the past generation, Somerville re-

Walker-Crawford House, Williston. A perfect example of the central-hall house, built in 1850.

tains the look and feel of a Deep South town. The town square, along with many dwellings along South Main, South Somerville, and Marginal Streets, is listed as a National Register historic district. The town's white frame, Greek Revival homes certainly convey the spirit and image of the antebellum planter, and among the more significant are the double Greek Revival porticoes of **Alba Villa** (1846) at 203 Maple, **Gentle Hill** (1852), a classic Greek Revival central-hall cottage at 417 Oak, and the **Higgason House** (1829) at 302 South Main. The local planter elite took services at the Gothic Revival **St. Thomas Episcopal Church** (1858) at the corner of West and Market Streets.

Somerville was incorporated in 1826, and within two years it had four hundred residents and at least one hundred dwellings. During the 1850s, another period of expansion and construction took place, largely in reaction to a railroad spur that connected the town to the main line of the Memphis and Charleston in 1854. Present Tennessee 76 follows the old railroad bed from Somerville to Moscow. Williston, which is midway between Moscow and Somerville, is a very interesting old railroad village that has the late 1890s **Crawford General Store** (now an antique shop), a small-town bank building (now the post office), and the historic **Walker-Crawford Farm.**

By Reconstruction, Somerville's population had climbed to just over two thousand, a number it has generally retained, enabling the town to retain its small-town environment. At the center of the square is **Fayette County Courthouse** (1925), designed in Classical Revival style by Memphis architect George Mahan Jr. Surrounding it are somber storefronts from one hundred years ago. The historic architecture, however, conveys little of the conflict that rocked this town, and all of the Tennessee Cotton Belt, in the late 1950s when African-American farmers, tenants, and sharecroppers tried to exercise their civil rights.

In 1959 the Original Fayette County Civic and Welfare League was devoted to improving the lot of Fayette County's African Americans, who made up about two-thirds of the population. But over the previous seventy years, only a few had been allowed to register and a mere handful allowed to vote. The Civic and Welfare League urged blacks to go to the courthouse and register. And local white landowners soon took strong action to quell the league's quest for equality. As soon as the year's cotton crop was in, for example, some seven hundred tenants who had sought voter registration were kicked off their farms.

To provide shelter for homeless tenants, the Civic and Welfare League established two tent cities on land owned by black farmers south of Somerville. Whites reacted by totally banning any trade with African-American patrons, which forced them to drive to Memphis for food and other necessities. But the black farmers of Fayette County soon discovered that they did not have to fight this battle alone. Groups from across the nation sent truckloads of food, clothing, and tents to Somerville in support of the locked-out and evicted tenants. After months of struggle, the federal government intervened and ended the commercial lock-out. Today a historical marker on Tennessee 76 on the southern outskirts of Somerville records this early battleground of the civil rights movement where Fayette's African-American citizens made a courageous stand against injustice.

Indeed, along the twenty-four miles of U.S. Highway 64 between Somerville and Bolivar, it is possible to imagine that brutal race relations have shaped the landscape as much as any other human action. According to a 1941 count, only two lynchings took place in Fayette and Hardeman counties in the first decades of the twentieth century, but those numbers do not account for the African Americans who were chased out of the county or who just disappeared when the iron code of race relations was somehow breached. Along with physical intimidation

The Pillars, Bolivar. One of the few relics of the plantation era in West Tennessee open to the public.

came the gross inequalities of Jim Crow segregation in public facilities. As much as possible, the ruling class kept African Americans uneducated and in the fields. In these two counties in 1941, over 20 percent of the blacks were illiterate. Among African-American males, 90 percent worked in agriculture, but only one in ten actually owned property.

Despite the violence and terrorism, African Americans felt a kinship to the land and shared a sense of place in the West Tennessee landscape. After all, the fields of cotton that can be seen today along the roadside have been carefully worked and nurtured by generations of black sharecroppers. Blacks established their own communities where cultural traditions and identity could be maintained and enhanced. Here were their homes, where they raised their families and lived out their lives. Here, too, were their unadorned churches, where they worshiped together. The Cotton Belt was as much their land as it was the whites'. Along U.S. 64, and the county seats of Tennessee's Cotton Belt, perhaps the physical setting of the African-American community is not as noticeable as that of the whites. But whenever visitors encounter an African-American cemetery, a decaying Rosenwald school, or an unassuming C.M.E. church, they are experiencing places of great significance to local African-American culture and history.

Bolivar, like Somerville, retains the look and feel of a Deep South

cotton town. Located on the southern bank of the Hatchie River, the town stands about one mile south of a very early settlement known as "Hatchie Town," which served as a Native-American village and later as a fur trade outpost. Its great antebellum prosperity is still evident in many striking buildings and residences that reflect the days of King Cotton.

Bolivar's initial success came as the head of steamboat navigation on the Hatchie River. From here, Hardeman County planters shipped their cotton via the Hatchie to the Mississippi River. Three properties mark the early river days. The **"Little Courthouse"** began as the county's original two-story log courthouse in 1824. Three years later, however, Levi Joy acquired the property, moved it to a new lot, added clapboards, and turned the courthouse into a fine Tennessee Federal residence. **Hazelgrove House** (1825) is the town's oldest residence (private, no access). **The Pillars** (circa 1828, 1837) was the Greek Revival townhouse of John H. Bills; it is now undergoing further restoration under the supervision of the Association for the Preservation of Tennessee Antiquities.

Southern agricultural prosperity during the 1850s certainly was felt in Bolivar, where new businesses and grand residences made their mark. In this decade, the New Orleans, Jackson, and Great Northern Railroad connected Bolivar to Jackson as well as to the Memphis and

Charleston line at Grand Junction. Important buildings from these years, on the south side of town, include **McNeal Place** (1858–61), perhaps the state's best example of an Italianate town house, the Greek Revival **Presbyterian Church** (1853), and the mammoth classical portico of the 1860 home called simply **"The Columns"** (all private, no access). The south side also has the historic **Polk Cemetery** (circa 1845); Ezekiel Polk, the grandfather of President James K. Polk, is buried here.

The north side of Bolivar dates more from the Victorian era. The North Main Street historic district has several architectural gems (all private, no access). One of the earliest dwellings is **Magnolia Manor** (1849) at 418 North Main, which is a late Tennessee Federal house with a Greek Revival portico. Also in the 400 block is the **Presbyterian Manse** (1869), an excellent small-town statement of Gothic Revival. **The Turrett** (1898) at 442 North Main is a Queen Anne cottage, while at 505 North Main stands **Mallory Manor** (1870), which reflects the vernacular "piano-box" style. This vernacular form has two gable wings connected by a long horizontal center section and takes its name from the shape of antebellum pianos.

Connecting the two neighborhoods is the historic town square, dominated by the **Hardeman County Courthouse** (1868), which gracefully combines Greek Revival and Italianate architecture. Around the courthouse are commercial buildings from the 1870s to the 1920s. On the east side stand unpretentious one-story commercial blocks, such as **Danny's Barber Shop** (1886). Four two-story blocks dominate the south side, with the Classical Revival **Bank of Bolivar** representing the most complete architectural statement. Also on the south side is the **Bolivar Post Office,** a Colonial Revival design by Louis A. Simon that was constructed by the Works Progress Administration. At the southwest corner of the square are three brick storefronts linked architecturally by an Italianate cornice. The best local example of Victorian architecture lies on the outskirts of town. The **Western State Hospital** on U.S. Highway 64 contains a historic district of Victorian and early-twentieth-century buildings associated with the development of the state's mental health program for the insane. Opened in 1889, the hospital's Administration Building is an excellent example of late Gothic Revival architecture, designed by the firm of McDonald Brothers.

The next route through the Cotton Belt is between Bartlett and Jackson on U.S. Highway 70. Here the two-land road closely parallels the tracks of the Memphis branch of the Louisville and Nashville as well as the western end of the Memphis-to-Bristol Highway. The highway also serves as the joint route of U.S. 70/79 from Bartlett to Brownsville.

Rural education is an important historical theme visible along or near this highway. Shelby County built more Rosenwald schools for African Americans than any other county in Tennessee. Near the Bartlett junction of U.S. 70/79 and U.S. 64 is the Oak Grove C.M.E. Church, which incorporates the original Rosenwald school for Oak Grove within its church buildings. Just north on the Brunswick Road, about five miles to the northeast on U.S. Highway 70/79, is the former Brunswick Rosenwald school for the many African-American families who lived and worked on the farms and plantations of east Shelby County. It was the two thousandth Rosenwald school built in the South; now it is home to a local Head Start program.

The Julius Rosenwald Fund, established in 1917 by Sears Roebuck magnate Julius Rosenwald, provided seed money for the construction of rural schools for disadvantaged and undereducated black children. The rest of the money had to come from both state sources and the African-American community. Creating an environment where black self-help and agricultural education would flourish was a basic goal for the fund. Another concern focused on improving the domestic environment of rural African-American communities. Rosenwald officials, according to historian Mary Hoffschwelle, believed that "rural blacks would be reformed first by building their Rosenwald school, which would unite them as a community, and then by the building itself, which would inspire hard work and clean living" (113–14). These advantages, however, failed to sway some white school boards that cared little about African-American education. So fund officials emphasized that the new schools would also tie local blacks more closely to the community while vocational education programs improved their labor skills.

Between 1921 and 1927, the Rosenwald Fund published several different sets of standardized plans for its school buildings. Usually painted white and made of clapboard, the buildings were plain and unadorned, except for the Craftsman-like bracketing under the roof eaves. Another common feature was the large unilateral bank of windows on one side of the classroom to allow adequate lighting. Interiors were also specified, providing for adequate blackboards, window shades, and modern desks for teachers and students alike. The fund further provided money for teacher's homes, and the cost was split between the fund and the local African-American community. Many dwellings were similar to

Former Rosenwald School, Brunswick. Recently renovated and covered with siding, this seventy-year-old school building still serves the local rural community as a Head Start center.

worker cottages, while other homes reflected either bungalow or Colonial Revival architecture.

The Rosenwald program's impact on Tennessee public schools was considerable, as is evident from those buildings still in use at Cedar Grove and Brunswick as well as from the abandoned school on U.S. 45W in Dyer. One state official observed that the attractive new schools had encouraged rural African Americans to achieve "better kept homes, better farms, and higher standards of living" (Hoffschwelle, 121). When the program ended in 1932, Tennessee ranked eighth out of fourteen southern states in terms of the number of Rosenwald schools. In all, there were 354 schools (mostly with one or two rooms) and nine teacher dwellings built in Tennessee. Public funding had provided most of the money, but donations by local African Americans had matched almost every dollar from the Rosenwald Fund. As historian Mary Hoffschwelle has observed, "Clearly blacks understood that new school buildings, whether or not they possessed the powers of social regeneration reformers ascribed to them, were essential to their struggle for a better life" (129).

On U.S. Highway 70/79 between Arlington and Stanton, small railroad towns and fields of cotton and soybeans dominate the landscape.

Green Gables, Arlington. A folk interpretation of Eastlake-Queen Anne architecture.

Arlington has such Victorian landmarks as the Gothic-style **Southern Comfort** (1867) and the Eastlake-influenced **Green Gables** (1880) (both private, no access). Arlington's old-fashioned Wilson General Store faces the railroad tracks. About eight miles to the northeast is another country general store, the C. T. McCraw store (1909) at Braden, in Fayette County. McCraw also operated a sawmill and cotton gin at this place, making it a rural crossroads for commerce in the first half of the twentieth century (private, limited access). In the early twentieth century, country merchants like McCraw were more than shopkeepers; they served as local bankers, and by granting—or withholding—credit at their stores, they could make or break local farmers and tenants.

The town of Stanton, eight miles northeast on U.S. Highway 70/79, is another agricultural crossroads. Created in 1856 as the railroad stretched its lines from Memphis eastward, Stanton exhibits classic antebellum symmetrical design since the town's historic business blocks, cotton gins, and sawmills face the tracks (see sidebar entitled "Common Railroad Town Plans," Landscape 20, this chapter). The town's historic Presbyterian Church, an excellent example of nineteenth-century Carpenter Gothic style, also faces the tracks. Located away from the tracks and closer to the highway, is the **Stanton Masonic lodge and school** (1871), which has recently been restored as a community building (pri-

vate, limited access). In the decades before adequate funding for public education, citizens who wanted schools and local fraternal lodges sometimes worked together to erect buildings that would serve both groups. In this case, the school was on the first floor and the secret meeting hall of the Masons was on the second floor.

In 1939–40, the federal Farm Security Administration established the Haywood County Farm Project near Stanton. It was one of thirteen model farm programs across the South intended to encourage farm ownership among rural African Americans. The Haywood County project provided modern small farms of ninety to 110 acres, complete with house, barn, and smokehouse, to thirty-nine families that rented the land with an option to purchase. With their economic independence somewhat secured, several Haywood County families became active in civil rights issues, attempting to create a local NAACP chapter in 1940 and obtaining the right to vote through the Haywood County and Civic Welfare League twenty years later.

These Depression era efforts to better the living conditions for rural African Americans in Haywood County took place near an area of rich land, which was well watered by the Hatchie River, that white settlers had controlled since the antebellum era. Three miles southwest of Stanton on U.S. 70/79 is Oak Hill Farm, established by Thomas Barksdale in 1828. His original farm of 250 acres of cotton, corn, and hay evolved over the next 150 years into a cotton and soybean farm of 444 acres. Adjacent to Stanton is the Tucker Place Farm, which has been in the Tucker family since 1885. The farm began small, with only 47 acres, but the second-generation owners, Charles and Almyra Tucker, turned the place into a showplace of progressive agriculture. Expanding the farm to over 700 acres, Charles used the nearby rail connection at Stanton to good advantage. He specialized in apples, which "were harvested in June and shipped by early refrigerated railroad cars to urban markets" (West, 291). He also raised prized hunting dogs, winning the field championship at Grand Junction in 1902. Today the farm yields more typical West Tennessee crops, such as cotton and soybeans, and the family has restored the property's original Greek Revival mansion, built by George Ware in about 1830 (both private, no access).

Agriculture was the foundation of the local economy and culture at Brownsville, the Haywood County seat, which is located twelve miles northeast of Stanton along U.S. Highway 70/79. One historian has noted that "Brownsville was a plantation county seat and grew not only because it was a court center but also because of the [numbers of] commissaries and mercantile establishments" (*WPA Guide,* 462). On the west side of town, at the **College Hill neighborhood,** a sense of the power and wealth of the local planters and businessmen is still conveyed through their former dwellings and mansions (private, no access). Many homes are identified by name and date, making it easy to take a walking tour of the neighborhood, while the former **Brownsville Female College** building (1852) and later high school has been turned into the Haywood County Museum at 127 North Grand Avenue.

The **Harbert-Hooper House** (1859) at 843 West Main is a grand Greek Revival townhouse that was built by James Bond, one of the state's wealthiest antebellum plantation owners. By 1860 he owned 220 slaves who cultivated hundreds of acres on five plantations. He even purchased his own steamboat to move crops to market. His wealth was ranked at thirty-seven times greater than that of the average farmer in Haywood County. At 727 West Main, the Bond family built **Whitehall** (1868), also in the Greek Revival style. Another important planter was H. C. Anderson, who built the Gothic Revival **Anderson-Austin-Moss House** (1867) at 823 West Main. Many other examples of nineteenth-century domestic architecture exist in this historic district, including the Second Empire style of the **Owen Burgess House**, which was moved here in about 1912, at 629 West Main and the piano-box vernacular form of the **Hall-King-Smith House** (1850) at 625 West College. An

Anderson-Austin-Moss House, Brownsville. Homes of the planter and merchant elite dominate the west side of Brownsville.

interesting twentieth-century home is the Tudor Revival style of the **Rotchschild-Hamer House** (circa 1925) at 514 West College.

East of the town square, on the combined routes of U.S. 70A/79, is another largely nineteenth-century neighborhood that reflects the wealth and prestige of Brownsville's business and professional elite. **Temple Adas Israel** (1882), at the corner of Washington and College Streets, is a rare example of a Jewish synagogue in a rural Tennessee town. Across the street is **Christ Church Episcopal** (circa 1850), which reflects a vernacular interpretation of Gothic Revival architecture clearly influenced by the earlier St. John's Episcopal Church in Maury County.

The beauty and grandeur of Brownsville's downtown, however, meant nothing to African-American residents. To find out more about black life in Haywood County during the mid-twentieth century, historian Richard A. Couto interviewed past and present residents. Ethel McElwee Black was the granddaughter of Samuel A. McElwee, an African-American attorney who had represented Haywood in the state legislature in the late 1800s. She recalled, "I did not like Brownsville. It was more like slavery than anyplace. It was sweet coming up because I didn't know any better. You could mind your own business and stay out of trouble, but there was no business to mind but what they said to do" (Couto, 106). When African Americans attempted to register to vote at the county courthouse in 1960, they faced petty and mean-spirited harassment: someone placed battery acid on the courthouse steps so no one could sit and rest while waiting in the hot summer sun; others threw pepper on the African Americans' clothes from upper floor courthouse windows. Attitudes and behavior changed slowly over the next twenty years. In 1981 the county historian agreed with the Tennessee Historical Commission that a historical marker in honor of Samuel A. McElwee should be erected on the courthouse lawn. But the county judge ordered its immediate removal, and the local historical society expressed no interest in finding another location. The marker ended up across from the entrance to Fisk University, where McElwee had received his diploma in 1883.

From the square at Brownsville, U.S. Highway 70 strikes almost due east toward Jackson. Today the interstate between the two cities carries most traffic so the federal highway becomes a very comfortable route to survey the rural landscape. At regular intervals along the road, there are cotton gins still operating. Indeed, during the fall picking and ginning season, especially at the peak period from mid-September to late November, the large trucks carrying cotton from the fields to the gins lose enough of their loads to make the road shoulders look as if a winter storm has just left a light dusting of snow.

Without the cotton gin, Tennessee never would have evolved into a major cotton market because the cotton fibers that grew here were too short for hand ginning or roller ginning, which could be performed on the long-staple cotton found along the coastal areas of South Carolina and Georgia. To separate short-staple cotton from the seeds, Eli Whitney developed the first cotton gin in 1792. Four years later, H. Ogden Holmes patented the saw gin, which replaced Whitney's original wire teeth with circular saws that improved the machine's efficiency and production. The first gin in West Tennessee was located in Jackson in 1821. Seven years later, both Jackson and Brownsville had gins in business.

In the nineteenth century, most planters operated their own gins, which were usually housed in a two-story building that included the storage bin, saw gin, and lint room. Outside stood a wooden screw press that turned the processed cotton into huge bales ready for shipping. By 1900 larger centrally located gins were in operation, replacing most of the individual gins except on the largest plantations. In 1938 only one plantation gin remained in operation. This decrease mirrors the trend statewide for all types of gins. In 1902, for example, the state had 833 cotton gins, but by 1958 only 297 gins operated in Tennessee.

The type of cotton processed by gins also has changed the ginning industry. Machine-picked cotton, compared to the earlier hand-picked cotton, demands automatic feeders and powerful dryers as well as new machinery for cleaning and extracting. A gin today is much more complex than the rather simple industrial machines of one hundred years ago.

The road between Brownsville and Jackson, with its cotton gins, rural churches, country stores, and farms, meant something different to African Americans who traveled along it or who lived beside the highway. The profits generated at the several cotton gins rarely reached their pockets. Sharecropping arrangements kept tenants strapped for cash, and no matter how hard they worked, few ever managed to purchase their land and take their own crop to the gin. The road to Jackson evokes more brutal aspects of the segregated South. Robert McElwee remembered the night in 1941 that a white mob kidnapped and lynched Elbert Williams for trying to establish a NAACP chapter in Haywood County. "I was lying on the porch and saw about twenty carloads," McElwee told historian Richard Couto. "It scared me pretty bad. They were carrying him [Williams] on down the road to kill him. I didn't know he was with them then, but I knew that later, and when he didn't show up in two days we knew something had happened to him" (147).

As U.S. Highway 70 enters Jackson from the west, it passes by the University of Tennessee's West Tennessee Agricultural Experiment Station. Established during the first two decades of the twentieth century, the basic goal of the agricultural extension program was to improve rural life and farm production. Here at Jackson, the university built a model bungalow residence, along with large barns that could house various farm activities, to demonstrate what a progressive farm landscape should look like. Extension agents taught farmers how to conserve their land, use fertilizer, and experiment with new crops and methods of cultivation. The federal Smith-Lever Act of 1914 permanently established this progressive effort to modernize the agrarian landscape of Tennessee, and regional offices, including the one at Jackson, have largely defined the crops and techniques that shape West Tennessee farmland. In fact, a new, spacious postmodern-style building opened in the late 1980s to continue the station's technical service to local farmers.

Jackson is one of the oldest towns in West Tennessee, but buildings of the twentieth century dominate the local urban landscape. On the west end of Main Street, the original route of U.S. 70 as it went through Jackson, is the Art Moderne architecture of the old Dr. Pepper Bottling Plant, which has recently housed an interior design firm. In the middle of the square is the **Madison County Courthouse** (1936), an excellent blending of understated classicism and Art Deco style, designed by the Nashville firm of Marr and Holman and funded by the Public Works Administration. To the east of the square, at 407 East Main, is the Streamlined Art Moderne of the **Greyhound Bus Station** (1938), designed by the noted modern architect Nolan Van Powell. Its sleek, blue porcelain exterior conveys a feeling of modernity and speed, perfect for a city where transportation, whether by road or rail, was so important.

Jackson's role as a transportation hub was closely related to its role in the regional agricultural economy. Three interesting side trips from here allow the visitor to continue exploring the region's agricultural history.

One of the earlier chapters in that history is documented by **Pinson Mounds State Archaeological Area,** about twelve miles southeast of Jackson on U.S. Highway 45. The park records the culture of the first farmers of West Tennessee, the Native Americans who developed Pinson Mounds during the Middle Woodland period of about A.D. 1 to 500. This National Historic Landmark contains a dozen ceremonial and burial mounds, with the seventy-two-foot-high Sauls Mound being the largest. The Ozier Mound (A.D. 100) is the oldest known ceremonial mound of its type in the country. The park museum has several exhibits

Greyhound Bus Station, Jackson. Streamlined Moderne architecture at its best.

that explain the site's significance and the continuing archaeological study of the mounds.

The Woodland period represented a transition from the lifestyle of hunting and gathering to a more agricultural way of life. Besides gathering nuts and berries, the Indians used such native plants as sunflowers, knotweed, and ragweed. Not long before Pinson was established, they began to cultivate tropical plants, including bottle gourd, squash, and the small-eared flint corn. They increasingly preferred to live nearer river basins, and Pinson Mounds is located on the Forked Deer River.

Another important agricultural center is also located along a West Tennessee river, but its history is much more recent. Twenty-four miles north of Jackson, on U.S. Highway 45W just south of the North Fork of the Forked Deer River, is Trenton, the seat of government for Gibson County. Incorporated in 1847, Trenton grew in size and prominence as the county's agricultural markets expanded, and entrepreneurs built cotton mills, flour mills, and sawmills during the late 1800s. In 1901 the county erected the eclectic **Gibson County Courthouse**, a wonderfully colorful and asymmetrical symbol of the county's aspirations for the new century, designed by W. Chamberlin and Co. of Knoxville.

South of the courthouse is the **Trenton historic district**, an intact residential neighborhood from the 1850s to the 1940s, which encompasses a wide range of domestic architecture, from traditional

Gibson County Courthouse, Trenton. This late example of exuberant Victorian architecture speaks to the agricultural prosperity of Gibson County at the turn of the century.

Greek Revival homes to the modernistic **Harder House** (1932). This marvelous blending of International and Art Moderne architecture at the corner of High and Sixth Streets was built by industrialist Sherman Harder, who operated the Trenton Cotton Mills, Inc. The most famous former resident of this area is novelist Peter Taylor, who was born here and lived his first seven years at **208 High Street** (both homes are private, no access).

East of the square, on Tennessee 77, is the **Freed House,** a striking upfront-and-wing Victorian house built by Julius Freed in 1871 (public). Freed was a Jewish merchant who came to Trenton during the Reconstruction era and became the town's leading capitalist during the late nineteenth and early twentieth centuries. His sons became very active in local politics, and the family, in general, became known for its humanitarian work, donating money for public fountains, parks, and ballfields. In 1976 Dr. Frederick Freed gave the city a unique and valuable collection of Veilleuse-Theieres (night-light teapots). The collection has become the city's symbol and is displayed at city hall.

From Trenton, travelers may continue east on the scenic route of Tennessee 77 for twelve miles to Milan. On the north end of town, along U.S. Highway 70A/79, is the West Tennessee Agricultural Museum, a project of the University of Tennessee's Milan Experiment Station. This new museum traces the historic development of West Tennessee agriculture and contains an excellent collection of farm tools and machinery, especially different types of plows.

Landscape 22: The Western Valley of the Tennessee River

Few roads travel along the lands that adjoin the west side of the Tennessee River. Twentieth-century engineering has turned the northern half of the river, from Paris Landing to Mousetail Landing in Perry County, into a huge reservoir. Old river hamlets, crossings, farms, and historic places are now under water. But the landscape of the southern half of the historic river valley can still be experienced by traveling two-lane back roads.

A very interesting circular drive is to take Tennessee Highway 69 from Bath Springs in southern Decatur County to Crump in Hardin County and then pick up Tennessee Highway 22 to Shiloh, the scene of one of the bloodiest Civil War battles. From Shiloh, take Tennessee 142 to Pickwick Dam where the road crosses the Tennessee River. To follow the east riverbank, go on Tennessee 128 from Pickwick Dam to Savannah, the seat of Hardin County. Next, continue on Tennessee 128, which parallels the river, to the historic town of Clifton in Wayne County. Here is a ferry that crosses the Tennessee River and allows access to Tennessee 114, which returns to Bath Springs.

This trip samples many different resources that have shaped the history of the Western Valley. With its ferry still in operation, Saltillo in Hardin County is a small river town with a few grand homes, such as the **Meady White House** (circa 1847) and Parker House (1906), standing on Main Street (both private, no access). At Shiloh Military Park is a complex of **Mississippian period mounds,** marking a much earlier period of settlement and agricultural history.

Pickwick Dam (1935–38), which is 113 feet high and 7,715 feet in length, records the impact of the Tennessee Valley Authority on the Mid-South landscape. From the visitor center, there is a tour of this mammoth and architecturally inspiring complex. "This building of dams and powerhouses, this setting up of transmission lines, with towers that looked like giant models of dressmakers' dummies, this orderly fury of construction," wrote R. L. Duffus of TVA's first projects in gen-

Tennessee River Ferry, Clifton. Ferry rides are a rapidly disappearing experience for Tennessee travelers.

eral, "was one of the most marvelous spectacles of its kind that have been seen in this generation on this or any continent" (78).

Directly north of Pickwick is the Hardin County seat of Savannah, where the large Victorian mansions of the **Savannah residential historic district** recall the wealth the river represented one hundred years ago. North along the river is the historic river town of Clifton, where the ferry, the historic **Presbyterian Church,** the Victorian-style Spurlock House, and **River Road historic district** (all private, no access) record life in an once prosperous river village. At a bungalow on River Road lived Tennessee writer T. S. Stribling, who wrote about the rural life of this region in the early twentieth century; in 1932 he became the state's first fiction writer to win the Pulitzer Prize for literature for his book *The Store.*

Route A: The Civil War along the Tennessee River

Shiloh National Battlefield is about five miles south of Crump on Tennessee Highway 22 in Hardin County. By all accounts, the Battle of Shiloh on April 6–7, 1862, was a turning point in the Civil War. The Confederates lost an opportunity to destroy a Union army and with it the reputations of commanders U. S. Grant and William T. Sherman. They also lost one of their most potentially brilliant generals, Albert S. Johnston. The loss of Shiloh strengthened Federal control of the Tennessee River and soon allowed the Yankees to take control of the Memphis and Charleston Railroad, which became a vital supply link in both the Vicksburg and Chattanooga campaigns of 1863. The bloodbath of the battle—some twenty-four thousand killed, wounded, or missing—shocked both southerners and northerners into the rather nasty reality that this war would not end soon in easy victory for either side.

The battle began in the early morning hours of April 6, 1862, when Gen. Albert S. Johnston launched a surprise attack on Grant's dispersed forces, camped near and about the Tennessee River between Crump Landing and Pittsburgh Landing, awaiting reinforcements from Gen. Don Buell. The Confederates struck fiercely and quickly pushed the Yankees toward the river. Gathering whatever men he could find, Union general Benjamin Prentiss formed a new line along a sunken road in a thick part of the forest. The Yankees mounted a stiff defense against wave after wave of Rebel charges. This place became known as the "Hornet's Nest" because the bullets flew by so fast and furious that the soldiers felt as if they were caught in a nest of hornets. Although facing murderous fire, including concentrated fire from sixty-two cannons, Prentiss maintained his position until dusk when he surrendered what was left of his original two divisions.

The heroic defense of the Hornet's Nest, along with an earlier stubborn stand at Shiloh Church, allowed Gen. U. S. Grant to gain time for reinforcements from Buell and to reorganize his scattered army. The next morning, a Federal counterattack gained back territory lost the previous day. Now the troops discovered to their horror unspeakable scenes of destruction from the first day of battle. As one soldier wrote, there were "gory corpses lying all about us, in every imaginable attitude, and slain by an inconceivable variety of wounds" (McDonough, *Shiloh,* 204).

The Confederate command was never able to reorganize its troops into an efficient fighting line, and sometimes the Rebels mistakenly fired on their own troops. By the afternoon, the Confederate command ordered a withdrawal, and the Rebels retreated to Corinth. No Yankees were in pursuit because Grant believed his troops had been too bloodied and shocked to chase the retreating enemy. The terrible Battle of Shiloh was over. Future President James A. Garfield recalled: "The horrible sights that I have witnessed on this field I can never describe. No blaze of glory, that flashes around the magnificent triumphs of war, can ever atone for the unwritten and unutterable horrors of the scene of carnage" (McDonough, *Shiloh,* 213).

Due to its isolated location, the Shiloh Battlefield has not suffered from extensive modern development. Created in 1894–95, the military park includes almost all of the significant places associated with the struggle. Its creation was part of a larger movement to create national battlefields so that the emotional wounds of the Civil War could finally be laid to rest. An excellent movie, museum, and interpretive guide await travelers at the visitor center.

Savannah, across the river from the battlefield, five miles east of the junction of Tennessee 22 and U.S. 64, is the location of the Greek Revival–style **Cherry Mansion** (1830), which was Grant's headquarters prior to the Battle of Shiloh. Also on the bluffs overlooking the town and river are several fine late Victorian residences, including the **Walker-McGinley House** (1899), a Queen Anne house at 311 Williams Street, and the **Irwin-Gray House** (1902) on Guinn Street, which was the residence of J. W. Irwin, the purchasing agent for the Shiloh National Military Park (all private, no access). The Hardin County Courthouse (1950), a Colonial Revival design by Nashville architects Marr and Holman, sits in the middle of a small downtown commercial district of buildings from the late nineteenth to mid-twentieth centuries.

CHAPTER EIGHT

The Mississippi River Country

The Mississippi River Country may be defined as the five counties—Lake, Obion, Dyer, Lauderdale, and Tipton—that lie adjacent to the mighty Mississippi River along the western boundary of Tennessee. Geologists call the land nearest the river the "Mississippi River Flood Plain," and, despite the best efforts of engineers over the last one hundred years, the waters of the Mississippi sometimes still wash over the riverbanks, although nothing in recent memory has matched the killer floods of 1927 and 1937. At that time, most of Lake County suffered severe flood damage because all of that county lies in the flood plain, including the largest towns of Ridgely and Tiptonville. While most of the land mass of the other four counties lies in the floodplain, the largest towns and county seats are located on the edge of the plateau overlooking the river bottomland. This location has kept the worst of Mississippi flooding away from the doorsteps of Union City, Dyersburg, Ripley, and Covington.

Worries today tend toward the more catastrophic. A geologist recently predicted a strong earthquake along the Mississippi; fortunately, he was wrong, but local people began to await fearfully the return of the earthquakes that forever shaped the landscape nearly two hundred years ago. From December 16, 1811, to mid-March 1812, a series of earthquakes jolted the region and were felt as far away as Washington, D.C. Geologists now believe that some of these quakes probably reached as high as 8.8 on the Richter scale, the strongest ever in North America. These extremely powerful quakes were centered at New Madrid, Missouri. Downriver at Hickman, Kentucky, which is just thirteen miles northwest of Union City, survivor Eliza Bryan wrote of the December 16 disaster:

> A violent earthquake shook, accompanied by a very awful noise, resembling loud but distant thunder, but hoarse and vibrating, followed by complete saturation of the atmosphere with sulphurous vapor, causing total darkness. The screams of the inhabitants, the cries of the fowls and beasts of every species, the falling trees, and the roaring of the Mississippi, the current of which was retrograde for a few minutes, owing, as it is supposed, to an eruption in its bed, formed a scene truly horrible.
>
> The river, falling immediately as rapidly as it had risen, receded within its banks with such violence that it took with it whole groves of young cottonwood trees which had hedged its borders. They were broken off with such regularity in some instances that persons who had not witnessed the fact could be with difficulty persuaded that it had not been the work of man. The river was literally covered with wrecks of boats . . . lately it has been discovered that a lake was formed on the opposite side of the Mississippi, in the Indian country, upwards of 100 miles long and from one to six miles wide, of a depth of from ten to fifty feet. (Coggins, 8)

This lake, of course, was famous Reelfoot Lake, now protected as the Reelfoot Lake State Park, between Tennessee Highways 21, 22, and 78 in Lake and Obion Counties. The terrible quake either formed or enlarged the eighteen-thousand-acre lake as well as creating new swamplands throughout the region. Described as the "jewel" of Tennessee's Mississippi floodplain, Reelfoot Lake is fourteen miles long and five miles wide, famous for the many cypress trees standing in its shallow areas (Luther, 5).

About ninety years ago, Reelfoot Lake was also a battleground between local farmers and fishermen, who had earned their livelihood from the lake for decades, and a group of entrepreneurs, who formed the West Tennessee Land Company in 1907. Through a series of slick legal maneuvers, the land company acquired exclusive control to Reelfoot in order to turn it into a private resort. Local residents fought back with violence. Over the next several months, night riders attempted to terrorize land company officials and murdered two attorneys. State officials then stepped in to settle the dispute, and by 1914 the state had acquired the property for public use. Reelfoot Lake has been a public park ever since.

This chapter also examines landscapes found on the higher Plateau Slope of West Tennessee. Millions of years ago, this land was at the bottom of a shallow sea; the western end of the plateau remains relatively flat and rises about two hundred feet above the Mississippi River. Railroads, not rivers, shaped history here, especially the tracks of the Illinois Central, which connected the small towns of West Tennessee to the major markets of Memphis, Mobile, New Orleans, and Chicago. Later in the twentieth century came U.S. Highway 51, once called the Jefferson Davis Highway, to link the cities and small towns of the region. That highway remains the single best way to explore the history of the Mississippi River Country.

Landscape 23: The Mississippi River

The mighty Mississippi enters Tennessee in the northwest corner of Lake County, but immediately curves northward to New Madrid, Missouri. It then winds its way southward, establishing the western border of Tennessee, except in places where the course has changed, thereby leaving land that had been east of the Mississippi in the early nineteenth-century *west* of the Mississippi. The tiny hamlet of Reverie, in Tipton County, is one such place. It can only be reached by Arkansas highways. The same is true of the historic Corona Farm (1836) in Tipton County, which is located on Centennial Island of the Mississippi River. Between 1836 and 1837, John and Elizabeth Bradley Trigg purchased over twenty-two hundred acres to establish a major antebellum cotton plantation along the banks of the Mississippi. The farm was very successful, expanding to thirty-one hundred acres. Then, in 1876, according to the family, the river changed its course, and "in two days time ate away one thousand acres of the Trigg place. The remainder of the land was severed from the mainland of Tennessee and was positioned then, as now, on the west side of the river" (West, 317). Within the last ten years, family members have raised corn, soybeans, peanuts, and wheat on this rich Delta land.

Memphis is the only river port of any significance along the Mississippi in Tennessee. But in the early nineteenth century, now-forgotten places, such as Randolph in Tipton County, actually handled more freight and goods. Tiny river towns still exist—Hales Point and Golddust in Lauderdale County as well as Heloise in Dyer County—but the river's periodic floods combined with the lure of railroad corridors along the nearby plateaus to keep most town builders away from the banks of the Mississippi. Along the river today are overgrown and mostly forgotten places that were once linked to the changing fortunes of the great Mississippi as it made its way to New Orleans.

Route A: Native-American Settlements in Shelby County

Hundreds of years before Columbus, the age of the great temple mound towns began in the South. This new Indian culture embodied advanced ceremonial and political concepts and has come to be called "Mississippian" because so many settlements concentrated within the river's valley. In West Tennessee, many temple mound sites from the Mississippian period are along the river and its tributaries, such as the Wolf, Hatchie, Forked Deer, and Obion Rivers. One place that is fully interpreted and open to the public is the **Chucalissa Village** in southern Shelby County, south of the I-240 loop in Memphis. From U.S. Highway 51, take Winchester Road west, toward the river, where the road becomes known as Mitchell Road before it reaches T. O. Fuller State Park. The Civilian Conservation Corps originally built the park as a segregated facility only for African Americans. The Chucalissa site and museum is located within the park.

In the summer of 1541, Hernando de Soto led the first group of Europeans to encounter Mississippian villages of present-day Tennessee, located probably either north or south of Memphis. Here he found Indian cornfields intermixed with fortified towns, some small and some large but all with impressive ceremonial mounds. Chucalissa was probably not one of those towns, but the site and museum are excellent places to explore regional history before European exploration and later settlement.

Different Native-American cultures have occupied the Chucalissa area over the last three thousand years. Archaeological investigations have uncovered scattered tools and projectile points left by people of the late Archaic and then the Woodland periods. The first permanent Mississippian settlement was brief and probably dates from A.D. 1000. Later settlements followed at approximately 1200, 1400, and 1500. The reconstructed village portrays the landscape as it would have appeared in the last settlement, or just before De Soto's 1541 visit to the Mississippi River.

Corn agriculture, supplemented by hunting, fishing, and trade, was the economic foundation of the settlement. Some southeastern tribes also grew different types of beans for their own use and for trade. The town was arranged around a central plaza, dominated by a large ceremonial mound for the dwelling of the town's headman and surrounded by a series of small mounds for the houses of other important village leaders. The town leadership lived in substantial homes, built of individual wall posts that were firmly planted in the ground, covered with split cane mats that were then covered with a couple of inches of clay-and-grass plaster. The thatched roof was either shaped like a pyramid or a gable. Others lived outside the ceremonial complex, on a nearby ridge or on top of several nearby hills.

The size of the dwellings reflected the owner's status and position within the village. The headman's house might be as large as fifty feet on each side, with large cypress posts supporting the pyramid roof. Dwellings around the plaza ranged between eighteen to twenty-two feet per side, while those behind the main mound were smaller, between fourteen and eighteen feet on a side.

These different elements of the Mississippian built environment are well portrayed at Chucalissa. The well-built homes and designed town plan directly contradict the all-too-common—and false—stereotype of Native Americans as nomadic wanderers of the American frontier. Chucalissa helps visitors confront the reality of Native-American culture. Its museum displays some of the artifacts found during the different excavations and provides a useful overview of the Mississippian period in Tennessee history. The park dates from 1939, when CCC workers, digging a new swimming pool for the adjacent state park, discovered the site. The government decided to support an archaeological excavation and to develop a park and museum. But World War II intervened and work stopped. During the 1950s, the Memphis Archaeological and Geological Society resumed the site's development. In 1962 the department of anthropology at the University of Memphis took control of the property, and the university operates the site for education and research purposes.

Native Americans are among the site's interpreters, and they provide an important sense of continuity between the prehistoric past along the Mississippi River and the later history of Chickasaw settlement in the eighteenth and early nineteenth centuries. West Tennessee was reserved as Indian Territory until 1819, and **Davies Plantation** (private, limited access), along U.S. Highway 64 in eastern Shelby County, was the location of an early-nineteenth-century Chickasaw farm. To reach the plantation, the traveler may return to Interstate 240 and follow this highway east for thirteen miles to its junction with Interstate 40. Continue east on I-40 for four miles to exit 16 where U.S. Highway 64 heads east to the historical markers outside the front gate of the property.

The Davies Plantation Road follows for several hundred yards an early Chickasaw trail that connected the Chickasaw Bluffs to Bolivar and then to the West Tennessee Chickasaw trail that linked the Tennessee paths to large tribal villages in Mississippi. U.S. Highway 64 generally follows the route of this prehistoric trail to Bolivar, representing one of the few examples in West Tennessee where a major federal highway did not closely follow railroad tracks. Local tradition dates the original log sections of the Davies home from 1807 (which makes it the oldest extant dwelling in West Tennessee). An Indian mound that probably dates from the Middle Woodland period (A.D. 1–500) also stands at the east corner of the house.

In 1821 Thomas Henderson acquired the land as part of a military warrant of 640 acres. Another early owner, Joel Royster, built the two-story log dwelling that remains today. By the mid-1800s, Logan E. Davies had acquired that property and other acreage to establish a large antebellum plantation. In time, Davies Plantation became one of the largest farms in Shelby County and was especially noted for its Berkshire swine.

The use of log construction by the original Indian residents of Davies Plantation is a good example of how native cultures adapted the technology of frontier settlers to their own purposes. The Chickasaws were permanent residents of West Tennessee when De Soto floated the Mississippi in 1541 and later when French traders and missionaries traveled the river in the late 1600s. Soon the tribe was involved in complex trade relations with French and English agents, who in turn introduced European items and technology to the Native-American way of life.

By 1782 the Chickasaws' extended economic relations even included the new settlers at Fort Nashborough when James Robertson established a supply depot for the Indian trade at the Lower Chickasaw Bluff overlooking the Mississippi River (the location of Memphis). Four years later, the American government and the tribe signed their first official treaty, which set aside the land between the Mississippi and Tennessee Rivers as the domain of the Chickasaws. In 1792 William Blount secured another Chickasaw treaty that strengthened the tribe's economic ties to the United States and largely ended American fears that the Chickasaws might reach a similar agreement with the Spanish.

Over the next two decades, the Americans intensified their contacts with the Chickasaws, hoping soon to receive major land cessions. In 1797 the government began to use an old Chickasaw road (better known as the Natchez Trace) to move mail between Nashville and Natchez. In 1802 the government approved the establishment of Fort Pickering—a federal trading post—on the Lower Chickasaw Bluff. Although the tribe's largest settlements were to the south, around Natchez, the Chickasaws used Fort Pickering as a river port to meet supply boats and traders. The fort soon attracted a number of permanent Indian settlers. According to an 1809 account, another large Indian village stood about five miles inland from the Mississippi. Around this time, from 1802 to 1809, an unknown Indian established the original log dwelling at Davies Plantation.

Trade with the United States, however, put many Chickasaws into debt, and increasingly the Americans demanded land in return. In 1805 the tribe exchanged a large section of land in Middle Tennessee to meet a $12,000 debt; another treaty in 1816 repaid the Chickasaw's allegiance and assistance during the War of 1812 by taking the tribe's remaining landholdings in Middle Tennessee. In 1818 federal commissioners Andrew Jackson and Isaac Shelby forced one final treaty on the Chickasaws that extinguished the tribe's title to all its remaining Tennessee land—some 10,700 square miles. When President James Monroe signed the "Jackson Purchase" in 1819, he brought an end to the centuries-old Chickasaw period in West Tennessee.

Route B: The Mississippi River during the Civil War

The best route to understand the role the Mississippi River played in the Civil War is to follow U.S. Highway 51 from Covington to Union City.

Control of the Mississippi River was of crucial importance in the Civil War. From its very beginning in 1861, the Confederate government in Montgomery, and later in Richmond, together with state officials in Nashville, took steps to defend the Mississippi. Six miles above Memphis stood the guns of Fort Harris. More powerful batteries were installed during the summer of 1861 at Fort Wright at the old river port of Randolph (private, limited access). To reach the town, the traveler may leave U.S. Highway 51 at Covington and turn west for about sixteen miles on Tennessee Highway 59 in Tipton County. Many elements of Fort Wright are intact, including an extremely rare brick powder magazine, portions of earthworks, and one of the original four redoubts, all built by slave labor.

Fort Wright enclosed about thirty acres, serving as a training base and field laboratory for the newly established Confederate army. Here Tennesseans attempted to build their first fortifications and to drill soldiers in the use of heavy artillery as well as to introduce basic rules of military discipline. Three famous future Confederate generals—Nathan B. Forrest, Pat Cleburne, and Alexander P. Stewart—along with a score of other important future commanders in the Army of Tennessee began their military careers at Fort Wright. The fort's history, however, was very brief. In late July 1861, Confederates abandoned the fort in favor of positions upriver at Fort Pillow and Island Number Ten. When Gen. William T. Sherman claimed the fort for the Union army in September 1862, he burned all buildings but one in Randolph and took whatever the Confederates had left at Fort Wright.

Fort Pillow was the next major Confederate fortification, and an 1864 battle there made this place one of the most infamous in the annals of the war. A National Historic Landmark, Fort Pillow is the only Confederate base on the Mississippi now open as a historic site in Tennessee. To reach the park, leave Covington and go north on U.S. Highway 51 about eight miles to Henning. Then turn west for eighteen miles on well-marked Tennessee Roads 87 and 207 to the entrance. The entrance takes the visitor through the Fort Pillow State Prison Farm. Located on the high First Chickasaw Bluff of the Mississippi River, the fort provided commanding views of approaching vessels for miles in either direction. The ever-changing course of the river, however, means that today the fortifications are about one mile away from the Mississippi.

Union gunboats first came within sight of the Confederate batteries on May 10, 1862, during the naval battle of Plum Point Bend on the river. Confederate boats repulsed this first Union thrust. During the next month, Union mortar boats bombarded the fort. Little damage was inflicted, but Union forces successfully swept by the fort and headed for Memphis. So as not to be cut off from the Memphis supply line, the Confederate command decided to abandon Fort Pillow on June 4.

Earthworks, Fort Pillow State Historic Area.

Unlike Fort Wright, which neither side used after 1862, Fort Pillow became a mainstay in the Federal occupation of the Mississippi River. In the spring of 1864, Maj. Lionel F. Booth commanded about six hundred Union soldiers at the fort, roughly divided between white and newly enlisted African-American soldiers. In an attempt to interrupt Union supply lines and distract the ongoing campaigns to the south, Gen. Nathan B. Forrest led his fifteen hundred troops against Fort Pillow on April 12, 1864. His larger force soon pinned the Union troops into a small crescent-shaped position. Forrest demanded surrender, but the Union troops refused. More fighting—and much needless bloodshed—took place until the Federal soldiers finally gave up. A recent careful investigation of the evidence uncovered that almost half of the Federal garrison died that day; indeed, African-American soldiers died at a rate twice that of the white Union troops. One Confederate sergeant recorded that "the slaughter was awful. Words cannot describe the scene. The poor deluded negroes would run up to our men fall upon their knees and with uplifted arms scream for mercy but they were ordered to their feet and then shot down" (Cimprich and Mainfort, 836).

The last of the major 1861 Confederate forts on the Mississippi was also the largest: the fortified Island Number Ten, which lay in the great river bend near Tiptonville in northwest Lake County. To reach the approximate site, the visitor may take U.S. Highway 51 from Henning about thirty-two miles north to its intersection with Tennessee Highway 78. Continue north on the state road for another twenty-three miles to Tiptonville. From there, go north on Tennessee 22 to two historical markers locating the original fort and the burial site of about seventy-five Confederates who died in the fighting.

Across from Island Number Ten, on a high river bluff at Columbus, Kentucky, the Confederate command installed a huge battery of 140 guns. Another Confederate force of 8,500 men and heavy artillery stood on the other side of the river at New Madrid, Missouri. Yet, Federal troops had little difficulty in taking these three Confederate fortifications. In March 1862 a Union army of 25,000, led by Gen. John Pope and supported by the naval boats of Flag Officer Andrew Foote, attacked the forts. A spirited Confederate defense held back the Federal advance for a few weeks, but on April 7, 1862, Gen. W. W. Mackall at Island Number Ten surrendered his entire garrison of 7,000 men, with 7,000 small arms and 158 pieces of artillery. Already inadequately supplied, the Confederacy could ill-afford such losses in men or equipment.

With the fall of Island Number Ten, Fort Pillow, and Fort Wright in the late spring of 1862, the door to Memphis was wide open, and on June 6, 1862, Federal troops occupied the state's biggest port city. The North controlled the Mississippi River Country for the remainder of the war despite periodic raids by Confederate cavalry. One interesting monument to those raids is the **Confederate Cemetery and Monument** at Summer and Edwards Streets (near the local middle school) in Union City. Travelers may reach Union City from Tiptonville by taking Tennessee 22 east for twenty-nine miles. In late December 1862, Nathan B. Forrest raided the Union supply lines and destroyed railroad tracks at Humboldt, Trenton, Kenton, and Dyer before attacking the Union troops stationed at the railroad junction of Union City on December 23, 1862. After the war, in 1868–69, local citizens erected the monument in memory of the unknown Confederate soldiers who had died that day. This was the first such monument to the unknown Confederate dead built in the South.

Route C: Farming the Mississippi River Country

Tennessee 78, from Dyersburg to Tiptonville in the northern corner of the state, and Tennessee 14, from Raleigh to its junction with Tennessee Highway 54 in Tipton County in the southern corner, are two highways that provide excellent overviews of the agrarian landscape of the Mississippi country

As soon as the Jackson Purchase was completed and approved in 1819, southerners rushed to the fertile land of the Mississippi River basin to establish farms and plantations. Cotton was the dominant crop here for over one hundred years, and every season followed the same pattern of work. In the summer, tenants (or, before emancipation, African-American slaves) would chop the grass and weeds away from the cotton plants. Once the weeds were gone, teams of mules would plow between the rows of cotton. The plants would then blossom, and in the fall came the time to pick the soft bolls of cotton. The entire tenant (or slave) family—men, women, and children—would take huge bags into the fields and painstakingly handpick the cotton.

Cotton cultivation demanded large tracts of land as well as large numbers of laborers. These two traits have left an indelible mark on the West Tennessee landscape. Almost any road in the region will give the visitor an opportunity to see large cotton fields, strategically placed cot-

Monuments and Memorials

Many different types of monuments and memorials are scattered across Tennessee. The most prevalent are memorials in honor of military veterans, from the Revolutionary era to the Vietnam War. Throughout the first half of this century, the most common was a statue of a brave and stoic Civil War soldier, invariably facing south if the monument was in honor of the Confederacy. An excellent example is the Sam Davis statue (1906) on the south side of the courthouse grounds in Pulaski. Most Civil War monuments were not built in the years immediately after the war—Union City's Confederate Memorial (1869) is an exception in this regard—but came later in the century or even in the early twentieth century. One impetus came from the desire to have statuary as part of larger urban landscaping plans. Memphis's Confederate Park, with its statue of Jefferson Davis, for example, dates to 1908 and was part of the broader City Beautiful Movement in Memphis.

The large number of Civil War monuments built from 1880 to 1920 also reflects the era's "Lost Cause" ideology, which used the sacrifice and heroism of the Civil War to justify and even expand brutal segregationist attitudes and public policies. Monuments to the war did little to honor the dead and heal the wounds of that terrible conflict; rather, they were potent symbols of a defiant South and of the racial hatred of that time.

After World War I, groups such as the Veterans of Foreign Wars began systematically to erect memorials to the soldiers of the twentieth century. On the grounds of the Campbell County Courthouse in Jacksboro, the National Youth Administration in 1938 built a joint memorial to local boys who had died in the Spanish-American War and in World War I. This early combination veteran memorial remained rare until after World War II. In the second half of this century, however, veterans' organizations have erected combination memorials to those who died in World War I, World War II, Korea, and Vietnam and placed them on almost every courthouse square. The first memorials to the veterans of the Persian Gulf War have already made their appearance, including at a small park in Tracy City.

In general, the twentieth century has proven to be a great era of monument building in Tennessee. Next to the veterans' groups, the Daughters of the American Revolution and the United Daughters of the Confederacy have been quite active in raising memorials to famous heroes, heroines, and places in Tennessee history. The latter group naturally has focused on the Civil War. Although the DAR has concentrated its activities on the early pioneer and revolutionary periods, several chapters have marked or manage historic sites that commemorate people and events from the early to mid-nineteenth century. In the last twenty years, previously neglected Tennesseans, such as the Cherokees and African Americans, have been honored with new monuments and memorials. The Tellico Reservoir covered the old Cherokee villages of Tanasi and Chota; impressive monuments mark their place today. The Tennessee Historical Commission has aggressively expanded its historical marker program to include significant places and people in African-American history.

Monuments and memorials do much more than identify people and places of historical significance. "Monuments tell us who we are, inform us where we came from, list the ideals we should honor, and suggest the goals toward which we should strive," emphasizes historian Gerald A. Danzer. They bind "a community together horizontally, but also vertically connecting the present generation with a heroic past and a fulfilling destiny" (1). Monuments document something about the person or event that is memorialized, but in the most cases they tell us much more about the people who built the monuments. The best example is perhaps the statue of Edwin Ward Carmack, sculpted by Nancy Cox McCormac, that stands in front of the state capitol. The prominence of the monument suggests that Carmack played a singularly important or crucial role in state history, although few historians would venture such an assessment today. The monument's prominent location, however, reflects the great passion of the prohibition debates of the early twentieth century and how Carmack became a symbolic martyr for that cause.

The close association between monuments and their makers is why travelers sometimes encounter decaying, neglected memorials. That spot or person once meant much to those who erected it. But once that day passed, the monument meant little to a new generation with its own symbolic needs and causes.

ton gins, the great plantation homes of classical architecture, the smaller vernacular cottages and bungalows of middle-class farmers, and the shotgun shacks of tenant farmers that are characteristic of Delta agriculture.

Just west of Tennessee 78 in the northern part of Dyersburg is the modern Classical Revival mansion used in the award-winning film *In the Heat of the Night* to portray the home of a rich southern plantation owner (private, no access). From this point, the visitor can travel north for about twenty-five miles to the county seat of Tiptonville through flat land once almost totally devoted to cotton production, but that now includes such crops as soybeans and milo. Soybeans are especially important. Before World War II, the crop was used mostly for hay or plowed into the ground as fertilizer. In 1940, however, chemists discovered a way to remove the unappetizing taste from soybean oil, and soon food processors and ordinary consumers developed a taste for this new product.

The land on either side of Tennessee 78 belongs to the Mississippi floodplain. But improvements and river levees built by the corps of engineers along the Mississippi and its major tributaries now largely protect this area from seasonal flooding except when sudden high water overtaxes the intricate corps system. Such was not the case in the nineteenth and early twentieth centuries, when the land flooded almost every year. The WPA writer who explored this area in the late 1930s marveled:

> The attitude of the bottom land people toward the annual phenomenon is amazing to the radio announcers and reporters who rush in as the rivers rise; housewives resignedly take up their carpets and move their furnishings to upper rooms, but very few think of leaving their homes. Except when levees break the water arrives sluggishly, its smooth brown surface rising almost imperceptibly. The men are usually drafted for levee work, to strengthen the banks with sandbags and brush and to perform patrol duty. Even before the water arrives the highway may be closed to all but those who carry passes, because the days have not passed when men from other areas—and even from across the river—attempt to relieve flood pressure on the levees nearest them by dynamiting levees elsewhere. (*WPA Guide,* 424)

Once visitors cross the Obion River Bridge and head down the river bluff into the community of Bogota, about ten miles north of Dyersburg, they have reached the heart of the river country. "To me,"

"Cotton Picking—New Style,"
1951–52 Annual Report of
Tennessee Department of
Agriculture. (Courtesy of Oscar
Farris Agricultural Museum,
Tennessee Department of
Agriculture)

says local farmer Don Childress, "when you come down that bluff, it's just like coming to heaven" (Hulme, 2: 353). There's not much in Bogota, but note its large cotton gin; every town in this area has one. In the late afternoons during the fall, the road is sometimes filled with cotton wagons and mechanical pickers coming home after a long day working the fields.

About seven and a half miles to the north is Ridgely, in Lake County. It is much larger than Bogota because of its historic connection to a spur of the Illinois Central Railroad. Large cotton-gin operations can be found along the railroad tracks. The town itself has an early-twentieth-century appearance. Landmarks on Main Street include the neoclassical facade of a local bank along with well-maintained bungalow and Classical Revival residences.

In the great Mississippi flood of 1927, the American Red Cross established an emergency relief camp at Ridgely, one of 154 established throughout the Mississippi valley. Here Red Cross workers provided food, medical care, and services to the local farmers and many sharecroppers, mostly poor and black, who had lost their homes in that natural disaster. The Red Cross encountered shocking social and medical problems throughout the disaster area. Most tenants suffered from a poorly balanced diet and from an almost total lack of medical care.

Margaret Wells Wood of the American Social Hygiene Association concluded that Delta folks were "worn out by the ravages of tuberculosis, pellagra, and venereal diseases, with little resistance due to unsanitary living conditions and lack of education." She believed that Red Cross camps provided "a Revolutionary step" toward improving this situation because the better camps introduced "rightful and healthful standards of living" to people who had known little but the direst of poverty. (Daniel, *Deep'n As It Come,* 123)

Almost exactly between Ridgely and Tiptonville is the hamlet of Wynnburg, the location of three of the county's oldest historic family farms (all private, no access). In 1870 William J. and Mary Barker Wynn established a large cotton plantation that expanded to 994 acres by 1887. Their son Samuel F. Wynn received 470 acres of this land in 1892 and later purchased an additional 480 acres. When the Illinois Central decided in 1907 to construct a new branch line from Dyersburg to Tiptonville, Samuel Wynn subdivided his farm and created the town of Wynnburg, donating land for the depot, local school, and churches. During the early twentieth century, family members sold about half of the farmland, and in 1939 the farm was subdivided into two properties now known as the Ed Sumara Farm and the Wynn Farm. Both farms still produce cotton in addition to soybeans and milo.

The historic Carter Farm, about one mile north of the Wynn property, has also yielded the same popular crops. Established by Richard and Temperance Bradford in 1861, the farm began with a mere 140 acres, but in the late 1800s, Bradford continued to amass land until he owned over twenty-seven hundred acres for cotton, corn, and livestock production. With his economic might came political power: Bradford was one of the county's organizers and served as the chairman of the Lake County court for many years. A nephew, William T. Auston, purchased fifty-five acres of the farm in 1880. He deviated from the agricultural norm and experimented with new crops. He planted the first alfalfa in the county and also bought the first local mechanical mower. Cotton was still an important crop, but Auston's progressive farming also gained profits from his alfalfa and cattle herds.

Tiptonville, four miles north of Wynnburg, dates from 1857, but the town stayed small until it became the seat of government for Lake County in 1870. Actual incorporation did not come until 1900. Two historic properties from this early period of settlement are the **Caldwell-Hopson House** (circa 1891), a Queen Anne dwelling built by a local merchant at 431 Wynn Street, and the local Presbyterian Church

Lake County Seed Company, Tiptonville. Industrial closings have devastated the local economy of Tiptonville, leaving its downtown business core almost completely abandoned.

(1880s), built in a Folk Gothic style. Located on a small rise, called the Tiptonville Dome, the town has always been spared the worst of Mississippi flooding, and it served as a Red Cross relief camp in both 1927 and 1937. The Lake County Oil Mill (1906–71), which produced cottonseed oil and other products, dominated the local economy for most of the twentieth century, and its large but abandoned and decaying works still stand along the railroad tracks near the junction of Tennessee Highways 78 and 21. Also note the several cotton gins along the tracks. The county once had as many as seventeen operating gins; as of 1987 only seven remained in business.

Across from the mill, on Tennessee 78, stands the boyhood home of Carl Perkins, whose combination of hillbilly music and rhythm and blues influenced the early days of rock 'n' roll. His home has been moved, and the loss of the original site lessens the visitor's ability to understand the physical world that nurtured Perkins. But the house itself is valuable because this unadorned frame dwelling was typical of the white tenant and working-class houses of the area, and few homes of this type are ever preserved.

The presence of the Illinois Central branch line gives a somewhat industrial character to the towns in the northwest corner of Tennessee. Down in the southern corner, along Tennessee 14 in Shelby and Tipton

Counties, is a rural area of old country roads and tiny towns that the railroads never served. The route begins in the heavily commercialized and developed suburb of Raleigh, which was the county seat for Shelby County from 1827 to 1868. Traveling northeast, Tennessee 14 soon leaves the restaurants, shopping centers, and gas stations and enters the world of rural Shelby County.

It is a landscape of mixed agriculture, with fields of soybeans, alfalfa, milo, corn, and even pastures for livestock sharing space with cotton fields. "From the 1930s to the 1950s," according to historian Pete Daniel, "the cotton South metamorphosed from a labor-intensive culture to one that increasingly used machines and chemicals, and the production of cotton moved ever westward" (*Breaking the Land,* 241). Much of this change occurred in the wartime years of 1944 and 1945, when southern farmers spurned cotton production for other crops. Workers were allowed to leave the land because there was no need for their labor; the days of one-crop, one-mule agriculture were largely over.

This route has constant reminders of the decades when cotton was king and tenants were lucky to scratch out even a measly living on worn-out land. Shotgun tenant houses are along the road or at the edge of the cotton fields. The shotgun is an example of African-American architecture, first transplanted from West Africa to Haiti and then to New Orleans by the early nineteenth century. This dwelling has the entrance at the gable end and consists of narrow, interconnected, multiple rooms (usually three) with no hallway. From these urban, African-American roots, the house evolved through the nineteenth and early twentieth centuries to become a standard dwelling for southern workers, whether they worked in the fields or in factories. "Shotguns" can be found in the large cities of Tennessee, but they are a recurring element in the rural landscape of West Tennessee, physical documents of earlier days of race and labor relations.

Another common tenant shack is a board-and-batten frame house with two front doors. These duplex dwellings crowded two tenant families into the same building. With the characteristic central chimney and the front doors balanced on either side, this dwelling was much like the earlier log saddlebag house of the Appalachian frontier and like the two-room, central-chimney frame quarters built for slaves in the colonial era (see sidebar entitled "Common House Plans," Landscape 5, chapter 3).

Landscape 24: The Uplands

The county seats along Tennessee's western border—except for Tiptonville, which is protected by miles of federally constructed levees—sit on a low plateau overlooking the Mississippi floodplain. At first, their history and economic development were closely tied to the plantations adjacent to the Mississippi or located along local tributaries such as the Obion, Forked Deer, and Hatchie Rivers. None of the towns was very large. Then the railroads came in the late 1800s. The tracks brought new opportunities, opened new markets, and bypassed the need for river transportation. Following the general industry rule that a siding was necessary every seven or so miles, the railroad also created towns where none had been before, including Henning, Newbern, and Ripley. Here on the plateau, safe from all but the worst floods and nurtured by the railroad, would grow the commercial centers of the Mississippi River country.

Route A: The Illinois Central Railroad

Established in 1851, the Illinois Central Railroad was the first federal land-grant railroad. Originally it connected the river port of Cairo to Chicago, but during the Reconstruction period, the railroad began to extend westward into Iowa and later during the 1870s into the South, headed for New Orleans. In 1882 the company took a long-term lease on the Chicago, St. Louis, and New Orleans, a company that represented a recent merger of two southern railroads that ran in Tennessee from Union City to Selmer.

The company's expansion was designed to take advantage of the recovering southern economy. West Tennessee was emerging as a major export market for timber and cotton. As the Illinois Central moved into central West Tennessee, the company paid close attention to the construction of a competing line near the Mississippi River. In the 1880s, the Newport News and Mississippi Valley Railroad—which later was called the Chesapeake, Ohio, and Southwestern—took an old pre–Civil War charter and began construction from Memphis to Paducah and on to Louisville. Throughout the decade, the new railroad line invigorated earlier county seats, such as Covington and Dyersburg, while creating such new towns as Newbern and Trimble.

In 1893, during a national period of railroad consolidation, the Illinois Central purchased the Chesapeake, Ohio, and Southwestern and linked the Mississippi River towns to its midwestern transportation empire. The historic buildings found along the towns of U.S. Highway 51 mostly date from the days of the Illinois Central, especially the period of 1910 to 1930, when the railroad poured millions of dollars into improving its trains, its tracks, and its depots.

After World War II, however, the importance of the railroad as a transportation corridor began to wane in comparison to U.S. Highway 51. First, the railroad stopped being a major employer along the line. From 1945 to 1966, the number of Illinois Central employees nationwide fell by almost 50 percent, from forty-one thousand to twenty-one thousand. Passenger service steadily dropped; by the 1980s, almost all of the small-town depots had been demolished. Businesses in small towns left the streets that paralleled the tracks for new lots next to the highways.

Despite these modern changes, the towns and cities along U.S. Highway 51 look like early-twentieth-century railroad towns. The impact of those bands of steel cannot be missed (see sidebar entitled "Common Railroad Town Plans," Landscape 20, chapter 7). The railroad improved access to major cotton markets, freeing small towns from the once all-powerful cotton factors in Memphis and New Orleans. New industrial mills, warehouses, and factories located along the tracks. The rural Delta was suddenly not so isolated from the mainstream of American business. The railroad, as historian Albro Martin has pointed out, "did nothing to destroy the sharecropping basis for poor southern labor, white and black, but it made perhaps the major contribution to the slow accumulation of capital that would ultimately make the real New South possible" (184, 186).

The best way to see the close connection between the railroad, town development, and the later creation of U.S. Highway 51 is to follow as closely as possible the old route of that highway, now marked as Tennessee 211, 210, 209, and 184. As a matter of fact, most of the current route of U.S. 51 is "interstate quality" between South Fulton and Dyersburg and then is a divided four-lane highway from Dyersburg to Memphis. Apart from detours to the towns and cities, there is not much to see except farmland, interchanges, gas stations, and shopping centers. But if travelers follow the old U.S. 51 route, they are never far from the tracks and the associated railroad structures and buildings.

At the crossroads of U.S. Highways 45 and 51, South Fulton is a small Tennessee town that shares the state line with the larger Fulton, Kentucky. On 305 West State Line Road (Highway 116) is the historic

Obion County Courthouse, Union City. One of the last PWA projects in West Tennessee, this courthouse is additional evidence of how the New Deal reordered the state's public landscape.

W. W. Morris House, an upright-and-wing house with Queen Anne architectural detailing. South Fulton is where U.S. 51 enters Tennessee, but the road quickly diverges away from the main line of the Illinois Central and toward the historic rail junction of Union City, which is thirteen miles to the southwest on U.S. 51.

Union City has always been a railroad town. In 1855 George Washington Gibbs provided a tract of land where the Mobile and Ohio Railroad could junction with the Nashville and Northwestern line. He first planned to call the town Junction City, but since another Tennessee community had selected that name, he chose Union City instead. The original town plat was designed by F. R. Helner, the chief engineer of the Nashville and Northwestern. The town experienced sustained growth after the Civil War due to the construction of the Newport News and Mississippi Railroad and the extension of the Illinois Central from Cairo, Illinois, to Jackson, Tennessee, during the 1870s. Here at the railroad junction developed a well-planned trade center and the largest town in the county. Two- and three-story brick buildings, homes to a variety of wholesale and retail businesses, faced the tracks and First Street, the town's primary business street. In the 1880s and 1890s, the local economy especially benefited from a large furniture-making industry.

Two events changed the urban face of Union City in the early twentieth century. The first resulted from a special election in 1890 that moved the county seat from Troy to Union City. Eventually, Washington Street became a civic plaza, linking the tracks, depot, and First Street businesses to the town's new public buildings. These included the **Union City Post Office** (circa 1916), designed by James Knox Taylor in the Colonial Revival style, and the **Obion County Courthouse** (1939–40), designed by Nashville architects Marr and Holman in the PWA Modern style and built by the Public Works Administration (see sidebar entitled "The New Deal Built Environment," Landscape 9, chapter 4). Reflecting the influence of the City Beautiful Movement of the early twentieth century, this plaza design gives Union City a look different from that of other West Tennessee county seats.

The second came when U.S. Highway 51 passed through town in the 1920s. The highway used First Street for its route, and that street soon eclipsed the tracks as the town's primary commercial artery. Businesses that once faced the tracks spruced up their former rear entrances to better entice traffic along the highway. Today many of these stores still maintain two entrances, one facing the tracks and the other facing

First Street. New buildings, including the grand Classical Revival Third National Bank, added to the street's image of vitality and prosperity. In the 1920s came Art Deco–style buildings, including the Capitol Theater (1927) and the six-story-high Davy Crockett Hotel, for travelers of U.S. 51. Built by E. K. Beck, the hotel has been converted into a senior citizens' center. Next door is the historic Salant and Salant shirt factory, part of the town's growing industrial base during these same decades. Also associated with the impact of the federal highways are the many extant gas stations around town dating from the 1920s through the 1940s. These buildings are a reminder of Union City's role as a major southern highway junction (U.S. 45 and 51) during the middle decades of the twentieth century.

Classicism is the dominant architectural motif in local church and domestic architecture. The First Christian Church (1912) on South Second Street and the First Methodist Church (1914) on East Main Street are valuable examples of Classical Revival design. Prominent homes in that same style are found along East Main Street, and the commanding porticoes of 704 and 804 East Main Street (private, no access) are especially noteworthy.

About seven miles south of Union City, on either U.S. 51 or Tennessee 184, is Troy, the seat of government of Obion County from 1823 to 1890. Even though the county seat has been gone for over one hundred years, the town's small business district remains organized around the old courthouse square. The next three villages along this route are historic rail towns and can be best viewed by taking Tennessee 211. Obion, about six miles south, is where U.S. 51 again closely parallels the tracks. This town, established in 1872, was once a key transfer point for goods being moved along the adjacent Obion River. W. M. Wilson designed a town plat of twelve hundred lots on either side of the tracks. South of Obion, near where the old road and railroad tracks cross the Obion River, is the **Trimble Covered Bridge,** the only historic covered bridge still standing in West Tennessee (private, limited access).

Established in 1873, Trimble is at the Obion and Dyer county line. As the initial southern terminal of the Newport News and Mississippi Valley Railroad, the village was named for the railroad's president. Its few brick commercial buildings that still face the tracks reflect the railroad's tendency to design new towns in a symmetrical fashion (see sidebar entitled "Common Railroad Town Plans," Landscape 20, chapter 7). Newbern, another seven miles south on Tennessee 211, has a rare surviving railroad artifact in its historic **Illinois Central Combination**

Depot. The Craftsman-style depot dates from 1920, a time when the railroad spent millions of dollars improving its southern lines. The building is called a combination depot because passenger rooms, freight house, and railroad offices were all housed under one roof. Across from the depot, the company even developed a small park to highlight the city's gateway to the national rail network. Passenger service stopped here in 1965, and the building was used for storage until the city government acquired it in 1990. The depot now serves passengers again as one of two Amtrak stops in West Tennessee.

Directly adjacent to the depot is a large cotton-loading platform where bales could be unloaded from wagons and placed on freight trains. Newbern, according to the 1939 *WPA Guide to Tennessee,* was "a cotton trade center, whose gins handle much of the cotton from adjoining counties." The nearby gins were constantly busy at harvest times. At Newbern, the WPA writer observed, "wagons and trucks laden with cotton stand in lines beside the gins, waiting to be unloaded. The cotton is fed through a chute into the teeth of the gins, which separate the seed from the lint. The lint is then blown into the press and compressed into bales, which are bound with jute bagging and steel ties" (420).

Dyersburg, the largest city in Mississippi River country, is about seven miles south of Newbern on either Tennessee 211 or U.S. Highway 51. Tennessee 78, 104, and 211 all lead to the **courthouse square his-**

Dyer County Courthouse, Dyersburg. The revitalized square of Dyersburg is one of the most active and interesting in the state.

toric district. The **Dyer County Courthouse,** built by Asa Biggs in a Classical Revival design, dates from 1911, but the city's history begins much earlier, at the beginning of white settlement in West Tennessee during the 1820s.

In 1825 Joel Dyer and John McIver donated sixty acres along the North Forked Deer River for the Dyersburg townsite, which had eighty-six lots surrounding a courthouse square. Situated at the river's head of navigation, Dyersburg grew steadily in size and influence, and it became the county seat and a center of trade, commerce, and culture. In 1836 the first steamboat, the *Grey Eagle,* arrived at the local docks. River travel at this time was preferable to overland travel because of the poor to nonexistent roads. Small steamboats could navigate the North Forked Deer River for nine months of the year.

Cotton, corn, and tobacco were shipped out of Dyersburg, but for its first fifty years, lumber was the economic mainstay. This area of West Tennessee was thick with virgin forests, and as settlement increased, slaves cleared land for cultivation and the owners sold the trees for more profits. After the Civil War, more and more land was cleared for cotton cultivation, and soon cotton joined lumber as the foundation of the local economy.

Between 1879 and 1885, Dyersburg experienced its first urban boom. In 1879 the A. M. Stevens Lumber Company launched the steamboat *Alf Stevens* to carry lumber to St. Louis. The Bank of Dyersburg received its charter that year and opened for business in early 1880. Five years later, the **Bank of Dyersburg** opened a new building, a stylish mix of Second Empire and Italianate architecture, at 100 South Main Street.

By 1880 the riverfront, which then occupied the land from the old U.S. 51 bridge over North Forked Deer River to the present site of the Dyersburg machine works, was again humming with activity. Four steamboats shipped products from Dyersburg to Memphis and St. Louis. The A. M. Stevens sawmill had opened for business, joined five years later by a planing mill. In 1881 another wood-products company opened a factory to make wooden bowls.

The arrival of the Newport News and Mississippi Valley Railroad in 1884 intensified the boom, and soon the railroad became the preferred way of shipping goods out of Dyer County. The new rail link also encouraged the establishment of additional industries and commercial services along the town square. In 1884, for instance, the Dyersburg Oil Company established a cottonseed plant that, with many expansions, remains in production today. The recent period of economic expansion naturally led to a growth in residential neighborhoods. Once, houses had clustered in and around the town square; now they were located north of the square along McCaughey, Masonic, Court, and Market Streets and between the railroad tracks to the east and river bluffs to the west.

These patterns of the urban landscape remained until the town's great turn-of-the-century expansion, when its population increased from thirty-two hundred in 1900 to seventy-five hundred in 1909, a 234 percent increase in just nine years. Residential growth continued to the north: the **King House**, for instance, a grand Classical Revival mansion at 512 Finley Street, was built in 1907. But most new homes were built eastward up and over the river bluffs, where the greatest concentration of historic neighborhoods is. During the early 1900s, Troy, Sampson, and St. John Avenues, along with the connecting streets of Oak and Gordon, became neighborhoods for the new business and professional classes that had crowded into Dyersburg. These homes provided an escape from the noise, grit, and grime of the industrial railroad corridor and riverfront.

Oak and Gordon Streets developed as a middle-class neighborhood, populated by doctors, attorneys, and entrepreneurs. Between Sampson and Troy Avenues, the two streets form a cohesive historic district, significant for its many fine examples of bungalow architecture. The builders in this area are especially known for having mixed classical details, such as Ionic columns, into the basic bungalow design. The residences at 120, 126, and 200 Oak Street, as well as 124 and 204 Gordon Street, are excellent examples of the many variations found in the bungalow style.

Six blocks of **Troy Avenue,** from about the 800 block to the 1400 block, took on the attributes of the City Beautiful Movement, complete with large, spacious lots, a landscaped median strip that divided the avenue, and street lanterns. Here the houses reflected the revival craze in domestic architecture during the years after World War I. These six blocks feature the Tudor Revival at 933 Troy, the Colonial Revival at 1005 Troy, and the Mediterranean Revival at 1031 Troy. During the 1950s and 1960s, builders completed the avenue by adding modern Colonial Revival and ranch-style homes. The **Latta House,** a mid-nineteenth-century example of a piano-box house at 917 Troy, marks the earliest period of residential development in Dyersburg.

New railroad construction fueled much of the early-twentieth-century growth. Between 1909 and 1914, Dyersburg became the junction for the Illinois Central Railroad, the Gulf, Mobile, and Northern Railroad, and the Birmingham and Northwestern Railroad. Only Memphis and Jackson matched its importance as a rail center in West Tennessee. A 1916 account proclaimed that Dyersburg, with a population of ten thousand, was home to more businesses than any other Mississippi country city, except for Memphis. The city boasted of several cotton mills, compress companies, a brick and tile company, milling and grain companies, cotton gins, lumber companies, and a grocery company. There was a new post office, designed by James Knox Taylor, and now home to the local library. Over the next decade, the downtown business district would be additionally graced by the Baird-Brewer Hospital (1919), the Mediterranean Revival Methodist Church (1924), the six-story Classical Revival First Citizens National Bank (1924), and the Classical Revival Baptist Church (1929), which was designed by architect R. H. Hunt of Chattanooga.

The Dyersburg Cotton Products Corporation opened in 1929, and it became the largest industrial firm in the county. The factory consumed about six million pounds of cotton each year from area farmers, keeping a large part of the population employed either at the factory or in the fields. Portions of the original factory and adjacent company housing remain intact. The owners built the factory at Dyersburg since the cotton was plentiful and the town's geographic location and rail connections allowed quick access to the vast midwestern trade area.

The construction of U.S. Highway 51 added striking modern buildings to the local urban environment. In 1938 the Greyhound Bus Company built a small Art Deco **bus station** just off the square at 304 West Court Street. On the southern outskirts of town, on the old route of U.S. 51, stands another interesting highway artifact, the Art Deco Courtland Square motor court. Its glass block windows and streamlined appearance certainly caught the attention of highway travelers sixty years ago.

Dyersburg began as a river town, but today the patterns of its urban landscape show the later influence of railroads and industrial development. The town of Halls, ten miles south of Dyersburg on either Tennessee 210 or U.S. Highway 51, is strictly a railroad town. At the site of the old town depot, a Illinois Central caboose has been turned into a local history museum that emphasizes the town's connection to the tracks that run through the town. On Tennessee 210, the way the highway eventually reoriented the town's business district is apparent: businesses moved away from the commercial strip facing the tracks to a new series of businesses on either side of the highway. In fact, the town library is in a converted service station of restrained Spanish Revival style.

Ripley, another ten miles south on old U.S. 51 (now marked as Tennessee 209), is the seat of Lauderdale County. Incorporated in 1838, the town developed as a minor center of trade and commerce between Dyersburg and Covington. During the Depression, the federal government added two landmarks to the downtown. In 1936 the Public Works Administration built a new **Lauderdale County Courthouse** in the region's popular PWA Modern style, designed by the Nashville firm of Marr and Holman. Five years later, the WPA added a new Colonial Revival–style **Ripley post office,** designed by Louis A. Simon, just off the square. The post office has a federally sponsored mural, Marguerite Zorach's *Autumn,* which depicts a pastoral scene of hunting and nut gathering.

Seven miles south of Ripley is Henning, a classic small railroad town in West Tennessee that became famous in the 1970s as the childhood home of Alex Haley, a major African-American writer of the late twentieth century. In 1873 Henning was established as a railroad town on the Newport News and Mississippi Valley line. Today an old Illinois Central caboose and small park commemorates the railroad days. The C.S.O. Rice Cotton Gin (1928) lies adjacent to the tracks. In the town's

Alex Haley's boyhood home, Henning. Haley first heard the stories for his beloved book Roots at his grandfather's bungalow in Henning.

walking tour pamphlet, Charles Rice, a recent operator, recalls that ginning could be dangerous: "Sometimes folks would be smoking cigarettes and drop a box of matches down into the cotton. When we'd start ginning it, here it would go up in flames. Then you'd have the problem of finding the things the children had left in the cotton while they played on it as their folks were picking." The former route of U.S. 51 then runs between the tracks and the small business district.

Henning's churches and dwellings are located behind this commercial strip. **Alex Haley's boyhood home** is open to the public as a state historic site. The house belonged to his grandfather, Will Palmer, who operated a lumber company and mill along the railroad tracks. Palmer's hard work and business acumen gained him respect among both whites and blacks in Henning. In 1918–19 he and his wife, Cynthia, constructed a ten-room bungalow, complete with library and music room, that symbolized his place within the local middle-class African-American community. In 1921 his daughter Bertha Palmer Haley brought her baby son Alex back home to Henning to live with her parents as her husband, Simon Haley, pursued graduate studies at Cornell. As Alex grew up, he became fascinated by stories from Grandmother Palmer about the family's ancestors, people including Kunta Kinte, Kizzy, and Chicken George, names Haley would later make famous in his very popular Pulitzer prize-winning *Roots: The Saga of an American Family* (1976). In *Roots,* Haley remarked, "When I had been thoroughly immersed in listening to accounts of all those people unseen who had lived away back yonder, invariably it would astonish me when the long narrative finally got down to Cynthia, . . . and there I sat looking right at Grandma!" (707). The stories Haley learned from his grandmother have become part of American culture not only through the popularity of the book but also from the tremendous response to the television miniseries based on Haley's writings. *Roots* inspired millions to search for their family history and to learn how their families have played a role in the drama of the American past.

Covington, the county seat of Tipton County, is seven miles south of Henning along U.S. Highway 51. Like Dyersburg, the town dates from 1825, when 106 lots on a seven-street grid were laid out on twenty-nine acres in the center of Tipton County. Unlike Dyersburg, however, the town never developed into an antebellum river port. Covington stood along a small tributary of the Hatchie River, isolated from the steamboat trade of the mid-nineteenth century. The board-and-batten **St. Matthew's Episcopal Church** (1858) on Munford Street is a splendid example of late antebellum Gothic Revival architecture in a rural town setting. It is one of the few remaining buildings from Covington's pre–Civil War history.

The town remained small and commercially insignificant until the Newport News and Mississippi Valley Railroad arrived amid much fanfare on July 4, 1873. Between 1873 and 1880, over six thousand new residents flocked to the commercial and industrial opportunities the railroad created at Covington. The new arrivals also included many African Americans, and before the days of Jim Crow, the black community elected J. W. Boyd to serve on the county court in 1878–79 and as a state representative in 1880. A disastrous fire in 1882, which destroyed most of the north and west sides of the square, slowed the town's momentum. Yet, between 1887 and 1888, Covington added its first two banks and topped this period of prosperity in 1889 by commissioning a three-story Victorian courthouse, which was built by W. F. Boone and Son of Clinton, Kentucky, that still stands proudly in the town square.

Covington's growth during the 1870s and 1880s was dwarfed by the economic expansion that followed after the Illinois Central's takeover of the railroad in the 1890s. Tied to a much more extensive north-south transportation corridor, local stores expanded goods and services and more professionals moved to Covington. The town received its first telephone service and electric street lights in 1894. In 1901 the **Hotel Lindo** was built on Liberty Street just west of the courthouse. Local contractor and brick maker Richard B. Shelton designed this three-story

brick hotel. Three years later, the Covington Milling Company opened a large four-story cotton gin factory along the railroad tracks.

During these years of expansion, an impressive residential neighborhood was evolving along **South Main Street,** directly south of the business district. Many homes date from the first years of the twentieth century, and they are an interesting mix of rather late Queen Anne homes with more up-to-date bungalow and Classical Revival styles. For instance, the Eastlake-influenced Queen Anne house at **315 South Main** dates from about 1886, and the **Conner House,** at 516 South Main, is also Queen Anne in style, although it was built over twenty years later in 1909. During this same time, from 1900 to 1920, eleven bungalows or American Four-Square houses were built along the street. The **Reid-Rast House** (1907), at 508 South Main, is a particularly good example of Covington's early taste for bungalows, which continued to be built in the district as late as 1941.

In 1923 the construction of the **First Presbyterian Church** at 403 South Main, a Classical Revival building with a portico of four Doric columns, introduced the language of classicism into the homes of Covington's elite. Four Colonial Revival residences were built in the following years. These dwellings reflected the town's earliest domestic architecture as represented by the Greek Revival central-hall cottages of the **Palmer-Sherrod House** (1853) at 615 South Main and the Simonton House (circa 1870) at 802 South College Street.

The most unique dwelling in this historic district is the

Lowenhaupt-Simonton House (1879–80) at 532 South Main. Jacob Lowenhaupt had been a Mississippi River riverman, but he could not compete with the new railroad lines serving the Delta. He retired in Covington and built a home in the French Colonial vernacular that reflected the architectural traditions of the grand plantations he remembered along the river in Louisiana.

Covington also shows how railroad decisions could directly affect a town's appearance. U.S. Highway 51 today runs just west of the town square. This route was once the roadbed of the Newport News and Mississippi Valley line, but after the Illinois Central Railroad acquired the line, it moved the tracks several blocks east of the Covington square, where the old depot now stands abandoned and decaying along East Liberty Street (or Tennessee 59). The construction of the new highway in 1924–25 followed the abandoned roadbed almost through the heart of town. Remarkable Art Deco and International-style buildings still exist along this corridor. The Coca-Cola Company often selected the Art Deco style for its local bottling firms. The exterior of the Covington bottling plant is intact, with a giant Coke sign on its roof, but the building is now a carpet store. At the corner of U.S. 51 and West Liberty is the Baxter Building, a striking International-style building. The Art Deco Coulston Electrical and Plumbing Supplies building stands just to the west at 204 West Liberty. An example of streamlined architecture is the **Elliston Medical Clinic** (1940s) on South Main Street.

Covington also has two remaining Art Deco theaters. The Ritz Theatre (1942) at 124 West Liberty is closed and awaiting restoration.

The **Ruffin Theatre** (1941), just west of the town square at 113 West Pleasant Avenue, is restored and is used as a community playhouse and auditorium. William F. Ruffin, a Covington businessman who operated a chain of thirteen movie theaters in western Tennessee and Kentucky, built and operated both theaters. The Ruffin was his flagship theater, originally constructed in 1936. Five years later, Ruffin updated the building's main facade and interior in the Art Deco style, with the new designs provided by the Clarksville architectural firm of Speight and Hibbs.

Suggested Readings

This list of suggested readings makes no pretense at being comprehensive; rather, I have attempted to list books and articles that I referred to throughout the book. I have also listed books and articles that provided me with direct quotes. The many county histories, especially the recent series by the Memphis State University Press, were of great value to my research, but most are not listed because they are difficult to find in bookstores today. I strongly suggest that readers check their local libraries for these sources, as well as for copies of the "Goodspeed" county histories from 1887. Another very valuable source for local history were the Tennessee nominations to the National Register of Historic Places, which are kept on file at the Tennessee Historical Commission in Nashville. In rural areas, the nominations are often the best sources available for local history research.

Ash, Stephen V. *Middle Tennessee Society Transformed, 1860–1870*. Baton Rouge: Louisiana State University Press, 1988.

Barclay, R. E. *Ducktown: Back in Raht's Time*. Chapel Hill: University of North Carolina Press, 1946.

Beesley, Gaylon N. *True Tales of Tipton*. Covington, Tenn.: Tipton County Historical Society, 1981.

Bergeron, Paul H. *Paths of the Past: Tennessee, 1770–1970*. Knoxville: University of Tennessee Press, 1979.

Bernard, Patricia A. "The Rise and Decline of a Working Class Community: Long Island, Tennessee, 1925–1986." *East Tennessee Historical Society Publications* 58–59 (1985–86): 112–40.

Biles, Roger. "Epitaph for Downtown: The Failure of City Planning in Post–World War Two Memphis." *Tennessee Historical Quarterly* 44 (1985): 267–85.

———. *Memphis in the Great Depression.* Knoxville: University of Tennessee Press, 1986.

Blumenson, John J. *Identifying American Architecture: A Pictorial Guide to Styles and Terms, 1600–1945.* Nashville: AASLH Press, 1977.

Burns, Frank. *Davidson County.* Memphis: Memphis State University Press, 1989.

Caldwell, Linda D., et al. *Growing Up with the L&N: Life and Times in a Railroad Town.* Etowah, Tenn.: Etowah Arts Commission, 1989.

Campbell, Carlos C. *Birth of a National Park in the Great Smoky Mountains.* Knoxville: University of Tennessee Press, 1960.

Carver, Martha. *Survey Report for Historic Highway Bridges in Tennessee.* Nashville: Tennessee Department of Transportation, 1993.

Chapman, Jefferson. *Tellico Archaeology: 12,000 Years of Native American History.* Knoxville: University of Tennessee Press/Tennessee Valley Authority, 1985.

Chumney, James R. "The Pink Palace: Clarence Saunders and the Memphis Museum." *Tennessee Historical Quarterly* 32 (1973): 3–21.

Cimprich, John, and Robert C. Mainfort Jr. "The Fort Pillow Massacre: A Statistical Note." *Journal of American History* 76 (1989): 830–37.

Cobb, James C. *Industrialization and Southern Society, 1877–1984.* Lexington: University Press of Kentucky, 1984.

Coggins, Allen. "The Earthquakes of 1811 and 1812." *Tennessee Conservationist* 55 (Jan. 1989): 7–10.

Conkin, Paul K. *Gone with the Ivy: A Biography of Vanderbilt University.* Knoxville: University of Tennessee Press, 1985.

———. *The New Deal.* New York: Thomas Y. Crowell, 1967.

———. *Tomorrow a New World: the New Deal Community Program.* Ithaca: Cornell University Press, 1958.

Connelly, Thomas L. *Civil War Tennessee: Battles and Leaders.* Knoxville: University of Tennessee Press, 1979.

Cooling, Benjamin F. *Forts Henry and Donelson: The Key to the Confederate Heartland.* Knoxville: University of Tennessee Press, 1987.

Corlew, Robert E. *Tennessee: A Short History.* 2d ed. Knoxville: University of Tennessee Press, 1981.

Couto, Richard A. *Lifting the Veil: A Political History of Struggles for Emancipation.* Knoxville: University of Tennessee Press, 1993.

Cozzens, Peter. *No Better Place to Die: The Battle of Stones River.* Urbana: University of Illinois, 1990.

Crane, Sophie, and Paul Crane. *Tennessee Taproots.* Old Hickory, Tenn.: Earle-Shields Publishers, 1976.

Creese, Walter. *TVA Public Planning: The Vision, the Reality.* Knoxville: University of Tennessee Press, 1990.

Cutler, Phoebe. *The Public Landscape of the New Deal.* New Haven: Yale University Press, 1985.

Dalton, Robert E. "Montgomery Bell and the Narrows of the Harpeth." *Tennessee Historical Quarterly* 35 (1976): 3–28.

Daniel, Pete. *Breaking the Land: The Transformation of Cotton, Tobacco, and Rice Cultures Since 1880.* Urbana: University of Illinois, 1985.

———. *Deep'n As It Come: The 1927 Mississippi River Flood.* New York: Oxford University Press, 1977.

Danzer, Gerald A. *Public Places: Exploring Their History.* Nashville: AASLH Press, 1987.

Davidson, Donald. *The Tennessee: The Old River.* New York: J. J. Little and Ives Company, 1946. Reprint, Knoxville: University of Tennessee Press, 1978.

Davidson, Faye T. "The Ames Plantation, Grand Junction." *Tennessee Historical Quarterly* 38 (1979): 267–76.

Dickinson, W. Calvin. "Frontier Splendor: The Carter Mansion at Sycamore Shoals." *Tennessee Historical Quarterly* 41 (1982): 317–25.

———. *Morgan County.* Memphis: Memphis State University Press, 1987.

Dickinson, W. Calvin, et al., eds. *Lend An Ear: Heritage of the Tennessee Upper Cumberland.* Lanham, Md.: University Press of America, 1983.

Doyle, Don H. *Nashville in the New South: 1880–1930* and *Nashville Since the 1920s.* Knoxville: University of Tennessee Press, 1985.

Duffus, R. L. *The Valley and its People: A Portrait of TVA.* New York: Knopf, 1946.

Dunn, Durwood. *Cades Cove: The Life and Death of a Southern Appalachian Community, 1818-1937.* Knoxville: University of Tennessee Press, 1988.

Durham, Walter T. *James Winchester: Tennessee Pioneer.* Gallatin: Sumner County Library Board, 1979.

———. "Wynnewood, Part I." *Tennessee Historical Quarterly* 33 (1974): 127–56.

———. *Before Tennessee: The Southwest Territory, 1790–1796.* Piney Flats, Tenn.: Rocky Mount Historical Association, 1990.

Durham, Walter T., and James Thomas. *A Pictorial History of Sumner County.* Gallatin: Sumner County Historical Society, 1986.

Dykeman, Wilma. *The French Broad.* New York: Holt and Rhinehart, 1954.

———. *The Tall Woman.* New York: Rhinehart and Winston, 1962.

Egerton, John. *Shades of Gray: Dispatches from the Modern South.* Baton Rouge: Louisiana State University Press, 1991.

———. *Visions of Utopia.* Knoxville: University of Tennessee Press, 1977.

Eller, Ronald D. *Miners, Millhands, and Mountaineers: Industrialization of the Appalachian South, 1880–1930.* Knoxville: University of Tennessee Press, 1982.

Evans, Carol Jo, and Helen Brown. *Then & Now: The Women of Englewood's Textile Mills.* Englewood, Tenn.: Community Action Group of Englewood, 1993.

Ewell, Leighton. *History of Coffee County, Tennessee.* Manchester: Doak Printing, 1936.

Faulkner, Charles H. "Industrial Archaeology of the 'Peavine Railroad.'" *Tennessee Historical Quarterly* 44 (1985): 40–58.

Federal Writers' Project of the Works Progress Administration. *The WPA Guide to Tennessee.* 1939. Reprint, Knoxville: University of Tennessee Press, 1986 .

Finger, John R. *The Eastern Band of Cherokees, 1819–1900.* Knoxville: University of Tennessee Press, 1984.

Fink, Paul. "The Railroad Comes to Jonesboro." *Tennessee Historical Quarterly* 36 (1977): 161–80.

Fite, Gilbert. *Cotton Fields No More: Southern Agriculture, 1865–1980.* Lexington: University Press of Kentucky, 1984.

Fogarty, Robert S. *All Things New: American Communes and Utopian Movements, 1860–1914.* Chicago: University of Chicago Press, 1990.

Ford, Jesse Hill. *The Liberation of Lord Byron Jones.* Boston: Little, Brown, 1965.

Foster, Austin P. *Counties of Tennessee.* Nashville: Tennessee Department of Education, 1923.

Garreau, Joel. "Beyond the Urban Core." *Architecture Minnesota* 18 (July–Aug. 1992): 18–19, 58–60.

———. *Edge City: Life on the New Frontier.* New York: Doubleday, 1991.

Garrow, David J. *Bearing the Cross: Martin Luther King, Jr., and the Southern Christian Leadership Conference.* New York: W. Morrow, 1986. Reprint, New York: Vintage, 1988.

Gebhardt, David. "The American Colonial Revival in the 1930s." *Winterthur Portfolio* 22 (1987): 109–48.

Glassie, Henry. "Meaningful Things and Appropriate Myths: The Artifact's Place in American Studies." *Material Life in America, 1600–1860.* Robert B. St. George, ed. Boston: Northeastern University Press, 1988.

Goodstein, Anita S. *Nashville, 1780–1860: From Frontier to City.* Gainesville: University Press of Florida, 1989.

Gordon, Susan L. "Home Front Tennessee: The World War II Experience." *Tennessee Historical Quarterly* 51 (1992): 3–18.

Gowans, Alan. *Styles and Types of North American Architecture: Social Function and Cultural Expression.* New York: HarperCollins, 1992.

Greene, W. P., ed. *The City of Paris and Henry County, Tennessee.* Paris, Tenn.: Paris Publishing Company, 1900.

Gregory, Rick. "Robertson County and the Black Patch War, 1904–1909." *Tennessee Historical Quarterly* 39 (1980): 341–58.

Hagedorn, Martha. *Historic Sites and Preservation in Upper East Tennessee.* N.p.: First Tennessee Development District, 1985.

Haley, Alex. *Roots: The Saga of an American Family.* New York: Dell Publishing Co., 1977.

Hall, Jacquelyn D., et al. *Like a Family: The Making of a Southern Cotton Mill World.* Chapel Hill: University of North Carolina Press, 1987.

Hargrove, Edwin C., and Paul K. Conkin, eds. *TVA: Fifty Years of Grass-roots Bureaucracy.* Urbana: University of Illinois Press, 1983.

Hoffschwelle, Mary S. "Rebuilding the Rural Southern Community: Reformers, Schools, and Homes in Tennessee, 1914–1929." Ph.D. diss., Vanderbilt University, 1993.

Huddleston, Ed. *The Civil War in Middle Tennessee.* Nashville: Nashville Banner, 1965.

Hudson, Charles. *The Southeastern Indians.* Knoxville: University of Tennessee Press, 1976.

Hull, Cordell. *Memoirs.* 2 vols. New York: Macmillan, 1948.

Hulme, Albert L. *Dyer County: Past and Present.* 2 vols. Dyersburg, Tenn.: First-Citizens National Bank, 1985.

I'll Take My Stand: The South and the Agrarian Tradition. New York: Harper, 1930.

Jackson, J. B. *Discovering the Vernacular Landscape.* New Haven: Yale University Press, 1984.

Jackson, Kenneth T. *Crabgrass Frontier: The Suburbanization of the United States.* New York: Oxford University Press, 1985.

Johnson, Charles S. *Statistical Atlas of Southern Counties.* Chapel Hill: University of North Carolina Press, 1941.

Johnson, Charles W., and Charles O. Jackson. *City Behind a Fence: Oak Ridge, Tennessee, 1942–1946.* Knoxville: University of Tennessee Press, 1981.

Johnson, Eugene J., and Robert D. Russell Jr. *Memphis: An Architectural Guide.* Knoxville: University of Tennessee Press, 1990.

Johnson, Leland R. *From Memphis to Bristol: A Half Century of Road Construction, 1928–1978.* Nashville: Tennessee Road Builders Association, 1978.

Jolley, Harley E. *The Blue Ridge Parkway.* Knoxville: University of Tennessee Press, 1969.

Jones, James B., Jr. *The Development of Coal Mining on Tennessee's Cumberland Plateau, 1880–1930.* Nashville: Tennessee Historical Commission, 1987.

Keith, Jeanette. "Country People: Tennessee's Upper Cumberland." Ph.D. diss., Vanderbilt University, 1990.

Kelly, James C. "Fort Loudoun: British Stronghold in the Tennessee Country." *East Tennessee Historical Society Publications* 50 (1978): 72–91.

Killebrew, Joseph B. *Introduction to the Resources of Tennessee.* Nashville: Bureau of Agriculture, 1874.

Klein, Maury. *History of the Louisville and Nashville Railroad.* New York: Macmillan, 1972.

Lamme, Ary J., III. *America's Historic Landscapes: Community Power and the Preservation of Four National Historic Sites.* Knoxville: University of Tennessee Press, 1989.

Lamon, Lester C. *Blacks in Tennessee, 1791–1970.* Knoxville: University of Tennessee Press, 1981.

———. *Black Tennesseans, 1900–1930.* Knoxville: University of Tennessee Press, 1977.

Lewis, Thomas M. N., and Madeline Kneberg. *Tribes That Slumber: Indians of the Tennessee Region.* Knoxville: University of Tennessee Press, 1958.

Lillard, Roy G. *Bradley County.* Memphis: Memphis State University Press, 1980.

Livingood, James W. *Hamilton County.* Memphis: Memphis State University Press, 1981.

Long, E. B., ed. *Personal Memoirs of U. S. Grant.* New York: Grosset & Dunlap, 1952.

Lovett, Bobby L. "Nashville's Fort Negley: A Symbol of Blacks' Involvement with the Union Army." *Tennessee Historical Quarterly* 41 (1982): 3–22.

Lowenthal, David. *The Past Is a Foreign Country.* New York: Cambridge University Press, 1985.

Luther, Edward T. *Our Restless Earth: The Geologic Regions of Tennessee.* Knoxville: University of Tennessee Press, 1977.

MacArthur, William J., Jr. *Knoxville: Crossroads of the New South.* Knoxville: East Tennessee Historical Society, 1982.

Manning, Russ, and Sondra Jamieson. *Historic Knoxville and Knox County: City Center, Neighborhoods, and Parks.* Norris, Tenn.: Laurel Place, 1990.

Martin, Albro. *Railroads Triumphant: The Growth, Rejection, and Rebirth of a Vital American Force.* New York: Oxford University Press, 1992.

McAlester, Virginia, and Lee McAlester. *A Field Guide to American Houses.* New York: Knopf, 1984.

McDonald, Forrest, and Grady McWhiney. "The Antebellum Southern Herdsman: A Reinterpretation." *Journal of Southern History* 41 (1975): 147–66.

McDonald, Michael J., and John Muldowney. *TVA and the Dispossessed: The Resettlement of Population in the Norris Dam Area.* Knoxville: University of Tennessee Press, 1982.

McDonald, Michael J., and W. Bruce Wheeler. *Knoxville, Tennessee: Continuity and Change in an Appalachian City.* Knoxville: University of Tennessee Press, 1983.

McDonough, James L. *Chattanooga: A Death Grip on the Confederacy.* Knoxville: University of Tennessee Press, 1984.

———. *Shiloh—in Hell before Night.* Knoxville: University of Tennessee Press, 1977.

———. *Stones River: Bloody Winter in Tennessee.* Knoxville: University of Tennessee Press, 1980.

TENNESSEE'S HISTORIC LANDSCAPES

McDonough, James L., and Thomas L. Connelly. *Five Tragic Hours: The Battle of Franklin.* Knoxville: University of Tennessee Press, 1983.

McNabb, William R. *Tradition, Innovation & Romantic Images: The Architecture of Historic Knoxville.* Knoxville: Frank H. McClung Museum, 1991.

Meinig, D. W., ed. *The Interpretation of Ordinary Landscapes: Geographical Essays.* New York: Oxford University Press, 1979.

Moffett, Marian, and Lawrence Wodehouse. *East Tennessee Cantilever Barns.* Knoxville: University of Tennessee Press, 1993.

Montell, W. Lynwood. *Don't Go Up Kettle Creek: Verbal Legacy of the Upper Cumberland.* Knoxville: University of Tennessee Press, 1983.

———. *Upper Cumberland Country.* Jackson: University Press of Mississippi, 1993.

Montgomery, James R. *To Foster Knowledge: A History of the University of Tennessee, 1794–1970.* Knoxville: University of Tennessee Press, 1984.

Mooney, Chase C. *Slavery in Tennessee.* Bloomington: Indiana University Press, 1957.

Mooney, Jack. "The Establishment and Operation of the Technical Training School of the International Printing Pressmen and Assistants' Union in Tennessee, 1911–1967." *Tennessee Historical Quarterly* 48 (1989): 111–22.

Morgan, John. *The Log House in East Tennessee.* Knoxville: University of Tennessee Press, 1991.

Morgan, William. *Collegiate Gothic: Architecture of Rhodes College.* Columbia: University of Missouri Press, 1989.

Morris, Eastin. *The Tennessee Gazetteer.* Nashville: W. Hasell Hunt, & Co., 1835.

Morton, Dorothy Rich. *Fayette County.* Memphis: Memphis State University Press, 1989.

National Park Service. *Trail of Tears National Historic Trail: Comprehensive Management and Use Plan.* Denver: National Park Service, 1992.

Noble, Allen G. *Wood, Brick, & Stone: The North American Settlement Landscape.* 2 vols. Amherst: University of Massachusetts Press, 1984.

Orr, Frank, et al., eds. *Notable Nashville Architecture, 1930–1980.* Nashville: Middle Tennessee Chapter of AIA, 1989.

Park, Marlene, and Gerald E. Markowitz. *Democratic Vistas: Post Offices and Public Art in the New Deal.* Philadelphia: Temple University Press, 1984.

Paschall, Douglas, and Alice Swanson, eds. *Homewords: A Book of Tennessee Writers.* Knoxville: University of Tennessee Press, 1986.

Patrick, James. *Architecture in Tennessee, 1768–1897.* Knoxville: University of Tennessee Press, 1981.

Peacock, Blanche. "Reelfoot Lake State Park." *Tennessee Historical Quarterly* 32 (Fall 1973): 205–32.

Peterson, Elizabeth, and Tom Rankin. "Free Hill: An Introduction." *Tennessee Folklore Society Bulletin* 50 (Spring 1985): 1–9.

Preston, Howard L. *Dirt Roads to Dixie: Accessibility and Modernization in the South, 1885–1935.* Knoxville: University of Tennessee Press, 1991.

Price, Edward T. "The Central Courthouse Square in the American County Seat." *Common Places: Readings in American Vernacular Architecture.* Dell Upton and John M. Vlach, eds. Athens: University of Georgia Press, 1985. 124–48.

Quin, Richard. "Ashwood, the Pillows, the Polks." M.A. thesis, Middle Tennessee State University, 1991.

Raskopf, B. D. *The Cotton Ginning Industry in Tennessee.* University of Tennessee Extension Bulletin, No. 303, 1959.

Raulston, J. Leonard, and James W. Livingood. *Sequatchie: A Story of the Southern Cumberlands.* Knoxville: University of Tennessee Press, 1974.

Reheder, John. "The Scotch-Irish and English in Appalachia." *To Build in a New Land: Ethnic Landscapes in North America.* Allan G. Noble, ed. Baltimore: Johns Hopkins University Press, 1992.

Relph, Edward. *The Modern Urban Landscape.* Baltimore: Johns Hopkins University Press, 1987.

Sarver, Ron. "See Rock City." *VISTA USA* (Summer 1987): 10.

Satz, Ronald N. *Tennessee's Indian Peoples: From White Contact to Removal, 1540–1840.* Knoxville: University of Tennessee Press, 1979.

Siler, Tom. *Tennessee Towns: From Adams to Yorkville.* Knoxville: East Tennessee Historical Society, 1985.

Sims, Carlton, ed. *A History of Rutherford County.* Murfreesboro: private, 1947.

Spoden, Hal T., and Muriel C. "Sycamore Shoals State Historic Area." *Tennessee Historical Quarterly* 36 (Spring 1977): 3–18.

Stilgoe, John R. *Metropolitan Corridor: Railroads and the American Scene, 1880–1930.* New Haven: Yale University Press, 1983.

———. "Two Archetypes of Landscape: Landschaft and Linearity." *Environmental Review* 4 (1980): 2–17.

Stover, John F. *History of the Illinois Central Railroad.* New York: Macmillan, 1975.

———. *The Railroads of the South, 1865–1900.* Chapel Hill: University of North Carolina Press, 1955.

Sulzer, Elmer G. *Ghost Railroads of Tennessee.* Indianapolis: Van A. Jones Company, 1975.

Taylor, Peter. *A Summons to Memphis.* New York: Knopf, 1987.

Tellico Blockhouse: U.S. Garrisoned Fort, 1794–1807. Knoxville: Tennessee Valley Authority, n.d.

Tennessee Overhill Experience. Pamphlet. Benton [?], Tenn., 1991.

Tretter, Evelyn K. "Doctor Woman." *Tennessee Conservationist* 54 (Nov.–Dec., 1988): 18–22.

Upton, Dell, and John M. Vlach, eds. *Common Places: Readings in American Vernacular Architecture.* Athens: University of Georgia Press, 1985.

TENNESSEE'S HISTORIC LANDSCAPES

Vieyra, Daniel. *"Fill 'Er Up!": An Architectural History of America's Gas Stations.* New York: Macmillan, 1979.

Vlach, John M. *By the Work of Their Hands: Studies in Afro-American Folklife.* Ann Arbor: UMI Press, 1991.

Waldrop, Frank C., ed. *Mountain Voices: The Centennial History of Monteagle Sunday School Assembly.* Monteagle, Tenn.: Monteagle Assembly, 1982.

Warden, Margaret L. *The Belle Meade Plantation.* Nashville: APTA, 1979.

Wedell, Marsha. *Elite Women and the Reform Impulse in Memphis, 1875–1915.* Knoxville: University of Tennessee Press, 1991.

West, Carroll Van. *Tennessee Agriculture: A Century Farms Perspective.* Nashville: Tennessee Department of Agriculture, 1986.

Wheeler, W. Bruce, and Michael J. McDonald. "The Communities of East Tennessee, 1850–1940: An Interpretive Overview." *East Tennessee Historical Society Publications* 58–59 (1986–87): 3–38.

————. *TVA and the Tellico Dam, 1936–1979: A Bureaucratic Crisis in Post-Industrial America.* Knoxville: University of Tennessee Press, 1986.

Whiffen, Marcus, and Frederick Koeper. *American Architecture, 1607–1976.* Cambridge, Mass.: MIT Press, 1981.

Whisnant, David. *All That Is Native and Fine: The Politics of Culture in an American Region.* Chapel Hill: University of North Carolina Press, 1983.

Willbanks, Ray, ed. *Literature of Tennessee.* Macon, Ga.: Mercer University Press, 1984.

Williams, Frank B., Jr. *Tennessee's Presidents.* Knoxville: University of Tennessee Press, 1981.

Williams, Samuel C. *Tennessee During the Revolutionary War.* 1944. Reprint, Knoxville: University of Tennessee Press, 1974.

Wolfe, Margaret R. *Kingsport, Tennessee: A Planned American City.* Lexington: University Press of Kentucky, 1987.

Wright, Gwendolyn. *Building the Dream: A Social History of Housing in America.* Cambridge, Mass.: MIT Press, 1981.

Young, Thomas D. *Tennessee Writers.* Knoxville: University of Tennessee Press, 1981.

Place Name Index

Name and Subject Index

TENNESSEE'S HISTORIC LANDSCAPES

262–63; Tennessee Immigration &
Land Co., 345; Tullahoma Land Co.,
343; West Tennessee Land Co.,
444–45
Lane, Isaac, 405
Lane, James F., 405
Lea, Cynthia, 168
Leake, Virginius, 393
Lee, Robert E., 216
Leech, Leonard L., 380
LeMoyne, F. Julius, 127
Lenoir, William B., 217
Lenoir City Car Works, 218
Legislation, federal: Factory Act of 1795,
198; Interstate Highway Act, 13;
National Industrial Recovery/Act,
211; Smith-Lever Act, 435
Legislation, state: Butler Act of 1925, 230–
31; General Education Act of 1909,
176; General Education Act of 1925,
230; Highway Act of 1923, 240
Lewis, E. C., 305
Lewis, John, 50
Lewis, Meriwether, 376–77
Libraries, 78, 79, 247, 288, 290, 340,
420, 405, 468; Carnegie, 28, 235
Lincoln, Abraham, 63, 144, 166
Lincoln League, 125
Literature, 18, 51, 52, 88, 169, 185–86,
261, 283, 321, 440, 470–71
Lodges, fraternal, 34, 92, 162, 221, 252,
264, 328, 348, 360, 380, 398, 429
Longstreet, James, 67, 81
Lowenhaupt, Jacob, 473
Lowenstein, Elias, 121
Lowenthal, David, 120
Lumber, companies: Babcock Lumber
Co., 3; Cumberland Lumber Co.,
245; Liberman, Loveman, and
O'Brien Co., 279; Little River
Lumber Co., 187–88; Scottish
Carolina Timber and Land Co., 142;
Sewanee Planing and Flooring Mills,
302; A. M. Stevens Lumber Co.,
466–67
Lumber, logging techniques, 279–80, 281
Lundy, Benjamin, 149
Lupton, J. T., 66
Luther, Edward T., 131, 237

Lytle, Andrew Nelson, 261
Lyttelton, William, 197

Mabry, Joseph A., 73
Mackall, W. W., 452
Magevney, Eugene, 118
Magic Chef Corporation (Dixie Foundry),
227
Maloney, W. A., 150
Mann, Robert N., 350
Mansker, Kasper, 32
Mars, Frank C., 356
Martin, Albro, 461
Martin, Joseph, 158
Martin, George, 400
Martin, Marshall, 400
Martin, William, 400
Mason, Eliza, 39
Mason, Thomas, 39, 220
Matthews, John, 357
Matthews, John D., 357
Matthews, Joseph, 357
Matthews, Sarah Walker, 357
McAdoo, William, 65
McClung, Charles, 71
McCormick, Nettie Fowler, 147, 149
McCraw, C. T. 429
McDonald, John, 55, 56, 87
McDonald, Michael, 181, 213, 225
McElwee, Robert, 434
McElwee, Samuel A., 432–33
McFerrin, Sam, 248
McIver, John, 466
McKee, John, 198
McKellar, Kenneth D., 116
McKinney, John A., 164
McKinney, Susan, 164
McLemore, John C., 109
McReynolds, Charles E., 269
McReynolds, Samuel, 269
McTyeire, Holland N., 101
McWherter, Ned Ray, 420
Meigs, Return Jonathan, 236
Melungeons, 162
Memphis Archaeological and Geological
Society, 447
Memphis Housing Authority, 113, 122
Mencken, H. L., 169
Mennonites, 372

Mentlo, Daniel, 317
Metropolitan Life Insurance Co., 327
Michaux, F. A., 151
Michie, Charles, 396
Military
—arsenals, 130, 365, 367
—Civil War, 18, 27, 39, 125, 144, 294,
310, 331, 393, 396–97, 404; Army
of the Cumberland, 331–32; Army
of Tennessee, 27, 63, 84, 331, 358;
Battles: Chattanooga, 19, 54, 63–64;
Franklin, 33–34, 358–59; Island
Number Ten, 452–53; Knoxville,
67, 72, 77, 81; Nashville, 84, 85;
New Johnsonville, 384–85; Parker's
Crossroads, 27; Shiloh, 440–42;
Stones River, 17–18, 331–33; Forts:
Ft. Defiance/Ft. Bruce, 301; Ft.
Donelson, 295, 298–300; Ft. Henry,
298–300; Ft. Harris, 449; Ft. Hill,
384; Ft. Negley, 33, 84–85, 399; Ft.
Pillow, 450–52; Ft. Wright, 450;
Fortress Rosecrans, 332–33;
Germantown Redoubt, 392–93
—early settlement era: Ft. Blount, 280;
Ft. Cass, 41, 202, 202; Ft. Caswell,
154; Ft. Patrick Henry, 136, 154; Ft.
Loudoun, 195–98; Ft. Marr, 210; Ft.
Nashborough, 83, 448; Ft.
Pickering, 449; Ft. Southwest Point,
236
—revolutionary war, 132, 136, 155, 157
—Seven Years War, 196–97
—Tennessee National Guard, 344
—World War I, 85, 286, 306, 344
—World War II, 69, 206; Camp Forrest,
344; Ft. Campbell, 14; Holston
Ordinance Works, 174; Manhattan
Project, 133–34, 182–85; Milan
Arsenal, 403
Mills, grist: Cortner's Mill, 342; Dungan
Mill, 154; Eureka Roller Mills, 150;
Ketner's Mill, 265; Pigeon Forge
Mill, 191; Pile-York Mill, 286;
Roller-Pettyjohn Mill, 160
Mills, paper, 3, 41
Mills, textile: Bemis Brothers Bag Co.,
406–7; Covington Milling Co., 472;
Dayton Hosiery Mill, 230; Dixie

Parks and reserves, state, *continued*
Montgomery Bell State Park, 378; Mousetail Landing State Park, 439; Narrows of Harpeth State Historical Area, 379; New Johnsonville State Historical Area, 384–85; Norris Dam State Park, 38; Old Stone Fort State Park, 3, 293; Paris Landing State Park, 439; Pickett State Park, 211, 238; Pinson Mounds State Archaeological Area, 387, 435–36; Port Royal State Historical Area, 202, 327–28; Red Clay State Historical Area, 200–201; Reelfoot Lake State Park, 444–45; Roan Mountain State Park, 132; Rock Island State Park, 246–47; Savage Gulf State Natural Area, 238; Sergeant York State Historical Area, 286–87; South Cumberland Visitor Center, 259–60; Standing Stone State Park, 211, 238, 283–84; Sycamore Shoals State Historical Area, 154–55; Virgin Falls State Natural Area, 238; Warrior's Path State Park, 159–60; Booker T. Washington State Park, 41–42

Parks, urban: Centennial Park, Nashville, 104; Church Park, Memphis, 124–25; Confederate Park, Memphis, 115, 454; Handy Park, Memphis, 124; Krutch Park, Knoxville, 74; McGregor Park, Clarksville, 301; Old Fort Park, Murfreesboro, 333; Overton Park, Memphis, 30, 127–28; Point Park, Chattanooga, 53–55; Ross' Landing, Chattanooga, 57–59; Riverfront Park, Nashville, 88; Percy and Edwin Warner Park, Nashville, 86

Parton, Dolly, 191
Patrick, James, 47, 152, 155, 317, 368
Patton, Mary, 157
Peabody Fund, 103–4
Pearson, Jacob, 221
Pearson, William, 27–28
Peaveyhouse, Elizabeth, 273
Peay, Austin, 79
Penn-Dixie Cement Co., 263
Perkins, Carl, 458

Peters, George B., 362
Pickens, Francis W., 396
Pickens, Lucy Holcombe, 396
Pillow, Gideon J., 121, 299, 367–68, 370
Politics, 66, 70–71, 86–87, 118, 125, 133, 144–45, 175, 215, 278, 303, 307–8, 317, 364, 418
Polk, Ezekiel, 426
Polk, George W., 368, 370
Polk, James K., 96, 121, 162, 333, 365, 426
Polk, Leonidas, 253, 368
Polk, Lucius, 368, 370
Polk, Samuel, 365
Polk, Sarah Childress, 333
Pope, John, 452
Porter, James D., 412
Post Offices, 43, 47, 61, 63, 74, 92, 116, 158, 217, 222, 247, 276, 286, 340, 343, 381, 400–401, 402, 411, 415–16, 417, 418, 463, 468, 469
Prentiss, Benjamin, 441
Presley, Elvis, 2, 31–32, 109, 115, 123
Preston, Howard L., 330
Price, Edward T., 339
Public Works Administration, 37, 86, 89, 96, 100, 210, 211, 317, 348–49, 378, 405, 435, 462–63, 469
Pyramid, 30–31, 114

Quin, Richard, 367

Race riots, violence, 50, 111, 182, 257, 338, 423–24, 434
Raht, Julius E., 206
Railroads, companies: Amtrak, 465; Atlantic, Knoxville, & Northern, 212, 215; Birmingham and Northwestern, 468; Carolina, Clinchfield, & Ohio, 172–78, 275; Chesapeake and Nashville, 312; Chesapeake, Ohio, & Southwestern, 460; Chicago, St. Louis, & New Orleans, 460; Cincinnati Southern, 229–30, 232–33, 275; Columbia, Lawrenceburg, & Florence, 371, 373; CSX, 33, 177, 389, 409; Duck River Valley Narrow Gauge, 352; East Tennessee and Georgia, 39–40, 67, 194, 220, 223,

226; East Tennessee and Virginia, 46–47, 67, 147, 150, 152, 174; East Tennessee, Virginia, & Georgia, 37, 40, 152, 164, 167, 218; East Tennessee and Western North Carolina, 174–75; Edgefield and Kentucky, 84; Gallatin and Scottsville, 312; Gulf, Mobile, & Northern, 468; Harriman and Northwestern, 235; Hiwassee, 40, 223; Illinois Central, 28, 49, 301, 388, 400–407, 445, 456–58, 460–61, 463–65, 468–69, 470–73; Knoxville and Bristol, 167, 168; Knoxville, Cumberland Gap, & Louisville, 167; LaGrange and Memphis, 389, 395; Lookout Mountain Incline Railway, 65; Louisville and Nashville, 29, 33, 37, 49, 68, 84, 87, 91, 107, 194, 212–13, 225, 301, 303, 305, 312, 324, 362, 371, 388–89, 402, 408–9, 411, 413, 418, 426–27; Marietta and North Georgia, 206, 212; Memphis and Charleston, 111, 388, 389, 391–98, 422, 425–26, 440; Memphis, Clarksville, & Louisville, 408; Memphis and Ohio, 408; Mississippi Central and Tennessee, 400, 404; Mobile and Ohio, 388, 398, 400, 404, 407–8, 463; Morristown and Cumberland Gap, 167; Nashville and Chattanooga 13, 18, 56, 84, 257, 264, 329, 331, 336, 341, 343, 345, 391, 409; Nashville, Chattanooga, & St. Louis, 13–14, 19, 49, 243, 245, 246, 264–65, 305, 344–46, 380, 389, 409, 414–19; Nashville and Decatur, 84, 355, 356, 357, 364; Nashville and Eastern, 25; Nashville and Knoxville, 276, 308; Nashville and Northwestern, 84, 380, 381, 383, 384, 399, 400, 409, 419, 463; New Orleans, Jackson, & Great Northern, 400, 425; Newport News and Mississippi Valley, 460, 461, 464, 467, 469, 471, 473; Norfolk